THE Sopranos

ON THE COUCH

The Ultimate Guide

ANALYZING TELEVISION'S
GREATEST SERIES

Maurice Yacowar

continuum

NEW YORK • LONDON

To my wife Anne,

with love and thanks

2007

The Continuum International Publishing Group Inc
80 Maiden Lane, New York, NY 10038

The Continuum International Publishing Group Ltd
The Tower Building, 11 York Road, London SE1 7NX

www.continuumbooks.com

Printed in the United States of America

Library of Congress Cataloging-in-Publication Data

Yacowar, Maurice.
  The Sopranos on the couch / Maurice Yacowar.—The ultimate guide.
    p. cm.
Includes bibliographical references.
  ISBN 978-0-8264-1922-4 (pbk. : alk. paper)
  1. Sopranos (Television program)   I. Title.
  PN1992.77.S66   Y33   2005
  791.45'72—dc21
                                          2003009240

Contents

"This fantasy of yours has meaning."

(Dr. Jennifer Melfi, I, 12)

Introduction to the Ultimate Guide

Season Six gives Tony the chance to transcend the criminal materialism of the first five seasons. After he is shot, at the end of the first episode, he returns as if from the dead with a new sense of the importance of life. At season end, Phil Leotardo's heart attack similarly raises his own need to change his life. Indeed, the opportunity to transcend one's accustomed life is the dominant subject in the first 12-episode installment of the show's extended wrap-up, with an eight-episode finale to follow.

A minor character in the opening episode encapsulates the theme. When longtime gunsel Gene Pontecorvo inherits two million dollars, his wife, Deanne, insists they retire to Florida. He promises Deanne he will be promoted after buying a new car and moving into Tony's neighborhood: "Tony and Silvio, all they understand is appearances." But—more like Charmaine than like Carmela—she wants out. Gene tries to buy his release from Tony, first with expensive watches and then with "a taste" of his legacy from his Aunt Edie. When Silvio conveys Tony's refusal—"You took an oath, Gene. There's no retiring from this."—Gene hangs himself. This minor plot combines several major motifs: the wife's superior morality and will, the criminal's possibility of an honest life, and ultimately the criminal's defeat by Tony's rigidity and his despair. Those elements will also prevent Tony's—and Carmela's—redemption.

In the season's most touching plotline, Vito Spatafore also tries to improve himself. With the minor challenge of his weight loss, he succeeds and advances his gang status (VI, 2). But when he tries to realize his homosexual nature he is defeated. After establishing a new life in a small New Hampshire town, he is drawn back by his family feelings and the thrill of the gangster life. Like Gene, he tries to buy a new life from Tony, running girls and drugs in Atlantic City. He vows to live heterosexually "straight." Tony is at first sympathetic with Vito's new sensitivity. When Tony yields to his advisers' prejudice, he is pre-empted by Phil Leotardo's sadistic avenging of his family's dishonor. In contrast to Gene and Vito's choosing to escape their old lives, Johnny Sacrimoni's jail sentence is forced.

By denying Gene and Vito their redemption, Tony fails to transcend his gang code. Over the season, he loses the new values prompted by his near-death experience. The family's Christmas harmony that ends VI, 12 pretends to devotion but celebrates Carmela and Tony's materialism. As Tony is tested, the season recalls *The Godfather Part III,* where Michael Corleone's possible redemption fails because of his despair and his persistent corruption.

A spiritual alternative to the Soprano life is established in the first episode's reintroduction of the characters. Instead of Sinatra's "It Was a Very Good Year" (II, 1), the episode is framed by William Burroughs's incantation from *The Western Lands* of the Seven Souls postulated in Egyptian mythology. As Burroughs intones, the first, *Rem,* is "the secret name" that "corresponds to my director" and "directs the film of your life from conception to death." This metaphor anticipates Tony's link between the baby carriage and wheelchair, between Janice's baby and Junior's dementia. Ever irreverent, Tony later translates Melfi's "circle of life" to the "circle jerk of life. Where's the dignity?"

Burroughs's reading, to music, establishes a spiritual context for the characters' emotional malaise and the futility of the materialistic response. His particular Souls sometimes parallel the character shown. Paradoxically, Gene and Deanne Pontecorvo celebrate his inheritance over *Sekem,* the emblem of energy and power—which even their windfall fails to provide them. The traitor Raymond Curto appears on his exercise bike over the sometimes treacherous *Ba,* the heart. *Ka,* "the only reliable guide to the Land of the Dead," attends Adriana's appearance in Carmela's dream in the house she is building to sell. Adriana rings ominous: "Who's gonna live here?" Carmela: "A family?" When Tony asks, "Was she going to buy it?" his phrase conjoins dying and buying. Carmela's dream admission— that despite all her affluence, "I am worried all the time"—undermines her house pride in her last speech of the season.

The season is pointedly structured. The first quarter—three episodes— pitch Tony into his coma and his visionary delirium. The halfway mark (VI, 6) leaves the persecuted Vito in his New Hampshire comfort, albeit cut off from his family and his friends. By agreeing to kill him, though, Tony slides back into pragmatic brutishness. By the three-quarter mark (VI, 9), Tony has regressed to his old crimes and encouraged Christopher's return to drinking. The season closes on the family's material and therefore shallow comfort, with only AJ promising to have grown from Tony's trauma.

Introduction to the First Edition

THE PHENOMENON

The Sopranos rules. In fact, it could be the best TV series ever made.

The show certainly captured a large, avid, and discriminating audience—which must be one criterion. In American pop culture the series was probably the most addictive program since cinemas had to turn on the *Amos 'n' Andy* radio show to lure people to the flicks. Quickly the HBO series attracted 3.7 million viewers on Sunday nights, 10 million in its four weekly airings; that topped the cable audience ratings. Its Season Two opener scored the highest cable show rating in history—without the *Dallas* dangle of a major murder mystery from the previous season's end. That the HBO audience of 25 million is only a quarter of the networks' audience makes the show's numbers and influence even more remarkable.

The Sunday telecast killed the restaurant business in some areas, as families preferred to stay in for the latest episode. Some ingenious restaurants—of the "If you can't lick 'em . . ." persuasion—offered a late special for appetites whetted by the Sopranos' cholester-rollicking dinners.

You can see the difference between the first two seasons' preview parties. Season One premiered downstairs at the Virgin megastore on Broadway, with a party afterward at John's Pizzeria on West 44th. For the Season Two premiere at the Ziegfeld and the party afterward at Roseland, 1,000 were expected but 1,800 showed up. HBO had to bus the overflow to its headquarters (Stephen Holden, pp. 170, 167). The phenomenon was secure.

In Canada, we heard about the series long before we had the chance to see it. In a brilliant coup, the private CTV network ran a nightly marathon of Season One *Sopranos* against the public CBC coverage of the Olympics. (For such relief, much thanks.) The nation thus hooked, seasons two and three followed on a cable movie channel, drawing closer to the American telecast, and were repeated on CTV.

For its "mesmerizing television," the show won the Peabody Award each of its first two years. Otherwise, the industry awards were surprisingly slow. Its first season netted 16 Emmy nominations—but only two won:

Edie Falco for best lead actress and David Chase and James Manos Jr. for best dramatic script, for "College," I, 5. (By my code here, that means Season I, episode 5. *Kapeesh?*) As Ralph Blumenthal suggested in the *New York Times*, "Maybe the Emmy voters never heard what happens to people who rob the mob"—or was it "the networks' reluctance to accept cable television channels as full industry partners?" (Holden, pp. 142, 145)

The 1999 Golden Globes were more just, with awards to Falco, James Gandolfini, and Nancy Marchand, along with Best Drama Series. Gandolfini was nominated for an Emmy the first two years and won Best Actor the second, when he was the show's only winner from its 18 Emmy nominations. In its first season the show swept the Screen Actors Guild for Best Drama Ensemble performance and for leads Gandolfini and Falco, the Directors Guild Best Director award for David Chase's pilot, the Writers Guild Award for "Meadowlands," the Producers Guild Award (David Chase, Episodic TV Producer of the Year), and the TV Critics Association awards for outstanding drama, new program, and individual achievement (which Gandolfini repeated the next year). The second season won the International Radio and Television Society Foundation Award, the Banff Rockies Award, the Chicago International Television Competition, and the CIBE Golden Eagle Award (for the season opener).

The verdict on its 22 Emmy nominations in 2001 was postponed twice by the September 11 terrorist attack and the US-led military response against the terrorists in Afghanistan. When the showbiz smoke had cleared, *The Sopranos* had won the top acting awards (Gandolfini and Falco) and a writing award (for III, 4: "Employee of the Month"). It lost the Best Drama and best supporting actors' awards to *The West Wing*. The show's importance in the national psyche is suggested in one of the very first jokes made about that tragic event. An Internet site posted a Soprano gang photo with the caption: "Just tell us where bin Laden is and fuhgedaboudit."

The myriad fan-sites on the net prove *The Sopranos* quickly grew from program into cult. Each new episode fired watercooler conversations for the next week. The argot crept into conversational usage. "Whacked" came to mean something other than what you did to your carpets—or what doing that made you feel. Newspapers and magazines chronicled its addicts' fidelity and fervor.

The Internet flogged a cornucopia of *Sopranos* merchandise, from Satriale's Pork Shop and Beansie's Pizza T-shirts to the classic elegance of the Bada Bing Babe ashtray, shot glass, beer stein, tumbler, and enough different coffee cups to give new meaning to the term "mug's game." Even after Big Pussy Bonpensiero was . . . whacked, actor Vincent Pastore "helped to develop" a cigar, hand-rolled in Dominica, for Don Diego. It zipped to the cover of *Cigar Afficianado*. You could harvest eBay for memorabilia—or relics?—of almost any actor/character on the show. Dominic Chianese (Uncle Junior) released a CD ambiguously titled *Hits*. CareerBuilder invited you to search for "jobs related to *The Sopranos*." But alas, they seemed legit, more like (lower case) family counseling than Tony's "waste management."

The actors became household faces and their characters household names. Paulie "Walnuts" Gualtieri (Tony Sirico) feels like everyone's favorite business "uncle," not just Meadow's and AJ's. Sirico remained a lovable eccentric spirit even after *Harper's* magazine ("Method Acting," June 2001, pp. 22–25) quoted from the transcript of his real-life trial for gangsterism in 1971. He allegedly threatened a New York club owner for seeking police protection: "I have an arsenal of weapons and an army of men, and I'm going to use them, and after I take care of those guys I'm going to come back here and carve my initials on your forehead." The transcript was posted on *www.thesmokinggun.com*. Nonetheless, Sirico became a popular regular on *Hollywood Squares*.

The confusion between art and life continued when 16-year-old Robert Iler (Anthony Jr.) was arrested with two teenage friends and charged with robbing two other teenagers of $45 on Manhattan's Upper East Side. Pleading guilty to misdemeanor-petty larceny, Iler was sentenced to three years' probation. He reportedly swore at the arresting officer and bragged "Don't you worry about me—I'm a millionaire" (*New York Times*, August 30, 2001).

When London's *Independent* reported the Philadelphia trial of Joseph "Skinny Joey" Merlino, it reached to *The Sopranos* for its context—" 'Soprano' snitch brings down Mob," blared the headline (July 22, 2001)—and its credibility. The 50 witnesses reportedly told stories that "would have given years of material to scriptwriters of *The Sopranos*." Tony Soprano provided a realistic allusion—and the diction—in a Salman Rushdie short story in *The New Yorker*: "The gangster Tony Soprano might be going to a shrink, but fuck him, he was fictional" ("Summer of Solanka," July 16, 2001, pp. 66–75). We know a fiction has permeated the collective mind when it provides the reality base for another fiction.

The show was popular enough to become a public target. It was accused of defaming the Italian-American community by portraying them as gangsters. The American Italian Defense Association—*AIDA v. Sopranos* instead of by them?—sued the program's distributor, Time Warner Entertainment, under the Illinois Constitution's dignity clause, which condemns inciting hostility toward "persons by . . . reference to religious, racial, ethnic, national or religious affiliation." On September 19, 2001, Cook County Judge Richard A. Seibel delivered his 11-page judgment that "The aria may be offensive to Verdi, but the Sopranos have the constitutional right to sing." Does *The Sopranos* perpetuate the Italian-American stereotype as "greedy mobsters lacking virtue," as AIDA claimed? Stay tuned.

THE QUALITY

All that is popularity. What's so *good* about *The Sopranos*?

For openers: it's brilliantly written, performed, and filmed. Each episode has the polish of an excellent feature film—with a tighter yet more complex, resonant script than most. For example, in the Italian wedding that opens I, 8, the detail and variety of character and activity is what we expect of a big-budget film, not a weekly TV show. The image is even more impressive when viewed—as in DVD—in the widescreen format in which it was filmed, instead of the one shrunk to the TV screen's proportions.

Yet the first season episodes were budgeted at only around two million dollars each, with an eight-day shooting schedule. (True, the pilot was shot in sixteen.) In every episode the polish exceeds the budget and the conditions. Remarkably, these one hour films were produced on the schedule of the normal 42-minute drama that makes up a one hour program on commercial TV. As director Tim Van Patten points out (Season II DVD, disc one) "This show is like making a feature in nine to twelve days"—and 13 of them in a row!

The show is also relentlessly entertaining. The characters are engrossing, the plot twists astonishing but coherent, and the dialogue mined with ironies and poetic resonance quite beyond what we are used to hearing on the boob tube or even on the commercial cinema screen these days.

Unique for a television series, details connect not just across the hour but across a season and beyond. Creator David Chase calls this the show's "connective tissue" in his commentary on the Season One DVD (disc four): the phrases, devices and themes that flesh out the plot skeleton. That complexity requires—and rewards—"active viewing" (disc one). The viewer has to dig for links and meanings beyond what's spelled out on the surface and is often left with mysteries. That makes this show more like European cinema than American cinema—and a complete departure for

American television. At the same time, *The Sopranos* provocatively raises major questions about how and why we live.

The show also emulates European cinema in its narrative pace. Though each hour contains an astonishing range of incident and theme, it feels slow. It pauses for the long silences that realistically represent a marital scene or (other?) therapy session but it can erupt into frenzy. The show is this flexible because it is not scripted for commercial breaks. Its structure serves its material, without the false climaxes that hook us for the sponsors.

The show uses the television medium brilliantly. TV's essential strength lies in its domestic immediacy. That could also be its weakness, as we may pay it the attention we give our wallpaper. But watching a family saga in our own living/rec room can be intensely involving. As shows like *Coronation Street* have proved, viewers tend to "adopt" their continuing TV family as a virtual extension of their own. That is what makes the soap opera—and such relatives as game shows and TV wrestling—the most characteristic television genre. The "family" connection feeds on the medium's domestic register.

Hence the sitcom based on a continuing though loosely related "family": *I Love Lucy* begat *The Dick Van Dyke Show* who begat *The Mary Tyler Moore Show* who begat *Bob Newhart* who begat *Seinfeld* who begat *Ally McBeal* who. . . . TV seems to bring one virtual family, whether real, *Friends*ly or workplace, to another, as a marriage extends families by connecting them. The Soprano family/Family life fits this aspect perfectly.

As well, the rich dialogue, with its heavily flavored accent—salty and spicy both—exploits the fact that—even with its larger screens and better visual definition—television remains a primarily aural medium. We *hear* more of a television show than we *watch*, as we read the paper, knit, or count our bags of money in the comfort of our own home while "watching" TV. More often with this series, however, the performances, camerawork, and Bada Bing dancers compel us to watch.

The serial format enables viewers to get to know a show's characters much more fully—and with deeper emotional engagement—than a one-shot drama or even a mini-series allows. When characters this colorful are developed into such complex beings, then a television show provides a slice of life as textured, nuanced, and involving as—a Charles Dickens novel. Remember: Dickens published his massive sagas in periodic installments, too, just like our weekly television series. The *Sopranos*'s 13-episode season allows for plausible inconsistencies and psychological twists that a shorter drama has no time for and that the sitcom's need for reassuring familiarity precludes.

Reviewing the first season in the *New York Times,* Vincent Canby wisely proposed *The Sopranos* be considered a "megamovie," in the tradition of Rainer Werner Fassbinder's fifteen-and-a-half-hour *Berlin Alexanderplatz* (1980) and Dennis Potter's original six-hour *The Singing Detective* (1988): "It's a stunning original about a most particular slice of American life, a panoramic picture that is, by turns, wise, brutal, funny and hair-raising, and of significance to the society just beyond its immediate view" (Holden, pp. 177, 179). I'd go a step further. In *The Sopranos,* a television series achieves the heft of a classic novel.

Finally, *The Sopranos* is very much an expression of its time. For one thing, it anatomizes the Me-First Generation. As Chase remarks on his DVD interview (Season One, disc four), the show's original, absurd joke is that "life in America had gotten so selfish" that even a mobster, whose business invented Me First, can't stand it any more so he needs therapy. That's what this outlaw society represents, however charmingly tempered by its nostalgia, loyalty, and *omertà*—the protective silence of the gangster who refuses to "sing."

Furthermore, as Dr. Melfi observes (in I, 1), many Americans share Tony Soprano's feelings of having come in too late, at the end, when the best of The American Dream is over. Where Tony's ancestors built the beautiful church, now you can't find two guys who can properly grout a bathtub.

So, too, the show's unprecedented candor. It has set new limits in the vulgarity of its language, its unflinching probe of its criminal characters' private and business lives, the candid dramatization of family problems, and the hypocrisies in church, school, and government, and the complexity of its moral positions. The serious ambition of its themes enabled HBO to transcend the archaic decorum and moral simplicities that paralyze commercial television. After all, ABC, CBS, and the Fox network all passed on the pilot script before HBO shot and adopted it.

HBO luxuriated in the greater freedom it enjoys over network television. The cable liberty paid off handsomely. With *The Larry Sanders Show, Oz, Sex and the City, The Sopranos,* and *Six Feet Under,* HBO rewrote the conventions of TV—and in 2000 outgrossed—in both senses of the word—all the major American networks. More importantly for us non-shareholders: Here are shows for grownups, who want paradox in their characters, moral ambivalence in their plots, and a sense that we are seeing life as those fascinating people would live it. As *The Sopranos* brought adult drama to the boob tube, it was as liberating to that long-stifled medium as, fifty years earlier, *A Streetcar Named Desire* was to American film.

After the *Sopranos*'s gutteral accent, the networks could admit more realistic speech, albeit in more measured tones. *The West Wing* producer Aaron Sorkin was prepared to let a character use the Lord's name in vain and to let the president's secretary describe his father with a five-letter anatomical term. *Philly* producer Steven Bochco proposed admitting a banned scatological reference (*New York Times*, September 2, 2001). Though shock radio (e.g., Howard Stern) and the reported foibles of President Clinton helped to broaden this climate, clearly *The Sopranos* led the way. It justified colloquial realism. From its premiere on January 10, 1999, *The Sopranos* was an oasis of reflective, intensely moving popular fiction in the desert of consumerist fantasy. It needed that realistic language. This liberty was another step in the Aging Boomers' revolution.

In a sense, *The Sopranos* is another form of "Reality TV." But it is more artful and less manipulative than all those *Survivor* shows we had to survive—that other phenomenon of the day. After all, *The Sopranos* is about how realistic characters survive in the urbane jungle—about their wiliness, ingenuity, dishonesty, and courage. It is about how those people get and how they get to keep those gaudy estates. But where the Survivor shows were artificial situations posing as real life, *The Sopranos* was art, brilliantly conceived and scripted, with the honesty of declared fiction.

The cast of largely unknown performers teased the audience by blurring the line between fiction and reality. As Tony's "waste management" firm evoked the real Gambinos' business front, the series packs the thrill of dangerous exposure. But the show always retained the resonance of fiction. In the HBO's own book on the series, *The Sopranos: A Family History*, Allen Rucker cleverly pretended to provide the "real life" background on the show's characters. In addition to chatty background on the show's creators and performers, it extended its characters' reality, through testimony from other characters, putative memos, and correspondence, even lists of some characters' garbage. This fictional dossier playfully extended the pretense to reality.

The realism draws on the (mainly) New Jersey location shooting. Creator David Chase insisted on that, even though "These days, movies and television series shoot for less in Canada. In recent years, Toronto has been a generic stand-in for Chicago, New York, and all suburbs in between." Though Chase has shot in Toronto, "It isn't New Jersey. It looks different, and that's the end of the story. . . . There's no collision of Hispanic, Italian or black around an 1890s brownstone square in Toronto. These are small, unimportant details, perhaps, but not to me" (Holden, pp. 129–30). While the interiors are generally shot in a Queens studio, the exteriors are shot on fresh locations that evoke gangland.

It also sounds real, with the salty vernacular and often poetic color of the characters' speech. "The feds are so far up my ass I can taste Bryl-cream," quoth Uncle Junior, under house arrest (II, 3). The quip has period color, preciseness, anger, and imagination. Or "It hurts like the fucking 'Pit and Pendulum' just to wipe myself" (II, 4). As the Hollywood D-girl, Amy, would say, "Very imagistic" (II, 7). The talk is so brilliantly written it rings unscripted. The complexity of the characters and the moral dilemmas they make reflect our real life. David Chase says: "I was looking for the notion that life is so complex now that even a wiseguy needs help sorting it out" (Holden, p. 103).

UNDERSTANDING *THE SOPRANOS*

Perhaps the series' basic pun is the title. Sopranos "sing"—which is also the argot for ratting to the cops/Feds. That's the sense of the term in II, 12, when Janice—having just killed her fiancé—tells Tony on his tapped home phone, "I can't sing. . . . I can't sing now. Think a minute, OK?" Sopranos sing at the highest range, the most female. That is, it is unmanly to betray one's gang. Note that the first gang member to turn state's evidence is the softie named Pussy Bonpensiero. (Ironically, his surname more or less translates as "good thought.") Over the whole series hangs the threat of someone "sing-ing" to the fuzz. More broadly, *The Sopranos* "sing" to the television au-dience about the secret lives, loves, and business ways of Gangland USA.

The series grew out of several established traditions in popular culture. From the American gangster films of the 1930s it drew the dynamic of gunfire, sexy music, and clubs, and the theme/value of individualism ram-pant against urban conformism. The hero climbs from the gutter to the top—and is brought down. The more Tony Soprano succeeds, the more riveting our wait for his doom. From the postwar American film noir, the series drew the awareness (not to mention the plot devices) of psychoanal-ysis. The wild, selfish Id escapes from the shadows of repression.

From postmodernism it drew its confidence that an audience will delight in irony, look for how this art draws from other art, and exult in transcend-ing borders and conventions. So these gangsters deliberately style them-selves after their favorite gangster films—especially Francis Ford Cop-pola's *Godfather* trilogy. (For a fuller discussion of this influence, see the appendix.)

From the Millennial turning point the show drew confidence that the times are ready for change, perhaps even something revolutionary, especially against censoring language and blinkering thought. The television audience was ready for a show about which it had to think and could argue. They would leave mush for meat. As James Gandolfini observed, "People are ready for a certain lack of political correctness. We do things with some respect" (Holden, p. 108)—especially (and this was radically new) respect for its audience's ability to deal with complexity.

The show's serious ambition was immediately recognized. As Stephen Holden introduced his anthology of *New York Times* coverage, "In forcing us to empathize with a thug whom we watch committing heinous acts, *The Sopranos* evokes a profound moral ambiguity" (p. xviii). For Peter Bogdanovich (Season One DVD, disc four), the interaction of the criminal and domestic worlds makes the family life more unusual, the gangster element more typical, and the resultant mix "strangely universal." Vincent Canby concluded, "*The Sopranos*, which plays as a dark comedy, possesses a tragic conscience" (Holden, p. 187).

J. Madison Davis, former president of The International Association of Crime Writers, North America, argued a Shakespearean dimension in *The Sopranos*. "The baseness of so many of the characters' acts and lives is contradicted by the nobility or the power of their emotions." Davis proposed that "the thrumming engine of the second season," Richie Aprile, is a New Jersey version of Shakespeare's Richard, duke of Gloucester, bent upon becoming Richard III—not to say just plain bent—with an outrageous marriage to help him along. "*The Sopranos* has always had a sense of high drama combined with a feel for the everyday, a sense of foolishness in the most serious situations, great dialogue, and, most important, a deep sense of humanity" (Holden, pp. 7–12).

How meaty can *The Sopranos* be? Let's consider the first shot of the first episode of the series. A suspicious Tony seems small between the foregrounded legs of a statue of a woman. He appears trapped by the woman he is looking up to, as if by scissors. The statue is not just a woman but the idea of Woman.

The male characters' sexual arrogance and insecurity form one of the series' primary themes. After all, Tony lives on Stag Trail Road and has named his boat *The Stugots* (that is, *cock* or, loosely, *balls,* connoting nerve and courage, gender-nonspecific). So the opening shot expresses the anxiety of a man insecure in his manhood, at once fascinated and frightened by Woman. The classical sculpture contrasts to the inflated dancers of the

Bada Bing, Tony's more natural habitat, over whom these men have such total control. In fact, the first shot inside the club foregrounds one stripper paralleling this bronze.

In Tony's unease before the nude sculpture we sense his vestigial Puritanism, his own twist on ethics, despite—or enabling—his corrupt profession. In his fear of Woman we get his fear of the womanly, specifically of being found to be weak, vulnerable, and—in particular—to break the code of silence. His female therapist, Dr. Melfi, will open his feminine side by making him talk and explore his feelings. Consistent with the towering Woman sculpture is the surprising strength of the women characters in this patriarchal clan. Carmela, Janice, Meadow, Livia, Melfi, even—briefly, fatally—Ralphie's whore, Tracee—all are strong, assertive women.

As the image stresses Tony's vulnerability, it sets off the series' most dangerous undertaking: It makes us sympathize with the Mafia killer. By immersing us in Tony's life, by rooting the fiction solidly in his perspective, the series challenges our moral judgment. It does an end-run around our usual morality. From Milton's Satan to Hitchcock's innocent criminals and criminal innocence, artists have known that evil has its own dangerous charm and that the best art will provide a moral test, not a polemic. Like the forbidden fruit in Eden, a moral work of art gives its viewer a challenge, not a confirmation.

As befits our percipient times, *The Sopranos* seems an exercise in moral relativism. Its hero hoods are not so bad—because we know them so well. They're not as bad as others who have not enjoyed the advantage of our identifying with them. That makes this series an exercise in moral judgment. As it betrays our knee-jerk responses, it tests us.

The complex dialectic of the opening shot—male vs. female, woman vs. idealized image of woman, strength vs. vulnerability, foreground vs. background—points to the series' central tension between the viewer's familiar morality and its violation by this criminal subculture. The viewer's rejection of the gang is itself complicated by their touching values of honor, family, and individualism. The result—from the first shot to the last—is an intense composition whose morality avoids the black and white in which we, confidently, naively, used to believe for the quicksands of reality grays.

AUTHOR! AUTHOR!

This guide now "reads" each episode of *The Sopranos* across its first four seasons with the closeness we gave that opening shot. Rare among television series, *The Sopranos* bears the critical analysis routinely accorded good literature, drama, and films. As a thoughtful construction, here is a TV series as rich as our best feature films in all it manages to say through its dialogue, camerawork, plot development, music, characterization, and the design of its image. But who is its author?

In literary fiction and drama, the author—the person responsible for the work, what it says, how its meaning radiates from how its elements are organized—is obviously the author, the writer. (Got that? The author is the author. Good.)

In film, authorship is more complicated. Because so much always happens in the laborious passage from the page to the screen, the author of a film is almost never the original screenwriter. On rare occasions the authorial control may be the producer, when he is as savvy and intrusive as a Darryl Zanuck or a David Selznick. Sometimes the controlling force behind a film may be the star (for example, Barbra Streisand, Marlon Brando on some occasions, or Orson Welles in *Journey into Fear* and perhaps in Carol Reed's *The Third Man*).

But usually we assume that the organizing intelligence behind a film is the director. The director may have full control of the writing and realization of a work—for example, Antonioni, Bergman, Fellini, Godard, Woody Allen, Steven Spielberg. Or s/he may work in (or as if in) the confines of a studio system, in tension with the assigned materials, for example, such *auteurs* as Dorothy Arzner, Ida Lupino, Fritz Lang, Vincent Minnelli, Douglas Sirk, Alfred Hitchcock, Howard Hawks, John Ford, Arthur Penn, Ang Lee, and others. Normally the director has the authority and responsibility for the vision and meaning delivered by the huge team of collaborators.

Television involves a different system of authorship. In a made for television movie, the author may well be the director, as in film. If the production system is similar, the difference may be only in the transmission. But a television series often deploys myriad writers and directors. In the first three seasons, *The Sopranos* credited 15 directors and 13 writers (who wrote sometimes alone, sometimes in twos or threes). This complicates the naming of one person as the source of the meaning and vision of the work. When that is possible in television it is usually the producer.

Except for the unique Alfred Hitchcock (who took his film persona to the small screen), Norman Lear was probably the first American television producer to stamp a series with his characteristic style and concerns. In fact, not just in one series but in a variety of them: *All in the Family, The Jeffersons,* and *Maude.* Network king Lear demonstrated that a producer can—and in a series normally would—provide the controlling impetus and cohesion for a continuing work. Similarly, James Brooks gave *Taxi* and the MTM range of sitcom series a characteristic stamp of values, tone, subject, and style. Today we can identify producer Aaron Spelling as the presiding author of his shows regardless of who else does the writing and directing. And it is clearly Steven Bochco's *NYPD Blue*.

The organizing intelligence behind *The Sopranos*, the person who "speaks" to us through each episode and their season collective, the "author" of the series, whoever may write or direct any component part, is David Chase. He conceived the idea, wrote and directed the pilot, and has been responsible for the work of his team—and for the meaning of their product—since. Chase continued to write some key episodes, including most season openers and closings: I, 1, 2 and 13; II, 4 and (with Todd Kessler) 13; and III, 1, 2 and (with Lawrence Konner) 13. He did "a lot of rewriting" on the early scripts before his writers absorbed his vision, he remarks on the Season One DVD (disc four) interview. And he insists on doing all the editing himself.

David Chase is the author—the creative source, voice, and vision—of *The Sopranos*. He knows the medium—having written for shows like *Kolchak: The Night Stalker*, *The Rockford Files*, and *Northern Exposure* since he was twenty-three. In 1988 he developed his first series, *Almost Grown*, another family drama with a popular music score. And given that his family name was DeCesare and he grew up in North Caldwell, New Jersey, he knows the cultural landscape. But "There was no cursing in my family," he assures us in his interview on the Season One DVD (disc four)—and he does not know anyone in the Mafia.

The series is full of Chase's personal touches. His daughter, Michelle, plays Meadow's friend Hunter. Uncle Junior's name comes from one of Chase's cousins (He's the man in glasses who leaves the Vesuvio with Uncle Junior in I, 1). The key speeches—after allowance for the characters' spin and dramatic irony—convey Chase's opinions about life, morality, honor, the excessive excuse of bad behavior in therapy, the remarkable achievement of the Italian-American community, and the short-sightedness of the Italian Anti-Defamation League. Clearly, it is David Chase who propels this unique series with his values, ambition, and vision.

Of course, no guide can be a substitute for the show itself. So let's cut to the Chase country.

Season One

I, 1: The Pilot

Written and directed by David Chase.

Gangster Tony Soprano consults psychiatrist Dr. Jennifer Melfi about his anxiety attacks and blackouts but is skeptical about the therapeutic process. He misses the duck family that settled in, then vacated, his swimming pool. He and his protege Christopher assault Mahaffy, a medical administrator, over a gambling debt. Tony fails to dissuade his Uncle Junior from using the popular restaurant of friend Art Bucco to kill an errant hoodlum. Tony has the restaurant burned down to save Art's reputation. Christopher kills a rival's nephew, Emil Kolar, to discourage competition for a big garbage contract. In his personal life, Tony's bitter mother, Livia, rejects any seniors residence, his daughter Meadow flirts with delinquency, his son Anthony Jr. is an underachiever, and his wife Carmela (correctly) suspects Tony of having a mistress.

As we have noted, the first episode begins with Tony nervous about opening up to a woman. Our first surprise is that Tony is consulting a woman psychiatrist. Tony's unease continues in Dr. Melfi's office, as he explains his panic attack, blackouts, and depression. Out of his element, Tony's black shirt obtrudes against the harmonized browns of Melfi's suit and her office.

As he will throughout the series, Tony fights the therapy: "It's impossible for me to talk to a psychiatrist." Of the four appointments in the first episode, one Tony skips and from one he stomps out angry (when Melfi asks him to discuss his feelings about the ducks). At the last he asserts that the Prozac has helped him so much he does not have to come any more. Tony's suspicion of therapy includes how his salutary talking reflects on his manliness. He cries when he realizes that he fears losing his family as he lost his ducks.

The flashback structure demonstrates the effectiveness of exposing buried memories. The past materializes for us. Tony's weeping shows how far his therapy has already taken him. Self-consciously he anticipates his tears. Of course, he feels this treatment has brought him down rather than up, made him weaker not healthier. Is he no stronger than simple Artie, who weeps at the loss of his restaurant? Tony consoles him with what he learned from Melfi: "Hope takes many forms." Not to duck the metaphor, behind that counsel lurks poet Emily Dickenson's line, "Hope is the thing with feathers."

Though Tony resists the treatment, there are early signs he will be erotically drawn toward Melfi. After asking her about her family's roots, he concludes "My mother would have loved it if you and I got together." But she corrects his casual "Hon" to "Dr. Melfi." When they happen to meet at the restaurant, Melfi seems nervous, but her unclinical language suggests some kinship: "Shut the fuck up," she tells her surprised date, Nils.

The first episode establishes the male fear of talking—especially if he's a gangster. Melfi scrupulously defines the line between doctor-patient confidentiality and her responsibility to warn the police if she learns of anyone's imminent danger. But Tony sneers at psychoanalysis: "I had a semester and a half at college so I understand Freud. I understand therapy as a concept." He prefers the Gary Cooper model, "the strong, silent type. There was an American." As "Guys today have no room for the penal experience," they join the Witness Protection Program instead of manfully taking the rap. Tony knows that if his cronies knew of his therapy he could be killed. Hence his nervous "confession" to Carmela who, of course, is overjoyed that he is seeing a therapist.

Already nervous about the RICO law's admission of government wiretapping and surveillance, Tony fears himself—or Melfi—being considered a squealer. When Tony first mentions RICO Melfi asks, "Is he your brother?" No, but it is heavy: RICO is the Racketeer Influenced and Corrupt Organizations Act passed in 1970 to help the government investigate and prosecute organized crime. From the Sopranos' perspective make that "persecute."

The opening episode also establishes the spectrum of parent-child tensions. Tony's son, AJ, has his thirteenth-birthday party postponed when Tony collapses at the barbecue. He collapses again while showing his mother the seniors residence. When Dr. Melfi encourages Tony to "Stay on your mother," what she means is "Pull back for some perspective on her." Carmela agrees that Tony's mother is his major problem. His avoidance of Melfi's question about his father suggests another major memory is buried there (which is revealed in I, 7 and III, 3).

Livia rails against Tony's neglect, rejects his gift CD player, and resists his encouragement to move into a well-appointed seniors home (with adjacent nursing quarters). Tony charmingly dances with his mother (to Connie Francis's appropriate "Who's Sorry Now?"). But Livia insists that daughters take better care of their mothers than sons do (an illusion entirely exposed when Tony's sister Janice erupts in II, 1). As Tony tells Melfi, his mother's current adoration of her dead husband jars with her life-long abuse of him, when she wore him "down to a nub." But Tony still envies his father who, although he didn't achieve Tony's rank, lived in an age of honorable gangsters who would never sing to the feds. In Livia's and Uncle Junior's bitterness about the current generation, Livia does not react to Junior's suggestion that something may have to be done to her son. That feeds his later plot to kill him.

Meadow rejects her mother's discipline and pleasure (their annual shopping visit to New York) as she chafes under teenage rules. The set design catches the pivot in Meadow's emotional state. Her bedroom abounds with the toys and dolls of her childhood, but a large butterfly on her wall suggests an imminent emergence. As if to realize Meadow's sense of her mother, Carmela brandishes a major military gun when she catches Meadow trying to sneak back into her bedroom. The militant mother lightly anticipates Livia's plotting against her son's life. "Mothers and daughters," Tony assures Carmela, "she'll come back to you."

Meadow would rather appeal her mother's ban of the Aspen ski holiday than hear Tony's pride in their ancestors who did the masonry and carpentry on the magnificent church. But Meadow grows thoughtfully appreciative in the scene. Here Tony speaks directly for David Chase, who was surprised to learn late in life that his grandfather and his brothers were master craftsmen from Europe who built some classic New Jersey churches.

By trying to save the reputation of friend Artie Bucco's restaurant, Tony irks Uncle Junior, his father's younger brother and himself the victim of a sibling's insecurities. Tony remembers him taking him to Yankees games and Uncle Junior remembers playing catch with him. The macho identify with athletics. Uncle Junior shattered Tony's self-esteem by telling his nieces that Tony would never make the varsity sports teams (hence his brief college tenure). Now Tony exuberantly attends Meadow's volleyball game (and plots business in the stands) and he will later spur AJ into football.

More dramatic is the Sopranos' marital tension. Tony strides into the kitchen bare-chested and slaps his wife's butt in the presence of their children and Meadow's friend, Hunter. Though Carmela devotedly attends his 6:30 A.M. medical examination, when he romanticizes their good times she snaps at him about his *goomah* (the wiseguy's obligatory mistress) and predicts he will go to Hell. Right after telling Carmela that she's the only person with whom he is "completely honest," Tony confirms her reference to his therapist as a "him." Despite her attack, Carmela gives him a warm, concerned wave as he enters the machine.

But Tony moves in a man's world, which wants to keep betrayal and infidelity in marriage where it belongs. This is demonstrated by the restaurant owner's smoothness in successive scenes. Tony brings Irina, his Russian mistress, one night and Carmela the next. "Mr. Soprano, months we don't see you," the restaurateur exudes for Carmela's benefit, "Where you been? Signora Carmela!" *The Godfather* theme music in the background confirms this man's world. Understandably, Carmela is surprised—and relieved—when what Tony "confesses" is not adultery but his other therapy.

In this bent world even language can't be straight. Hence, the gangsters' professional euphemism. Tony tells Dr. Melfi he's "a waste management consultant," which is literally and metaphorically, but not exhaustively, true. He manages more kinds of waste—and wasting or whacking—than the term usually covers. At the restaurant, Tony tells Melfi that her "decorating tips" really worked. Insofar as his improvement is still superficial, the Prozac is a kind of decorating tip. When he tells Melfi that he and debtor Mahaffey "had coffee," we watch Tony gleefully run him down with Chris's new car in an office park in Paramus, N.J., then beat him into submission. But as Mahaffey drops his tray of coffees when he sees Tony coming, the euphemism is not untrue.

Situations can be as deceptively innocent as language. Mahaffey is persuaded to take Hesh as a partner, and to tap medical insurance for fictitious operations, when Hesh and Pussy take him to a bridge overlooking a deep chasm and a waterfall. Except for Pussy dropping his ice-cream cone down the deep gorge, the threat is unspoken. Mahaffey feels the most sinister pressure when he hears the ice-cream truck depart, leaving the men alone. The most innocent sound can carry a brutal subtext.

Tony's unsteady "nephew" (son of Carmela's cousin) Christopher is introduced as a weakling, late on his assignments, more concerned about his $60,000 Lexus than in kicking the loan-welcher, Mahaffey, at foot. Later, Chris almost blurts out the reason why Artie's restaurant, aptly named Vesuvio, was blown up. Christopher is of the yappy, indulgent generation that Tony rues. Open with his feelings, Chris objects that Tony did not congratulate him for killing Emil Kolar. When Chris mentions his autobiographical screenplay Tony explodes: "What you gonna do, a Harry

Hill on me now?" Hill was the hero who betrayed the mob in Martin Scorsese's *GoodFellas* (1990), the film David Chase calls his Koran (Season One DVD, disc one commentary).

In fact, Chase cites this scene as the precise point "we left network television behind." On the first day's shooting, this scene was the first shot. The script called for Tony to slap Chris, as if waking him out of his fantasy. But Gandolfini suggested his character would be much angrier at the danger of exposure. With his on-a-dime turns from concern about Chris, to rage at his threat, to warmth again, as he straightens Chris's clothing, Gandolfini made Tony both violent and cuddly. With that touch the show abandoned the usual sentimentalizing and excusing of the gangster hero.

Confirming his influence by films, Christopher kills Emil Kolar amid full-screen black and white stills—close-ups from the poster in the background—of Humphrey Bogart, Dean Martin, and Edward G. Robinson. To prepare for Emil's arrival Chris strikes Kung Fu movie poses. He sees himself as acting in those stars' gangster tradition. The song over the murder is Bo Diddley's swaggering, "I'm a Man." But Chris's heroic self-conception is undercut by the pig heads piled behind his left shoulder—not a flattering audience.

With the cocky insensitivity of the young and the shallow, Chris calls Emil E-mail. The image of Chris and Pussy swinging Emil's corpse *at* the dumpster wall instead of *up into* it is an emblem of Chris's frustrated aspiration. He will always want to swing higher than he can. The gangsters may model themselves after their film heroes, but Chris wants to enter that fantasy world.

Against all that artifice stands Tony's fascination with the wild ducks. They are a miraculous eruption of nature in his denatured life: "It was such a trip to have those wild creatures come into my pool and have their little babies." Mystifying his family, Tony wades into the pool to feed them. He offers to build them a better ramp. Tony's depression begins when the ducks leave. In his dream, his penis falls off. When he runs to get his Lincoln mechanic to restore it, a bird swoops it away. When Tony realizes "I'm afraid I'm gonna lose my family like I lost the ducks," his mood is caught by Sting's "I'm so Happy I Can't Stop Crying."

Perhaps the pastoral wistfulness of the duck family also lay behind his naming his daughter "Meadow." The name recalls an ideal lost and forgotten in the seamy New Jersey setting—especially the landscape surveyed in the show's title sequence (see our Conclusion) and especially distinguished from the "Meadowlands" where the gang beat and bury their enemies. Like the ducks, Meadow's name suggests a natural refuge from Tony's bleak world. But even nature can be deceptive and dangerous—as Mahaffey senses high above the waterfall.

From her first appearance, Artie's wife, Charmaine, resents the gangsters' patronage of the Vesuvio. Throughout the series she remains the one character of uncompromised conscience and values. Standing against a mountain of garbage, Artie has to give Tony back the "free" cruise tickets by which Tony hoped to get Artie to close his restaurant so Junior couldn't kill his gunsel there. Typical of Tony's poisoned life, he destroys his friend's prized restaurant to protect him. In this twisted ethos, Charmaine's ethics and Uncle Junior's stubbornness push Tony to arson. However irregular, it is generous.

Some witty editing enforces the sympathetic ambivalence. Right after Charmaine insists "someone donated his kneecaps for those tickets," Mahaffey hobbles into view in a knee-high cast and on crutches. After Mahaffy admits taking the tranquilizer Zolof, his tormentor Tony gulps Prozac as he practices his golf swing. The predator is as nervous as his prey. Just as Tony assures Chris, "Beautiful day—what could be bad?" we see the bitter Livia, being driven to AJ's party by Uncle Junior.

The episode closes on Tony's pool. Carmela pragmatically greets Livia and Uncle Junior: "OK, everyone, let's eat." As everyone heads off to dinner, Meadow's friend Hunter announces she won't eat. (Typical of the show's gathering ironies and coherence, in II, 2, Hunter is in the Eating Disorders ward at the hospital and in II, 3, she tells Meadow she uses bulimia as a strategic threat to control her parents.) Then three little boys run past laughing—and aiming a toy gun, like the men they may join their dads' business to become. The camera holds on the vacated pool, a benign shimmering blue, vacant of the partygoers, the divided families united within The Family, but vacant too of the glimpse of more natural family life that Tony found in his ducks. As the closing Nick Lowe song concludes, "God help the beast in me."

- A poll on the HBO website—HBO.com/Sopranos—on the favorite line of dialogue in Season One chose AJ's response to Livia's refusal to come to his birthday party: "So what? No fuckin' ziti now?" In its unsentimental concern for the appetite the line may be an homage to Clemenza's classic line from *The Godfather*: "Leave the gun. Take the cannoli."
- Because this pilot was filmed two years before airing, some of the characters look much younger than in episode two. The actors playing Irina

and Father Phil were replaced. And Satriale's Pork Store was built to replace the original Centanni's Meat Market. (In *The Godfather Part II*, we learn *cent' anni* is a toast: "We should all live happily for a hundred years.")

■ Typical of the show's subtle detail, this dysfunctional family's coffee is Chock Full o'Nuts.

I, 2:   46 Long

Written and directed by David Chase.

In the season's only pre-titles scene, Tony's relationship with Uncle Junior is shivered when Chris and his friend Brendan Filone steal a truckload of DVD players fr0om a company protected by Uncle Junior. Meanwhile, Tony has his crew replace the stolen car of AJ's science teacher. Livia, after a kitchen fire and a driving accident, is moved into the Green Grove seniors' residence. Tony is infuriated by Dr. Melfi's suggestion that he hates his mother.

In the only pre-titles scene of the season, a television discussion in the background deals with the confusion and instability of the underworld, while in the fore Tony and his crew count their mountain of money. The staging emphasizes the speakers' remoteness from the Sopranos' life. U.S. Attorney Braun claims that because of drugs and squealers the gangsters have forever lost their heyday. This foreshadows Pussy's treachery and fall. But gangster-turned-author Vincent Rizzo argues that there will always be organized crime to serve such popular needs as gambling, drugs, and pornography. Twice in the first scene Silvio cheers Tony up with his Pacino imitation (from *The Godfather Part III*): "Just when I thought I was out they pulled me back in." The joke and all that money make the writer seem the wiser of the talking heads—even though Rizzo turned rat.

Perhaps the central metaphor of this episode derives from the newspaper item Pussy reads out in that prologue, a proposal to clone Princess Di. Silvio's impersonation of Pacino is a comic form of cloning. More broadly, Tony takes the traditional view: Only God can make life. But cloning is part of the new technology that, with its consequent compromised ideals, defines this episode. When Tony replaces Mr. Miller's stolen Saturn (implicitly to improve AJ's D+ in Science), it's with a different stolen car. The repainting makes it a bathetic kind of clone. The DVDs that Chris and Brendan steal and the new telephone equipment that befuddle Livia and Bing bartender Georgie point to the complexity of new technology that replicates image and voice.

This is also seen in Paulie's tirade against the ubiquitous gourmet coffee shops that exploit the superior Italian. "We invented this shit and all these cocksuckers are getting rich on it." In righteous indignation—"They ate *pootsie* until we gave them the gift of our cuisine"—he steals an espresso machine. Paulie feels swamped by the cloning of Italian food and coffee—from which only the "real" Italian, that is, he, should profit.

But even cloning can't replicate the family warmth Tony finds in the three photographs left in his mother's emptied house: the young woman, the mother with young Tony, his parents holding their baby boy. Tony falls, breathless, after seeing the pictures, because—like the lost blessing of his ducks—they represent a contentment he cannot recover. Worse, he never had it. The only loving experience he can recall for Dr. Melfi is the time Livia and her children all laughed when their father tripped and fell down the stairs. Even their one positive memory is based on cruelty.

Tony struggles to reconcile his mother as helpless little old lady and as psychological monster. Though his sisters have abandoned her, Tony feels guilty despite all his generous effort. Of course, for this mother nothing is ever enough. Even as Tony has gorged on her Virginia ham, she insists from her sick-couch, "You never let me feed you." To Carmela's offer, "You know you can come live with us," Livia replies: "I know when I'm not wanted." Yet Tony tells Melfi that Carmela won't let Livia live with them. His one specific praise—"She's a good woman. She put food on that table every night."—better suits his *focaccio*-winner father.

The idea of "Mother" is so strong that it makes the Bada Bing dancers drop everything to come over to Tony when they hear Livia is in trouble. Later, they only pause vaguely when Tony beats up the phone-fumbling Georgie. The parallel connects violence and sentimentality. In the episode's last shot, the three pole-dancers personify the confused emotions of a valueless order.

Tony shares that confusion. Rather than acknowledge his anger at his mother, he stomps out of his last session with Melfi, insisting he won't talk to her again. Tony is ashamed and afraid of his emerging anger, despite Melfi's advice that "Sad is good; unconscious isn't." Clearly Livia has left Tony as "scathed" as the DVD truck driver asks his robbers to leave him. Like the over-dedicated son, the trucker provides the rope with which the robbers can—to save his job—leave him helpless.

The family betrayal spreads into Family betrayal when Chris robs the company paying Uncle Junior protection. Uncle Junior drags the cancer-stricken boss Jackie Aprile from his sickbed to award his tribute. Ironically, we will later learn that Uncle Junior had once hijacked Jackie's trucks, necessitating a "sit-down" to clear the air. Now Tony's loose cannon, Chris, has his own, looser cannon, Brendan, who again robs that company of a load of Italian suits. (Fancy dressing is one of the conventions of the gangster genre.) When the robber's inability to drive the truck leads to fatality, this Family conflict parallels Livia's accidentally running over her friend.

The dangerous disorder is pervasive. Tony is undermined by his mother's negativism in the one family and by his "nephew" Chris's unruly ambition and his own uncle's rigidity in the other. When Chris is denied admission into a popular club and gangster-film maestro Martin Scorsese (Anthony Caso) is welcomed in, Chris renews his resolve to parlay his life into a Hollywood film.

The narrative order confirms the duplicity and disintegration. Just after Tony tells Carmela how proud he is that Livia chauffeurs her less capable friends ("It gives me hope"), she drives into her passenger. When Tony insists Livia's black caregiver Perrilyn will stay, the camera holds on Livia's ambiguous close-up: Is she resigned or plotting? Carmela finds Perrilyn leaving in a rage, for reasons of which Livia pretends ignorance: "These blacks—who knows what they're gonna take the wrong way?" (Perhaps being referred to as "These blacks"?) Though Uncle Junior approves her hiring, as soon as Tony is gone Junior mutters: "A smoke he hires. For his own mother." The particular term works against Junior: Livia needs that "smoke" to prevent another kitchen fire. Tony is only slightly less prejudiced: "No ganji," he warns her at their first meeting.

In this show nothing positive goes undeflated. So Tony assures Livia that Carmela does not want her fine jewelry yet; they both want her to enjoy a long, healthy life. But when Livia says she gave all her jewelry to a cousin Tony explodes: "All I got was a vibrating chair?" Contrary to the nursing home director's reassuring Italian proverb, it will take more than time and patience to turn the mulberry leaf Livia into anything like silk. She's closer to the proverbial sow's ear—with a bullet.

In this world of imitation and copies, characters often project their weakness on others. When Livia claims Perrilyn stole "that beautiful plate that Aunt Septimia took from that restaurant in Rome," she projects her family's theft upon the innocent Trinidadian. So, too, Silvio wonders if the Royal Family had Diana whacked.

In one example of successful cloning, Pussy's car repair shop is named Bunuel Bros. The reference to Spanish film director Luis Buñuel declares the spiritual source of this series' black comedy and scathing anatomy of social hypocrisy and familial dysfunction. "I'm a big Buñuel fan," Chase remarks on the Season One DVD interview (disc four), with particular respect for his Surrealist dreams.

- When Pussy tracking the car thief jokes "I'm a fuckin' Rockford over here," he alludes to Producer David Chase's earlier career as a writer on *The Rockford Files*.
- The episode title, "46 Long," alludes to Silvio's intention to steal a suit from the thieves but is also a sum of money—$46,000.
- James Gandolfini (Tony) was born in Westwood, N.J., graduated from Rutgers, worked as a bouncer and nightclub manager, and broke into Broadway in 1992. He—along with Aida Turturro (Janice)—appeared in the 1992 Broadway revival of Tennessee Williams' *A Streetcar Named Desire*, starring Jessica Lange and Alex Baldwin. His pre-*Sopranos* films include *A Stranger among Us, A Civil Action, 8 mm, Get Shorty, The Juror, Crimson Tide*, and *True Romance*. In 2001, he played a gay hitman who becomes Julia Roberts's confidante in *The Mexican,* the prison warden who tyrannizes Robert Redford in *The Castle*, and the corrupt store-owner in the Coens' *The Man Who Wasn't There*. Even without the colorful Soprano language, he retained his expressiveness and remarkable physical presence.
- Edie Falco (Carmela) is the daughter of jazz drummer Frank Falco. She studied acting at SUNY, Purchase. Her films include *Bullets Over Broadway, The Funeral, Private Parts, Copland*, and the lead role in *Judy Berlin*.
- Jamie Lynn Sigler (Meadow) made her professional theatre debut at 12 in the musical version of *It's a Wonderful Life*. As she's quoted on the *Maxim* website, "I'm Cuban, Greek, Romanian and Sephardic Jew, so I couldn't get further from Italian." Robert Iler (AJ) began doing television commercials when he was six and has appeared on *Saturday Night Live* and the film *The Tic Code*.
- In his Season One DVD interview (disc four), Chase applauds his teenage actors for their direct, accurate portrayals. They contrast to all the unrealistically cute, bright, "empowered" children and youth on TV.

I, 3:   Denial, Anger, Acceptance

Written by Mark Saraceni, Directed by Nick Gomez.

Meadow and Hunter coax Christopher into getting them some speed to get them through their SATs. An elderly Hasidic Jew seeks Tony's help to get his daughter's divorce. Artie and Charmaine move into a cheaper home, still ruing the loss of their restaurant. At Livia's suggestion, Uncle Junior has Christopher roughed up and Brendan killed for their unruliness.

In this episode the collision between the gangster world and the religious takes two forms. The first contrasts the Hasidic Jewish and the Italian cultures. "Ah-seed-em but I don't believe 'em," quips Paulie, encapsulating their difference in belief and vision. The second ethical arena is domestic.

When they meet under the pig atop Satriale's Pork Store, the very location undercuts the orthodox Jews' venture. Clearly this partnership will not be kosher. Elderly Hasid Shlomo Teittleman offers Tony $25,000 to persuade Teittleman's son-in-law, Ariel, to grant his wife a divorce, without the half-share of the motel Ariel demands. For his help Tony demands a 25-percent share of the motel.

As the Jewish divorce is called a "get," it makes for some smooth wordplay: Tony will help Teittleman get the *get;* "Let's understand each other from the get-go;" "We got you your *get.*" But this harmony in language belies deeper differences. When Paulie suggests shooting Ariel instead, Silvio observes "It's taboo for his religion"—as if their Catholicism were not troubled by that nicety.

As usual in this series, the gangster world is reflected in the supposedly respectable one. Silvio reports that the DA put the "rabbi's goon squad" out of business. The deal runs against both Hesh's advice to Tony "not to get involved with these people"—by which he means not Jews but "fanatics"—and Teittleman's son Hillel's advice against dealing with gangsters. Both warnings prove prescient.

Ariel proves an indomitable adversary, a spirited Hasid who talks like the hoods. He's known Shlomo "since before I had hair on my *petzel*" (Yiddish, colloquialism: "little penis"). In that cocky quip lies the seed of his doom. Ariel draws from the Jews' heroic defense against the Romans at

Masada, where 900 Jews staved off 15,000 Romans for two years: "They chose death before enslavement. And the Romans: where are they now?" "You're looking at them, asshole," Tony replies. Silvio is impressed: "If we don't kill this prick we should put him to work."

Hesh advises Tony that castration is a more effective threat to a Jewish fanatic than death: "Finish his *bris*." Even a fanatic would rather die than live castrated. Hesh knows whereof he speaks: He is in bed with a beautiful young black woman. When Ariel settles with Teittleman for a 15-percent share in the motel, the old Hasid tries to renege on Tony's share, but Tony prevails.

In the family tension between ethics and expediency, Uncle Junior needs to rein in Christopher and Brendan, who are hiding behind Tony. He spurns Mikey's advice of violence: "Take it easy. We're not making a Western here." Livia capriciously shares Tony's love for Christopher because he once put up her storm windows. She suggests Junior have Christopher roughed up and Brendan shot: "Maybe Christopher could use a little talking to. You know. The other one? Filone? [pause] I don't know." Having planted her plot, she typically retreats, but reiterates her motive for revenge: "I'm a babbling idiot. That's why my son put me in a nursing home." In a parody of parental concern the unsuspecting Brendan remarks: "Kids. You think you can protect them. But you can't." Brendan takes a predator's pleasure from that conclusion.

In a double act of charity Carmela overrules Tony to host a fundraiser for the Pediatric Hospital. Hiring Charmaine and Artie to cater it adds expediency to her ethics. The good cause advances Carmela's social prospects and helps her friends. But the personal charity is not entirely successful. Charmaine is insulted when Carmela summons her with the same hand gesture she used for her Polish maid. Less to assuage Carmela's concern for her than to counter Carmela's condescension, Charmaine reveals that before they were married Charmaine dated and slept with Tony. Carmela is oddly unassured by this.

Their husbands' relationship also quivers when Tony attacks Artie for still bemoaning his restaurant. Tony is in close-up when Artie rhetorically asks: "Who would burn down a perfectly good restaurant? It's stupid. Insane." In Tony's "I'm sorry, Artie" an apology hides behind ritual sympathy. Feeling both guilty and justified, Tony explodes at Artie in the kitchen. After expletives the men playfully hurl food at each other. It starts when Artie's rhetoric unwittingly points to Tony's guilt: "What the fuck do you know about it?" Like the charge, the cold cut sticks to Tony's forehead.

As Carmela innocently smiles at the food fight, behind her we see almost lost in soft-focus the more suspicious Charmaine.

The Charmaine-Artie relationship gathers weight. In earlier episodes Charmaine criticized her husband's involvement with Tony, ostensibly because she rejects the mobster world. But Charmaine's resentment toward Tony may have some root in their old affair. Perhaps she needs to convince herself more than Carmela that she is happy with her marital choice (especially when she will leave Artie in III). In any case, the disclosure helps explain why Charmaine has distanced herself from her close friend Carmela. Certainly she is more aggressive and effective than Carmela in influencing the husband. But as Artie points out, Charmaine is inconsistent in agreeing to work the Sopranos' fundraiser but refusing Tony's help to restart their restaurant. She is more scrupulous than the other characters in defending her ethics against expediency. In an opposite virtue, Adriana persuades Chris to supply Meadow's speed to save her from the dangers of Jefferson Avenue.

Tony's meetings with Dr. Melfi dramatize the title's movement from denial through anger to acceptance, especially regarding his friend and Acting Boss Jackie Aprile's fatal cancer. Tony is disturbed when two pictures in Melfi's waiting room of a barn and a rotted tree remind him of mortality. In his Russian *goomah*'s bedroom, he is bothered by the image of a desert motel with an empty canvas chair in front of it, another image of departed humanity, though it reminds Irina simply of "David Hockey." As usual, the malapropism makes new sense: There is ice—or at least cold comfort—in that Hockney desert. Also as usual, Tony stomps out of the second session with Melfi. In the last visit he stays to wonder about our gift of knowing we will die.

Along with his quick anger, Tony shows stirring of a thoughtful nature. After all, he paused over those two pictures. Then he contemplates Ariel's willingness to die "if it's for something." In contrast, Jackie Aprile is helpless before his cancer. Tony's gift—a stripper busting out of her nurse's uniform checks Frankie's "vitals"—provides futile relief. His next visit dispels Tony's confidence that "Jackie's so fuckin' mean he'll scare that cancer away." Now Jackie is wasting away, too preoccupied to enjoy Ariel's conversion.

With Melfi, Tony considers Teittleman's charge that he's a Frankenstein monster, or its Jewish counterpart, the Golem—monstrous, inhuman, unfeeling. The dramatic montage that concludes the episode shows Tony is a man of feelings, but is operating in a world of savagery. Similarly, Ariel's beating is intercut with Carmela's civilized reception, especially her "schmoozing" with a Jewish woman.

In homage to the climaxes of all three *Godfather* films (not "a Western"), Uncle Junior's attack on Christopher and Brendan is intercut with Meadow's choir's performance of "All through the Night." This episode begins with the two bloods returning the hijacked truck as Tony's favor, not Uncle Junior's. It concludes with Junior's retribution for that act. Mikey brings the plot full circle when he greets Brendan with "Hijack, bye Jack." The interwoven chorale puts gangland justice in the context of spirituality and grace. The song over the violence lends a lyricism to the otherwise gratuitous shots of the last twitch of Brendan's toe and his last cigarette floating on the surface while blood swirls into his bath. In Chris's mock execution, he confesses he gave Meadow speed and befouls himself. He's left on the blood-red boards, his bravado exposed by the gun's blanks.

Within the choir scene, Meadow's and Hunter's choir and solo singing are intercut with close-ups of Tony watching, proud and obviously moved. His sentiment is genuine notwithstanding the violence in his business life. In this scene his family provides a blissful respite from the compromises of his Family. Tony's challenge is to sustain his family feelings against the callousness required in his Family role. His Family style encroaches upon his family bliss.

When Tony comes late to the recital he joins Carmela and takes her hand. She withdraws it quickly. In one of those resonant ambiguities that so distinguish this series, her particular motive is uncertain. Is she irked that he has—as usual—come late to an important family event? Does she suspect he is coming from his mistress? When Carmela brushes her nose, is she sniffing for that presence? Is she still disturbed by Charmaine's disclosure? Or does she want to indulge her pride in her daughter's performance without being reminded of Tony's compromising role in her life? Does she spurn his real hand to enjoy the idealized moment of her daughter?

Carmela's action suggests a complexity of emotional possibilities. This is the lot of a human nature whose impulses and activity range from the savage to the saintly. Ending on the choir's last note of "All through the Night" provides a counterpoise to the first episode's close on "God help the beast in me." But the end-credits' song returns to the gloomier theme of responsibility in the face of death. In "Complicated Shadows" Elvis Costello and the Attractions remind us, "Well, you know your time has come / And you're sorry for what you've done."

▪ Lorraine Bracco (Dr. Jennifer Melfi) won an Oscar nomination as Henry Hill's wife in *GoodFellas*. Because she played that gangster's wife she declined the offer to play Carmela here and opted for the shrink. She also appeared in *Hackers, Getting Gotti, Even Cowgirls Get the Blues, Medicine Man, Radio Flyer*, and *Sea of Love*.

I, 4:   Meadowlands

Written by Jason Cahill. Directed by John Patterson.

Tony's alienation from Uncle Junior intensifies, as he avenges Christopher's beating. After Jackie Aprile dies at only 44—paradoxically for a gangster, of cancer—the captains support Tony as boss. But to make peace with Uncle Junior Tony submits to his leadership. Meanwhile, Meadow explains their father's gangster life to Anthony Junior.

In the opening shot Tony and Dr. Melfi present their faces in the same frame. Usually they are shot separately, as if they were speaking from separate worlds, or one is viewed beyond the other. This shot begins what turns out to be Tony's nightmare that his associates know about his secret therapy. The dream approaches reality when Paulie has a dental appointment up the hall. The nightmare presents scenes of increasing implausibility, from Tony openly admiring Melfi's legs, to Heshie having a therapy session with her, Silvio having sex, and Paulie and Pussy waiting outside. Melfi turns into Livia. Discovering AJ behind a door anticipates his learning about his father's real profession. The episode concludes on a wiser AJ leaning on a tombstone at Jackie Aprile's funeral. Finally aware of the family's Family life, he gazes stolidly back at his father's wink.

This episode deals with the shifting of power on both the personal and professional planes. When AJ fights his former friend Jeremy at school, the larger boy backs down after his father is frightened by Tony—innocently holding an ax—at a garden supply shop. But Tony is never simply innocent. He pressures the clerk to sell him some banned DDT. In the marriage, Carmela threatens divorce to keep Tony from ending his sessions with his therapist, whom he continues to let her assume is a man. ("He's got more degrees than a thermometer.")

In the most chilling show of strength Uncle Junior orders Tony out of his cafe and commands him to "come heavy" (that is, armed) if he ever returns. Their leadership rivalry feeds Junior's familial resentment: "A son who throws his mother in an asylum." Livia refuses to enjoy the $4,000-per-month retirement home Tony provides. After Jackie Aprile's death Tony returns to Junior's Sit Tite Loungenette, "heavy, like you said, but I don't want to use it." Contrary to Silvio's expectations ("Adios, Junior"), Tony makes peace by offering his uncle the leadership (for two prize territories, for Tony to "save face"). As he assures his aides and the other captains, though, Tony expects to be involved in his uncle's every decision. Tony applies to Uncle Junior the strategy Melfi proposed, to give Livia the illusion of being in control.

Another power shift involves Detective Vin Makazian, who covers his gambling debts and two alimonies on a $40K salary by doing odd investigations for Tony. Another loose cannon, Tony finds him urinating outside Livia's seniors residence. Hired to follow Melfi, Makazian stops her date's car and beats him up. The once confident tax lawyer Randall cowers in his house.

In their session Melfi reports this to Tony. "It's not your fault," she replies, when Tony says he's "sorry" about her friend's assault. As with Artie, Tony's formal sympathy allows him a safe "apology." As he set the cop on her tail, here the therapist is in ignorance and the client has the broader knowledge and counsel. The power has briefly shifted. Melfi is distracted when Tony recalls seeing his first corpse at the age of fifteen. She has lived "a sheltered existence," out of touch with "the climate of rage in American society" and "casual violence" that Vin Makazian has just shown her.

Christopher is the episode's primary loser of power. He's widely teased for having befouled himself during his beating. In a collision of language, after Adriana asks if he really "made number two in his pants," he proposes to go get some "shit" from Brendan. Adriana's decorum seems childish in Chris's world. Having been humbled in the (definitely non-pastoral) Meadowlands, he's afraid to step outside. The gangster is as traumatized as the tax lawyer. Assuming Tony ordered his assault, Chris screams at Meadow for tattling about her speed. When Tony does turn on Christopher, it's when the young man ignores Tony's sorrow at Jackie's death and urges war against Uncle Junior.

In the climactic power shift, Jackie Aprile's death shakes the society. Tony weeps at the news when he hears it on the television. In awe, one of the Bada Bing dancers stands under the set: "I'll never forget where I was this day." Her sad life seems briefly ennobled by the passing of this ostensible hero, the JFK, RFK, or Martin Luther King of the Bada Bing. The stripper's comment deflates her pathetic reverence and the gangster's false status.

At Jackie's funeral, Uncle Junior benignly receives the captains' respect, a small vainglory in the face of death. In surrendering the leadership to Uncle Junior, Tony seems to have created the monster that Teittleman called him in the previous episode. But, as he assures the wary *capos*, "I still love that man." The organ and the lyrics of Mazzy Star's "Looking down from the Bridge" give the end credits an elegiac wail.

▪ In his delirium, the dying Jackie Aprile says two nonsensical things that assume ironic significance later. The first—"The fish is in my pocket"— anticipates the association of Pussy Bonpensiero's murder with fish. The second is unintended, a dramatic irony created by time (specifically, September 11, 2001), not the scriptwriter: "I'm at the World Trade Center." That line may be removed from future reruns. After all, in the fear of mailed-anthrax spores the networks withdrew the *Seinfeld* episode in which George's fiancée, Susan, dies from licking bad invitation envelopes.

▪ Nancy Marchand (Livia) was already suffering from lung cancer and emphysema when the series began. She was on bottled oxygen between takes. Her character was supposed to die in the first season, but she proved so riveting that she continued into the second. Ms. Marchand died on June 18, 2000. Her acting career extended from the classic television show *Marty* in 1953, where she played Marty's (Rod Steiger) date, to her four-Emmy (1978–1982) career as the stately WASP publisher, Mrs. Margaret Pynchon, on *Lou Grant*. Her films included *Tell Me that You Love Me, Junie Moon; The Hospital; Regarding Henry;* and *Jefferson in Paris*.

▪ Livia's character derives somewhat from creator David Chase's memories of his own mother: "The way she acted was very sad. As she got older, she started insulting more and more people, taking umbrage at things they said and cutting herself off from the world. . . . 'I don't cater to anyone,' she used to say. But there was a kind of self-awareness of what she was doing. . . . She was aware sometimes that she was being outrageous and provocative. . . . She would say 'I hate it' and later say 'I didn't say I hate it; I don't know where you got that from.' " She wielded "the tyranny of the weak" (Holden, pp. 18, 22–23). But of course Chase's "mother is not Livia. By any stretch of the imagination. In the first season, in the first few shows, in the pilot, some of Livia's dialogue is actual dialogue from my mother. My mother had a very Livia-like attitude. She was very unintentionally funny. Because she was so downbeat" (Rucker). As it happens, Mario Puzo said that he based his *Godfather* hero, Vito Corleone (Marlon Brando), on the strength and wisdom of his mother.

I, 5: College

Written by Jim Manos Jr. and David Chase. Directed by Allen Coulter.

When Tony drives Meadow to Maine to visit three prospective colleges, he spots a former associate who turned state witness then disappeared into the witness protection program. Tony and the frightened man stalk each other. While Meadow is at her second interview, Tony ducks out and kills him. Carmela is visited by Father Phil, who seems to have a romantic interest in her—and in her cooking—but his overnight stay ends up innocent.

The pre-visuals sound of church bells resumes from I, 3 the combination of religious music and secular violence. In a similar mix of culture and savagery here Tony kills the traitor while Meadow is at her Bowdoin College interview. The episode contrasts Tony's very warm and open scenes with his daughter to his strangulation of Fabian Petrullio, now "Fred Peters."

Two statements contend for the title of "central theme" here. The first is Father Phil's response to Carmela's questioning the "major contradictions" in Jesus's words. The priest's faith in love—"Hopefully, some day we'll learn to tolerate, accept and forgive those who are different"—seems vacuous amid the moral complexity in this series and especially in this episode. As the priest flirts with seducing Carmela, his "love" is rather ambivalent. Indeed, the predatory priest validates the second statement, the Nathaniel Hawthorne quotation that Tony reads on the wall of the classic writer's old college:

No man can wear one face to himself and another to the multitude without finally getting bewildered as to which may be true.

As Carmela suggests, we have to "face" the major contradictions in our own various faces, to discover our integrity and to understand others. So Hawthorne's statement trumps Father Phil's.

In a comic version of confusing faces, Peters has problems with lips on the busts he makes. Christopher mistook the Sinatra bust in Jackie Aprile's rec room to depict Shaquille O'Neal (not that common a confusion in life): "He fuckin' needs to practice a little on lips." Excessive lips are an apt weakness for someone who talked too much to the FBI. Tony confirms his identification of Peter when he spots the Ronald Reagan bust in the travel office—with Shaq's lips. Tony's "Hello Rat" could express a closet Democrat.

Though the squealer has gone to great lengths to put on a new face, he has not changed. Peters loses our sympathy when he aims to shoot Tony and when he tries to hire two drug buyers to kill him. The post-mob Peters remains shady. He threatens his druggies, "Want the cops to find out who burned down your historical house?" Petrullio/Peters gives a second meaning to Tony's unflagging purpose: "You know one thing about us wiseguys? The hustle never ends." As Petrullio "flipped" after he was busted for selling heroin, he foreshadows Pussy's predicament.

Tony's murder is shockingly interwoven with his squiring Meadow to university interviews and confronting her suspicions about his career. As Stephen Holden reflects on the first season, "As much as it banalizes its mobsters, it refuses to trivialize their viciousness. Tony's brutality is all the more disturbing because it erupts from within a social framework of apparent normalcy. That framework includes a devout young priest, who, like Dr. Melfi, skillfully sidesteps the deeper moral issues of Tony's life" (p. xviii).

The Hawthorne quotation applies to all the major characters in this episode. At its simplest, it shows when Christopher pushes his offer to fly to Maine to dispatch Peters. "I'm your soldier," he insists, so his duty requires that he do the job for Tony. But then he lets slip his true motive: Whacking Peters would ensure Chris's promotion. When Chris says he's "a cunt hair away from being made" and Tony kills Peters himself, Tony becomes that cunt hair. In III, 7, Junior declares himself to be the cunt hair separating Tony from owning all New Jersey. In both usages, womanizing men—immoral, insecure—denigrate woman. As both speakers are violent toward their lovers, the image expresses the insecurity behind their callous power.

The Hawthorne theme of faces is varied in Tony's scenes with Meadow. They leave the first campus in the familiar tension about what a daughter can safely tell her father. In this case, it involves the sexual liberty that undergraduates take at the respective colleges. Later, Meadow volunteers—"because you were honest with me today"—that she and her friends used speed. But Tony overreacts:

TONY: Right under my nose. You'd think you'd know.
MEADOW: No, Dad. You won't.

Meadow is reminded that a daughter has to balance the faces of Ostensible Innocence and Honest Experience. For his part, Tony prefers to see her positive faces: the college student, the Italian magazine model.

Meadow earlier put Tony to that test when she directly asked if he is in the Mafia. At first he is offended by the stereotyping of Italian waste managers as Mafiosi. After his reflex denial ("There is no Mafia"), under her steady stare Tony admits that some of his "money comes from illegal gambling and whatnot." Meadow is grateful for his candor: "At least you don't deny it, like Mom." Earlier Meadow beamed when he admitted (what she already knew) that he "got into a little trouble" as a kid. At their candlelit dinner Tony opens up even further: "My father was in it, my uncle was in it. There was a time there when the Italian people didn't have a lot of options." But Meadow challenges his rationalizing: "You mean like Mario Cuomo?"

Notwithstanding this candor Tony continues to deceive her, when he chases the "old friend" he spotted. Tony shows how good he is at proffering false faces when he smiles away his bloody interest in the man and later explains away both his dangerous chase and the murder evidence, his bleeding hand and muddy shoes. We approve his deception even as we appreciated his earlier honesty.

Of course, Tony's marriage is a dance of false faces. We are reminded of this when, before he phones Carmela, Tony phones his Russian mistress. Irina is upset that her one-legged cousin, Svetlana, has landed a husband after only two months in America. Tony's strategic excuse is that he has two children approaching college, not that he loves and would never leave Carmela. In another apt malapropism Irina tells Tony not to "throw up in my face" what he has bought her.

The Sopranos' domestic front is more dramatic at home, where Carmela has stayed behind with the flu. Sensitive to AJ's face, after he has brought her breakfast in bed, she sends him off to play video games with a friend. She is less prepared for Father Phil, whom this episode exposes as a negative paradox.

The priest is young, handsome, goateed, in a word, "cool." He drops Yiddish colloquialisms he learned growing up in the Yonkers melting pot. His first word in this episode is the ecumenical "*Oy.*" Aptly, he teaches her *schnorrer* and *schlep*. A rather catholic Catholic, in one breath he defends

Islam against its popular misrepresentation, then praises even more avidly the Chianti. For a celibate he seems excessively given to the appetites. On his entrance, he "confesses" to Carmela that he has "a jones for your baked ziti." The phrase seems a euphemism for "having a boner" for something, that is, an excited desire for it. Similarly, in I,1, he almost uses his Lord's name in vain: "Jeez, Louise!" Here it's "Aw, jeez."

Their conversation shifts between the religious and the secular. They discuss Willem Dafoe's Jesus in Martin Scorsese's *The Last Temptation of Christ* (1988), which was originally intended for Robert De Niro. "Bobby D.," quoth the priest, steeped in the text. Father Phil even impersonates Jesus *via* De Niro. When Father Phil offers that all Jesus' known speeches total only two hours, Carmela adds that all the Beatles's songs total 10. Behind this apparent non sequitur may lurk John Lennon's observation that the Beatles were more popular than Christ. In this priest's conversation, religion always fades into popular culture. His world serves up five times as much Beatles as Jesus. Eager to watch the DVD of *Remains of the Day,* Father Phil defends his appreciation of Emma Thompson: Observing a beautiful woman is the same as admiring a sunset, a Douglas fir, or any other example of God's handiwork. A flash of lightning behind him makes his explanation seem demonic.

The priest's intimacy with Carmela intensifies as they watch the film together on the couch. They touch each other as the Thompson and Anthony Hopkins characters do in the film—when the butler softly objects "You are invading my private time." Carmela is so moved by the film (and by Father Phil's physical contact) that she cries. The priest caresses her: "Carmela, if I can help, please." "How?" she turns on him abruptly. After a pause that should only be called pregnant, the priest retreats from the secular potential to propose to hear her Confession. Their exchange wavers between the religious and the carnal. "I'm a terrible person," she says. "No," the priest replies, with suspect gendering, "You're a wonderful woman."

Here Carmela lets several false faces drop. "I haven't truly confessed in 20 years," she begins. She admits that she has forsaken what is right for what is easy, she has admitted evil into her house, she has said or done nothing about her husband's "horrible acts." She has thus endangered her children's moral development, and all "because I wanted things for them." This recalls Meadow's silent skepticism in I, 1, when Carmela said "you can't just lie and cheat and break the rules you don't like." Meadow knows her parents' model.

As if to prove her point, the scene cuts to the motel, where Tony is carrying a drunk Meadow to her cabin and Peters has Tony in his gun sights, only to be distracted. We see Tony threatened right after Carmela says she expects God will compensate her "with outrage for my sins." At this point, Peters also embodies the danger that Carmela might betray Tony. But she still loves him: "I still believe he can be a good man."

Tony's bending over to kiss Meadow goodnight is intercut with Father Phil giving Carmela communion, with close-ups on her sensuous acceptance of Christ's body and blood. Carmela's reception of the wafer and wine is repeated, closer, to emphasize the physical sensation. The priest finishes the wine with secular aplomb. As he kneels to embrace her, we get a close-up of her blissful smile.

AJ's phone call, asking to sleep over at his friends, awakens Carmela from her sleep on Father Phil's shoulder. She has to crawl over the priest's lap to get to the phone. The priest remains visible in the background, reacting to their having the night alone. He caresses her back until they verge on a kiss. Then Father Phil quickly rises and runs to the bathroom to vomit (fulfilling Irina's earlier malapropism). In the priest's absence, Carmela phones Tony for reassurance but hangs up; his voice reassures her more than anything he might say.

Yes, the Lord moves in mysterious ways, all right.

The next morning, while Carmela drinks her coffee in the foreground, Father Phil awakens in his T-shirt on the sofa. He is uncertain whether they did "anything out of line?" "You have nothing to apologize for," Carmela assures him, but she keeps her back to him. When he admits he was tempted, she deflects him by reworking Bogart's line in *Casablanca*: "Of all the *fanook* [Americanized colloquial for 'gay, bent'] priests in the world, why did I have to get the one who's straight?. . . . It's a joke." The priest is obviously struggling with his faces as man of the cloth and as man of the flesh, while Carmela juggles her faces as faithful and betrayed wife, needy woman, and good Catholic.

Amid all these temptations, deceptions, and betrayals in deed or in intent, Tony strangles "Peters" because "You took an oath and you broke it." For Tony, betrayal of his friends justifies murder. Betraying his wife justifies carefulness.

At home Tony correctly infers from the vanished ziti that "Monsignor Jughead was in"(relating the priest to the always-hungry sidekick of the *Archie* comics). Tony's quip catches both the popular culture and the appetites that characterize Father Phil. Tony is skeptical when Carmela says the priest stayed overnight alone with her "but nothing happened." What did they do for twelve hours, play Name that Pope? "He spends the night here and all he does is slip you a wafer?" When Carmela says he's verging on sacrilege Tony apologizes: "I didn't mean to verge." He may loom but he would not verge. Ironically, given the range of his experience just in this episode, Tony is flummoxed at the idea that Father Phil stayed overnight innocently: "You know what? This is too fucked up for me even to think about."

But our Carmela trumps Tony again: "Your therapist called. [pause] . . . Jennifer?" She exits smartly, leaving Tony fumbling to recover his face as faithful husband. It's only therapy: they just talk.

The episode fades out on a shot of the vacated kitchen hallway. The empty space echoes the suspicions in the Sopranos' marriage. There are no song lyrics over this episode's conclusion, just music, because words have been broken or are false. When Carmela learned that Dr. Melfi is a woman she asked Father Phil rhetorically, "Why does he have to lie? What is he hiding?" The priest's assurance was as self-serving as Christopher's: Tony should supplement his therapy with work on his soul. In this episode no major character operates with a single, honest face.

- HBO executives argued against having Tony kill the traitor. "HBO said you can't do this. . . . You've built up the most interesting protagonist on television in the past 25 years, and now you're just going to lose it." Chase responded that that "we'd lose viewers" if Tony failed to kill the rat (Holden, pp. 155–56). The result was a story of powerful ambivalence and ironies that won the best dramatic series Emmy. In his interview on the Season One DVD (disc four), Chase calls this "the ultimate *Sopranos* episode" that could be "a film noir in and of itself."

I, 6: Pax Soprana

Written by Frank Renzulli. Directed by Alan Taylor.

Tony's cronies ask him to temper Uncle Junior's unilateral decisions, such as over-taxing Hesh, killing a drug dealer who sold his tailor's grandson drugs, and not sharing the spoils with his *capos*. Meanwhile, Tony has sexual dreams about Dr. Melfi and tells her he loves her. Father Phil discourages Carmela's thoughts of divorce.

This episode exposes varieties of male power, primarily through Tony's exchanges. His tension with Uncle Junior contrasts Tony's subtlety with Junior's direct force. Uncle Junior's power image is undermined when in his first appearance he is revealed to be pantless (he is being measured for a suit). In the last shot of the episode, the FBI promotes his picture from Capo to Boss. Beginning as a pantless preener, Junior ends as the image of authority, the FBI's target icon. But as the captains have accepted him only as a front man, his power is primarily image.

Tony is sensitive enough not to oppose his uncle openly. He solicits Livia's help, but she would rather manipulate Junior against Tony than for him. Then Tony works through Johnny Sack to get a sitdown on behalf of Tony's longtime friend, Hesh. There Tony plays ignorant of the issue and appears to side with his uncle. Similarly, before proposing his compromise, Johnny flatters Junior: "If there are any flies on you they're paying fuckin' rent."

Tony may have learned this style from Hesh whom, as Livia warns Junior, Tony regards highly. Hesh brings Tony his complaint in a soft tone, as they stroll along the street. Accepting the principle of the tax but questioning only the amount, Hesh appears far less agitated than Tony. After Uncle Junior reduces the tax without losing face, Tony persuades him to satisfy his five *capos* by sharing Hesh's back-tax among them (Tony returns his own share to Hesh). In a more sinister case of subtle power and image, a waiter at Uncle Junior's testimonial snaps photographs with a hidden camera for the FBI.

Tony is less successful in asserting his sexual power, especially when he targets Dr. Melfi. In one dream, accompanied by the black rhythm and blues tune, "What Time Is It?" (The Jive Five: "It's time for love"), Irina's blowjob turns out to be by Melfi. "Tony, I love your cannoli," Melfi says in Irina's voice. In another she appears naked to summon him into her shower.

In their real sessions, Tony sets out to seduce Melfi. To introduce their potential as lovers he cites Carmela's suspicion. He struggles to define her— "She didn't know you were a girl—you know, a woman—Excuse me, a doctor—a woman doctor."—outside his usual range of "woman."

He attributes to Carmela the burn wound that Irina jealously gave him and her anger at the suggestion she dress more like Melfi, to give his libido "a jump start." Here "jump" has a sexual undertone. After this seductive lie he compliments her "killer body under there." His sexual address begins when she charmingly laughs at his joke about prostate examinations: "Hey,

I don't even let anyone wag their finger *in my face!*" When she evades his kiss, he says he loves her. But it's his lies about Carmela that show he's trying for Melfi. This falseness coheres with his summary of psychoanalysis: "What you're feeling is not what you're feeling and what you're not feeling is your agenda."

Interestingly, Tony is so confident in his masculinity that he is unperturbed by Melfi's rejection and walks away tall. For her part, Melfi stands up to him, as unflinching as when she agreed to take him on as a client. Nor—for a man who so lives by his gun—is he as shaken by the drop in his libido as we might expect. When Carmela raises that issue, he blames his Prozac, citing Melfi. In Carmela's emphatic "*She* says that?" she remains more upset at his doctor's gender than by his diminished libido.

Carmela's current anger begins with Tony's neglect at their anniversary dinner, when he consults with Johnny Sack. In his sensitivity to Uncle Junior's feelings Tony insults Carmela's. As Tony erodes her self-respect her consoling spree at Roche-Bobois catches his attention.

Oddly, the new furniture does not change our impression of the house. If *The Godfather* displays the Corleones' respectability and Old World class— from Vito's first stolen carpet on—all the Sopranos' house "says" is that they have money. The house and its contents are bland, featureless, with neither the character of the antique nor the energy of the modern. "I don't have antiques. My house is traditional," Carmela says in III, 1 (after Martha Stewart). They might just as well, as Tony snaps, go live in the Roche-Bobois store, for all the hominess and personal character their home has.

In her materialism, however, as in her tolerance—even grateful appreciation—of Tony's *goomahs*, she is (as Father Phil points out) not sinless in complying with Tony's godless life. (The priest is right? As Tony reminds us, even a stopped clock is right twice a day.) Carmela is more worried about losing Tony than about her own soul.

Tony's sexual power is least effective with Irina, who—as his dream reveals—has been replaced in his lust by Melfi. In return, Irina ignores him when he calls her over. Paradoxically, the episode concludes on the peak of Tony's sexual power: his submission to his wife. As she joins him by the duck-less pool, he assures her that there is nothing to "this Melfi thing." To Carmela's dedication Tony replies "Carmela, you're not just in my life. You are my life."

As in love, so it is in management. The most effective power is that secured by other direction and by sharing. In that other macho arena, the parents' bleachers at the Little League baseball game, Tony tries to advise his uncle through a historical parallel: Augustus Caesar enjoyed a long, peaceful reign because he shared with his captains his power and its rewards. Junior proves impervious to history. But he responds to Tony's recalling Junior's old story about a bull teaching his son. The young bull suggests running down to a herd to screw a cow; the older sage prefers walking down and screwing them all. Power inheres in its measured use, not flash.

The male's sexual and political powers are again connected when Junior accepts Hesh's compromise on his tax: "What did I say? Hold on to your cock when you negotiate with these desert people." His joke extends the Jews' distinguishing circumcision to castration (and recalls Hesh's advice re: Ariel). It also coheres with the episode's theme of impotence, the threat to the "cannoli." Junior's joke about "the desert people" is undercut when Tony visits Hesh's plush, green horse farm. So much for ethnic stereotypy, whether of the desert Jews or of the Mafia Italians.

The horse farm scene also rebukes Livia's prejudice: "Just don't let certain people take advantage of you. . . . How's your Jewish friend? . . . Who ever heard of a Jew riding horses?" Junior imperils both himself and Tony by following her suggestions. Though Junior realizes Livia wants to punish Tony for putting her in a home, he acts on her advice anyway. With Tony, Livia also feigns innocence: "I don't know that world. . . . I don't want to get involved." But she continues to feed Junior malevolent ideas.

Livia will play her games: "Who is it?" "It's me, Ma." "Who?" At home in I, 1, she similarly pretended not to recognize her son. In I, 8, she immediately recognizes Carmela's voice at her door. She fakes not recognizing AJ's voice in II, 7 (maybe it's a male thing). Here Livia walks brusquely out of Tony's dance, as if she doesn't want to feel affectionate or close to her son. In the next episode—and even more in III, 3—we will learn that Tony's traumatic memory of his father, murder, sex, and meat also includes Johnny Boy's frisky dancing with Livia—and her evasion of him.

Melfi suggests that Tony chose an Italian-American woman as his therapist, over two Jewish males, because he thought that "by coming clean" with her he would be "dialoging with" the key Italian women in his life—Livia, Carmela, Meadow. She attributes Tony's love to their analytic progress: "You've made me out to be everything you're missing in your life—and in your mother."

As Livia's advice to Junior demonstrates, an ostensible gift can be an imposition of power. Because Melfi knows gifts can be used to control the recipient, she refuses even Tony's small gift, the decaf coffee. When he has her car stolen to replace its starter, she is frightened and outraged at his "violation of my privacy." But he didn't want to see her robbed, he explains. Replacing her car's "starter" relates his good deed to his wanting her "jump start" on his own sexuality. In a non-sexual context, he uses the term "kick start" instead (I, 12). Nor is there any generosity in the gifts Uncle Junior exacts, like his new tax on all poker games or his new tax on Hesh with a $500,000 back penalty. Gifts, whether volunteered or exacted, show the boss's power.

The episode's title derives from Tony's Roman model for popular rule— with the implicit danger of betrayal—the Caesars from Octavius to Julius. Ironically, in the BBC production of *I, Claudius*, Augustus's scheming, evil wife (played by Sian Phillips) is also named Livia, an irony that undercuts Tony's parable for Junior. Still, the *Pax Romana* model—augmented by Tony's bull—brings the *Pax Soprana* to both the business and home fronts, for the while.

- Dominic Chianese (Uncle Junior) toured in Gilbert and Sullivan's *The Mikado* and *Patience* in 1952. His television work includes *Kojak, East Side West Side*, and *Law and Order*. He also appeared in *Gotti, Dog Day Afternoon, All the President's Men, Fort Apache: The Bronx, Cradle Will Rock*, and the remake of *The Thomas Crowne Affair*. In *The Godfather Part II* he played Johnny Ola, the Corleones' Miami connection who "turned" Fredo and is killed with a coat hanger. Chianese is an accomplished lounge singer, as we see on his two CDs and in his performance in III, 13.

- Michael Imperioli (Christopher) has appeared in over 40 movies since 1980, including Steve Buscemi's *Trees Lounge, I Shot Andy Warhol, Dead Presidents, Malcolm X*, and *Lean on Me*. He was a writer/producer and appeared in Spike Lee's *Summer of Sam*, recalling the summer of paranoia caused by serial killer David Berkowitz.

I, 7: Down Neck

Written by Robin Green and Mitchell Burgess. Directed by Loraine Senna.

Anthony Junior's delinquency at school prompts Tony to recall his own boyhood mischief and to wonder what his children know about his work. He discusses his memories with Dr. Melfi. As Tony's alienation from Livia worsens, we infer that she has always been a problematic mother.

This episode reflects upon how our personal history wields an uncertain effect on our future. As Dr. Melfi puts it, our genetic and cultural pasts may reveal our predispositions but they do not predetermine our fates. We remain responsible for our choices. Santayana's famous dictum—unless we know our history we are doomed to repeat it—here applies to both social and psychological history. In the penultimate scene, Tony watches a History Channel program about the Battle of Midway while running on his treadmill. The allusion sets the present midway between the knowable past and the unknowable future.

Tony learns from his past. As his father's cronies took their daughters to the fairground, he will arrange for several mothers to be placed in the same seniors home, as a front for their meetings. His first remark to Christopher draws on his therapy: "You're doing an excellent job. Allow yourself to take pleasure in that."

Tony's work scene contrasts to his meetings with the school authorities, after AJ is caught stealing sacramental wine from the school chapel and tested for learning disability and psychologicial problems. At work Tony is a stickler for order, using hard-hat Christopher as a "Union Safety Official" to bring a construction manager into line. But at his son's school the specialists hold sway.

During his meeting with Father Hagy and school psychologist Dr. Galati, we share Tony's skepticism about the new jargon ("Anthony has misbehaved. He should be consequenced"). Tony rejects the school psychologist's report because he considers AJ a 13-year-old boy, not a case. The specialists turn every problem "into a disease." Tony is frustrated that the modish "consequencing" does not include the time honored "whack upside the head" or the traditional tarantelle on the bottom. His own father's favorite "child development tool" was the belt. The school officials who reject spanking give AJ "a complete *battery* of testing."

We probably don't approve Uncle Junior's extreme *laissez faire* either: "Whatever happened to 'Boys will be boys'?" Ever unhelpful, Livia tells the family dinner that Tony stole a car when he was 10 and that because of his constant mischief she practically lived in the vice-principal's office.

As Tony and Carmela wonder what their children know about their father's work, they agree they should talk at least to Meadow "about the business . . . as a family." Whether it is the upper or the lower case, "family" is left ambiguous.

Tony's "history" begins with brief flashes back to Meadow's questions on their college tour and to his murder of the snitch, Peters. The flashes' briefness suggests Tony is trying to suppress them. As Livia scolded him earlier (projecting), "You only remember what you want to remember." The flashes swell into memories of entire scenes from Tony's childhood.

The episode's title refers to his hometown, where he remembers watching his father beat up Rocco Allitori, a debtor, to the sound of Eric Burdon and the Animals's "Don't Bring Me Down." Tony remembers seeing his father arrested at a fairground, along with Uncle Junior and a clown. Tony's spying on his father's Sunday trips with Janice is caught in Them's "Mystic Eyes." After his brief arrest, his father returns home while the Italian rock group, The Young Rascals, play "Lonely Too Long" on *The Ed Sullivan Show*.

The latter rock group's name suggests the American culture's affection for the outlaw, the rascal. Rocco is the first to congratulate Johnny-Boy, despite having been so badly beaten by him. Rocco even invites Johnny-Boy to join him on the Reno venture that made him a billionaire. But Livia refused: She would rather smother her children with a pillow than let them live in Nevada. Now Livia denies ever keeping her husband from doing anything he wanted. She shouts her familiar disclaimer: "I don't know what you're talking about!"

Tony's fondness for the History channel speaks to his curiosity. That abstract interest turns to the compelling concern whether his son is doomed to be like him, that is, whether his history will replay in his son. He hopes AJ is proud of him but he wants him to be different. Tony projects onto Carmela his own fears that AJ may be restricted to Tony's genetic limitations and character. Anticipating this point, Tony is shown in close-up when the school psychologist cites AJ's difficulty in both "following rules" and "weighing consequences." Tony initially believes in predestination: "You're born to this shit. You are what you are." On the other hand, genetics does not always rule, as he cites Pussy's three kids at college and—conversely—successful businessmen siring Leopold and Loeb.

Tony's sessions with Dr. Melfi open his troubled relationship with his parents and the silence in which their issues festered. He recalls his mother threatening to poke her fork into his eye if he did not stop nagging her, his jealousy of older sister Janice, and Uncle Junior hitting him with a pitch when he was distracted. *Plus ça change....*

Tony responds childishly when Melfi raises his "intimate feelings" for her. He tells her about his twenty-four-year-old mistress: "How old are you?" "I find it interesting that you took so long to tell me you have a girlfriend," Melfi says in her slow, soft manner. Tony playfully parodies her. He is as belligerently guarded against Melfi's rejection as he was with his parents as a child.

When he tells Melfi what Johnny-Boy did for a living he pauses after the initial euphemism: "Retail meat and provisions—and a little numbers, loan sharking, extortion." The problem of providing for one's family appears in AJ's first response to the psychiatrist's image of a riderless horse: The rider may be off getting its food. Then AJ projects a more comfortable alternative: he is watching the first *South Park* episode, where Cartman's anal probe from aliens results in flaming flatulence. However influential the genes, AJ has his father's way with analysts.

Tony's colleagues have similar issues with their children. Silvio's daughter complains that the Bada Bing "objectifies women"—despite his paying them $1,500 a week. "Boys are different from girls," observes the large man named Pussy. To Silvio's "It's hard to raise kids in an information age," Tony adds, "To protect them." This line rings as false as Brendan's version did in I, 3. Tony's motive is to protect himself from his child's knowledge and rejection. The "information age" hardly applies to AJ learning from his schoolmates of his father's work, although a web site about the Mafia did feature Uncle Jackie Aprile. Replaying this fear of openness, Tony criticizes Chris's daylight theft of watches.

On AJ's visit to Livia (part of his punishment), he lets slip that Tony has been seeing a psychiatrist. After Livia's initial skepticism—"That's crazy. That's nothing but a racket for the Jews."—she immediately concludes that he goes to complain about what she did to him. Ironically, Livia delivers the patented self-pity of the Jewish mother.

The episode closes with Tony, sweating from his History Channel workout, pausing for a quick exchange with AJ. Like their earlier chat, over the flat tire, when AJ admitted his suspicions about his father's work, this points to their potential closeness. The episode closes on the Jefferson Airplane's musical injunction (in "White Rabbit") to "Feed your head." Tony first recalled this song when driven to his morning Prozac. When AJ says his punishment for the wine theft is not fair, Tony pats him affectionately and agrees: "You got that right." Making them both sundaes, Tony delinquently squirts whipped cream into their mouths, creating one of the better father-son memories that will feed their heads into the future.

Of course, there is an alternative reading for that last scene. Tony's quest for health is limited and self-defeating. He follows his strenuous physical workout with a huge sundae, replete with nuts, sprinkles, M&Ms, and the side shots of whipped cream straight. In his physical regimen as in his sessions with Melfi, Tony seems to take two strides back for each stutter forward. However painful his self-exploration, he undoes it with his impulsive indulgence. Self-destruction is the history he chooses.

■ David Chase may have two personal inflections in this episode. He recalls that his mother prevented the family's move to California, when his father had the opportunity to go build printing presses there. As well, Chase would sympathize with Tony's acceptance of AJ's "fidgeting." As a schoolboy in Clifton, New Jersey, the A-student Chase got an F in deportment: "I was always jiggling" (Holden, p. 22).

I, 8: Legend of Tennessee Moltisanti

Written by Frank Renzulli and David Chase. Directed by Tim Van Patten.

Rumors of indictments against New Jersey gangsters send the Family heads scurrying to destroy or to hide evidence. Dr. Melfi resists her family's pressure to refer him to another therapist. But at their session Tony erupts in an insulting rage. Meanwhile, Christopher tries to write a screenplay ("Mob stories are always hot").

This episode straddles the characters' private and public lives and focuses on the ambivalence of the Italian-Americans' image. The public life is represented by the opening scene's *Godfather*-style wedding, which dissolves on the rumor of federal indictments. The Mafiosi hustle their wives home for spring cleaning.

When Carmela comes to take her to brunch Livia is immediately suspicious. Her instinctive dread is right: Carmela's hidden agenda is to enable Tony to stash his guns and cash in Livia's closet. So the nervous music starts up when Carmela has Livia safe in her car. Meanwhile, the newspaper and TV news make the gang families' private lives too public for comfort.

Searched by the FBI, Tony grows tenser at work and in his sessions with Dr. Melfi. Despite their growing affection, he explodes when she reminds him he will be charged for missed sessions. "I don't appreciate pouring my heart out to a fuckin' call girl," he says, who's shaking him down. "Of course, this is what it's all about, right? Motherfuckin' cocksuckin' money." Paradoxically, it is because he now has "intimate feelings" for her that he turns so abusive. As so often in this series, apparently inconsistent behavior has a psychological consistency.

Tony remains properly concerned for Chris despite claiming "I wipe your ass with my feelings." But even at his ugly worst Tony is too human for Melfi's ex-husband Richard's dismissal as "Evil." So, too, Livia, who when she tells Uncle Junior about Tony's psychoanalysis, begins with self-pity, plants a destructive innuendo, then withdraws from responsibility: "I'm sure he's told the psychiatrist it's all his mother's fault. . . . God only knows what he says. . . . But I don't want there to be any repercussions." As Richard rightly guesses, the Italian-American male client has "mother issues." As the ad said: "You don't have to be Jewish."

Though the story still centers on Tony, here more attention is paid Dr. Melfi and Christopher. In our first glimpse into Dr. Melfi's personal life, her parents and ex-husband want her to refer her dangerous client to someone else. When Richard peremptorily dismisses Tony he blames the Italian gangsters for creating the negative stereotype of Italian-Americans. Similarly, Tony accuses FBI agent Grasso of betraying his people and the FBI of prejudice in turning an Italian against him. Of course, to "grass" is to "sing" or to betray.

As *The Sopranos* has been broadly charged with stereotyping, these scenes provide an Equal Time rebuttal. As Richard argues, the 5000 Mafia members (at its peak) should not define the country's 20,000,000 other Italian-Americans. The Sopranos list major Italian inventors and innovators. Antonio Maiucci invented the telephone, but Bell gets the credit. (Incidentally, it's at a Maiucci Festival that Vincent kills Joey Zaza in *The Godfather Part III*.) Tony is proud that more Italians fought for America in World War II than any other ethnic group. But Meadow casts a pall on the dinner when she raises the history of the Mafia. These scenes rebut claims that the show perpetuates the negative stereotypy of Italian-Americans.

Rare for this series, these discussions seem arch and preachy. Lacking the usual mischief and irony of *The Sopranos,* they rather resemble the sobriety of its rival quality series, *The West Wing*. On the other hand, when Melfi's father proposes a toast—"To we, the twenty million."—he makes the Italians the subject of the phrase ("we") instead of the object ("us"). His grammatical error makes the Italian Americans the force not the victim.

But this show does not capitulate to the critics. Melfi counters Richard's paranoia. Go after Hollywood movies, she advises, not her client. "With all the poverty, starvation, ethnic cleaning and generally horrible shit in this world, you devote your energies to the protection of the dignity of Connie Francis." In light self-satire, Melfi's son Jason refers to "ginzo gravy," as Chris calls himself a "skinny guinea." Even Richard speaks Soprano when he tells Melfi not to "bust my balls with Freud by numbers."

In their paean to the Italian-American, Tony and Carmela exchange enigmatic smiles at the climactic mention of "Francis Albert"—Sinatra. A romantic privacy plays around that public figure. Sinatra is the presiding legend in this series—more here than the titular Tennessee Williams. In I, 11 Mikey and JoJo Palmice's kid is named Frankie Albert. For Sinatra made it in America, beyond showbiz. While he hobnobbed with presidents he retained the glamour and courage of his gangster style and associations. When Chris buys the newspapers reporting his criminality, over the end credits we hear Cake's song, "Frank Sinatra."

In another ethnic balancing, Melfi, Richard, and Jason consult a Jewish therapist who takes a wacky pride in having a maternal relative who worked for Lepke. "Those were some tough Jews," he gloats. This Jew relishes the identity that the Italian resents. As it happens, the actor playing the Jewish Dr. Reis is Sam *Coppola*—confirming the *paisan*'s kinship with "the desert people." Dr. Reis suggests Melfi refer Tony to a therapist who specializes in "Mafia depression," an admittedly unfunny joke that provokes Reis's self-approving wheeze and his clients' stunned silence.

As unfunny as the Jewish shrink is the comedian working the old folks' home. Completely out of touch with his audience, he is mediocre, to boot.

His jokes broaden the show's ethnic stereotypy. In the Polish version of *Rashomon* everyone remembered the rape the same way. The Jewish Doctor Goldman abandoned tree surgery because he fainted at the sight of sap. This joke may apply to the squeamish who recoil at the show's bloodshed. Clearly any Italian-American stereotypy is only part of the show's satire. Here is Equal Opportunity offensiveness. Richard may see this as another example of Melfi's "cheesy moral relativism," but satire has its own validity.

The episode's primary psychological focus is on Christopher. It opens with his surreal nightmare that combines Czech pork sausages, the murdered Emil, and girlfriend Adriana (who in his nightmare turns into Carmela, as she dreads). Christopher seems to fear being replaced (as Adriana's sustenance) or engulfed by sausages, that is, reduced to meat himself. In the opening shot, the cartoon pig wallpaper behind Chris recalls the real carcasses behind him when he murdered Emil. Later, when Paulie says Chris's apartment is "like a sty" the "pig" is implicit, and a reminder that Chris's life and mind are a mess as a result of that murder.

Christopher hungers for the publicity the others dread. He is indignant that Brendan is cited as a "soldier" and he is not. He ignores his "mommy's" phone call until she mentions that he has been named among the "scumbags" in the paper. Then he rushes out to buy up all the copies— out of pride rather than shame. Chris hungers for the shame of his success.

Christopher Moltisanti is also frustrated by his laptop and by his writer's block. The episode title comes from Adriana's assurance that he is her "Tennessee William"—and he is rather singular, both as a lover and as a writer. Chris has the familiar artist's problem but with no artistic purpose: "I love movies, you know that—the smell in Blockbuster." That last phrase is even more disdainful of cinema than its homonym, "the smell of blockbuster," because it settles on cheap viewing, not success.

To judge by his (mis)spelling, Chris does not know "loyal" or how to "manage." He grows increasingly moody and irrational, complaining both to Paulie and to Pussy that he has no identity. His life does not have the "arc" (that is, the transforming experience) that a screenplay is supposed to give its lead character. The survival-bent Pussy replies: "You know who had an arc? Noah."

Christopher explodes at a bakery clerk for a perceived slight. After shooting the floor to hasten his service, he gratuitously shoots the boy's foot. "It happens," Chris says. It did. The scene and the impulse come straight out of Martin Scorsese's *GoodFellas*. There hero Henry Hill remembered that even as a young gangster he never had to wait in line at the bakery. More important, Joe Pesci's irrational character plays "cowboy," specifically Cagney's Oklahoma Kid, at a card game. To speed the boy's drinks and sandwiches he shoots at the floor, making him "dance." Then he shoots the boy in the foot—and at the next game kills him.

The bakery scene here is not just a homage to Scorsese's film—or that close relative, a rip-off. It's central to Chris's characterization. Frustrated at his attempt to make a name for himself by writing a screenplay (titled *You Bark, I Bite)*, he acts out a scene from a genre classic. Reversing the usual conundrum—the artist who writes what he cannot achieve in life—Christopher here lives what he cannot write. Tony calls that behavior—and digging up Emil's corpse—"cowboy-itis," the action of someone who wants to be caught. Chris knows he wants to make a name for himself. He doesn't realize his methods are self-destructive.

There is another twist. The actor who played Spider, the boy Pesci shot in *GoodFellas*, was young Michael Imperioli, who plays Christopher here. In a kind of meta-filmic effect, the roles seem continuous. The actor shot then, shoots now. The victim has grown into the victimizer. The casting allusion suggests that a cycle of violence operates beyond the level of the immediate plot. Finally, our gangsters worship *The Godfather* but live Scorsese's meaner streets.

- Steven van Zandt (Silvio Dante) is a guitarist in Bruce Springsteen's E Street Band, with no previous acting experience. In an in-joke, Silvio is reported to have owned rock clubs in Asbury Park. His real-life wife, Maureen, an actress and dancer, plays Silvio's wife, Gabriella.
- Tony Sirico (Paulie "Walnuts" Gualtieri) grew up in Bensonhurst and developed a resume of 28 arrests (mainly for armed robbery) and two jail sentences (five years). Excited by an ex-cons traveling theatre group, he made his film debut in 1974 in *Crazy Joe*. Then followed *The Godfather Part II, Miller's Crossing, GoodFellas, Mickey Blue Eyes,* and his Woody Allen period: *Deconstructing Harry, Celebrity, Everyone Says I Love You, Mighty Aphrodite,* and *Bullets Over Broadway.*
- Vincent Pastore (Big Pussy Bonpensiero) was a club owner in New Rochelle, when regulars Matt and Kevin Dillon talked him into acting. His films include Sundance winner *True Love, Jerky Boys, GoodFellas, Gotti, Witness to the Mob, The Last Don,* and *The Hurricane.*

I, 9: Boca

Written by Jason Cahill, Robin Green and Mitchell Burgess.
Directed by Andy Wolk.

Uncle Junior's macho status is threatened by report that he is skilled at cunnilingus. He learns that Tony is talking to a psychiatrist. The gang fathers pressure their daughters' successful high school soccer coach not to leave for a university post. But when they learn he seduced one of his Grade XI players they plan their own justice.

This extraordinarily brave episode set a new benchmark even for this benchmark series. It combines the coarsest humor with ethical challenges in two serious plots. Both involve responsibility in sexual relationships and the tension between individual liberty and societal constraints. Finally, in both stories licentious behavior conceals Puritanical fears.

In the lighter plot, Uncle Junior takes his girlfriend Bobbie to Boca Raton, where for sixteen years they have escaped for carefree pleasure. When Bobbie flatters his "real instinct" for cunnilingus, Junior reminds her that his society holds it "a sign of weakness" for a man to give oral sex. It is manlier to receive than to give. A soft, generous man is vulnerable. Indeed, in the previous episode, just before Christopher shot the bakery clerk, he indignantly asked "Do I look like a pussy to you?" In this insecure, macho society, it is derogatory to associate a man with the feminine, from pussy to palaver. "You always have to talk about everything," Junior charges Bobbie.

When Carmela learns of Junior's penchant, she can't resist jokes at dinner. Having coaxed out her secret, Tony taunts Uncle Junior at their golf game, getting back at him for recalling Tony's game-losing fielding error in Little League. Tony seethes in close-up before he starts teasing Junior on the taboo.

When Junior confronts Bobbie with the leak, he restrains his impulse to punch her but shoves her lemon meringue pie in her face. This reflex derives from the famous scene in *The Public Enemy* (1931), where gangster James Cagney shoves a grapefruit in Mae Clarke's face. When Junior calls Bobbie a "stupid fucking blabbermouth cunt," he works up to the climactic rejection of the feminine part that he has most prized. A close-up on him outside, teary-eyed and alone, suggests Junior lost more than Bobbie when—

reduced by the overhead shot—he scurries away from a 16-year relationship of open sexuality and love. In effect, he abandons his softer nature. When he mentions her again—in II, 11—he has forgotten his responsibility for their split.

As Junior feels more vulnerable he grows more anxious about Tony's psychiatric sessions. When Mikey suggests that Tony's mysterious twice-weekly meetings are with the Feds, Junior reports Tony is seeing a shrink. The two are telling the same story, but Mikey has it wrong. In the men's locker room, Junior thinks violent: "Anthony wants to play games. I taught him how to play games. I taught him to play baseball." Goaded by Livia, feeling humiliated by Tony, and sensing his nephew's weakness, Junior considers killing him.

As the stakes rise, the plot is peppered with outrageous puns. There are gags about giving head, "going down" to/in Boca, "whistling in the wheatfield," "sushi," "South of the Border, where the tuna fish play," the acquired taste for that "sweet, sweet girl," the Kalahari bushman, and Tony's ingenuous confusion of the golfer's "rough" with "muff." But then, the job Junior got Bobbie is with the Joint Cutters Union. This frisky language belies the deadly seriousness of insecure men's games.

The oral sex jokes color even the innocent language. When Bobbie remarks, "If only they knew the other side of you," Junior replies: "They'd eat me for breakfast." And Tony: "You *mange*, Uncle Joon. She'll come back." Conversely, when Tony playfully calls Allie Alphonse, his gender-blind address contrasts to her seduction by her soccer coach.

It is also hypocritical—as Carmela points out—for the men who themselves may practice cunnilingus—as Tony does once a year, presumably on Carmela's (or Columbus's) birthday—to look down on it. So, too, in the more serious plot, when the gangsters learn that Hauser has seduced a student. Silvio alternates between wallowing in the transgression and fearing for his daughter: "My daughter should know this shit? My daughter should have to think about that filth? . . . That self-righteous prick put his dick in my little girl's soccer teammate!" Silvio moves between indignation and relishing the sordidness, with appropriate hand gestures.

Of course, Silvio considers Hauser self-righteous because he rejected Brandy's free blowjob at the Bing. The coach declined, whether out of respect for his wife or because he prefers his lovers adolescent. The men's ambivalence about sex and the female is nicely caught when we cut from Tony's compliment to Meadow and her teammate—"Good job, girls"—to the naked pole-dancers at the Bada Bing.

The fathers are excessively involved in their daughters' game. Silvio offers his daughter "a hundred bucks for a goal." When the referee orders him off the field, Silvio pauses to kick dirt at him. Again, a character emulates some dubious film hero. The men's passions at the game are only exceeded by their machinations outside. In appreciation, the Bada Bing gives the Coach drinks and Brandy "on the house." Her name reduces her to a free drink for Tony or Silvio to dispense.

When Hauser is reported leaving for a university post the hoods try to persuade him to stay, first with the carrot—a free fifty-inch television— then with the stick—Christopher's implied threat to the Hauser dog. At least against the television the coach stands defiant: "Don Hauser will not be intimidated." Earlier, Hauser strutted his independence by quoting the most famous line from—what else?—*The Godfather:* The University of Rhode Island "made me an offer I couldn't refuse." Of course, even the desire to keep the coach is selfish, because the fathers want him to stay till their daughters graduate.

When the men learn that the girl who had slit her wrists, Allie, had been seduced by her school soccer coach, their passions roil against him. Their immediate urge is to give Hauser an "after-school special." This could be castration, now that detentions are illegal (I, 7).

In this drama Artie is a significant figure. Without his friends' power, he feels intensely their shifting attitudes toward Hauser: their appreciation, their resolve to keep him, then their rage. In fury, Artie hacks out his frustration on the weeds in his garden. After Charmaine talks him around he tries to dissuade Tony from vigilante justice. He argues that the men's revenge would satisfy only themselves. Artie counsels leaving Hauser to the police. But Tony fears he will escape with a light sentence, then "go to Saskatchewan and teach girls soccer there." When Tony throws out Artie and Charmaine's wisdom, he denies the balance of feminine sense. He is persuaded when Dr. Melfi supports Artie's/Charmaine's argument.

The issue redefines manhood. Artie wishes he had "the balls" to punish Hauser himself, instead of leaving it to Tony. But Charmaine assures him: "Arthur, you do have balls. That's why you're not like him." For Charmaine, the vigilante hood is less of a man than the responsible citizen is. The gang tweaks Artie's manhood when Charmaine calls him home from the Bada Bing. More lightly, Artie jokes that if the coach's soccer success gets Artie's daughter a scholarship, "I'll blow the guy at midfield." Artie seems laughably presumptuous when he tells Tony Soprano what to do. But he is manliest when he wields his wife's wisdom against the macho boss.

In this episode Tony is a champion of social responsibility. He orders a young man to remove his baseball cap at the classy restaurant. Having stared the boy down, Tony then sends the couple a bottle of wine. He rewards those who obey him—and would punish those who don't. When Tony discusses the coach's transgression, Melfi returns to the same question: Why does Tony assume the responsibility to set the world right? There is a thin line between the citizen's proper responsibilities and a self-flagellating compulsion. Trying for that balance, Tony apologizes for his previous session. Calling Dr. Melfi a whore "might have been overstating the case a bit." But he still plots his vigilante justice for Hauser.

In an ironic statement of this theme, when Uncle Junior reiterates his need for Bobbie's secrecy, he dismisses her logic with "What are you going to do? I don't make the rules." Of course, as Family godfather he does make the rules. More broadly, everyone in the society of this series makes his/her own rules, or chooses which laws or conventions to accept, which to modify, which to ignore. Meadow's girlfriends, including Silvio's and Hauser's daughters, will drink in the park but will go only so far in working for a coach they can't stand. From AJ's mischief to Livia's mothering, *The Sopranos* reflects a society where people live without governing absolutes. They are responsible for themselves. They make their own rules.

Even after throwing Artie out, Tony wavers whether or not to unleash Silvio outside Hauser's house. We don't know his decision until the TV news reports that an unnamed school friend of the victim reported Hauser to the police and he has been arrested. Tony staggers home, falling-down drunk from his Prozac cocktail, and before passing out at his wife's feet mumbles "Carmela, I didn't hurt nobody." For once his profession of innocence is true.

Parallel high-angle shots, which shrink the subject, comment on manhood. The first undercuts Corrado's macho pretensions when he scuttles away from Bobbie to preserve his shallow manliness. The second, here, reduces Tony physically but reflects a manlier self-control, despite his drunken silliness.

Meadow watches this scene from upstairs, strong and clear-eyed. Perhaps she was the informer, the Soprano who took on the Hauser problem—through the legal system. After all, in the last scene she holds the high ground when Tony crashes in, hands clean for once but out of control, as if he could not do the right, the responsible, the female sensible thing without getting drunk first. Tony seems to have lost another virginity, in for the first time *not* taking brutish action; he needed to be bolstered by drink to prove this manhood too. Besides, we've seen Meadow confront Hauser before. "Go fuck yourself," she tells him, then runs her 20-lap punishment, and only then quits his team. Who blew the whistle? I suspect Meadow. After all, she has her father's sense of justice and initiative. And as a goalkeeper, Meadow is the pivotal loner of last defense.

▪ The pie/grapefruit allusion to *The Public Enemy* evokes one of David Chase's favorite films: "Even now, he can—and does—recite most of *Public Enemy* complete with a description of camera angles. 'It blew my mind. It hooked me. I don't know why, but it did' " (Holden, p. 24). The film figures more extensively in III, 1, where we see the grapefruit scene.

I, 10:   A Hit Is a Hit

Written by Joe Bosso and Frank Renzulli. Directed by Matthew Penn.

Tony and Carmela socialize with their respectable neighbors. Christopher sponsors Adriana's launch into music management by funding the demo of a rock band fronted by an ex-boyfriend. A black rap mogul pressures Hesh to pay back-royalties to the survivor of one of his music performers from the past.

The titular "hit" is both a mob and a musical term. This episode provides a variety of pecking orders—societal and musical—and the temptation to try to rise in them.

In the opening scene Paulie, Chris, and Pussy make a huge score by killing a drug runner in New York for invading their territory. In this context, they are punishing an invader, reaffirming his exclusion. As if for balance, later Tony is denied membership in the private golf club because the membership is full. Old members have to die before new ones can be admitted.

If Tony spurns the obvious strategy, it is because he does not really want to join that supercilious society, the "mayonnaisers." He is concerned what his friends would think if he were to hang out with what his father called "Wonder Bread Wops." Tony's "whites" means assimilated Italian, not Caucasian. In an episode about the racial tension between blacks and whites, the term suggests there is hegemony within races as well as between them.

Because Carmela wants to broaden the family's social sphere she and Tony mingle with non-mob (as distinct from non-criminal) American-Italians at a barbecue. The men freeze their stock market talk when Tony enquires, yet they pump him for Mafia information. At the private golf club Tony feeds their fantasies. How "real" was *The Godfather*? Did Tony have to bleed his finger for an oath? They exclude him from their circle but want the secrets of his.

At first uncomfortable, Tony proceeds to one-up them. He invents a story about John Gotti outbidding him at an auction of an ice cream truck then driving him home in it, ringing the bell all the way. His listeners know they have heard something true and poetic but they can not figure out what it means. The anecdote recalls the sinister ice-cream truck in Mahaffey's conversion scene in I, 1. The golfers are also thrilled when Tony calls Dr. Cusamano "The Cooze," because they feel admitted into mob argot. Tony later assures Dr. Cusamano that the word no longer connotes "pussy."

Even these Italian-Americans reduce other Italian-Americans to the mob stereotype. At the dinner party Dr. Cusamano relishes the scene in *Casino* (Martin Scorsese) where Joe Pesci pops a rival's head in a vise. That is, all along the social ladder people draw reference points and attitude from the gangster movies. At the other end, Paulie, when Chris uncharacteristically leaves an orgy to take Adriana to dinner, quotes another gangster classic (Mervyn LeRoy's *Little Caesar*, 1930): "Mother of Mercy, is this the end of Rico?" Of course, when Adriana becomes the FBI's target at the end of Season III, she becomes the "end" (that is, objective, target) of RICO (the Racketeer Influenced and Corrupt Organizations Act).

Tony tells Melfi that the golf game taught him what it is like to be used for someone else's amusement, "like a dancing bear." He recalls that as a kid he and friends similarly exploited Jimmy Smash, a boy with a cleft palate. When they were bored they had him sing for them, so they could laugh. The kid craved to hang out with his exploiters but he cried his way home.

But the newly sensitized Tony again makes Jimmy a joke. After explaining Jimmy is doing 20 years for robbery, Tony comically imitates the man's voice, by which he was identified in a bank robbery despite his mask. Tony persists with his joke even now he is aware the joking was wrong. His politically incorrect instincts continue unrestrained. Typically, Tony's incorrigibility is the basis of both his evil and his charm. As Carmela admits, about his episode-ending mischief with the sandbox, "You look kind of cute when you're being a bad boy."

Perhaps that dynamic is also at work in the episode's first scene, the New York mugging. The murder scene is entirely at odds with the comedy in the rest of the episode. While the episode satirizes the Italian-American film stereotype, the opening plays a cliché scene straight. Tony repeats the ridicule he is embarrassed to have made, feeding the golfers a fiction that fulfills their expectations, the episode itself starting off with a gangster film cliché—in each case the art plays to a prejudice.

As Carmela grows insecure about what she would do if "something happened" to Tony, she acts on a stock tip she gleaned from her society outing. Her first purchase does well. A headline reports that because of its successful impotence drug, American Biotics tumescently splits three for one. Presumably, the women learned the promise of this drug from their husbands, whether from their bull market or their bed.

But Carmela will never enjoy their comfort level. The respectable wives know they are secure: "We don't just play [the stock market and, one assumes, anything else]; we win." And they're legitimate. In fact, Tony earlier plans to invest his windfall score in something "legit"—like "some insider trading shit." This, Cusamano's cronies—and their wives—clearly practice.

Because Adriana doesn't want to be a housewife like Carmela, she talks about running her own restaurant or managing musicians. As the ambitious/frustrated Christopher envies the glamour of Massive Genius, the black rap mogul, he decides to launch her. But Chris remains Chris. To encourage the lead singer he smashes a guitar on his head. When he drops the mediocre band and suggests Massive Genius was interested in her, not them, Adriana charges that Chris is still trying to "keep me down." As for his macho silence: "You're either screaming your head off or fucking dead." Having discovered her own ambition, she now resists her recessive role in the relationship.

Chris flashes his bigotry when he's impatient for service at the burger shop. To a black customer Chris replies: "I'm looking for a burger, not converted rice." This Uncle Ben aspersion recurs around Tony's aversion to Noah in III, 2. Despite his racism, Massive Genius accepts Chris as a useful tool.

In fact, Chris's racism only confirms Massive Genius's assumption about the Italian and Jewish gangsters. In a collision of pecking orders, Massive Genius expresses his respect for Chris's "people" by praising *The Godfather*, which he saw "200 times." Moreover, he pretends to a special sensitivity by defending *The Godfather Part III* as "misunderstood." Regrettably, he does not elaborate. Perhaps he relishes the honky overlord's suffering—diabetes, debility, heartbreak, and death. Or he may simply be trying to ingratiate himself, as Chris called out to "Martin Scorsese" about another unvalued film, "*Kundun*—I liked it!" (I, 2).

Massive Genius flexes his new power by trying to shake Hesh down for $400,000 in royalties he says Hesh owes the family of Little Jimmy Willis, one of Hesh's old music partners. The singer died penniless, having—as Silvio quips—blown on horse (heroin) the money Hesh invested in his horse farm.

Massive lumps Hesh in with the history of whites, especially the Jews in the entertainment industries, who exploited the black. Hesh claims "My people were the white man's nigger when yours were still painting your faces and chasing zebras." That animal combines the white and the black worlds, so it is an appropriate emblem for Hesh to confront Massive. When Hesh calls Massive "Tatteleh" (Yiddish: "little father," but not quite "Daddy-O"), he provides his own ethnic version of "Bro."

In contrast to all the episode's wannabes Hesh is a self-sufficient, solid integrity. He seriously considers Massive's moral and legal argument before deciding not to pay. Threatened with a lawsuit—with Massive's *Jewish* lawyers—he counters with pertinent savvy. Hesh notes that one of Massive's hit songs plagiarized one of his songs' rhythm track. More than a legal ploy, this proves that Hesh knows rhythm and blues music. That is, he has a plausible claim for composer royalties on the songs Massive contends Willis wrote alone. Of course, in I, 6, Tony teased Hesh by joking that he took the credit for songs the black kids wrote. But Tony could have been teasing his friend. Here, when sound engineer Squid criticizes Adriana's singer for poor structure in his songs, he shows how Hesh might have contributed to Little Jimmy's composing.

Later Hesh dismisses Chris's group's demo—and Chris's charge that Hesh's musical judgment is obsolete. Unaffected by Chris's ambition, Hesh judges from his own solid core. If the song he calls a hit—Dori Hartley's "Nobody Loves Me but You," from his album, *Blue Djinn*—happens not to have been a hit, that only confirms the independence and solidity of Hesh's judgment: He's talking quality, not sales. Whether Adriana's group is called Defiled or Visiting Day, Hesh knows they are not good. In contrast, Massive Genius likes "any music that turns shit green" (that is, makes money).

The zebra also emblematizes the assimilated Italian-Americans. When viewed in their natural habitat—the Cusamanos' dinner party—they reveal their own pecking order. One guest wonders how Mafia neighbors affect their god, "property values." Dr. Cusamano shares the Monte Cristos (Cuban cigars, illegal) Tony gave him, but condescends even in his defense. With its bribery and bugging, "Sometimes I think the only thing separating American business from the mobs is fuckin' whackin' someone." The "closed" membership at the Cooze's golf club recalls Tony telling Chris that the "made" membership is full. As the doctor's diction has been inflected by exposure to Tony, the distinctions between legitimate and illegitimate business have blurred. Melfi bravely opposes one woman's denigration of the Sopranos' taste: "I like Murano glass."

But Tony has the last laugh. He enigmatically asks his neighbor to keep a package for him for a few weeks, which The Cooze and his wife assume is important and likely illegal but are too nervous to open. It is just sand. Here Tony's evil is safely "so much fun." When the episode closes on the Cusamanos scared of their box, we are brought full circle to the opening scene, where Tony's gang grabbed someone else's stash. The closing tone is much lighter than the opening. A playful hoax is not a bullet between the courier's eyes.

And yet . . . and yet, we and the Cusamanos hear a couple of pained screams from next door. They recall the screams that Dr. Melfi heard when she left the dining room to see Tony's house from the Cusamanos' bathroom. Tony denied hearing them, when she asked, but she heard definite screams. Now we see their source: Tony, as he strains under the weights in his basement exercise room. Logical enough in their literal import, the screams additionally express the strain and the pain of someone trying to improve his condition, in a melting pot America that maintains prohibitive social barriers not just between but within its ethnic hierarchies.

In the episode's most delicate exchange, Dr. Melfi tells Tony that she was at the Cusamanos for dinner and she saw his house. She does not tell him that she went out of her way for the excuse to go to the bathroom, flushing for a cover, and that she climbed the bidet for her glimpse. Nor her delicacy in taking a piece of toilet paper to lower the seat, a gesture that reminds us how far apart Melfi's and Tony's natures are. As Tony leaves he pauses in the doorway, then says "You saw my house." With another shuffle he is gone.

His line hangs in the air. That she saw his house suggests to him that she wanted to look at it. She has sought an insight, an intimacy, outside their sessions. Perhaps Tony even entertains the thought that Jennifer Melfi may have been impressed by it. Moved to regard him more respectfully, she may perhaps now be more open to him. We detected her squirm when The Cooze said his patient gave him the Monte Cristos because he was "very happy" with his referral (that is, Melfi). Though none of this is spoken, in the glimpse, the report, its consideration, the shrink's relationship with her client has reached a new intimacy, despite the patient's aggression and the therapist's recoil.

I, 11:   Nobody Knows Anything

Written by Frank Renzulli. Directed by Henry Bronchtein.

Pussy collapses in a brothel from his back problems. A police raid on Jimmy Altieri's social club uncovers a cache of weapons in the pool table. Pussy and Jimmy are arrested, but Pussy is released immediately. Vin, Tony's police source, reports that Pussy has been wired to incriminate him. Meanwhile Livia, angry that Tony has sold her house, tells Uncle Junior that Tony meets with three other *capos* at the seniors residence, where they have put their mothers. When Vin is arrested in a brothel raid and suspended, he kills himself. As Tony concludes that Jimmy is the traitor, Uncle Junior decides to have Tony killed.

This episode unleashes a variety of betrayals against one surprising and maverick loyalty. As the first season nears its conclusion the emphasis is on the disorder still to be settled.

Much of it deals with Tony's pain at the idea that Pussy might be the traitor. "Like him, I fuckin' love him" he tells his detective Vin Macazian. But Pussy is the Feds' favorite target for "flipping" because he "loves his family above all else." Trying to prevent his treachery, Tony assures Pussy that he would never be out of options (that is, bound to the Feds); he has friends who would die for him. But when Tony jokes that the convalescing Pussy is a "beached whale" he anticipates his marine death.

To ascertain whether Pussy is indeed wired, Paulie takes him to a steam bath. Pussy pleads his doctor's insistence that a *schvitz* (Yiddish for sweat) would be bad for his high blood pressure. Tony insists on being "110-percent sure" before ordering what he has to. He requires Paulie to see the wire on him before acting. This is Othello's "ocular proof." If he demands less evidence before shifting his suspicion onto Jimmy, it's because Tony does love Pussy and fears wrongly condemning him. When Pussy disappears, Tony physically attacks Paulie for perhaps having acted prematurely.

Tony's loyalty to Pussy—and Paulie's loyalty to Tony, in taking on Pussy's punishment for him—contrasts to Livia's betrayal of her son. Livia maintains her martyred innocence in the face of Carmela's bluntness: "I want you to cut the drama. It's killing Tony." Livia fires Uncle Junior against her son, when she seems to let slip Tony's conspiracy with the other *capos*. As usual, her dangerous innuendo begins as a complaint: "I suppose he would have found it harder to have his meetings at my house than in the nursing home. . . . Maybe it was you they were talking about, who knows? . . . Now I just don't like being put in the middle of things." When Junior decides to have Tony killed, "Blood or no," Livia feigns concern: "Oh, God, what did I say now?" Junior is so paranoid that more than one meeting of the *capos* becomes a disease: He says "pleurisy" for "plural."

The other regulars have minor roles in this episode. Melfi allows that Pussy's bad back could result from his secret and guilt. At breakfast Meadow remarks upon America's backwardness in still criminalizing prostitution and in persecuting the president (presumably Bill Clinton, unnamed) for his vagrant sex life. Tony confirms his loyalty to old values (as to old friends): "Out there it's the 1990s. But in this house it's 1954."

The episode's most surprising case of loyalty is Tony's bought detective, Vin Macazian. When Vin objects to Tony's insults, we assume Tony disdains of Vin for being disloyal—albeit to the police. Disloyalty is bad in itself. But we later (in III, 3) learn that in Tony's most traumatic childhood experience, his father used his brutality to teach Tony not to gamble. So Tony hates Vin for gambling. In II, 8, Tony tells Melfi that his victim Davey is "a fuckin' degenerate gambler." In I, 1, he called Mahaffey "a degenerate fuckin' gambler." To his face here Tony calls Vin "a degenerate fuckin' gambler with a badge." Even Livia dismisses the elderly Millie at Green Grove as "a degenerate gambler." Johnny-Boy made the phrase a moral unit. Of course, whatever risks he may take Tony does not gamble.

Moreover, as that trauma associated gambling and raw meat with violence and sexuality in Tony's mind, there is also an irony in Vin's earlier quip (in I, 4) to Melfi: "You have prime rib at home. Don't be going out for hamburgers." Assuming Melfi is one of Tony's conquests, Vin cites Tony's weakness, his phobia for meat, as if it were his strength. Again, the irony in the language shimmers across episodes.

To some extent, Vin embodies the weaknesses that Tony has suppressed in himself. Tony is surprised at this bond. Having assumed that Vin's service is out of strictly mercenary motive, he is touched when the madam Debbie tells him that Vin always liked and trusted Tony. She recalls his assurance: "As long as he had you in his corner there is nothing really to worry about. . . . At least with Tony Soprano you know where you stand." In the episode's last scene Tony stands contemplative under the bridge from which his unappreciated friend dove.

In an earlier conversation Tony found something of his own experience in the turned cop's. As a boy, Vin recalls, he used to hide under his bed all night to escape his parents' violence. Especially now Tony knows the need for such refuge. He could also identify with Debbie's summary of Vin: "He was not happy with himself. How he turned out." The reason why may be inferred from Vin's pinning his badge back on before diving to his death. When Vin sarcastically applauds Tony's "amazing ability to sum up a man's whole life in a sentence," his complexity and ambivalence parallels Tony's.

For years Vin went to Debbie for friendship and mutual support. Tony comes to regard that relationship as a variation on his with Dr. Melfi. As Debbie remarks, "Who wouldn't want to sleep with their shrink? . . . You would be amazed how much easier it is to open up when you're naked and in the arms of someone who cares for you." Although we do not see much of the Vin-Debbie relationship, it seems warm, understanding and healthy—especially when compared to the vituperative marriage between Mikey Palmice and JoJo. The latter bristles harsh even after Mikey hears Junior has ordered Tony's murder, which would lead to Mikey's promotion.

In this episode about trust and betrayals there is a metaphoric resonance in Paulie's report from the doctor: "When it comes to backs nobody knows anything, really."

I, 12: Isabella

Written by Robin Green and Mitchell Burgess. Directed by Allen Coulter.

Worried about Pussy's disappearance, Tony is overcome by depression, despite his diet of Prozac and Lithium. For Uncle Junior, Mikey puts out a contract on Tony. Chris unwittingly thwarts the first attempt by parking in the assassins' way while spying on Tony. On the second, Tony wrestles the assassins in turn through his car windows, has one shoot the other, then grabs the second's gun. Laughing exuberantly at having escaped, Tony smashes his car and is briefly hospitalized for stitches on his ear. He spurns the FBI's offer of the Witness Protection Program. His encounter with a beautiful, nurturing Italian exchange student is revealed to be a fantasy. AJ goes to his first prom, escorted by Silvio and Paulie in a limousine.

From the opening shot, the corpse of the woman Uncle Junior nostalgically remembers giving him his first handjob behind the chicken market, this episode is about death in life. The outdoor shots show the trees turned yellow, the autumn of desiccation and chill. When Jimmy Altieri tells Junior "How many of these [funerals] do we have to go to?" we know he has just his own left. Suspected of informing the Feds, Jimmy will be killed in the next episode. Uncle Junior points to the spiritual void of his time when he wonders why Saints cards don't sell like baseball cards: "Thousands of bucks for Honus Wagner and jackshit for Jesus." In addition to the righteousness and alliteration, the phrase shows how Junior, not unlike the Metaphysical poets, unites the profane and the religious in one passion.

When Tony is not cowering slit-eyed under his blankets, he stumbles through his days in a depressed stupor. In his first session he and Dr. Melfi are unusually framed in the same shot, as if he needs her to prop him up. Denying any pain, he says: "I don't feel nothin'. Nothin'. Dead. Empty." He stumbles out of bed to his drugs, against the Tindersticks's song, "Tiny Tears," a spare, melancholy lyric about someone lying in bed week after week, "too busy looking into your head, To see the tiny tears in her eye."

Tony's one vitality in this episode turns out to be a fantasy. He sees a beautiful young Italian woman hanging white laundry next door. He walks over and sniffs the slip he picks off the grass. Isabella is an exchange student studying dental surgery, house-sitting while the Cusamanos are golfing in Bermuda. When he meets her downtown and takes her to lunch she guesses his people are from Avelino. Tony envisions her in a rural house, nursing their baby. We might infer he's projecting a fantasy of them together, but he later tells Melfi the fantasy was set around 1907 and she was whispering to baby Antonio not to cry, not to worry, everything will be alright, she loves him. The sexual, idealized Isabella is the mother Tony never had.

When Cusamano returns Tony realizes that he imagined the entire experience. But for Melfi it points to Tony's need for a loving, caring woman in his life, at a time when Livia keeps reporting news stories about mothers murdering their children and when she has prodded Uncle Junior to kill him. Tony denies his mother's possible involvement in what he insists was a carjacking. The FBI and the TV news say it was a failed assassination attempt; Silvio and Chris assume it was at Uncle Junior's order.

There are careful clues to suggest Isabella is a fantasy figure. For one thing, she's too beautiful to be true. Her whiteness and full-bosom ethereality recall Claudia Cardinale wafting through Federico Fellini's 8½ (1963). Tony meets Isabella outside a pharmacy that has an antique window display and a sign, CHEMIST SINCE 1907. Their conversation bristles with the fugitive metaphors of a dream. She knows where he's coming from (including Avelino). If she's studying dental surgery it's because Tony has a cavity to fill (and has an episode ago had a flat tire while driving AJ to a dentist for his braces). When Tony—and a close-up—focuses on her perfect mouth, her beauty may embody the pre-sexual orality of the child. Her interest in gum tumors and soft tissue points to Tony's need for a woman of healthy softness, who would replace his malignant undermining (the tumors/rumors of his mother wanting him whacked). His own anxieties reflect in her wondering why a "hero" would be trapped in a sandwich and why his foundation should be shaken by a "hurt-quake."

When Carmela sees the woman she is concerned that he took her for lunch ("If I had an ounce of self-respect I would cut your dick off"). But that verification of Isabella is immediately undercut. The shot of Tony in bed rotates 90 degrees, so that the prone Tony seems erect, and the maid tells him Carmela has gone to New York to buy a suit for AJ's prom. As we know Carmela has already done this, the line declares this exchange—and therefore the previous one with Carmela—fantasy. Even as Tony fantasizes a nourishing woman he generates a balancing punishment. Both his fantasy love and his fantasy of his wife are a way to avoid thinking of his mother.

Of course, Livia is at full venom. She drives Tony from the dinner table with her insults. Why should he be depressed, she snorts: "Nobody threw him into the glue factory and sold his house out from under him." A scene outside a cinema could be either real or part of Tony's fantasy. As she and Junior line up for tickets, Livia details how dead Tony already acts and how non-existent he is as a father. "Don't talk about Tony any more," Junior snaps, "It's done." This scene is so consistent with the plotters' realistic scenes that it could be happening. On the other hand, as everything in the scene is gray and it is blown with the same strong wind that blows around the radiant Isabella, it could be Tony's fantasy, in which his subconscious finally admits the conspiracy against him. This confusion between reality and dread confirms the death-like state of Tony's life at this point.

The characters react variously to the failed assassination. When he hears of the first failure Junior vomits out of his car. After the second he panics over Tony's likely revenge. Carmela wants to take up FBI agent Harris's offer of witness relocation: "This is our chance to get out." But Tony would not break his oath of *omertà*—nor retire to sell souvenirs roadside or to ranch rattlesnakes in Utah.

As she watches the TV-news report with Uncle Junior, Livia is shocked: "How could this happen. . . . My son got shot—and he got away! . . . He's my only son." She shifts from the obligatory shock that Tony was shot, to the genuine disappointment that he got away, to maternal rhetoric. Her first words to Tony are unconsoling: "Your ear—it's disfigured." When she doesn't recognize Meadow, Junior angrily confronts her about her convenient loss of memory. She gives her usual bold reply: "I don't know what you're talking about." A chastened Junior senses that his dangerous action was based on an unreliable, vengeful old woman.

Tony's session in Melfi's car seems almost romantic. When Carmela drives him to the dark country road, she avoids looking at Melfi as if she were his *goomah*. "Did you ever tell anyone about you and me?" he asks Melfi, as if they were furtive lovers. Though she answers that truthfully, she tells a lover's white lie: that the cigarettes in her car are her son's. We know (I, 8) Jason moved to a smoke-free dorm. Her eyes fill with tears as she explains how his fantasy of a nourishing Isabella addressed his situation with Livia. When they part, he caresses her cheek with his knuckles.

And how does Tony feel after his brush with death (from the other end of the scythe)? "To tell you the truth I feel pretty good." Getting shot "gives you a nice kick start," he tells Dr. Melfi. (In this violent context he says

SEASON ONE · 71

"kick start," vs. the "jump start" he used in the sexual context in I, 6). When in his depression he wanted to die, now "every fuckin' particle of my being was fighting to live."

We glimpsed his revived spirit earlier, when Father Phil dropped in to express his concern and suggested a circle of prayer: "Why don't you grab a sandwich and we'll talk later. You are sleeping over, aren't you?" The incorrigible Tony S. is back alive and kicking—especially at the freeloading family priest. Fitting that the episode closes on Cream's "I Feel Free." The last line we hear could speak for Tony's post-assault cockiness: "I can walk down the street and there's no one there." Of course, it also reflects his solitude, the solitude that comes with the mark of Cain.

■ As usual, the script sparkles with incidental information. Carmela opens the windows on Tony: "In Alaska they wear these little light hats in the winter so they don't get depressed." And as Silvio points out, "Winston Churchill, he drank a quart of brandy before breakfast. And Napoleon, he was a moody fuck, too." No theme is too bleak to go unlightened by this series' dark comedy.

I, 13: I Dream of Jeannie Cusamano

Written by David Chase. Directed by John Patterson.

As Livia shows increasing signs of Alzheimer's she is transferred to the nursing unit. She tells Artie that Tony burned down his Vesuvio. When Artie confronts Tony with a shotgun he is talked out of his anger. Tony violently attacks Dr. Melfi for suggesting that Livia might have been involved in his assassination attempt. But he is persuaded when the FBI plays their tapes of her Green Grove conversations with Junior. Tony, Chris, and Silvio kill Junior's two aides, but before they can get to Junior he is arrested in an FBI sweep. Junior refuses the FBI offer to implicate Tony instead. When Tony comes to the hospital to smother his mother he is thwarted by the fact she has suffered a stroke. In the last scene Tony, Carmela, and the children, trapped in a heavy storm, are given refuge in Artie's restaurant.

In the first season's finale there is a general clearing of the air and the conclusion of several issues. Tony secures his position by having traitor Jimmy Altieri and Junior's two henchmen, Chucky Signore and Mikey Palmice, killed. Though Junior is saved by his arrest, his power shifts to Tony. Tony finally realizes his own position when the FBI plays tapes of his mother and Junior plotting against him.

Livia continues her subtle destruction. When Artie visits her she pretends confusion—remembering that husband Johnny-Boy, not Tony, played Little League with Artie—before letting slip her lethal revelation: "You're such a good boy, Artie. . . . After what my son did to you, how can I look you in the face? . . . You don't blame him for starting the fire? I guess we have to be grateful that nobody was incinerated to death." Between the compliment and the relief comes the shiv.

Tony's denial to Artie is false but it is literally and emotionally true: "I didn't burn down your restaurant. I swear on my mother." In fact, he only commissioned the arson; nor would he object if Livia suffered divine retribution. To Artie's correct statement of Tony's motive for the arson Tony makes the only possible defense: "Here's a question for you. Am I that fuckin' stupid?" Thus persuaded, Artie smashes his rifle on his own station wagon—not the action of a smart wiseguy—and speeds off, even more overwrought than on his arrival.

Even after Tony knows about his mother's and uncle's plot, he hosts them at the traditional Sunday dinner. In this world the relatively virtuous can be as duplicitous as the vile. "I don't have to admit anything," Livia responds to an innocent remark by Carmela. Over dinner Livia pretends not to remember Artie Bucco.

In a bedroom chat Tony blames himself: "What kind of person can I be, if my own mother wants me dead." Carmela wisely shifts the blame to Livia. When she adds that she's a peculiar duck, the innocent colloquialism recalls Tony's dream (I, 1) of a bird flying off with his penis, which to Melfi represents Livia emasculating her son. Tony blames his razzing of Junior and the fear of what he may have told Melfi for the war: "Cunnilingus and psychiatry brought us to this." For Tony, that is a doubled fear of the feminine. Tony declares that he will take of care of Junior and Mikey "and I'll get some satisfaction. But inside I'll know"—the inexpressible: that his own mother tried to have him killed.

In the episode's most dramatic scene, Tony leans over his mother as she is being wheeled up the hospital hallway and tells her: "I know what you did. Your only son. . . . I heard the tapes!" When the orderlies say she can't understand, Tony fights off them and their illusions about her: "Look at her face. She's smiling." Under her oxygen mask, the indomitable Livia seems indeed to be.

Artie's explosion against Tony clears their air as well. When Artie later thanks Father Phil for his counsel, we infer that the priest has been urging Artie to tell Charmaine and the police that Tony was responsible for burning down the Vesuvio. His "You must be strong" apparently means "strong enough to turn Tony in—or to let Charmaine do it for you." All the while Father Phil has been assuring Carmela of his concern for Tony and enjoying his steaks and DVD player, he has been counseling Artie against him. The priest is disappointed when Artie finds peace in not squealing. Doubting Tony "would only add to the quotient of sorrow in the world," Artie rationalizes, like a good sermon.

After Carmela learns that Rosalie Aprile gave Father Phil her Jackie's watch and finds them snuggled over the lunch she brought him, Carmela rebukes Father Phil's pretended interest in Tony and affirms her independence from her priest:

He doesn't give a flying fuck. . . . I think that you like the . . . whiff of sexuality that never goes anyplace. . . . I think you need to look at yourself. . . . I think you have this m.o. where you manipulate spiritually thirsty women. And I think a lot of it is tied up with food somehow as well as the sexual tension game.

In her wisdom and articulate coolness, Carmela shows a remarkable strength here. Her self-awareness ("spiritually thirsty women") and courage to abandon a false support contrast to the helpless Livia's demonic strength. Carmela's strength is all the more impressive given that she has been shaken by the sweeping arrests and by seeing Mikey's wife crying on television about her husband's disappearance. The reaction shot shows Carmela identifying.

Unable to respond, Father Phil retrieves his DVD and leaves. He represents the supposedly superior alternative to Tony but is exposed as equally self-serving, self-indulgent, and predatory. As exasperated Carmela points out, "I get exactly the same 'who me?' shit from Tony." From the priest's sanctimoniousness Tony is attractively free.

This scene begins with Carmela coming home with groceries and finding the priest in her kitchen, having checked the fridge. He brought a DVD that Carmela does not want to see (in her one curious lapse of judgment Carmela is not a Renee Zellweger fan). The only *One True Thing* about Father Phil is the title of the film he says he brought for Carmela's interest.

Far stormier is Tony's confrontation with Melfi. Tony hears her apposite definition of a "borderline personality disorder." But when she suggests Livia may be behind the assassination attempt he leaps on her, swearing and threatening. Tony has to overcome her fear before Melfi admits him again—having slipped precautionary scissors up her sleeve. In their brief discussion Tony says his only dreams have involved him having sex with Jeannie Cusamano, doggie-style, and he refers to her "big ass," which as Melfi observes does not apply to the slender Jeannie. As he fantasizes to avoid confronting the real women in his life, he turns to others' cheeks. When Tony warns that Melfi's life may be in danger she slips into the mob argot: "I can't lam it. . . . Jesus fucking Christ!" But—still not of Tony's world—she calls Pussy "Booty" by mistake.

When Tony tells his three aides about his therapy and invites their response, they react sympathetically. "I'm sure you did it with complete discretion," Silvio offers, confident he also speaks for the still absent Pussy. Paulie surprises: "I was seeing a therapist myself about a year ago. I had some issues. Enough said. I lacked some coping skills." Chris doesn't know what to think—"Was it like marriage counseling?"—so he just runs out.

The first season closes on a note of familial warmth and grace. When Artie lets Tony bring his family in from the storm he overrides his suspicions about the arson and Charmaine's rejection of the mob. As Tony toasts his family, he beams at his children: "You two'll have your own families someday soon. And if you're lucky you'll remember the little moments. Like this. [pause] That were good." The pause suggests that perhaps most of the family's "little moments" may not have been so good.

The prospect of these children having their own families harkens back to the episode's start. Livia's unexpected visit interrupted Meadow petting under a boy on the sofa and AJ masturbating in his room. The road toward having children indeed begins with such fumbling adolescent sexuality.

More seriously, this conclusion returns to the season's opening episode. The nostalgia about "little moments . . . that were good" recalls Tony's remarks to Carmela in I, 1, when she attended his CAT scan: "We had some good times. Some good years." In the first episode Tony cried when his lost ducks portended his loss of his family. His toast here shows that the 13 episodes of tribulation and self-discovery have reconciled him to that natural cycle of growth and life. Though the last episode is propelled by the energy of Buddy Holly's "Rave On" and Bruce Springsteen's "State Trooper," two classical pieces—Gabriel Faure's *Pavane* (a rock version of which was played in "*Pax Soprana*," [I, 6]) and Samuel Barber's *Adagio for Strings*—close the season on notes of peace and warmth.

- There is an uncharacteristic continuity error. In the previous episode Livia complains that Tony has sold her house. In the next episode, it has not been sold, so it accommodates Janice's romance with Richie. This is a minor trespass in a series of such remarkable coherence. For example:

When the FBI agent tells Junior he really wants to get Johnny Sack and his superiors, Junior replies: "I want to fuck Angie Dickinson. See who gets lucky first." Junior dreams he marries Angie—still in the context of turning informer—in his anesthetic dream in III, 7. One presumes Junior loves the Angie of *Rio Bravo* (Howard Hawks, 1959; cp. IV, 1; IV, 5), not that of the later *Police Woman* television series.

When Tony pulls a gun out of a fish's mouth to kill Chucky Signore, he sets off a string of "sleeping with the fishes" incidents, alluding to *The Godfather*. It culminates in the murder of Pussy—and Tony's torment thereafter.

- With regard to Tony's "Cunnilingus and psychiatry brought us to this," Chase considers this line too literary, self-conscious, and arch—"but I couldn't resist it" (Season One DVD, disc four).

Season Two

II, 1: Guy Walks into a Psychiatrist's Office

Written by Jason Cahill. Directed by Allen Coulter.

Pussy returns to a suspicious Tony. Tony's older hippie sister Janice comes from Seattle to care for Livia, who has recovered from her "stroke" but is still hospitalized. Christopher cheats to get his stockbroker's license so he can operate a crooked brokerage firm. Tony has the jailed Uncle Junior's gunsel aide Philly Parisi killed. Tony suffers panic attacks but cannot find a therapist.

The second season opens in the un-Soprano setting of a classroom, with an authoritative black man in a suit presiding over a room of individual desks and computers. An Oriental man about to take the stockbroker's exam identifies himself as Christopher Moltisanti. Chris requires this certification for a new scam that derives from Tony's plan to invest the windfall (I, 10) score in something "legit." The surprise and meaning of this scene depend on our knowing what Christopher looks like and is. This in-joke is a playful way to welcome back a familiar audience.

A montage reintroduces the major characters, accompanied by Frank Sinatra's "A Very Good Year." In addition to the song's usual nostalgia, here it implicitly celebrates the series' successful beginning. The montage begins with a pan from an IV to a hospital patient—Livia, apparently recovering. Then we see Tony playing the emblematic solitaire, the gang passing in a bag full of money, Junior in jail, Carmela cooking, the FBI labeling Tony's picture as the new "Street Boss," Dr. Melfi meeting clients in a motel, Silvio flashing new shoes and suit, AJ starting to take an interest in his looks, Livia at therapy, Paulie (ditto) screwing a stripper on the Bing pool table, Chris snorting coke in front of an Edward G. Robinson gangster film on TV, Meadow taking a driving lesson from the affectionate Tony, Carmela still cooking, Tony under his mistress Irina, then tiptoeing home, throwing his perfumed shirt in the washer, then joining Carmela in bed. She awakens long enough to turn away from him.

While it is business as usual, some old habits (Carmela, Paulie, Chris, Tony) are interwoven with new beginnings (Livia, AJ, Silvio, Meadow, Melfi). There is often a fugitive connection between the Sinatra phrase and the visual it attends—e.g., a comment on woman's vanity for Silvio and AJ preening, the mellow sense of life as vintage wine, from the brim to the dregs, over Tony and Carmela in bed together—usually ironic.

The plot resumes with a threat and its apparent resolution. When Tony goes out for the morning paper he recoils from a suspicious car in the driveway. Out steps the long-missing Pussy, whose suspicions of Tony are reciprocated. Pussy says he went for back treatments to Puerto Rico, where he became involved with a 26-year-old acupuncturist. Now he's back because he needs the money to support his family, two kids in college and one marrying. He hadn't contacted anyone because his friends had turned "their hearts of stone" against him. They read his weakness as treason. He knew he was in trouble when out of the blue Tony came at 3 P.M. to assure him he had friends. He knows Tony's embrace is to frisk him for a wire. His bad back may denote a suspect spine. Even as his cronies welcome him back and convey (most of) his territory earnings, Tony has Paulie check out Pussy's story. At the Bing, when Silvio performs his *Godfather* Pacino for Pussy, he concludes with the prophetic: "Our true enemy has yet to reveal himself."

In addition to the treacherous Pussy, Tony is afflicted with his older sister, Janice, a Seattle hippie who now calls herself Parvati (after a Hindu goddess). Janice's scam is total disability insurance for her chronic carpal syndrome. After promising to take Livia back to Seattle, to look after her, Janice tries to prevent Tony's sale of Livia's house and to grab what she can from Livia. Janice is equal parts New Age Flake—looking to the Chelsea set to fund her new video—and schemer, as she reveals in her poolside chat with sister Barbara. Notwithstanding her lack of work ethic and her general dysfunctionality, Janice plans a self-help video titled "Lady Kerouac; or, Packing for the Highway to a Woman's Self-Esteem."

With no Melfi to help him, Tony disintegrates. At first he seems in control. Though he is off therapy he is self-medicating and confident. After whacking Philly, Tony feels secure enough to tell Melfi that she can safely resume her normal business. She is shocked and angry that he knows her motel phone number and seems to be watching her. Being as safe as Tony does not mean she is safe from him.

Apart from Pussy's danger, Tony's main problem at work is Christopher, who neglects his duties as their brokerage's SCC Compliance Officer. The operation hustles sales of a bad company to fixed-income pensioners. Even Tony's lawyer, Neil Mink, has sold some of his Disney to buy the inflated "Webistics," (a name that summarizes the costly electronics snare). Chris's two loose-cannon aides, Matt Bevilaqua and Sean Gismonte, assault one broker for giving a client honest advice. When Chris corrects them, he demands a cut of their car thefts. He slaps Adriana for mentioning his drug use in their presence. When we cut from Chris's assault of Adriana to Tony's approach to Melfi, Chris seems to personify Tony's negative potential. That is, he represents Tony's Achilles Heel not just in the gang but in his own psyche. Both men need "to exercise impulse control," as Tony counsels Chris.

From this stress Tony's composure crumbles. Happily driving along to Deep Purple's "Smoke on the Water," when his CD sticks he loses his temper and blacks out. Happily, the airbag saves him from injury and the crash cures the CD. At his barbecue, Tony is enraged by Janice's machinations. Carmela orders him to join his friends for some fun. Even with them, he is belligerent and almost passes out. When he goes to a male therapist, despite claiming to be "Mr. Spears" he is recognized. The therapist refuses to take him on as a patient. He has seen *Analyze This* (1999), Harold Ramis's comedy of a shrink (Billy Crystal) and his gang-boss patient (Robert De Niro). (Once again, film demonstrates its dangerous public effects.)

Realizing Dr. Melfi is his last hope, Tony imposes himself on her at a roadside diner. They sound like ex-lovers. "That was a different time for us," Melfi responds to his nostalgia. Though Tony is apologetic ("I don't deserve your help"), Melfi remains angry. When his danger forced her practice into a motel, one client killed herself. She orders him out of her life: "How many other people have to die for your personal growth?"

In the closing scene Tony drifts around Carmela at home in the afternoon. She nukes him a bowl of cold pasta, fixes his collar while he eats, then sits with him to check the mail. Their silence expresses marital comfort. This scene provides a mellow conclusion to the season opener, which has refreshed our memories of the characters and introduced Tony's problems old (Livia), new (Janice), and resurrected (Pussy). Their kitchen comfort is a rebuke to what Livia told Carmela on her wedding day: "This is a big mistake. Tony will get bored with you." The closing song, Skeleton Key's "Nod Off," ironically comments on patterns of marriage and their violation: "Someday, she'll marry someone just like Daddy." Carmela's husband would not be commanded off—as her father is—to buy canned peaches for a pound cake.

● Aida Turturro (Janice) played James Gandolfini's wife in the 1992 revival of *A Streetcar Named Desire.* Her films include *Bringing Out the Dead, Mickey Blue Eyes, Sleepers, Manhattan Murder Mystery, What about Bob?,* and *Play It to the Bone.* She also played Fran on *As the World Turns.* She is the cousin of actors John and Nicholas Turturro.

II, 2: Do Not Resuscitate

Written by Robin Green, Mitchell Burgess, and Frank Renzulli.
Directed by Martin Bruestle.

Tony has tense visits with Uncle Junior, first in prison then, when he is on house arrest, at the doctor's office. When Tony takes over Junior's territory he leaves him reduced earnings and the title of boss (to keep the FBI's focus on him). When FBI agent Skip Lipari drives Pussy home from therapy we learn that Pussy has been informing the Feds for two years, but remains reluctant to rat on Tony. Rev. Herman James Jr. leads a picket of the Massarone Bros. Construction site, demanding jobs for black joint-fitters. Tony pays him a private kickback after providing goons to break up the next demonstration.

The range and intensity of betrayals in the Soprano circle still surprise us. The joint-fitters plot is a parable of betrayal. Reverend James co-opts his 83-year-old war veteran father in his campaign to win construction jobs for African Americans. But under the reverend's "business arrangement," Tony charges the construction company for breaking up the next demonstration—five non-existent positions on the payroll. Tony and the reverend share the money for these "no shows." No African Americans are hired. The reverend betrays both his community and his father (who dies ignorant of the deal). The revelation poignantly reflects on what the father told Tony: "Never underestimate a man's determination to be free." For his son, the freedom of choice is to "fill his pockets," what he accuses the white bosses of doing.

The father represents a genuine piety of which his son—like Father Phil—is a self-serving pretender. Herman James Sr. is so real he even has his original teeth. He dies right after we—and Tony—meet him. Cynically, the kickback payment follows the reverend's philosophizing: "When the last one goes we become the old ones at family functions." Herman Sr.'s passing is the end of the church's "Old School."

There is no equivalent to the virtue of Herman Sr. in Tony's ambivalent relationship with Uncle Junior. They agree to whack Green Grove owner Freddy Capuano, whose indiscreet gossip includes Tony's attempt to smother his mother. Junior tries to salvage his own honor by exhorting Tony to make peace with Livia. "Nobody played me," he avows, "She didn't know she was setting you up to get whacked." But Tony insists: "She's dead to me." Livia shadows Junior's invective use of "motherless." (For example the prison guards are "motherless fucks who listen to everything.")

Despite their tensions, however, when Junior falls in the shower Tony rushes over to help him. He carries him out like a bride, to the end-credit song "Goodnight, My Love," by Ella Fitzgerald and Benny Goodman. Ella's "Remember that you're mine, sweetheart" provides an ironic twist to this irregular relationship. Despite their animosity, the uncle and nephew remain devoted.

There is a false suggestion of betrayal when Uncle Junior appeals for medical release from prison. When he compares the electronic bracelet to Nazi Germany, his Jewish lawyer senses that Junior has offended the Jewish judge. In a soft, oily voice the lawyer suggests "I don't think we should let our shared sorrows or biases enter into this, Judge." That is, he tries to exploit their ethnic connection. But the honorable Judge Jacob Greenspan rejects this manipulation and imposes the bracelet to prevent Junior's flight.

The domestic machinations continue. At dinner Janice evades Tony's ban by talking about how wicked Livia is. To ingratiate herself she calls Meadow's driving examiner a "Fascist martinet"; as soon as Meadow gets her license she is maneuvered herself. From Meadow Janice learns that Livia likes "that Mario Lasagna guy" (translation: Mario Lanza). Janice flatters Livia with opera records and fond memories of watching the tenors on *The Ed Sullivan Show* together every Sunday eve, though she admits to Meadow "I hated that shit." But Livia knows her daughter: "You're here because you want to take my house." When Janice proposes to live with her, Livia switches to prefer Green Grove.

Despite Livia's malevolence she is archetypal: "Some day I hope you have children of your own and they treat you like this." Livia generously offers Janice "some of my tapioca"—from which she has recoiled. With more mischief than care Tony agrees to take the house off the market and let them live there: "You deserve each other. It'll be like *Whatever Happened to Baby Janice.*"

As with Tony's therapy, AJ unwittingly betrays him by telling Livia that Janice and Tony discussed her DNR—the DO NOT RESUSCITATE instruction that the nurse requested, in case of emergency. Livia uses this knowledge. Why should she move home with Janice, "So you can not resuscitate me?" Livia teases Janice with suggestions that she has stashed a large sum of money. Livia phones Carmela, insisting she doesn't know what she did to upset Tony and warning her that Janice is "a snake in the grass." Faithful to her husband, Carmela hangs up on her. In its snarl of manipulations and betrayals *The Sopranos* adds the grab of a good soap opera to the wit of classic drama.

II, 3: Toodle-Fucking-oo

Written by Frank Renzulli. Directed by Lee Tamahori.

A friendly policeman calls Tony to Livia's house, where Meadow's party has been taken over by druggies. Carmela rebukes Janice for interfering in their daughter's discipline. After Richie Aprile is released from prison, he bullies and beats pizza seller Beansie, for refusing to pay him tribute. Richie courts Parvati (Janice) at a yoga class. Dr. Melfi is embarrassed when she, in a group of imbibing women, encounters Tony with his gang.

The episode's title comes from Melfi's embarrassment at the restaurant. As she tells her psychiatrist, Elliot, when she met Tony she departed with the coquettish "Toodle-oo." When her "Jennifer" dominated her "Doctor Melfi," she "regressed into the girl thing to escape the responsibility of abandoning him as a client." She regressed because "young girls are not accountable for their behavior" (a view both Meadow and Janice implicitly share here). Hence, too, Melfi's nightmare—which we see as an event—where Tony's panic attack causes his fatal car crash, accompanied by the "You're out of the woods" song from *The Wizard of Oz*. Oz represents

Tony's strange world and his death, her recovered safety. Clearly, he affects her still.

The loss of control, both of others and of self, is the theme of the episode's other two plot lines. Both plots are covered by Janice's "That's what this is all about—ego and control." In the first, Meadow's party runs out of control when it is crashed by delinquents with designer drugs. That design causes chaos. The combination of health and danger in the teens' grab for independence is caught in the stretcher case who overdosed on Special K and Ecstasy.

Discussing her punishment, her parents know they no longer control their teenager. While Carmela insists Meadow must face consequences, Tony is more pragmatic: "I yelled. What the fuck else am I gonna do?" The parents should not overplay their hands "Cause if she finds out we're powerless we're fucked." Meadow knows this. She discusses her strategy with Hunter, who controls her parents through threats of bulimia: "Start purging. They won't say anything." Meadow's proposal—that she be punished by the brief withdrawal of her credit card—leads to ritual negotiation. The teens are in control. Meadow leaves her parents the same illusion of authority that the gangsters leave the cops. For Meadow, her parents' punishment is hypocritical: "How do you think my father makes a living?"

Other characters assert independence by changing their names. Livia tells Richie that Janice became Parvati just to shame her mother. In return, Janice's son Harpo has—not surprisingly—changed his name to Hal and moved to Montreal with his father, Eugenio, who is with the *Cirque du Soleil* (a less metaphoric circus than the Sopranos).

In another form of domestic control, Richie Aprile tries to reclaim his territory after 10 years in jail. Richie shaking down the pizza dealer parallels Meadow's shakedown of her parents—wangling extra cash to make up for the lost card. In their first meeting, Richie smashes Beansie's face with a coffee pot, then bashes him with a chair and fists. Later he shoots at him, then runs over him with his car, permanently crippling him. Richie's behavior is worse than Meadow's revolt, of course, but both show a lack of self-control and both reject Tony's authority. As Tony loses control over Meadow, Richie promises to serve Tony but he casts his lot with Uncle Junior. To Junior's rhetorical "What are you gonna do?" Richie responds "Whatever you tell me. . . . I'm yours, Junior."

Janice/Parvati unites Tony's domestic and business tensions when she interferes in Meadow's discipline and resumes her teenage affair with Richie. In both plots Janice undermines Tony but proves inconsistent, even hypocritical. Having supported Meadow's independence and opposed her punishment, she turns against her when—"beyond outrage"—she sees the damage done "her" house. In their yoga she and Richie both claim to have advanced their consciousness since they first dated. But there is little yoga in Janice's scheming or in Richie's sadism.

Richie's double entendre here suggests a non-spiritual bent: "Did you ever think you'd see Richie Aprile doing Downward Facing Dog?" That yoga position suggests the traditional "doggie style" that Tony dreams of doing with Jeannie Cusamano (I, 13) and that we will later see (II, 10) Richie and Janice engaged in (pistol to head optional).

When Richie tells Janice he did "a lot of stretching" in jail, more is involved than his work on his physical flexibility. Having served his "stretch," he is now bent upon over-reaching. In fact, his courtship of Janice is precisely ambiguous. It mingles Richie's family and his Family ambitions. That scheme is implicit in this exchange:

TONY: Go fuck yourself.
RICHIE: How's your sister?
TONY: Hey. There's no need for that kind of talk.

Richie opposes Tony by courting Janice through Livia, bringing flowers to the hospital. This romance would advance his status in the Soprano crew. Actor David Proval suggests Richie's feral cunning, from his hard but warm voice to his steely nose-to-nose confrontation of Tony. Richie uses Janice's affection—like Uncle Junior's suspicion—against Tony. After their yoga meeting, we cut from Richie thoughtfully watching Janice walk away, to Tony scratching his back as he waits for Richie in the mall. Romancing Janice is Richie's phantom stab at Tony's back.

Perhaps a minor theme lies in the running reference to fellatio, as it is associated with macho power and selfishness. In the first restaurant scene Tony lets his leering cronies assume Melfi is a conquest. "Pipefitter Lips," Pussy poetically names her. Richie's release is celebrated by homages at the Bada Bing Club and a blowjob in the backroom. Though the latter was Silvio's treat, Richie insists on paying: "Whose joint did you just cop, mine or his?" Richie insists on control. Men will be boys. As he tells Tony, "What's mine is not yours to give me."

Against the macho posturing, violence and strategizing loom two strong characters. Carmela shows her integrity first in criticizing and then in reconciling with Janice. It would not be Christian to let Janice leave their home, she tells Tony, after asking Janice's forgiveness. Carmela's family sense overrides such heated differences. In the parallel world, Beansie, so crippled he needs Tony to blow his nose, reiterates his "Old School" fidelity: He won't tell the police. In contrast, Richie's "Old School" warning to Christopher is not to beat Adriana (Richie's niece) unless he marries her first.

The episode ends as it began, with Tony surprised to find Meadow at his mother's house. This time she is scrubbing the floor, gagging at its stench. The episode closes on Tony's thoughtful close-up, as he considers his daughter's new responsibility. The Mafia-American Princess shows a surprising self-control as she persists in her nauseating task. This duty no-one urged on her. In her emerging maturity perhaps Tony sees he may not need to try to control her much longer.

- Director Lee Tamahori is a New Zealander who made a remarkable international reputation with his first feature film, *Once Were Warriors* (1994), which won a PEN Award. Two years later he made his American directing debut with *Mulholland Falls*. He went on to direct *The Edge, Along Came a Spider, In Search of the Assassin*, and *10th Victim*.

- Melfi's shrink, Dr. Elliot Kupferberg, is played by the well-known film writer and director Peter Bogdanovich. He directed *Targets; The Last Picture Show; What's up, Doc?; Paper Moon; Daisy Miller; Nickelodeon; Saint Jack; Texasville;* and *Noises Off*. As an actor, he appeared in several Roger Corman B-classics (*The Wild Angels, The Trip*) before moving up to Agnes Varda's *Lions Love*. His documentaries about filmmakers are especially well regarded. His experience as a film critic and historian is apparent in his interviews with David Chase on the Season One DVD (discs one and four).

- David Proval (Richie Aprile) studied acting with Uta Hagen and William Hickey. In *Mean Streets* he played the genial bar owner, Tony. He also appeared in *The Shawshank Redemption, Innocent Blood, Four Rooms, The Star Chamber*, and *The Siege*. He won the Toronto Film Festival Best Actor award for the title role in *Nunzio*. After he was killed later in this series (read on) he played a rabbi opposed to capital punishment on *The West Wing*.

II, 4: *Commendatóri*

Written by David Chase. Directed by Tim van Patten.

Paulie smashes a stolen DVD because it won't play. Two hoods carjack a family's Mercedes ML430, which Tony's gang will sell to partners in Italy. Tony takes Christopher and Paulie to Naples to meet boss Zi Vittorio. Meeting with the Number Two man, Tony offers to supply the Mercedes ML cars at $90,000. Don Vittorio is wheeled in by his beautiful daughter, Annalisa, whose husband is the acting boss but serving a life sentence. Tony agrees to sell Annalisa the cars at $75,000 provided she lets him have her best man, Furio. Meanwhile, Angie tells Carmela and Rosalie Aprile that she wants to divorce Pussy. When Pussy's meeting with his FBI contact is interrupted by a friend, Elvis impersonator Jimmy Bones, Pussy kills him.

This major episode critiques its male heroes' ethic and satirizes the self-importance of their style, both their Italian and their macho. The title, *Commendatóri* ("commanders" or "knights commander"), is the honorific with which the Naples hotelier greets our heroes. Paulie enjoys the title, but when he addresses some locals with it they ignore him. The episode questions male honor both in Tony's trans-Atlantic business world and in Angie's and Carmela's discussion of marriage.

In a comic version of this theme, the wus rages at the men who stole his new Mercedes: "Fuckin' niggers! . . . Well, who else?" But this is in the safety of his family, after the thieves are safely out of earshot. Far from resisting, he cowered with his family. Of course, the Sopranos are the "Who else" behind the theft.

In the opening scene the gangsters' silly strength turns to destructive frustration. When they can't get their stolen DVD to run their advance bootleg of the—what else?—*Godfather* outtakes, they break the machine. The episode opens on a close-up of the FBI warning that starts the DVD. That makes the FBI comically futile: A bootleg copy of buried material is about to be played on a stolen machine.

"You know the scene I love most?" Paulie asks. Of course, what and how men love is one of the episode's major questions. " 'It was you, Fredo.' " In that scene in *The Godfather Part II*, Michael Corleone grips his brother's (John Cazale) head and identifies him as the traitor. To keep the mood light, Paulie does not finish the quote: "You broke my heart!" Now Pussy—Tony's traitor—asks about his visit to Junior. After resisting the men's "favorite scene" nonsense—"What, you gonna call Coppola with ideas how to fix it?"—Tony relents. His favorite scene is the Don's trip to Sicily, with the crickets in the silence at Don Cicci's villa. (For the implications of Tony's choice, see the appendix.) But in the event, Tony's Italian experience does not live up to the *Godfather* model. The Don's modernistic villa does not live up to Don Cicci's.

In Italy, Tony's discipline contrasts to his colleagues' weakness. Though Christopher is determined to view the topless beaches and the crater of Vesuvius, he misses both—and neglects Tony's assignments—by sharing a hard drug stupor with the hood Tanno. Chris rushes to buy Adriana's Italian presents from the Duty Free at home.

Paulie wants to discover his roots in order to match his doctor (!) brother's experience. Italy is his "mother country. Here they make it real." But he proves a misfit in that reality. At the first dinner Paulie rejects the Italian food and asks for macaroni and tomato sauce, to the disdain of the Italians: "And you thought the Germans were classless pieces of shit." Paulie wants to rush back to the hotel to avoid the restaurant toilet. He bores the prostitute with his delight that she is from his grandfather's home town. Another local, assuming the American must be from NATO, blames him for cutting the ski lift cable. But at the airport Paulie reports "I felt right at home" and urges Pussy to visit his roots there as soon as possible.

Tony's business trip is a success. His final deal doubles Uncle Junior's profit. And he secures Furio Giunta, who speaks English and is from the Old School. That is, he honors the code of silence, respects the family, and shows his strength of character when he beats up a young boy who frightened the entourage with firecrackers. While the mother cries for mercy, the boy begs to join the gang, and the *carabiniéri* drive discreetly away, Furio pounds the kid while others hold him. "This is Naples University." From Tony's pensive response to the sight we may infer revulsion, but it is covetous respect.

None of our Italian-American heroes understand the spoken Italian, so they are helpless without our privilege of subtitles. Furio translates Nino's "Why is he busting my balls? Tell him to get to the point" to "Happy to be at your disposal." This shows (1) Furio may be a brute but he is diplomatic, and (2) the Italian thugs speak the same language as the American even if it is different. Tony's first negotiation with Annalisa ends with her "Fuck you" and his "Up your ass." The American rap record Annalisa's son plays is paralleled by the Italian rap played over the end-credits (Jovanotti's "Piove").

It may even be an uncharacteristic success for Tony *not* to screw Annalisa. He shows an unexpected honor. When she leads him into the Cumae, a pagan sybil's cave, the layered hallways present them as archetypes. Behind Tony is a fountainlike column, behind Annalisa an open cave. The contrast suggests the Romantic balance of the archetypal Male and Female. Against that background they reach their agreement and she offers herself. Tony declines because of conflict of interest: "I don't shit where I eat."

In this surprising abstention, that business principle may be less important than some other factors, such as the self-awareness to which Dr. Melfi has led him or his guilt at not having brought Carmela along. Or he is comfortable only with submissive women, like Paulie with his Neapolitan whore. Annalisa is a hard case: "My husband. Fuck you. He is never coming back, so you have to fucking deal with me." Tony can do his business deal with her but he cannot deal with such a strong woman, albeit available. In motivation the show prefers the enigmas of life over literary simplification.

Annalisa's power is ambiguous. With wiry strength she commands the all-male operation, while sustaining her warmth and softness as a mother and in caring for her incoherent father. The song in her domestic scene is Wyclef Jean's "Blood Is Thicker than Water." As Annalisa relates the myth of the sybil and burns her toenails (to keep them from any enemy), she is a primitive parallel to Melfi's psychoanalysis—yet she is an effective modern manager. The close-up on Annalisa's mouth, devouring a prawn, recalls the close-up of the dream with Isabella's luxuriant mouth in I, 12. But like the villa, this reality falls short of Tony's fantasy expectations. In contrast to Isabella's feminine delicacy, Annalisa's robust chew suggests a masculinity that could lead a gang.

Tony's dream of fucking Annalisa—from behind, Roman wolf-style, the woman in a hiked toga and the man in the classic breastplate—parallels Pussy's nightmare about a "too quiet" Jimmy. Whether it is the Jimmy Bones he fears will squeal on seeing him with the FBI agent or the Jimmy Altieri who was killed (so is now bones) in Pussy's place (an unwitting impersonation), the nightmare reveals Pussy's guilt and fear for talking to the Feds. He protects Tony by reporting that Raymond Curto took over Junior's stolen car exports.

When our heroes drive home, Paulie, who found the trip miserable and frustrating, beams while Tony, who enjoyed such success, broods. Tony's pensiveness may center on Annalisa, recalling Uncle Junior's continuing regret that he "never went." "It ain't over yet," Tony consoled him. But the "serious man" Junior remembers is now a wheelchair invalid who is only interested in reciting American place-names. His "Wheel-share Pool-apart" refers to his own immobility more than LA's Wilshire Boulevard. The senile Italian's blurry fascination with American clichés parallels the deracinated Italian-Americans' remoteness from the real Italian.

Carmela's disappointment at being left home feeds the marriage doubts prompted by Angie Bonpensiero's decision to leave Pussy. In fact, an Italian love song bridges Angie's "I'm getting a divorce" with the romantic shot of the men's plane flying the night sky to Naples. At lunch with Carmela and the widow Rosalie Aprile, Angie's happy pretense crumbles. She thought she missed Pussy and was worried but his return made her want to vomit. She shocks her friends by saying she wants a divorce.

Although we know Pussy is profoundly preoccupied, Angie thinks his insensitivity proves their marriage a waste. When she mentions her biopsy, her husband goes back to putting WD40 on his pocketknife. Even after hearing the good news, she is so nervous she drops a dozen eggs. But he responds: "Good, I'll be back later." When he wordlessly brings her roses she whips him with them, then runs upstairs. Pussy is not entirely without sensitivity. Angie says he cried when he heard their daughter could not bear children. But—manfully—he buries it.

Angie wonders how he could dare "To just come and go like that." "Have you reached out to him?" Carmela naively asks, sounding more like a marriage manual than a woman who lives a similar void. Carmela defends the sacrament of marriage and reminds Angie of her responsibilities to their three (grown) children. When Angie reports her lawyers will file for divorce on Tuesday, Carmela assumes she is taking another day to rethink it. No, Monday is a Jewish holiday so Angie's lawyers are unavailable.

Carmela's opposition to divorce rationalizes her own marriage with reflex arguments. Her thoughtful close-ups after these exchanges suggest she doubts her position. Perhaps for her as for Angie, it is—as Sarah Brightman and Andrea Bocelli sing her favorite song—"Time to Say Good-bye."

In her feminist wisdom Janice defines Italian men as "swaggering mama's boys, fuckin' hypocrites . . . emotional cripples . . . [who] expect their wives to live like the fuckin' nuns at Mount Carmel College." Annalisa confirms this view when she tells Tony why she's accepted as a leader: "Italian men in love to their mothers so obeying woman is natural." Janice seems to have persuaded Carmela until she avows that prison made Richie sensitive to the plight of women. At that Carmela can only laugh, but she stops for a serious thought anyway.

Among themselves the gangsters' women can be as tough as their men. This Tony learns from Annalisa, as well as from Carmela, who in the next episode slams the door on Uncle Junior when he comes to the reception for Furio. Here in the restaurant, the melancholy widow, Rosalie, yells at the woman at the next table. The Family ladies can give as good as they get. That's perhaps why they rule out divorce.

When Tony comes home, Carmela is upstairs, putting away the laundry. Tony, bearing his usual gifts, is diminished by the high-angle shot—what director Van Patten calls his "high-wide-and-stupid shot" (Season II DVD, disc one)—while Carmela fills her screen. As she remembers Angie she wonders if Tony's return is more nauseating than nice. Or would she rather stash her family's laundry than air it? In any case, the wives have lost their respect for their *Commendatóri.*

- According to director Tim Van Patten's excellent commentary on the Season II DVD edition (disc one), the show's general rule is to shoot the gangster scenes with a wider angle lens, bringing them closer to the viewer, and the family scenes with a longer lens, giving them a softer register, more detached. He reports that it is not uncommon in Italy for strong women to take over their man's gang, though they tend not to last long as leaders.

- Because of scheduling problems, the Naples restaurant and hotel interior scenes were filmed in New York and New Jersey, with the Italian actors flown in for their parts.

II, 5: Big Girls Don't Cry

Written by Terence Winter. Directed by Tim Van Patten.

Though Furio's advent disturbs Tony's crew, he handles a brothel owner's unpaid debts more persuasively than Chris did. Chris takes an "Acting for Writers" workshop with some evasion, some success, and a violent outburst. Tony is infuriated to learn Janice is trying to get a bank loan on their mother's house. Dr. Melfi takes Tony back as a client.

As the title suggests, this episode deals with how different characters handle their emotional pressures. "Each his own, Tony. Each his own," as Richie explains his interest in Janice, after Tony remarks: "There are men in the can better looking than my sister."

As the show shifts away from Carmela, the primary "Big girl" here is Dr. Melfi, who discusses with her therapist her guilt for having abandoned Tony. Under her client's absent influence, Melfi is eating more, gaining weight, and against her will thrilled by his danger. She even stomps out of her first session à *la* Tony: "Fuck you. You think this is funny. You smug cocksucker. Fuck you." Dr. Jennifer Melfi's Soprano accent raises her therapist's eyebrows.

When Melfi tells her shrink that seeing Tony "will be very therapeutic for me," she reverses her responsibility. When Kupferberg asks if Tony lies behind her over-eating, she retreats to a Livia line: "I don't know what you mean." Melfi admits "feelings on a personal level" for Tony but denies they are sexual: "He can be such a little boy sometimes." But this context is harsher than his box of sand (I, 13). The scene cuts to Tony in his car, enjoying his cigar to the sounds of Furio torturing the brothel owners. When Melfi puts down her glass of wine to call him, her invitation seems romantic. Though Tony declined, he appears at the appointed hour, like a lover who has feigned disinterest.

Chris finds a release for his emotions in the acting workshop Adriana gave him for his birthday. When the teacher describes the actor as the instrument for conveying ideas, she also covers Chris's Family role, in which he has just been out-performed by Furio. Feeling socially inferior to the other students, especially Mitch, a BA (English) now selling Porsches, Chris introduces himself (not entirely wrong) as working with stocks. He evades the assignment with which he can not identify: the Gentleman Caller in *The Glass Menagerie*. When Chris can not understand why this "player" would try to screw Laura the gimp, he reduces the character to his own experience. The play recalls the singular reduction of Adriana's "my Tennessee William."

Chris performs passionately as Jim in *Rebel without a Cause*, weeping as he begs his father's help. His emotional release confirms the irony of the episode title, because men as well as "Big girls" are expected not to cry. In a more abstract exercise at the next class, Chris explodes at the actor who played the father, punching and kicking him. As Adriana suggests, because his father died so young Chris has unresolved issues, which emerged in the class and drove him out of both workshops in which he revealed himself. When he rises at night to throw out his screenplay he again runs away from self-exposure. His false class-name, "Chris McAvity" suggests he senses he has a cavity to fill but hides it (even in his pronunciation: Mac-a-vee-tee).

Furio's arrival creates some possible problems for Tony. He coaxes Artie into providing a job front for Furio's immigration, as master cheesemaker. Only later, meeting outside The Lou Costello Memorial, does Tony inform Paulie. The site suggests the comical sidekick that Paulie fears he is becoming. Lou's statue stands parallel behind Paulie in one shot, and looms over him, hat befouled, in another. But that is rather Pussy's fate, as Tony promotes Paulie and Silvio and leaves Pussy to report to them.

Embittered by this slight, Pussy asks "Foolio" if he stomped the grapes for their wine. When he is pointedly excluded from a discussion, Pussy leaves ("I've gotta make a call anyway"). Then we see him and FBI agent Skip Lipari both complaining about being bypassed for promotion. The respectable world again parallels the mob's. When Lipari says Tony doesn't "give a flying fuck" for Pussy, his phrase recalls Carmela's description of Tony's feelings for Father Phil and the church (I, 13). In this parallel Tony is trapped between opposing expectations, his gang code on the one side and conventional morality on the other.

No such dilemmas for young Furio. He amuses little children at his welcoming party, warmly engages with all, and is delighted to be in the land of AFC old movies. Now at his spiritual home, he trims the title of his favorite TV show to "PD Blue." Yet the same affable Furio wreaks efficient havoc at the brothel.

As Tony imported Furio to distance himself from his dangerous business, he is all the more concerned when he loses his temper. At word of Janice's mortgage, Tony smashes the phone, to AJ's shock and Carmela's anger. "Why don't you grow the fuck up?" she properly advises. Angry that Irina is feeding Cheezies to the boatside ducks (!), he attacks the Russian next boat for suggesting Irina date his brother.

We don't share Melfi's surprise to see Tony back for his appointment. For we've seen him impose on Hesh with long outpourings about his short fuse. Tony is oddly reassured when Hesh tells him Johnny-Boy, Tony's father, used to get stress attacks once or twice a year and once cracked his head open on a cigarette machine.

From their sessions, Tony tells Melfi, he wants to stop the panic attacks and blackouts so he can "direct my power and my fuckin' anger against the people in my life who deserve it." The "power" may come from a manual but the rest is pure Tony. Addressing his mix of self-defense and self-destruction, Melfi asks how he felt about Furio's devastation in the brothel. "I wished it was me in there." "Giving the beating or taking it?" Tony tries to smile away her somber question, but he considers it. Perhaps the episode's last shot—Christopher throwing his self-expression (his screenplay floppies and hard copy both) into the dumpster outside and striding back into the dark house—speaks for Tony too, as he swaggers back to the supposed strength of silence. Big guys do not cry—or even talk.

- The feral Furio is played by Naples-born Federico Castelluccio, who came to the United States in 1968. In 1982 he earned a BFA in painting and media arts at the School of Visual Arts in New York. Since 1986 he has had remarkable success acting on stage, film, and television, while maintaining his career as a painter.
- The Lou Costello Memorial honors the junior partner of the Abbott and Costello vaudeville and B-film comedy team. He was born Louis Francis Cristillo in Paterson—where Castelluccio grew up. Costello is yet another great Italian-American who is not connected with the Mafia.

II, 6: The Happy Wanderer

Written by Frank Renzulli. Directed by John Patterson.

At their high school College Night, Tony and Artie meet school buddy Dave Scatino and his son Eric. Tony rejects Dave's request to let him into the Executive high-stakes poker game that Tony took over from Junior. At Richie's game Dave runs up a $7,000 debt, which Richie demands be paid before he plays again. Richie explodes when he finds Dave playing in Tony's Executive Game, where he incurs another $45,000 debt. When Artie can not lend Dave $20,000 for "breathing space" he gives Tony Eric's jeep. Meadow's joy at getting the SUV turns into anger when she learns its source. She and Eric have been rehearsing "Sun and Moon" (from *Ms. Saigon*) for the school's Cabaret Night to score extra-curricular activity points for college admission. Eric turns on Meadow and walks out on Cabaret Night, damaging his college chances. This leaves Meadow with the advantage of performing a solo, "My Heart will Go On," the theme from *Titanic*.

The loser's pall hangs over this black comedy. Perhaps because the characters' ambitions are so twisted satisfaction is impossible. Here even the winners are losers. Meadow's triumphant solo comes from the film about the sunk Titanic so it is a success based on a disaster, as her getting the jeep was based on Eric's dad gambling losses. Meadow's cabaret success pales beside the loss of her friend, because of their respective fathers' doings, and her realization that—as Tony yells—"Everything this family has comes from the work I do."

Innocent Meadow is herself compromised by having to scramble for non-academic points to bolster her college application. As the Brown College representative advises, admission is highly competitive: "Get all your academic and extra-curricular ducks in a row."—that fugitive promise of Tony's lost ducks again—"Leave nothing to chance." In one way the students' plotting for college admission is antithetical to the gamblers' world of chance and risk. Yet university acceptance does not depend on academic standing but a system of maneuvering, not entirely unlike the mob poker game. Thus one friend parlays her black mother into early admission to Wesleyan. Whether she wants to or not, Meadow "wins" by getting both the jeep and the solo. Eric loses the first innocently and abandons the second. Both fine kids are damaged by their fathers' wrong-headed ambitions.

The loser's gloom is introduced lightly in the second scene. When Tony jokes about what heroes Dave and Artie were at school, he implies that they are since fallen. Great and boisterous quarterbacks Y. A. Tittle and Joe Namath shrink to the merely affable Phil Donohue and Alan Alda. A close-up holds on Artie's sad recognition. Perhaps it was Tony's gibe that spurred Davey on to the risky, high-stakes game in which he "got no business being."

Though Dave has a successful sporting goods store, he's doomed by his compulsion to gamble. His weak face and nervous eyes stamp him a loser, as both card games prove. While Tony naps at the Executive Game, Dave raises his initial debt from five to forty-five thousand dollars. Tony's five-percent weekly interest charge puts Dave's business and his family at risk. With Mickey and Sylvia's "Love Is Strange" playing in the background, Dave tries to borrow money from one friend, Artie, to stave off another, Tony. His faith in his friends' love is naive, desperate, and irrelevant. For Tony as for Richie, the financial screws on Davey are purely business, "Nothin' personal."

Dave fares even worse as a father than as a gambler. When he takes back Eric's jeep, he pretends to punish him for "going off-road" (Eric drove the cheerleaders onto their practice field). "Accountability is everything,"

Dave shouts to his wife and son. This hypocrisy loses any sympathy we might have given him.

At least Tony scores points for his relative integrity. He warned Dave not to play in the Executive Game, warned him not to expect favors on his "short-term" loan, and then does what he has to do to save face in his world. For that reason, too, he "taxes" Richie for "disrespecting" Tony's game. Tony is also the more—albeit harshly—honest with his child. He admits that Eric's father "something like" sold him the truck. Not to mention his: "So take that high moral ground and go sleep in the fuckin' bus station if you want." Though everything is going well for Tony, he suffers from his anger at his mother, his defensive anger at his therapist, and his veering between self-respect and guilt.

Adding to the Sopranos' history of loss and sorrow, Uncle Junior tells Tony that there was another brother, Hercule (reduced to Eckley), born between Junior and Johnny-Boy, who was as strong as a bull, handsome like George Raft, but "slow." As was the custom, the brothers kept him in a home until he died. Tony tweaks Uncle Junior when he recalls Livia "talking about my father's feeble-minded brother. But I always thought that was you."

The episode focuses on Tony's anger. He tells Dr. Melfi that he is so upset he could smash her face into hamburger—but won't. She has turned him into one of those yappy "fuckin' pussies," not the strong, silent Gary Cooper type he always admired. Tony's confusion points to the heart of the episode: "I got the world by the balls and I can't stop feeling I'm a fuckin' loser." Though Tony rejects Melfi's claim that his parents kept him from joy, whenever Livia surfaces—at the cabaret, at a funeral—her very presence enrages him anew.

As Tony describes his free-form anger, when he sees someone happy, "always fuckin' whistlin' like the fuckin' Happy Wanderer," he wants to tear out the whistler's throat. "Why should I be angry at guys like this? I should say *asalut'*. . . . Good for you. . . . Go with God." Later Melfi suggests Tony should be heartened by the death of sister Barb's father-in-law, who the day after retiring is fatally blown off his roof while installing a satellite dish. Without Tony having to do anything, the man "joined the ranks of the unlucky." And isn't Ercole "enough of a sad tragedy that you can join the rest of the douche bags" who are always whining at their therapy? Seeing such others fail, she suggests, should enable Tony to see Melfi without guilt. Since resuming their sessions Melfi is more aggressive toward Tony.

The episode closes on a tauntingly happy note. Gudrun's opera solo at the school cabaret—a soaring German song about a heavy heart—gives way for the end credits to "The Happy Wanderer."

Because of Tony's values, built into his every success is inevitable frustration. He and Silvio luxuriate in now owning the Executive Game, which his father and uncle started 30 years ago and from which Uncle Junior used to chase them away. Even as he nets $80,000 from this game, though, Tony "loses" because of his entanglement with Dave, the mixed blessing of the jeep, and the deepening of his differences with Richie.

After the funeral service's "not the first to rise from the dead," the camera pans from a sleeping Livia to her malevolent resurrection in Janice. She goads Richie against Tony, saying the $50,000 Tony gave him on his prison release is what her father gave someone in that situation thirty years ago (equivalent to half a million now). Richie brings Meadow a bigger bouquet than Tony's. Tony's every satisfaction brings more loss.

In contrast, at Richie's game Artie cashes out when he is ahead. He is free from the macho vanity that keeps Dave losing: "I got to go now or Charmaine will have my balls on the menu." This episode satirizes the macho element in the high-stakes card game. Though Christopher tells his two aides this is no "nickel and dime" game, he slips matches under the scales to reduce the cost of seafood for fifteen—then accuses the clerk of cheating. His two gunsels pettily complain at being treated pettily. Silvio ludicrously explodes at one aide for trying to sweep up the cheese under his chair.

Among the players are real-life celebrity Frank Sinatra Jr.—whom Paulie calls "Chairboy of the Board"—and fictional Dr. Fried, whose specialty is penal implants. Only Tony and Dr. Fried smoke Tony's Macanudos. Sometimes a cigar may be just a cigar, but not in this context. Especially not a Macanudo, with its heft and outlaw strut. Foreshadowing the resurrection of Meadow's Cabaret solo, Paulie reports that a crate of Viagra is being lowered to "raise" the Titanic. In an apposite pun, Silvio opines that Dave "ain't got dick." Similarly, when the idealistic Hasid, Hillel Teittleman, complains at partner Furio's taking so many rooms free for his whores, he loses the high ground when a prostitute admits his custom.

In the moral universe of *The Sopranos,* there is no uncontaminated virtue. Meadow clearly does not have the voice or training that Gudrun has, but she still gets her solo in the cabaret—because she is a Soprano. However much she tries to distance herself from her father's work, Meadow suffers its advantage. All that keeps Tony from being the Happy Wanderer himself is his inability to know joy, his refusal to sing.

■ In the card game, Sunshine is played by Paul Mazursky, who acted in *Blackboard Jungle* and directed such films as *Bob and Carol and Ted and Alice*, *Blume in Love*, *Harry and Tonto*, *An Unmarried Woman*, *Down and out in Beverly Hills* and *Scenes from a Mall*.

II, 7: D-Girl

Written by Todd Kessler. Directed by Allen Coulter.

On a joyride in Carmela's Mercedes, AJ breaks the sideview mirror. When scolded, AJ defends himself with the Existentialism he has learned in school from Camus' *The Stranger*. Tony asks Pussy to advise AJ. Agent Lipari pressures Pussy to wear a wire to AJ's confirmation party at Tony's house. Meanwhile, Chris meets his lawyer cousin Gregory's fiancée, Amy, a woman in film development (the titular D-Girl), who introduces him to director Jon Favreau. She reads Chris's discarded screenplay, *You Bark, I Bite* (of which Adriana faithfully preserved a copy). After Chris has sex with Amy he turns more callous toward Adriana and Tony. At the confirmation party Tony gives Chris ten minutes to decide either to dedicate himself completely to his service or to leave Tony completely. After thinking about it outside, Chris returns to the fold.

In the series' most openly philosophical episode, Chris as much as AJ comes of age. AJ "stumbled into Existentialism" (in Dr. Melfi's sympathetic phrase; Tony blames the "Fuckin' Internet"). The concept exposes Chris's shallowness: "I love movies. But I want to be a player." He won't bother with "all that other shit" such as working, acting, qualifying, that is, actually becoming something instead of just affecting the role. He wants to be a player rather than learning to play a real role.

As AJ questions the meaning of life in an Absurd order, the other characters are defined by whether they respond with dedication or with betrayal. They are all as insecure as AJ. For defending her brother's proper "education," Meadow is sent to her room. Pussy is torn between serving the FBI to stay out of jail or to serve Tony.

Adriana is clearly dedicated to Chris, despite his unreliability and his evasion of marriage. Mind you, Tony's advice to Chris doesn't help her case: "When you marry you'll appreciate the importance of fresh produce." But Adriana is herself star-struck and upset when Chris toured Amy and Favreau through his old neighborhood without her.

Livia, as usual, instinctively thwarts Tony. She nourishes AJ's adolescent *angst*: "Who says everything has a purpose? The world's a jungle. You want my advice, Anthony, don't expect happiness. You won't get it. People let you down. I won't mention any names. But, in the end, you die in your own arms. . . . It's all a big nothing. What makes you think you're so special?"

In the series' most self-referential episode, Amy brings Chris to Jon's set, where the two lesbian heroines—played by Janeane Garofalo and Sandra Bernhard—shoot each other. Chris becomes a hero by proposing Sandra's last epithet be "*puchiacha*" (cunt) instead of "bitch." "Cunt. I like that," concludes Favreau.

Despite its Brooklyn authenticity, however, from another perspective Chris's suggestion is wrong. "Cunt" would not be the ultimate pejorative for a lesbian that it is for these men. Chris's bright suggestion may be true to its social background but it remains a man's view, a male invective. (True, Svetlana uses the term in III, 3, but that's her Profanity as a Second Language. Gloria uses that term for Irina in III, 12, but that episode is about characters proving their "balls.") The term seems inappropriate for the lesbian character to call her lover, even in dying anger.

Chris fascinates Jon with his gun and with his stories, including the Sinatra background to the Johnny Fontane plot in *The Godfather*. But a playful skirmish terrifies Jon. As Amy is fascinated when Chris dominates the Morgan Stanley rowdies at the bar, Jon is taken with Chris's gun and his aura of danger. But Amy pursues her attraction. Critiquing Chris's script, she starts listing the seven-part hierarchy of human needs that motivates characters. By the third, "the need to understand," she is on him.

Later Chris discovers Jon's new script has stolen Chris's story about Joey Cippolina, who poured acid on a she-male for seducing him. "*Crying Game*," says Amy, who lives through the filter of film. Later, to Chris's rueful expression of affection she replies "This is getting kind of William Inge here, isn't it?" Though he betrayed Adriana and Gregory with Amy, Chris feels betrayed and endangered by their use of his anecdote.

Chris's introduction to the filmmaking world parallels AJ's confirmation. As Chris learns its systemic lures, exploitation, betrayals, and abandonment, he loses the innocence that tempted him to drop Tony and Adriana for Hollywood. Chris becomes a man when he drops his improbable Hollywood fantasy and rededicates himself to Tony. Even if that means exchanging one Hollywood role for another, the writer for the hood, the dedication is better than the vain and treacherous pursuit of a phantom.

AJ's existentialism is equally shallow. His passengers' mortal risk in his joyride prompts: "Death just shows the ultimate Absurdity of life." Not without grounds does Tony question AJ's claim to manhood. Two years after bedwetting at camp he is reporting "Nitch's" claim that "God is dead."

Pussy's youngest son Matt shows more authority. After correcting AJ's "Nietzsche"—that is, AJ has not yet found his proper niche in philosophy—Matt rejects Nietzsche for his lunacy and Sartre as "a fucking fraud [who] copped it all from Husserl and Heidegger." Matt recommends Kierkegaard: "Every duty is essentially duty to God." Not bad for a gunsel's kid who has just proved his prowess in the batting cage and who dismisses current Rap as "marketing."

Pussy says his kid won't hit sacrifice flies. But Pussy is about to sacrifice Tony—and thereby himself—to avoid serving "thirty to life for selling H." At the beginning of Pussy's end, the cemetery lies just behind Pussy's house when agent Lipari coerces him against Tony. Pussy is so torn that he assaults Angie when she almost catches him wiring himself for AJ's confirmation party. Matt has to pull his raging father, bleeding from the mike, off her.

In his first session with Dr. Melfi, Tony is less disturbed with AJ's delinquency than with his brooding. Melfi spells out the implications of Existentialism. In a world without absolute values—"In your family even motherhood is up for debate."—people are solely responsible for themselves. The only absolute is death. Though he agrees "the kid's on to something," with AJ Tony hardens his position: "Even if God is dead you're still gonna kiss His ass" (that is, be confirmed).

When AJ is caught smoking pot Carmela confirms the family's religious approach: "What kind of animal smokes marijuana at his own confirmation?" Is it too much to ask to "be a good Catholic for fifteen fuckin' minutes?" But AJ defends his grass: "Even Grandma says the world has no purpose."

When Tony asks Pussy—as AJ's godfather (no film reference intended)—to counsel AJ, he leaves his *Waste News*. But Pussy's "You gotta learn to appreciate the value of things" refers to the dented Mercedes. There is some self-justification in Pussy's advice: "Sometimes you got to do things you don't want to." Pussy approaches AJ after the marijuana incident: "I'm your sponsor. We need to talk. You need to listen." The line is ironic, because the "We need to talk" really means "I need to talk to you" and the

"You need to listen" hides the fact that the FBI agents are listening on Pussy's wire, hoping Tony will incriminate himself. Instead, all the agents hear is Pussy telling AJ what a generous man Tony is. "He'd take a bullet for you. . . . He's a stand-up guy."

Absent from the family picture ("Where's the godfather?"), Pussy is up in the bathroom sobbing because he is betraying his best friend. This godfather has crumbled into Fredo. In the last sequence, the high passion of opera, Emma Shaplin singing "*Vedi, Maria,*" unites Chris's decision to serve Tony and Pussy's to betray him. Chris and Tony both face the Existential choice the hero of Chris's screenplay faced: to shit or go blind.

The Kierkegaard line—"Every duty is essentially duty to God"—shadows every small duty and its converse betrayal in this episode. For example, Pussy weeps because fidelity to Tony would be closer to serving God than serving the FBI would be. The irony of AJ's brush with Nietzsche is that his father has the makings of the Nietzschean hero. At his best—that is, worst—Tony Soprano rises above convention, above the law, above the reflexes of traditional morality, and stamps out his own code and values. What pulls him short is his regression into societal convention, his "Old School" nostalgia and the colleagues who betray him. Tony is especially Nietzschean in the instinctiveness of his ethic, uncontaminated by philosophy or instruction.

▪ Jon Favreau wrote and produced *Swingers* (1966) and directed a TV movie, *Smog* (1999) and a feature *Made* (2001). He is also well known as a film and TV actor.

II, 8: Full Leather Jacket

Written by Robin Green and Mitchell Burgess. Directed by Allen Coulter.

Meadow hopes to go to Berkeley, but Tony and Carmela want her closer to home. Chris proposes to Adriana. He and his two aides, Sean and Matt, crack some safes. The new hoods embarrass themselves by addressing Tony in the toilet, then visit Richie who says "If there's ever anything you can do for me let me know." Richie begrudgingly agrees to have his nephews, the Spatafores, build a ramp at the crippled Beanie's house. To improve their relations, Richie gives Tony a prized old leather jacket and is devastated to find he gave it to his maid's husband. Hoping to impress Richie, Sean and Matt shoot Chris. Chris kills Sean and when Matt seeks help, a furious Richie chases him away.

This show's major theme is "leaving the nest" and the parents' or mentors' challenge of knowing when to guide and when to withdraw. As Richie quotes the Tao: "You got to shut one door before another one can open." This high-blown sentiment is undercut by Bobby closing a car trunk in the background, while Junior says: "Was that so hard to do?"

As usual the family drama is played out both in Tony's home and in his business. And where they merge: Richie gives Tony the jacket he admired as a boy because "I got to let go of the past." The gesture shows an unexpected sentimentality in the vile Richie. He is understandably hurt when Tony—because he wants to let go of the same past—gives it away. In giving Tony the jacket—and then mentioning it at every opportunity—Richie seeks to recover his position as Tony's senior and benefactor. It's a way to win their war—as the title parodies Stanley Kubrick's war film *Full Metal Jacket* (1987). Tony's slight increases Richie's discomfort with him as boss. To mollify Tony Richie agrees to build his victim Beansie a ramp but proceeds half-heartedly. For his part, Tony wants Richie "where I can see him." "That's what we mean when we say 'family,' " Carmela replies, with a kiss.

A second metaphor inflects the first: the "profile toner" advertised on TV. Often the mentor's "generosity" here is insincere, a matter of improving one's public appearance. Concerned about his "profile," Richie threatens Beansie for presumably asking Tony for the ramp instead of asking him. In a comic version, Richie jokes with Matt and Sean about Chris's "camel nose," which is emphasized at the end when the camera pans down his unconscious body's profile. Carmela strives to improve the "profile" of Meadow's college application because marks are not enough anymore.

When Meadow challenges Carmela's right to have her room cleaned, Carmela suddenly agrees. On the verge of leaving home for college, Meadow is old enough to look after herself. "What right do I have to interfere?" Carmela also corrects her attempt to hide Meadow's letter from Berkeley, requiring additional materials for her application.

Before that recognition, however, Carmela first asked her neighbor Jeannie, then approached Jeannie's lawyer sister Joan, for a reference to help get Meadow into Georgetown, Joan's alma mater. "You don't understand. I want you to write the letter," Carmela tells the lawyer firmly, having softened her approach with a ricotta pie. The Soprano pie with peaches becomes an offer Joan can't refuse. Perhaps the threat of a broken leg may lurk in Carmela's remark that her mother's foot specialist is in the neighborhood. When she returns the pie plate Jeannie conveys her sister's face-saving insistence that she was persuaded to write by Meadow's remarkable transcripts and her teachers' comments. Apparently, honest lawyers—not to say apparently honest lawyers—need to tone their profile as much as Mafiosi do. Joan's acquiescence undermines her earlier advice to her sister: "You want to be a doormat for the rest of your life? Just deal with it."

Carmela first helps her daughter, then lets her mature. In contrast, when Chris proposes Adriana's mother—who risibly preserves her bottled sexpot image—interferes and threatens her daughter: "When you get hurt next time, this door is closed to you." If Carmela will continue to "interfere" in her daughter's life, she will keep a lower profile.

In his session with Dr. Melfi, Tony wonders why he gave Meadow her friend Eric's jeep when he knew "she would freak out." Melfi suggests that unconsciously he must have wanted to stop shielding Meadow from his work—especially since the gambler Dave was such a respectable citizen. Tony was helping Meadow adjust to the reality she will inevitably meet when she "leaves the nest" ("Not those fuckin' ducks again!"). Tony wonders how he can be accused of doing something noble when "I give my girl a car to rub her nose in shit." Helpless before yet another psychiatric paradox, Tony pledges silence—but at least he does not stomp out.

Tony's surrogate child, Chris, is grateful that Tony straightened him out with his ultimatum of the previous episode. After some great sex with Adriana (which always helps one appreciate education), Chris summarizes his mentor's lesson: Stay focused, no distractions or drugs, keep your eye on the prize.

Chris is less fortunate in the hoods whom he chooses to mentor. Sean and Matt are transparently immature and indiscreetly eager to meet and to impress Tony. Matt won't marry because he can hire women for all his domestic relief. Not that Chris is much more mature. In post-coital candor he blames his fights with Adriana on his failure to "communicate my needs," as if she might not have any.

Indeed, there is an ironic cut from Tony advising AJ to "crack the books" and the safecrackers. Sean's habit of leaving a bowel movement at the safe-crack scene confirms his infantilism. When Matt is whacked in II, 9, he wets his pants and cries for his "Mummy." Both men feel insulted that Tony sent Furio for his money and that Furio exacted an additional grand. Hoping to win Richie's favor by whacking Chris, they prove their independence premature. Paulie is spooked into nightmares.

Ironically, when Sean is killed because he can't get out of his seatbelt, he seems to justify Livia's irresponsible warning AJ against seatbelts (II, 7). But life is a tragedy of the Absurd. So Chris is nearly killed just when he assumes a new maturity. Or as Pussy in the next episode mechanically tells Tony, he believes in God even though He moves in mysterious ways his wonders to perform.

"How could this happen?" Tony asks rhetorically at the end of the episode. How could it not happen in a world of unbridled ambition and misdirected mentoring? With no music over the end credits, the beep and thwock of Chris's life-support system attest to the starkest level of existence.

■ Beansie was earlier described as a Mummy in his hospital bed, after Richie ran him over (and over). Here, as Richie approaches them, Uncle Junior describes a black market film scam to Tony: "He had *The Mummy* before it was in the theatres." Even without the sharp focus of a pun the language often provides such fugitive echoes and coherence. So, too, in the next episode Carmela is moved to concerns for religious vision, after hearing that a hood's *goomah* has borne a child "by C-section." *The Sopranos*'s scripts offer extraordinarily intense language.

II, 9: From Where to Eternity

Written by Michael Imperioli. Directed by Henry J. Bronchtein.

After coming out of a clinically dead state, Christopher tells Tony and Paulie that he crossed over to Hell, where he saw his father. The dead Mikey gave him a message for Tony and Paulie: "Three o'clock." Tony dismisses this but Paulie is spooked into nightmares. Meanwhile, Carmela wants Tony to have a vasectomy. Overwrought, Tony snaps at Dr. Melfi and at AJ. Tony and Pussy whack Matt Bevilaqua for trying to kill Chris.

In a script written by Michael Imperioli (who plays Christopher, aspiring screenwriter), Chris's shooting moves the characters to reevaluate their lives. For several, it's a wake-up call to their mortality. But over the episode presides Otis Redding's "My Lover's Prayer," a love song in religious language. It plays over Adriana's vigil at Chris's bedside, through Carmela's quarrel with Tony and over their reconciliation at the end.

In business as usual Tony and his men don't tell the detectives anything about the suspect, Matt Bevilaqua. Christopher's mother proves more of a virago than we expected of the woman angry that the paper named her son among the "scumbags" (I, 8). Here, amid the muted grays of the hospital and the somberly dressed family, she rages against the shooter: "I want that motherfucker to suffer." "Don't worry," Silvio assures her, "we'll do the best we can." Like the "bad eminence" of Milton's Satan, here "the best" means "the worst."

When Chris regains consciousness he is certain he has visited Hell—an Irish pub where every day is St. Patrick's Day. There his father loses every hand he plays and he is painfully whacked again every midnight. Tony is skeptical about Mikey's message. After all, would all "the heavy-hitters" Paulie has whacked choose Mikey as their leader? As Tony summarizes his religious beliefs: If in India you go to Hell for eating steaks and in New Jersey you don't, then "None of this shit means a goddam thing."

Unassured, Paulie stays awake to see 3 A.M. tick by safely. He dreams he's being dragged to hell. He argues that Christopher visited purgatory not Hell (no horns on the bouncer, not very hot). So Paulie negotiates himself a deal: His life's crimes will only require 6,000 years there, which he could do on his head, like a couple of days here—just "a little detour on the way to Paradise."

His séance is a comic collision of the mundane and the supernatural. The psychic, his suburban furnishings, the other clients, all are spectacularly ordinary, as if they came from Wal-Mart. Tea and cookies will follow the messages from Beyond. Despite this bathetic normalcy, the psychic contacts Sonny Pegano, Paulie's first hit, and reports Mikey Palmice's tease about Paulie's poison ivy. At this Paulie runs amok, throws a chair and yells "fuckin' queers" before stomping out. With that reaction the séance parallels Tony's discomfiting sessions with Melfi. But where Paulie drags "a bunch of fuckin' ghouls around," Tony's baggage lives.

In a delicious irony, Paulie cuts off his parish priest. After 23 years of donations Paulie "shoulda had immunity for all this shit." The racketeer is angry that his church has not provided the protection he bought. Father

Felix, a bald man who sits at his desk coolly smoking, looks like a "Waste Management Boss," especially with the big trucks passing outside his window. He dismisses the medium as a charlatan, but makes no case for his religion, just: "You should have come to me first and none of this would have happened."

That defense is exactly what Don Vito Corleone (Brando) tells his first supplicant, the undertaker, at the beginning of *The Godfather*. When the priest echoes the Godfather, his moral vacuity justifies Paulie's charge. The church is equivalent to the mob's protection racket. The allusion validates Paulie's goofball assumption: "You left me unprotected. I'm cutting you off for good." After a scolding glare at Jesus, Paulie leaves the church, slamming the door on God for having broken their deal. The down-shot leaves Jesus balefully viewing his diminished territory.

Notwithstanding Paulie's comic function, this episode also provides our sole glimpse into his warmer nature. In two scenes he relates to his obviously loving mistress and her children. Paulie's comfort with them is as dramatic—and more touching—than his large (and real) tattoo. As in the Tony and Melfi plots, Paulie's gangster experience intrudes upon his more important private life.

Against that Catholic background, the Jewish Hesh provides more pragmatic consolation. He assures Adriana that Chris is in the best trauma unit in the Tri-state area, then questions the doctor from a position of medical knowledge.

In contrast, Carmela prays to Jesus to save Chris and to "Deliver him from blindness and grant him vision . . . [to] see Your love and gain the strength to carry on in service to Your mercy." Her faith seems confirmed when Chris recovers and Tony tells her Chris saw Heaven. But Chris tells her it was Hell he visited and to Hell he was told he was going. Though she doesn't confront Tony with his lie, it confirms Carmela's insecurity: "If you can't be honest with me at least have the balls to be honest with yourself."

Carmela also wants Tony to have the balls to get a vasectomy. She is affected by the gossip that Ralph Rotaldo's Brazilian *goomah* had his child. Carmela fears her children's humiliation if a mistress bore Tony's child. Tony denies he is having an affair: "I told you I cut it off." Normally, he would say: "I broke it off." But "cutting" it off hangs in this episode's air, from Paulie "cutting off" Father Felix to Carmela's demand of a vasectomy. Even in his care Tony is insensitive: "I had her tested for AIDS!" Outraged, Carmela stomps out to sleep alone. Otis Redding marks Tony's solitude: "What you gonna do tonight / When you need some lovin' arms to hold you tight?"

Despite their anger, when Chris's emergency brings them back to the hospital, Tony and Carmela enter holding hands. Their differences are suspended in the crisis—but they resume. Tony takes his nerves out on AJ for dropping a dish of pasta after dinner: "I'm supposed to get a vasectomy when this is my male heir?" To make amends Tony brings a pizza and pop into AJ's room to apologize. He assures AJ that he sees himself in his son. "I gotta learn to control my emotions around the people I love. . . . I couldn't ask for a better son, AJ. I mean that."

When Carmela overhears Tony's apology, she rejects the "snip snip." Touched at Tony's fatherly warmth, she considers having another child. Of course, she came to get Tony for Pussy's call—the summons to deal with Matt.

At episode end, Carmela plugs Tony's habitual pledge of fidelity with "Just prove it." In perhaps their most intimate scene in the series, Carmela is tender toward Tony, massaging him, holding him, as if to alleviate his burden she subconsciously knows he feels from having just avenged Chris. In the last shot, the camera pans away from the couple's lovemaking—with its corporeal climax in their clenched hands—past a row of approving ornamental angels, still to "My Lover's Prayer."

For all his stress, Pussy enjoys his community here. In the hospital Pussy consoles and hugs Adriana. He rejects Richie's "negative energies" and wants "positive vibes only" around Christopher. But in an opening pan across the waiting room, over Carmela's prayer, while the others sit together in their private thoughts, Pussy is isolated alone in the background. Perhaps to ease the FBI pressure, he tells Lipari that Tony seems to suspect he has turned. But Skip assures him: "You're the one who's seeing through different eyes."

When someone does report Matt's whereabouts—"for points,"which is what Matt tried to score with Richie by shooting Chris—it's to Pussy. Is he being blessed for his treachery? Or do singers of a feather attract each other? Tony insists on shooting Matt himself—with his faithful Pussy—rather than delegating the duty.

From whacking Matt, Tony and Pussy go to dine at the restaurant Pussy first brought him to on the night Tony "popped [his] cherry." Whether that initiation was sexual or his first murder, in Tony's vulnerability toward his betrayer he is once again like a virgin. The stained glass window behind Pussy recalls Paulie's abandoned church, to which the men's steak dinner is a heartier alternative. Pussy affirms his faith in God, whose mysterious ways have helped him, but that glass recasts him as Judas.

The character who fares least well through this drama—with the obvious exception of gunsel Matt—is Dr. Melfi. After Paulie bolsters himself with his ludicrous calculation of Purgatory, we find the more intelligent Melfi crumbling. She is unusually aggressive with Tony and shakey in her own position.

Tony's self-justification is as transparent a rationalization as Paulie's tally for Purgatory. Tony contends that he and Christopher won't go to Hell. Hell is for molesters and sadists, Hitlers and Pol Pots: "We're soldiers. Soldiers don't go to Hell. It's war. Soldiers kill other soldiers. Everybody involved knows the stakes." His logic seems undercut by his impulsive, animal scratch. His argument parallels Carmela's prayer—"We have chosen this life in full awareness of the consequences of our sins"—but where she acknowledges her sin Tony strains to justify himself.

Angered by Melfi's skepticism, Tony argues history (incidentally also answering the critics of the show's treatment of Italian-Americans). The American government opened the floodgates for Italian immigrants "because they needed us, to build their cities." But not all wanted to lose their identity. Some wanted to preserve their culture of family, honor, and loyalty—Tony's "Old School." Not all wanted to remain "worker bees," feeding the moguls, "Some of us wanted a piece of the action." At Melfi's skepticism, Tony turns on her: When he's worried about the "nephew" he loves, "This is the time you pick to take a stand?"

We next see Melfi crying to her therapist, Elliot, guilty for having been insensitive to her patient. "Do I hate him?" she wonders. She has been drinking alone, to face Tony's "moral Never Never Land." Having taken a moral position, now she's scared and regrets having told Tony her son's college. Melfi's strong character has been shattered.

While everyone reacts to Chris's crisis differently, Chris finds his own characteristic response. While his friends and family come and go, his cronies avenge him, his mother rages, Carmela prays, Chris quietly ratchets up his morphine drip.

II, 10: Bust Out

Written by Frank Renzulli and Robin Green & Mitchell Burgess.
Directed by John Patterson.

A witness makes Tony a suspect for Matt's murder, which tightens the FBI hold on Pussy. Tony uses Dave's sporting goods store as a front to order goods that will not be paid for. Carmela sympathizes with Dave's wife Christina about her husband's gambling. Carmela and Christina's brother, Vic Musto, are instantly attracted to each other. He retreats after Dave tells him that Tony has bankrupted him. Faced with jail, Tony draws closer to his children. When Richie tries to turn Uncle Junior against Tony again, he is warned about Janice.

This episode is about the relationship—sometimes direct, sometimes ironic—between the immediate experience and the larger contexts beyond our awareness. According to the end-credits song, Journey's "Wheel in the Sky," "The wheel in the sky keeps on turnin' / I don't know where I'll be tomorrow." This song also accompanies Carmela's attraction to Vic. However sentient and focused a character may be, there is always some influence beyond his awareness. The arc is redefined by its whole, the unseen, larger circle. As superstition evolves into religion, those invisible forces are what Annalisa's sybils, the medium Colin's séance, Father Phil's Christianity, and Dr. Melfi's psychoanalysis are supposed to access for us.

At the plot center, Tony's confidence about Matt's whack is shaken when he learns that a witness espied Tony and a "heavyset" accomplice leaving the murder scene. Suddenly Tony faces the threat of jail—or of fleeing to "Elvis country" (where there are no Italians or Jews). As he tells Dr. Melfi, "I could be goin' away for a very long time—for something I didn't do." That he rewords from a broader context: "I didn't do nothin' wrong." As the witness is not identified, Paulie cannot dissuade him. As Melfi detects in Tony's swagger—"the government can do what it wants" to him, once AJ has left home—Tony for the first time appears scared.

Here the turning wheel is felt first in the witness, then correctively when the newspaper identifies Matt as a Soprano associate. The witness is an intellectual: he plays avant-garde music and reads *Anarchy, State and Utopia*. He is caught between the hope for a crime-free Utopia and the more immediate dangers of criminal anarchy. He tries to be a responsible citizen (that is, "a flag-salutin' motherfucker") but when he learns of the Soprano involvement he understandably panics. With his wife's support ("I knew it. I knew it. But no, you had to be The Big Man!") the witness rejects the FBI ("lying cocksuckers"), withdraws his identification and leaves Tony safe again.

Even in Tony's relationship with his children the visible moment is redefined by the larger context. He misses AJ's swim meet because he's stashing, with lawyer Neil Mink, $400,000 to be paid out to Carmela in the event of his absence. Where Carmela sees only the apparent neglect, Tony's larger movement serves his familial care.

The parent's relationship with the child is affected by both the larger patterns of the parent's other concerns and the natural cycle of the child's maturing toward independence. As Melfi describes this "bittersweet" stage, "You're glad that they're growing up but you're sad to lose them." When Tony suggests they share a movie and pizza, AJ is committed to meet his friends at the mall. When Meadow finds Tony maudlin from brandy she sends him to bed (as he earlier did the game-playing AJ). "Sometimes we're all hypocrites," she says, negating her earlier criticism of his profession.

In the last scene, Tony having "dodged the big bullet" takes AJ sailing. In their exuberance they are unaware of the larger arc they are cutting, as they unwittingly capsize a small boat in their wake. Oblivious of the danger in their power, the father lets his son steer *The Stugots* in all its—dangerous, suspect—masculine glory.

The theme also applies to the Janice-Richie scenes. When they make love—on Livia's sofa in the living room, as if they were still adolescents—Richie holds a pistol to her head and she spurs him on with hot monosyllabics. He can handle the "Boss" and "You're the best" but he withdraws from her "It should be you." "I can't think of shit like that when we're having sex," he complains, limply: "You're not in the moment." Richie's lust for power is checked by his compulsion "to be loyal . . . I'm Old School."

When Richie sympathetically needles him about Tony's abuse, Uncle Junior warns him about Janice's dishonesty. Now the arc of fealty is redefined by the larger arc of betrayal, which is redefined by another arc of fealty. So, too, the traitor Pussy's "Thank God" when Tony learns the witness is not an insider. On the other hand, Pussy feeds the FBI information (the list of duped investors in Webistics). Yet Pussy does not betray Tony's murder of Matt.

In contrast, in Carmela's impulsive dalliance with Vic Musto—the "artist in wallpaper"—both characters are swept away by their feelings. It is ironic that Vic introduces himself to a Soprano as "bonded, state-certified but I'm still dangerous." He soon learns about that family's danger. Carmela, we know, is virtuous and faithful. Vic, we learn, was the perfect husband through his wife's fatal breast cancer. We see his generous character when he confronts Dave and resolves to pay for Eric's college. (In Tony's Executive poker game Dave lost his son's education fund.) But when checking out the confining powder room, Carmela and Vic seem driven to their kiss. They both pull back, apologizing simultaneously, shocked at their own impulses.

They are cooler but still forced to have contact with each other when they agree on the phone that Vic will work alone the next day and Carmela will prepare a gourmet lunch. When his co-worker Ramone arrives instead, Carmela's (and our) hopes are dashed. Vic has shown his extraordinary virtue—and his sensible fear of Sopranos—again: resisting the force of the wheel driving him to Carmela. In addition to their powerful attraction, Carmela is influenced by her marriage difficulties, Tony's insensitivity toward AJ, and of course, the literature she is reading *(Memoirs of a Geisha)*. Vic's control of his temptation contrasts to his brother-in-law Dave's self-destruction.

When Tony learns he is safe he is watching a History Channel program about Patton, another figure who both turned and was turned by the wheels of history. As the show intones, Patton too "knows the controversies that have swirled around him have tainted his reputation." Tony would also identify with the TV remark that Patton's "hatred of his enemy is matched only by his concern for his men." When Tony goes into the powder room for a deep sigh of relief, he is unaware of the second threat he has dodged: Carmela's romantic temptation within that same tight space, with its vertical-bar wallpaper and the camouflaged door out. In moving to a private space to express his relief Tony celebrates one close call on the site of another.

As with the capsized boat, Tony is often the larger wheel that influences other's lives. In this case his destruction of Dave frightens Vic off Carmela. Just the Soprano name renders the murder witness amnesiac. Tony drives Dave into bankruptcy by ordering large quantities of designer bottled water, coolers, designer running shoes, and airline tickets on his store account. We see Tony's invisible reach when Artie offers Christine and Carmela the water Tony gave him "such a deal on" (at the expense of Christine, who nominally owns Dave's store). More positively, Tony thanks the crippled Beansie for agreeing to accept his $50,000 cash gift. For her part, Carmela meets with other mothers to plan their kids Graduation Night parties, hoping to impose a circle of their control on the celebrants' exuberant arcs.

We also find this dynamic in the editing strategy of ironic bridges between scenes. For example, right after the police tell the witness that it's people like him who enable the police to stop criminals, we see the merry-go-round where Tony meets Richie. It images the police's inability to break out of the circle of arrest and release, charge and acquittal, identification and withdrawal. Similarly, Tony will pass Richie's complaint—that Baronc Sanitation is over-charging him—on to the company, of which Tony is half owner. In this example of the arc governed by the circle, Tony gives Richie a runaround. The merry-go-round metaphor relates back to the police and ahead to Richie.

Similarly, we see Dave playing Russian roulette on his pool table at home so we know he has a gun. When Tony finds Dave sleeping in a tent in the store, they have a candid chat. Tony admits he let Dave into the disastrous game because "I knew you had this business. It's my nature," as in the fable of the scorpion and the frog. Dave breaks down when Tony says the end is Dave's bankruptcy. When the scene ends with a gunshot, we assume that Dave has killed himself. But the shot is the starter's pistol in the next scene, AJ's swim meet.

The scene bridge is something that relates back to the previous scene and is redefined in the next one. The element means one thing in the context of the first scene, but something else in the next. Thus a woman concerned about "Little Eric" (presumably Dave's and Christine's son) turns out to be a character in a television-soap opera to which Uncle Junior has become devoted. The sausage-spewing machine that could represent Richie's and Junior's churn of malice is what Livia is watching on her TV. When it turns to make chocolate pasta Livia gives Meadow $20 to celebrate her college admissions at Berkeley and NYU, her wait-listing at Columbia and Georgetown—and her unaccountable rejection at Bowdoin and Penn. The student proposes and the college disposes—more mysterious grindings of an unseen wheel.

In this theme *The Sopranos* replays on the level of dramatic irony one of its recurring issues: At what point are we responsible for our selves and our actions? When Tony tells Melfi about Annalisa's "You're your own worst enemy," Melfi replies: "The question is 'How do you stop?' " Tony stops—the therapy—and goes sailing with his son instead. As he gleefully revs up his 120 seahorse-power *Stugots* he upsets the smaller boat. The tangled web of responsibility and determinism ensnares us in every action, large or small. Our soul—like God and the devil—is in the details.

II, 11: House Arrest

Written by Terence Winter. Directed by Tim Van Patten.

Restricted to his house, Uncle Junior reunites with an old friend, Catherine Romano, whose late husband was a cop. At lawyer Neil

Mink's suggestion, Tony starts biding his time at his garbage company office, instead of at the Bada Bing. He's disturbed that Richie—with Junior's approval—continues to sell cocaine along his collection route. From his stress Tony collapses, has breathing difficulties, and develops a severe rash. Meanwhile, Dr. Melfi braces herself with a long vodka before Tony's session and is ordered out of a restaurant for quarreling with a smoking woman.

Confinement and nostalgia form the cohering theme of this episode. It is introduced in the song when Carmela leaves Tony alone to go for her eyebrow treatment. As Tony contemplates changing his life habits, that aging symbol of 1960s' liberation, Bob Dylan, sings "You're gonna have to serve somebody."

Literally, Uncle Junior is confined under house arrest. Abhorring restriction, he rejects the bedpan because "I'm not a cat. I don't shit in a box." When Michael McLuhan of the marshal's ("Marshall's") office restores his electronic bracelet, Junior learns that the tedium is the massage. In even closer confinement: he spends six hours with his hand stuck in the kitchen drain—and needs to be relaxed and lubricated by Richie to be freed. Junior's physical condition, apnea, literalizes his feeling smothered.

When Junior fails to attract the young nurse, Tracy, he is forced to acknowledge that he can no longer score with the women that he would have as a younger man. So he settles into a relationship with Catherine Romano. He assures her that her dead husband Lou, "a real straight shooter," was not on the take. In the funhouse mirror of this world, "straight shooter" means a sympathetically bent holster. The futility of living on the past is expressed in the closing song, Johnny Thunders' "Can't Put Your Arm around a Memory." In contrast, Catherine relishes Junior's company because of their common past: "I enjoy you, Corrado. I always did."

Richie feels confined by his small garbage route and high costs, especially when Janice wants an $850,000 home. He chafes under Tony's restrictions—for example, forbidding his drivers' dangerous sale of cocaine—and takes risky initiatives. In the opening scene—to The Pretenders's "Space Invaders"—Richie has a garbage truck dump its load in front of a deli whose owner complained at having to pay double for missed pickups. Parodying a guarantee, the company gives the complainer double his garbage back. Continuing to turn Junior against Tony, Richie deploys Livia's evasive innuendo: "I don't want to say anything disparaging."

Of course, another form of constraint is a nagging memory, the past that won't stay buried. That's what Livia marshalls when she tells Junior that her Johnny-Boy once said that the nice, sweet Catherine let him feel her up behind The Sons of Italy Hall. Even the innocent are confined by their storied pasts. Earlier, Junior briefly recalls his lost Roberta, the 16-year affair he ended when she betrayed his cunnilinguistic genius (I, 9). He is heartened that she has bought a house: Bobby saw her buy a fountain of a urinating boy.

As Tony complains to Dr. Melfi, he is so bored even a polished thriller like *Se7en* is uninteresting: "It's all a series of distractions till you die." Interestingly, when Tony mentioned watching a Brad Pitt and Gwyneth Paltrow movie, Melfi assumed it was *Sliding Doors*—though Pitt isn't in it— an optimistic movie about discovering one's alternative life. But Tony sticks to his gangsters. Even his passion for history now fails him. He does not rush down to see the gang's shipment of World War II memorabilia, including the jeep Patton drove in Sicily, Eisenhauer's dinner service, and Goering's guns. In ominous comedy, the false Pussy parodies the TV-and-Hollywood Nazi: "I know nothing. Nothing. . . . Vee have vays of dealing vit you, Mr. Soprano."

When Tony's lawyer advises him to insulate himself from the gang's shenanigans, this turns into a self-imposed, painful form of house arrest. For long days at his garbage company office Tony doodles, scrapes his rash till it bleeds, and sets up an office basketball pool. When his doctor suggests he talk to his therapist about "stress management" Tony takes a more direct approach. In his office he screws (doggie-style) the stacked secretary ("a Born-again Christian," he was warned), while a dog barks madly in the background. Stress spreads.

Another form of constraint sounds in the characters' language. Though the profanity seems outlaw, even blasphemous, it slips into the formal order of a pattern. Junior's "Mother of fuckin' Mercy" is echoed by Tony's "Son of a fuckin' bitch." The black Michael McLuhan from the marshal's office seems unaware of the larger pattern that his name and occupation set on him, even when the nurse calls him Marshall McLuhan. Like the song by the other 1960s icon, Dylan, this man's name serves a larger pattern. Similarly, the country club's reception sign, "Couples Invitational," assumes a second meaning from our downview on a passing cleavage.

Dr. Melfi herself is restricted by her relationship with Tony. She feels she cannot refer him to another doctor, yet she suffers from their association. When she humiliates her son in the restaurant, Melfi claims her concern was for his well-being. So, too, she insists Tony is not ready to be referred elsewhere. When her son says he is studying Lacan's deconstructivism, Melfi jokes that his grandfather was a contractor. But the subject's irony relates rather to her disintegration. She finally accepts Kupferberg's prescription for an anti-obsession drug. When Tony finds her "mellow," we credit her vodka bracer.

In a variation on the theme of constraint, perhaps Melfi has her own compulsive behavior in mind as well as Tony's when she cites the psychological disorder, alexithymia: "The individual craves almost ceaseless action which enables them to avoid acknowledging the abhorrent things they do." Without this activity, they have to face their feeling empty and the self-loathing that has haunted them since childhood, so "they crash." In one shot Tony and Melfi both seem to be patients, turned away from each other, their heads held in the hand in opposite directions. Of course, Melfi resumed seeing Tony for her therapy as well as his.

Melfi's disintegration proves Tony destructive. Under his unintentional influence even someone of Melfi's sensitivity, knowledge, wisdom, and both psychological and moral self-awareness proves helpless. She breaks down from trying to bridge the abyss between Tony's charm and his evil. When Melfi embarrasses her son at the restaurant, she expresses her pent-up rage at not being able to control her life—a frustration perilously close to what she was treating in Tony. Stress spreads.

In different ways, the characters are moving out of themselves. Uncle Junior falls asleep in front of the televsion with Catherine holding his feet. To subdue his snoring she puts his oxygen mask on him. At last he has friendly, relaxing company—and she packs a seductive *manicott'*. Carmela broadens her horizons by hosting a book-club discussion of Frank Mc-Court's memoirs, which focus the Italian-American women on the Irish characters' dysfunctional families and drinking problems. Melfi promises Dr. Kupferberg that she will go to an AA meeting.

Tony escapes his office rut—and rutting—by returning to the Satriale backroom for gags with the gang. A car crash takes them outside. There the lads shuffle around, Tony lights up his Cuban, and Paulie suns himself under a reflector. FBI Agent Harris drops by to introduce his new partner, Joe Marquez. The rising camera takes a detached, clinical view on the street life below. This is not the microscope used to burn live ants (as Tony joked was his pastime), but a bemused and sympathetic gaze down on people making the most of their empty day. In the absence of high drama, the pulse persists.

These last mundane details—like the comforts of Catherine and Junior—exemplify the "series of distractions" by which we divert ourselves until we die. This consolation helps to bridge old animosities. If no lion lies with any lamb here, at least Tony and Agent Harris comment amiably on the Nets's basketball game, the erstwhile quarrelers Hesh and Chris play cards, and Pussy shares a girlie magazine with his once resented Furio. The peace survives the collision caused by Carmine's speeding.

II, 12: The Knight in White Satin Armor

Written by Robin Green and Mitchell Burgess. Directed by Allen Coulter.

Pussy starts to fancy himself an FBI employee. Though Tony and Carmela throw an engagement party for them, Richie plots to kill Tony but Janice kills him in a domestic tiff. Tony breaks up with Irina but is drawn back when she attempts suicide.

The season's penultimate episode returns to the tension between loyalty and betrayal. Of course, the most dramatic case is Janice's engagement to marry Richie, heralded as the union of the Sopranos and the Aprilos. Scene after scene opens in harmony and dissolves into bitterness, because the sentiments are false.

The opening seems to be a dream: An unfamiliar couple dance elegantly through the empty mansion. When Tony and Janice carry in a loveseat, and the couple are identified as Richie's son Rick and his competition ballroom dance partner, it seems the dream has become reality. In their loving speeches at the engagement party Janice and Richie avow as much.

But that dream scene carries the seeds of its destruction. If Tony enters ("ass first," director Allen Coulter instructed) helping Janice carry in the love seat, he exits telling her to "shove it up [her] ass." So, too, the young man dancing turns out to be Richie's son, Richard Jr. As Tony expects and Janice denies, his dance career profoundly disappoints Richie. Jackie Aprile Jr.'s introduction is also ominous, as his cigar suggests he aspires to become another Tony.

The fatal kitchen incident is defined by the TV-boxing match, which plays behind Janice as she nags Richie. Initially, he is irked having to make decisions about the wedding, then by the mounting house costs, then by Janice's snarling hatred of Tony ("Tony just can't handle that our house is nicer than his fuckin' house."). In return, she objects to Richie's attitude. She drugged Livia so they could have sex but says that is unlikely now.

The irritants collect. Richie flares up when she calls his son "Ricky" instead of Rick and wishes he had a son like Jackie, not a dancer. When Janice would accept Rick being gay Richie punches her mouth. Removing the *New Jersey Bride* magazine from his chair, Richie sits down to eat, and says coldly: "You gonna cry now?" Janice gets the gun they use for sex and kills him.

Ironically, this happens right after Tony has authorized Silvio—who glowers like the mask of Tragedy or the hunched bitterness of Richard Nixon—to kill Richie. The murder verifies Uncle Junior's last advice to Tony (as to Richie earlier): "You have to wonder where Janice is in all this. My little niece." With her new hair, wardrobe, and domestic assertiveness, the hippie niece is transforming into mob wife—until she arrests the engagement.

Though both Richie's violence and Janice's murder are shocking, they are consistent. In Richie's first appearance (II, 3), he warns Chris about slapping Adriana: "You want to raise your hand, you give her your last name." That is how Richie is from the Old School. Janice's violent outburst confirms the shallow faddishness of her various New Age idealisms.

In her post-murder need Janice turns to the brother she has been sabotaging. In the opening scene Tony explains he is hosting the engagement party, despite his hatred of Richie, out of obligation to his sister. Janice is even more aggressive against Tony than Livia is. To provoke Richie, Janice reports that Tony does not want him near his kids. But when she needs help she calls Tony and he saves her. Tony enters the kitchen warily, his gun drawn, as if he might be entering a trap.

Despite their differences, Tony sympathizes with his sister. Livia is delighted to hear Richie did not come home: "He probably jilted her. That's the story of her life." Tony defends Janice: "What chance did she have, with you for a mother?" Livia passes through an encyclopedia of emotional pretense here, inviting Tony's kiss and dismissing him as "cruel." When he falls on his face outside, Livia laughs—as in Tony's only warm memory from childhood (I, 2), when the family laughed at Johnny-Boy's fall. At the bus station Tony tells Janice that his shrink has diagnosed Livia as a narcissistic personality who cannot allow joy. This episode shows Janice as an equally destructive narcissist.

In contrast to Janice's and Livia's betrayal of Tony stands the quiet, unquestioning loyalty of Silvio, Chris, and Furio. And ostensibly Uncle Junior. At first, Junior's frustration and financial needs ($400,000 just to challenge the wiretap evidence) make Junior sympathetic to Richie's desire to whack Tony. But when he "couldn't sell it" to Albert Barese, Junior concludes Richie is "a fuckin' loser." He is better off with Tony.

When Junior warns Tony about Richie's plot he claims his cocaine selling (earlier his "lifeline") was a strategic ploy. "I've been playing him." Junior hides his self-interest in avuncular warmth: "If I didn't come to you your fuckin' wife would be a widow and your children wouldn't have a father. Go fuck yourself." But however self-serving, Junior still loves his nephew. Even when he's angry enough to want him killed, he still loves him. In the Family family, blood is thicker than . . . bloodshed. Uncle Junior's simple homeliness is expressed in his kitchen, with its pictures of kittens, the domestic instruments, and cake-plates. When he hears of Richie's failure the green half-wall behind him seems an image of his nausea.

Dr. Melfi, who seems to be recovering her composure and stability, remains Tony's faithful counsel. She indignantly denies ever being judgmental about his—or any other client's—sex life. She even tries to temper Tony's guilt about Irina:

TONY: I was bangin' her for two years.
MELFI: Was that a hardship on her?
TONY: That's cute.

Now that Melfi seems to have regained control of her negative feelings toward Tony and their relationship, Tony again enjoys their exchanges.

In Pussy's tension between loyalty and betrayal, he moves from his closeness with Tony to wear a wire to the engagement party and to turn in Chris for hoisting a truckload of Pokémon cards (more "nickel and dime" stuff for the unwise guy whose brokerage certificate was a "license to steal" via the stock market). Tailing Chris, Pussy puts a 7–11 clerk into a coma, smashes his son's car, and needs Skip's intervention to avoid the charge of leaving an accident. More than the capsized boat victims, the clerk is a serious reminder of the innocents our heroes hurt.

To resolve his conflict, Pussy generates a new loyalty. He defines himself as an FBI employee. He suggests that after this assignment he could resettle under the Witness Protection Program in Scottsdale, Arizona, and give lectures to the FBI. He acts like an operative, giving Skip a present and using official language and code on his reports: "This is the Fat Man." "Who? Sal?"

Pussy rationalizes his switch of loyalty: Tony treated him like "an errand boy" when he sent him to find the teacher's car. He conveniently overlooks

Tony's more recent trust in their whacking Matt Bevilaqua together, though—to show how comfortable he now feels "in" the FBI—he admits his involvement to Skip.

Like Pussy, Carmela loses faith in Tony when she smells Calvin Klein One on Tony's shirt after he claimed to have left Irina. Of course, Carmela understands her situation. When Janice tries on her wedding gown (thanking Jesus for her cleavage), Carmela advises her: "In a year, tops, you're going to have to accept a *goomah*." As the scene is shot almost entirely in a mirror the image of radiant bridal bliss seems an illusion. Mirrors always suggest pause for reflection.

Nor does Irina's suicide attempt arouse Carmela's sympathy. When Janice phones Tony for help, Carmela moves from suspicion—"You better get it. Maybe she slit the other wrist"—to skepticism. She phones Livia's to check if Tony is there.

The characters' lives make for inverted values. So Richie tells Junior, "This country is going through boom times. There's more fuckin' garbage than there ever was." Amid the formal elegance of the bridal shop, Janice reveals Richie's need to hold a gun to her head during sex: "It's ritualistic. Fetishistic. That's all." Anyway, "usually he takes the clip out." After her suicide attempt, the Russian Irina refuses to talk to the hospital psychiatrist because he's Rumanian. She is depressed because she's too old to model for salad spinners. Though her salad days are over, she is still green in judgment.

When Carmela thanks Vic for "thinking" and "being strong" for both of them in curtailing their relationship, she suggests a possible future: "Maybe someday I will be free." When the scene opens, the sound of the paint-mixing machine sounds like machine gun fire, especially as it follows Albert Barese's refusal to join "a move against Tony Soprano." The sound-cut connects Vic's and Barese's submission to Tony. In Tony's life, murder is as common as redecorating. But Carmela resists the idea that Vic withdrew simply out of fear of Tony. Director Coulter kept Vic and Carmela in profile to express their unease with each other (Season II DVD, disc 4), with the paint-chip rack between them "like a ski-slope toward her." Again, this TV show has the visual artistry of a feature film.

At the end, Carmela asserts a new independence. She announces that after Meadow's graduation she and Rosalie Aprile will take a three-week holiday in Rome to shop and perhaps to meet with the Pope. Tony will chauffeur AJ and find Meadow a tennis clinic "because if I have to do it, Tony, I just might commit suicide." The wife assumes the rights and strategies of the *goomah*. The scene begins with a pan up from Carmela's Italian travel brochures. At the end Carmela walks out, leaving Tony shrunk between the living room column and the wall, as usual behind a rock and a hard place.

In his own way, Tony maintains fealty if not fidelity to his lovers. When he breaks up with Irina it is partly to force her to make her own life, to get a career, to find someone who will marry her and give her children. This explanation is not just a rationalization. Irina is unhappy in their sporadic relationship. Her friend Svetlana's Bill carried her off when her prosthetic leg fell off in the—where else?—Gap store. So it's understandable that Irina will ask: "Where is my knight in white satin armor?" The malapropism admits Irina's desire for a wedding gown, like Janice's, that would be her armor against the world.

In part, Tony leaves her so she will find her knight. His response to her suicide attempt shows that he is concerned for her, in his fashion: "Fuckin' ambulance. They pumped her stomach. Cost me three grand." Having suggested modeling prospects and a therapist, Tony finally breaks with her by sending Silvio with $75,000 cash and his usual sage advice: "Time is a great enemy" for a woman, but "Something always comes along. . . . It's called *Passages*. It's a book."

Primarily, Tony breaks off with Irina because he loves Carmela. Dr. Melfi is surprised that he ends the affair now, given his obvious feelings for Irina. But now his concern for Carmela outweighs his vagrant lust. He protectively refuses to tell his wife what happened to Richie: "Carmela, after eighteen years of marriage, don't make me make you an accessory after the fact." Despite the discretion of his words, his first hand gesture suggests a gun. But with Carmela his words and deeds are rarely at one.

When she hears that Richie is "gone" and Janice decamped to Seattle, Carmela concludes: "That was not a marriage made in heaven." The camera provides a couple of different views of Tony and Carmela sitting together on the sofa, like Carmela and Father Phil in I, 5, and Chris and Jon in II, 7, apart but together. Particularly given Carmela's recollection of her wedding—

CARMELA: Remember how radiant I looked walking down the aisle?
JANICE: You must be depressed.
CARMELA: No, not depressed. I leave that for others.

—her marriage was not made in heaven either. It was made on earth, where real people live, with real problems and few illusions, and it has adjusted to the challenges and compromises necessary to sustain it. The white satin wedding gown is not a suit of armor, not a protection against outside threats, but a ritual no stronger than the people's loves within it. In that spirit of familial acceptance Tony can see Janice off with "All in all, I'd say it was a pretty good visit."

As all the relationships are tested and redefined in this episode, it seems to grow out of the previous one's Dylan song, "You're gonna have to serve somebody." But when the dust has cleared Tony can relax with a more satisfied song over the end credits, The Eurythmics's "I Saved the World Today": "Everybody's happy now / The bad thing's gone away / Everybody's happy now / The good thing's here to stay." The Richie and Irina threats are gone and the Tony and Carmela marriage remains, in whatever new terms she may negotiate.

II, 13: Funhouse

Written by David Chase and Todd Kessler. Directed by John Patterson.

Livia is rejected by her daughter, Barbara, and by the Green Grove Retirement Home for having abused the staff. When she insults Carmela, Tony washes his hands of her by giving her two first-class airline tickets to go live with her sister in Tucson. Tony and Pussy meet at an Indian restaurant to collect on their new prepaid phone card scam. Suffering severe food poisoning, Tony experiences six nightmares, mostly set on the Asbury Park boardwalk in winter. In their climax, a tilefish with Pussy's voice admits having betrayed him to the FBI. Tony finds Pussy's wire under his cigars. Tony, Silvio, and Paulie take Pussy out on a boat and kill him. On the eve of Meadow's graduation the FBI arrest Tony for possession of stolen airplane tickets. Out on bail, he attends the graduation ceremony and party.

David Chase concludes the second season with an episode focused on purging and cleansing. Not all the examples are scatological. The literal purge, of course, is Tony's epic reaction to food poisoning. Tony spends a night of cramps, upchuck, and the richest orchestration of flatulence since *Blazing Saddles* (Mel Brooks, 1974). The less sensitive Pussy had "a slight touch of diarrhea but that all passed." Of course, apart from the safe-cracker's wind-breaking in II, 8, the only previous note of flatulence in this series was also struck by Pussy on his release in I, 11. The purge theme gives new meaning to the framing Rolling Stones song, "Through and Through" and Tony's episode-end regret, "I blew an easy one. I blew everything. . . . I got predicates up the ass."

In a psychological form of purge, Tony's nightmares pour out his waking anxieties. The dreams grow out of Tony's playful surrealism when he claims his coat has grown hair and is attacking him (It's the sable for Carmela). His suicide flame in the first nightmare points to the *gee* which Artie blames for the food poisoning. In India that clarified butter is used to prepare the body for the funeral pyre. His first nightmare transforms the supplier of Carmela's new fur, Patsy Parisi, into his brother Philly, whom Tony had whacked in II, 1. Pussy is notably absent from Tony's suicide.

In another dream Tony watches himself shoot Paulie—then admit to Melfi that this was an excessive punishment for Paulie's sending out a family newsletter every Christmas and whistling television commercials, especially since he is such a good earner. (He doesn't mention Paulie's worst trait: repeating—in self-congratulation—his own jokes.) This dream prepares Tony for the execution of a close aide.

In the second dream Dr. Melfi speaks through Annalisa, agreeing that he is still his own worst enemy. In the next dream his new clean-up guy Furio hands Tony a roll of toilet paper as Adriana and Chris drive Tony to find Pussy. Tony's subconscious is zeroing in on Pussy.

In a dream session with Dr. Melfi, Tony enters wearing his sweatshirt and a fairly impressive erection (actually a strapped-on dildo, according to Director John Patterson, in his commentary on Season II DVD, disc four). This Melfi refers to as his "friend," then his "friend Pussy." This recalls the confusion in I, 1, between Pussy Malanga (whom Junior planned to kill in Artie's restaurant) and Big Pussy Buonpensiero. As Tony told Hesh, "You think he's going to fuck with Big Pussy? My Pussy?" Now Tony is uncertain whether Melfi is talking about Pussy or pussy: "I got pussy on the brain. Always did. I want to fuck you. Always did."

The ambiguity confirms Pussy as the unacknowledged source of Tony's anxiety, his uncertainty about his safety and identity. Tony has Pussy on the brain but suppresses his intuition that his best friend has turned. As Pussy has been singing to the FBI, he is Tony's weak spot, the lowest-case soprano. This dream ends with Tony taking Melfi on her desk, as his weakness for pussy edges out his vulnerability to Pussy one last time.

In Tony's last dream his anxiety would not be deflected. From a market stall a tilefish confesses in Pussy's voice: "You know I've been working with the government, Tony. . . . Sooner or later you've got to face facts. . . . You passed me over for promotion." In telling Tony what he already knows, the fish surfaces Tony's suppressed intuition. Through the magic of digital imaging, the fish is morphed with Pussy's mouth.

As Tony has to get past the pussy to Pussy in his nightmares, he has to go beneath the Cuban cigars in Pussy's bedroom to find the wires, mike, and mini-recorder that confirm his treachery. As if to indulge a Freudian analyst, Pussy hid his betrayal under his cigars. Pussy's identification with fish was set up in the opening restaurant scene, when a waiter passed Tony's and Pussy's table with a platter of fish.

The confrontation on the boat is poignant, as it unwinds over the surreally inapt, "Baubles, Bangles and Beads," by the god Sinatra. As the song is about small mementos that evoke a shared, loving past, perhaps it does suit the scene where the three men kill the traitor who was "like a brother" to them. As well, the "singer" Pussy is confronted on the line "Her heart will sing, sing-a-linga."

After a reflex denial Pussy minimizes what he gave the FBI: "Picayune shit. . . . They know about the calling cards, Scatino, the phone card scam." From his defense of helplessness—"I was going away for pushing H. . . . Thirty to life. I had no choice"—he turns to brag about deceiving the FBI: "I'm mind-fucking those donkeys like you wouldn't believe." After a few tequilas Pussy recalls his 26-year-old acupuncturist in Puerto Rico: "Her ass was the second coming." The men laugh along until Tony punctures the illusion: "Did she even really exist?"

Exposed, Pussy still asks, "Not in the face, ok? Give me that? Keep my eyes?" In *GoodFellas*, Tommy (Joe Pesci) is shot in the face so his mother cannot have an open coffin. As Pussy is at sea he should be beyond that concern. But then his admission that his "inner ear balance is off" speaks to a failure in balance as well as conscience.

Tony's physical purge points to several other poisons. From the Green Grove point of view—shared by Barbara's husband, Tom—Livia has been properly expunged. Tony thinks he has managed that, too, until his scam tickets backfire, she is stopped by airport security and he is arrested.

Meadow seems to purge herself of any last shame about her father, especially after her friends see him taken out in handcuffs. As she assures Carmela: "This is who Dad is. My friends don't judge me. And fuck them if they do. I'll cut them off." Coming after Tony's submission to the arresting FBI boss—"You think this bothers me, you fuckhead?"—Meadow's line shows her father's strength.

The sable coat is enough to wash away Carmela's recent anger at him. The WATCH US MAKE IT sign on the Saltwater Taffy shop bridges their making love and the first of his boardwalk nightmares. The juxtaposition suggests the flow between his real and dream lives.

Even Dr. Melfi comes clean. She tells Tony that she didn't push him to confront his mother's "psychic injuries" to him because she was afraid of him. Now she declares his flaming rage—as expressed in his dream of self-immolation—is his distraction from the profound sadness he refuses to confront. Tony pretends to confident cheer, with his feet on her table, arrogantly. He exits jauntily singing down the hall: "Maybe, baby, I'll have you." As he projects into life the sex he dreamed, he continues to ignore his sorrow.

Pussy has purged himself of his qualms about betraying his best friend. As he tells Agent Lipari, "President Franklin is my best friend and he's in there"—the envelope in which Pussy regretfully turns over his take on the phone-card scam he has just exposed.

Dave's animosities are also purged when he meets Tony over the—of course, given Dave's luck—empty coffee machine. Without blaming anyone, the haggard Dave reports that son Eric was accepted into Georgetown but is going to State College for financial reasons. Dave invites Tony to hang out with him on the ranch outside Las Vegas, where he has taken a job. That is not the most promising location for a compulsive gambler with "cowboy-itis." It is no surprise when, in the next season, Meadow reports that Dave is in a mental ward.

The last episode of the second season closes the elements introduced in the first. Tony's dream replays Silvio's Pacino performance for Pussy: "Our true enemy has yet to reveal himself." The stock hustle started there is closed down here. Tony nominates Chris for "the button." As Chris, like Meadow, graduates, he shows far more control and maturity than in the first episode. Melfi is back in normal business and has reconciled herself to dealing with Tony. As before [II, 1,] Angie wonders where Pussy is and is angry he isn't there—so she could leave him. Other characters—Chris's two sets of useless aides, Richie, Janice, Irina—are one way or another out of the way. As Tony exults at the start of the episode, "All my enemies are smoked." But he still feels angry with himself for the airline ticket mess. Otherwise, Tony has survived his depression.

Paralleling the season opener's montage, the last episode intercuts Meadow's graduation and the family's celebrations with a survey of the Soprano business interests: a Barone garbage truck, a porn theater, the phone cards, a junkie Hillel has to clean away at the Teittleman/Soprano motel, the gutted brokerage office, money raining down on the Executive card game. These support Meadow's celebration. As Tony smokes his long (and did I mention illegal?) Cuban, all seems well in his world. But Melfi knows the profound sorrow Tony is hiding.

The closing shot of the pier and the swelling, frothing tide, the waters at which Tony stared when he left Pussy to the deep, remind us that there are hidden depths under Tony's security that may not prove so peaceful. Not if there is a Season Three. Fear of what the tides might wash up adds a sinister note to the love song that ends the season: "Waiting for a call from you." When the phone rings in the Soprano home, everyone holds their breath.

- Yes, Virginia, there was an actual Big Pussy and a Little Pussy in New Jersey crime, back in the 1940s. David Chase adopted the names.

Season Three

III, 1: Mr. Ruggerio's Neighborhood

Written by David Chase. Directed by Allen Coulter.

Their phone taps having failed, FBI Agent Ike Harris and his team plan to wiretap Tony's basement. To plant a mike in a lamp, they tail each resident. Meanwhile, Tony is concerned about the melancholy of Patsy Parisi, who was brought over from Uncle Junior's crew after Tony had Parisi's twin brother Spoons whacked. AJ tries out for the football team, Meadow deals with college and her troubled roommate, and Carmela gets a new tennis coach.

David Chase launched the third season with a humorous program that focused on Tony's FBI hounds as much as on the Soprano family. The title reference to Tony's plumber, Mr. Ruggerio, parodies *Mr. Rogers' Neighborhood*. The FBI's covert operations evoke the notorious "Plumbers" of Richard Nixon's White House. The FBI focus makes this a shaggy dog story—like Paulie's lunch monologue about befouled shoelaces. It belies the opening scene suggestion that the topic will be—as Tony's morning paper headline puts it—MOB COMPETITION FOR GARBAGE CONTRACTS HEATS UP—VIOLENCE FEARED.

The agents' tailing of the household reintroduces the characters more fluidly than the montage in II, 1. Again, the familiar audience is flattered with in-jokes—this time at the FBI's expense. The earnest agents have everything wrong. Pussy did not end up in some compost heap but in the ocean. Livia is one mother who would testify against her son—even *sans* immunity. The more certain they are, the more wrong: "Richie Aprile! No doubt about it—the cartel had him whacked." They still have Tony's picture labeled "Underboss," when he has effectively become the boss.

When the Sopranos rush home to their basement flood, the agent is certain it "must be a crisis with one of the children." The FBI man is right about the family's devotion—hence Carmela's "Save the pictures!" But they don't know a leak when they get one. They say they have no idea what went wrong—but they knew Tony had a problem water heater.

Even when the agents are onto something they prove wrong. Watching the video tour of Tony's basement, an agent spots a rust point in the 120-gallon hot water tank. Skip Liparski, a plumber's son, confidently predicts the tank will blow in six months. Wrong again: the tank blows the following Tuesday, aborting the bug. In their dealings with the Sopranos the FBI can't deal with even that leak

The FBI is also comic in how it follows the law. The agents are hobbled by the legal limits on how long they may listen to their bug. They hear Tony assign a "messy job" but it is only their maid's husband planning a sump pump. When they return they hear Tony and Carmela discuss his roughage, dental floss, and the problems therewith.

The series plays the FBI as if they were a gang like Tony's, only not as effective or smart. The FBI and the mobster have more in common than their Black and Decker. The agents case the joint. They pick locks to get in. The agent watching Carmela can't stop ogling Adriana, as she joins Carmela's tennis lessons and attracts the apparently lesbian coach. He even sounds like a wiseguy: "How green was my fuckin' valley." The spotted spy reports "They fuckin' made me." The FBI's need to move before "our warrant goes stale" parallels Tony's tank blowing post-warranty. The FBI "agency" is similarly parodied when Tony says he hired his mother's Russian caregiver from "an agency." She is his ex-mistress Irina's one-legged cousin, Svetlana.

The agents have their own argot. The agent has no idea "what went down." They report on the family as "Bings," with Meadow "Princess Bing," AJ "Baby Bing" and Tony "Der Bingle," in homage to Bing Crosby—like whom perhaps they hope he will "sing." The home is "the sausage factory." Having laughed at Pussy for playing his word game (II, 12), we can't take the real FBI agents seriously either.

In contrast, the gangsters show a surprising knowledge of Shakespeare. For example, in II, 12, Uncle Junior resolves "to screw [his] courage to the post" (after Lady Macbeth's "Screw your courage to the sticking place"). In I, 4, Junior is "waiting here like fucking Patience on a monument for discipline to be handed down" (*Twelfth Night*). Even Johnny-Boy was reaching for his Coleridge when he called young Livia "a fuckin' albacore around my neck" (I, 7). Here one of Tony's mugs describes Patsy in a paraphrase of Hamlet's "That a man may smile, and smile, and be a villain."

Of course, I am not accusing the Mafiosi of reading Shakespeare. In their alert intelligence they accrue language—and literature—the way they snap up business opportunities, as Tony does the Teittlemans' motel and Mahaffey's medical practice. That is how Tony uses what he learns from Dr. Melfi. He is not always accurate, as in I, 2, when he mistakes Melfi's Cape d'Antibes as "Captain Teebs." But usually the gangsters are more alert, opportunistic, and clear than the FBI. The crooks can seem classier than the cops.

Nor is the FBI entirely trustworthy. When the judge warrants two entries to plan and to place the hidden microphone, he insists they "limit both entrances to the basement only." But one agent rifles the family's mail and sneaks a peek into the kitchen fridge. Perhaps to extend the target beyond Italian-Americans, one agent is off to Denver for state espionage at a *mosque*. The agents seem fastidious about process when they debate whether to move the table back to its original placement, after the flood. On the other hand, one agent runs Stasiu's name past Anti-Terrorism "just for laughs." Well before September 11, this was an unjustified intrusion. After, that satire is nullified.

In fact, Stasiu is—understandably—embittered about America. He answers all his wife's Citizenship Exam questions with "Martin Luther King" and insults the composer of "The Star-spangled Banner." She scolds him for losing a test point by translating the sign STOP MEN AT WORK as "Stop all men who are working." But that is Stasiu's experience of America. In Poland, he was a mechanical engineer who supervised twenty employees and had a full time grant for autonomous research. In America he drives a cab. But that's no reason for the FBI to investigate him. While they track him, his wife steals the Soprano silverware and glass.

In a more somber scene, Patsy Parisi stumbles drunk into Tony's yard and aims his pistol at him to avenge his twin's murder. But his resolve weakens and he lowers the gun, weeping. He satisfies himself by pissing into Tony's pool. When Parisi aims to kill Tony the FBI agents watch him— and don't know what to do. Preventing the murder would blow their cover. They don't even say what they said when they spotted the flawed water tank: "It's a shame we can't warn him." Tony is protected by the would-be killer's weakened will, not by these Keystone Kops, ensnarled in their strategy, whose only "executive decision" is to move back the basement table.

Later, Parisi assures Tony that he is happy to be working with him, feels well rewarded, and has "put the grief behind me." The camera holds on his stolid non-commitment when Tony suggests Parisi bring his young son over to "hang out with AJ" and "go in the pool." The irony is both verbal—there are two ways to "go" in the pool—and dramatic—Patsy won't want his son to go in the pool that he "went" in. The "Hamburger Patties" sign behind Tony is framed as "Hamburger Pat" when he probes Patsy's mood, as if to suggest what Pat's wrong answer might make him. The episode's most somber scene—Patsy's intention to kill Tony—turns into comedy and Patsy stays the patsy.

The central characters' natures are also advanced in this episode. Tony's handling of Parisi is generous, certainly more humane than Paulie's "option," whacking him like his brother. The "excellent jersey" draws AJ out of his apathy to try out for the school football team. When his training scene is introduced by the FBI agent's cry of "Touchdown!" (re: the completed bugging), the FBI agent is again played unaware of his context. Meadow handles her college and New York freedom better than her at first frisky, then depressed roommate, Caitlin. And Carmela finds herself again shunned romantically, when the new tennis coach lusts for Adriana.

The Sopranos gain sympathy by how they are victimized here. Jeannie Cusamano nearly betrays them to the undercover agents, their maid steals, and—reduced to that level—the FBI subverts their privacy. Each time Tony wafts down the driveway for his morning paper, in his open robe, T-shirt and boxer shorts, he seems open and vulnerable, a sympathetic figure. When the FBI pretends to be a mosquito-control unit, they treat the Sopranos as their target pests. They are more honest when they claim to protect their power line.

The program advances two plunging lives. In the last dorm scene Hunter tells Meadow that Eric Scatino hates Montclair State and has been doing a lot of LSD. As Meadow knew him as "straight," he becomes another victim of Tony's amiable profession. Similarly, the Caitlin who partied so freely in her first scene here falls into obsessive depression. This recasts her earlier confidence that "New York is an experience that unalterably changes a person."

Notwithstanding these shadows, the episode remains comic. Its lightness informs the choice of music. Tony sings along with Steely Dan: "I'm a fool to do your dirty work," when he drives to work, unaware of the FBI's dirty tricks against him. At the end, as the camera zooms in on the miked lamp, Elvis Costello (in "High Fidelity") asks "Can you hear it?" At several points the FBI's seriousness is undercut by the theme from the old *Peter Gunn* series. That was another hero whose solitary search for justice showed up the law-enforcement institutions. Satirizing the FBI's skullduggery, the Gunn theme is mixed with Sting's "Every Breath You Take," with the spy's threat: "I'll be watching you."

■ Paulie's tirade against the danger of germs on one's shoes has its own poetry. In contrast to men's washrooms, some women's are so clean "you could eat maple walnut ice cream from the toilets." But the riff fits: He's paranoid about bugs, including the FBI breed. Tony frequently has the Bada Bing toilet "swept" for bugs. Furio's delicate dusting of Tony's car plays into this concern about cleanliness and against his rather rougher nature. This cleanliness fetish harks back to II, 9, where Paulie wipes his hands with some cleaner, to Pussy's disdain, in the hospital waiting room.

III, 2: *Proshai, Livushka*

Written by David Chase. Directed by Tim Van Patten.

Tony tells Meadow's college friend Noah Tannenbaum, an African-Jewish-American, to stay away from her. Livia dies. Janice's return revives familiar tensions. Carmela and her father add a welcome candor to the falseness of Livia's funeral.

Again the episode begins with the garbage gang war. This opening scene fulfills the violence promised in the previous episode's opening, then veers off into the tragic-comic mode, with Livia's death.

The title comes from her brusque Russian caregiver's toast: "Good-bye, little Livia." As Svetlana admits, Livia was a difficult patient and "She defeated me." But to honor Livia's wishes Svetlana insists on keeping her very valuable collection of opera and American show-tune records that Janice tries to pry away. Janice's search for Livia's supposed stash of cash in the basement wall cuts to another hood's being wired for Livia's wake. The greed and malice unleashed by Livia's death make this a black comedy. In its funeral context, Les Paul's "I'm Forever Blowing Bubbles" over the end credits lightly reflects on the evanescence of life and its petty acquisitions.

Livia's funeral occasions massive hypocrisy. Everyone struggles to be respectful toward the not very dear departed. "At least she didn't suffer" is the most common obsequy. Tony's chorus is "What are you gonna do?"—which is what the crooked Reverend James said at his—far superior—father's passing (II, 2) and what Tony said about Spoons Parisi's death (III, 1). From the background, Fanny—still in the wheelchair from when Livia ran her over—offers that Livia was her "best friend" because she always called to tell her who had just died.

When Janice forces the confessional circle, the coerced Hesh musters something like a compliment: "She didn't mince words. Between brain and mouth there was no interlocutor." Hesh always rises to the occasion. Ironically, he provides a more appropriate reflection on Livia in the Jewish joke he told at the funeral home earlier. In his story, the only positive anyone has for the deceased is "His brother was worse." In contrast, the stoned Christopher irrelevantly questions the claim that "there's no two people on earth exactly the same." His conclusion—that there could be "another Mrs. Soprano just like her"—consoles nobody.

When Artie is about to recount Livia's report of Tony's arson, Carmela cuts him off: "This is such a crock of shit!" Obligated not to teach her children hypocrisy, she remembers Livia as dysfunctional: "She gave no one joy." Carmela's father rises (against her mother's silencing) to support her: "We suffered for years under the yoke of that woman. She estranged us from our own daughter." Carmela notes that Livia's children did not disobey her until after her death, when they staged the funeral Livia had forbade. She didn't want a funeral because she was afraid no one would come. Livia neglected her grandchildren's memory books because she thought no one loved her enough to read them. In her frank criticism Carmela shows a sympathetic understanding of the poor soul.

Janice's true feelings also emerge, despite the artifice of her expression and the "California bullshit," as Tony banned it, of her confessional circle. Though she planned not to come—until Tony paid her fare—Janice arrives at the Sopranos' in full weep. She uses her homage in the "circle" to promote her own "visual interpretive skills" and declares her critical mother "the reason I make videos today" (presumably, instead of pursuing the drawing and painting on which Livia was "tough" but "right"). To introduce Tony, Janice reports that Livia preserved all Tony's schoolwork but none of hers and Barbara's. Janice's homage is as self-serving as Charmaine's announcement that the desserts now ready are by the New Vesuvio's newer pastry chef.

Tony feels guilt for feeling relieved his mother is dead. Though he can tell Melfi his mother was a "selfish, miserable cunt," he cannot accept that she planned his murder. But she was the source of all his problems: "So, we're probably done here, right? She's dead." Of course, Tony tries to end his therapy in most of his sessions with Melfi.

Tony finds refuge in the classic Jimmy Cagney film, *The Public Enemy*, several times. Where Junior relived its grapefruit-in-the-face scene (I, 9), Tony emphasizes the dying gangster's last scenes with his maudlin mother. The video applies to Tony's family life in two opposite ways. First, its hero's loving, supportive mother is a pole away from Livia. When gangster Tom (Cagney) is wounded his mother says "I'm almost glad it happened," because now he will return to her. As Livia wanted her son's murder, she was disturbed that he survived. If Tony identifies with Tom, it is by their contrasting mothers; their fathers were harsh disciplinarians, Tom's a cop and Tony's a hood. Tony does not cry at his mother's death until he's overwhelmed by the last scene in the movie. Tom's corpse falls through the doorway while his mother is cheerfully readying his room for him upstairs. Before another sip of scotch stops him, Tony cries—less for Livia's death than for the mother's love he never had.

Second, that video recalls Meadow's alienation when Tony banned her friend, Noah Tannenbaum, because he was half-black (and the other half Jewish). For Noah, in this film "Cagney is modernity"—and Tony personifies archaic racism. But Noah seems naïve in his zeal for the college film course titled "Images of Hyper-Capitalist Self-Advancement in the Era of the Studio System." For that theme applies equally to the post-studio system, to *The Sopranos* as a mass media entertainment like the old genre films, and to both Noah's father's and Tony's jobs. Like so much academia (and books analyzing American TV series), the pompous academic overstates the obvious. If *Public Enemy* is "modernity," *The Sopranos* is postmodern in its shifting viewpoints, non-linear narrative, cultural allusiveness, and reflecting back on itself.

Hence this episode's rare bit of technical gimmickry. When Carmela finds Tony unconscious on the kitchen floor, she asks: "What happened?" The scene—including Tony's exchange with Meadow and Noah—is run backward to its starting point, then replayed. This device emphasizes the filmic nature both of *The Sopranos* and of the Sopranos' experience. It is especially appropriate for a scene that deals with (i) Noah's filmconsciousness and (ii) Tony's regressive nature, seen especially in his racism. It also suggests that in life, too, we can move backward, though only in the sense of regressing. You can't rewind life to edit it. The rewind reminds us we're watching a movie.

This technical self-consciousness parallels the moral self-consciousness of the title with which the video introduces the Cagney film: "Tom Powers in *Public Enemy* and Rico in *Little Caesar* are not two men, nor are they merely characters—they are a problem that sooner or later we, the public, must solve." Clearly, Tony Soprano is a problem that we have to solve, a moral question that troubles our affection for him, though not in the pseudo-sociological terms of those two films. *The Sopranos* clearly shares the intention of *The Public Enemy*: "to honestly depict an environment that exists today in a certain strata [sic] of American life, rather than glorify the hoodlum or the criminal."

In another form of self-reference, Furio describes a plan to hijack the popular *Survivor* television series by scoring protection money from the competitors. With his own spin on "surviving," Furio would bring that show's artificial reality closer to his reality—that is, to the reality already inflected by the gangster film. As the fictional and real worlds meld in the media, we glimpse (the dead) Pussy in the hallway mirror when Tony opens the door. As it is not Tony's perspective, our memory is imaged within the fictional world.

When Tony returns from the garden to find Carmela, Meadow, and AJ arrayed in wait, our assumption—and probably his—is that they are set to attack him for insulting Noah. Instead, they sympathetically report his mother's death. His first response is "You're kiddin'. I mean, Jesus Christ!" Then he repeats "She's dead"—as if to make sure. The homilies follow: "She was in no pain, Tony" (Svetlana); "We all know—how much you loved her" (Silvio); "I can imagine how you feel" (Paulie). Tony's first expression of genuine emotion after Livia's death is his "Goddam fuckin' bitch!" (which refers not to his dear departed mother but to Janice, who plans to miss the funeral).

In an interlude, Meadow helps AJ write an essay on Robert Frost's poem "Stopping by the Woods on a Snowy Evening." Its discussion of death and the rigors of life reflects on the Livia plot. When Meadow relates the "miles to go before I sleep" to Death as "The Big Sleep," Robert Frost meets film noir (*The Big Sleep*, Howard Hawks, 1946). The poem also reflects on Tony's rejection of Noah. Meadow explains that the cold, white snow is an image of death. "I thought black was death," AJ replies. "White, too," Meadow says. As she now sees the half-black Noah as a life force, she associates Tony's racism with death, emptiness, and the chill in their relationship. In a related joke, Tony assures Janice that the Richie murder investigation is "colder than your tits." As the motherhood of Livia and Janice (whose son is now a street-person in Montreal) is cold and killing, Tony's rejection of Noah places him in their camp.

Tony exults in racist terms for Noah that avoid the N-word. In III, 2, he calls him "Moe," as the generic Jew. There is glee and vitality in his anti-black barrage: "charcoal briquette," *ditsou, moolinyan,* "Those old Tarzan movies?" "Maybe if I say it in Swahili." In III, 3, Noah is "Sambo." In III, 9, he is "Jamal Ginsberg, the Hasidic Homeboy" and in III, 10, "the Oreo cookie." In III, 5, the black cop Wilmore is "this fuckin' smoke" and "affirmative action cocksucker." Colorful, clever, Tony's offensive language is as unscrupulous, dangerous, and charming as his more criminal behavior.

As they watch her graciously accepting condolences, Tony remarks to Carmela that Meadow is becoming "a robot, like the rest of us. . . . All her innocence is gone." Her cold look at her father confirms his fears that she is no longer his little girl.

III, 3:   Fortunate Son

Written by Todd Kessler. Directed by Henry Bronchtein.

After Christopher is finally "made"—that is, admitted into the gang's inner circle—he has trouble meeting his new responsibilities. Janice moves into her mother's house and steals Svetlana's prosthetic leg, to leverage her demand for Livia's record collection. Dr. Melfi probes the causes of Tony's panic attacks. Meadow confirms their alienation and AJ succeeds at frosh football.

As the title suggests, this episode centers on the ambivalence of being a son—the mix of benefit and burden. In the central episode, Tony remembers that when he was 11 years old, he saw his father chop a finger off the butcher Satriale for not paying his gambling debt. As Dr. Melfi points out, Tony's current panic attacks are triggered by his associations with meat. His latest attack was not, as we assumed, prompted by the Uncle Ben rice logo and his "frank conversation with Buckwheat" (that is, Noah reduced to a Little Rascal), but by the capicola. The cold cuts knock Tony cold.

His first faint was after the Satriale episode. Before the roast beef dinner, young Tony watched his father and mother dance. His father's badinage mixed sex and meat: "You like it with the bone standing in it," he says, ostensibly about Livia's menu. "The lady loves her meat," Johnny-Boy jokes, squeezing Livia's buns. She rejects his *All of Me* dance. Her only good mood was the day of the meat delivery. Tony has since associated raw meat with violence, blood, his first intimations of sexuality, and his responsibility "to bring home the bacon." Tony's cold cuts are Proust's madelaine, his floodgate to memory.

At the same time, Tony remembers that he was fascinated, not repelled, by the violence. His father praised him for watching the attack on Satriale, instead of "running like a little girl." So rather than "getting the belt" for disobeying his father's injunction to wait in the car, little Anthony is praised for stomaching the violence.

The traumas of the father are visited upon the son. Tony encourages AJ's football effort. On AJ's first heroic play, a fumble recovery, he crawls out from under the gang tackle with his vision and hearing slowed, as if he were concussed. His father's cheers seem like animal growls until they focus. When AJ is appointed defensive captain, he faints. He doesn't want the responsibilities of being "made" this way; AJ went into football just to wear the cool jersey. Now his father's support becomes a pressure on him. AJ offers to visit Meadow just to escape Tony's lecture over a television football game.

AJ bristles at Adriana's tease about cheerleaders because frosh football is too marginal to have cheerleaders. Perhaps he doesn't want football to become a way for others to project themselves onto him, whether it's Adriana's sexuality or Tony's own linebacker success. The frightening burden of his success at football may prompt him to reject college because of its smarter "freaks."

Tony's pressure on AJ extends to two surrogate sons. Tony promised Jackie Aprile to look out for his son, Jackie Jr., and to keep him out of crime. Though Tony asks Chris to keep an eye on him as well, Chris exploits Frankie's idea of robbing the Amnesty International benefit concert at Rutgers (the featured performer makes this a Jewel robbery). At their lunch meeting Jackie acts like an alienated son when he arrives late, in unnecessary shades, and overreacts to Tony's advice.

Tony has always treated Chris "like a son," watching and promoting his "nephew" (for example, I, I), though he is actually the son of Carmela's cousin. When Chris is "made" this relationship is formalized. "This Family comes before anything else"—including one's family. Tony is like a father to all his "made" men, to be brought any problems they may have. Ironically, Chris's induction gift is the football gambling business, which exploits the weakness Johnny-Boy taught little Tony to avoid. When the chorus of "Where's the Money?" (Dan Hicks and his Hot Licks) attends the end-credits, Chris's predicament—struggling to meet the responsibilities of a "son's" maturing—stands for the entire episode and all its sons, real or virtual.

All these sons chafe under the "roles" their fathers impose on them. At the school football game, the peridontist Romano swears at the referee like a wiseguy. Daughters resist the same pressure, as when Meadow favors the forbidden Noah. She makes a point of telling Carmela she is spending the weekend with him at the Connecticut home of his parents' friends (from NBC yet!).

Carmela is caught between her daughter and her husband. To prevent their confrontation, she discourages Tony from coming to visit Meadow, but defends him. He comes "from a place and a time where he thinks he has your best interests at heart." This statement is fair to both. In a more sterile relationship, Adriana's mother can't lend Chris money because "she's still paying for her hysterectomy."

Janice proves an even more problematic daughter when she campaigns for Livia's record collection. She claims several motives for wanting the old records back. "These old albums, they're a window into her soul," she tells Tony. Then she is making a documentary on the power of popular music in the lives of Livia's generation. In the next episode she tells the Russians "These records are all I have to remember my mother by." But Tony knows Janice wants the records to sell on the Internet. When she takes for hostage Svetlana's $20,000 artificial leg (with the Kenneth Cole calfskin boot), she indirectly draws Tony into her conflict—and into another unwilling encounter with Irina, now engaged to be married. Svetlana demonstrates her assimilation when she dismisses her old leg as "Russian piece of shit" and urges her fiancé to ignore Janice: "Bill, don't waste breaths. This cunt is gonna be sorry she fuck with me."

In the opening scenes, first Chris tells Adriana, then Tony tells Chris, they have seen "too many movies." Adriana fears that Paulie's call to be made may rather be to his murder, as happens in *GoodFellas* and *Donnie Brasco* (Mike Newell, 1997). But the only violence in this visit is Paulie's fashion statement: "Shoot your cuffs," he preps Chris.

Parodying the parent/mentor relationships, Janice's current fiancé is a 19-year-old who "can go all night." Similarly, when the newly made Chris and his sponsor Paulie say they love each other, the next shot is of two

strippers kissing as they dance g-string to g-string, another ritual performance of "love."

■ Carmine from New York knows all about Tony's blackouts and his
psychiatrist and assures him "There's no stigmata these days." That is,
Tony won't be martyred for such modern phenomena.

> ## III, 4: Employee of the Month
>
> *Written by Robin Green and Mitchell Burgess. Directed by John
> Patterson.*
>
> Ralph Cifaretto takes over Richie Aprile's garbage business and Jackie
> Aprile's widow, Rosalie. Ralphie ingratiates himself with her son
> Jackie Jr. by paying him for helping beat up a debtor. New York boss
> Johnny Sack moves to a mansion in New Jersey. Svetlana sets two
> Russian thugs upon Janice to recover her artificial leg. Dr. Melfi is
> beaten and raped in her office parking tower. When the rapist is
> released on a technicality Melfi considers unleashing Tony's justice.

The most powerful episode to date centers on the fragile state of our
civilization. Dr. Melfi's rape is shot to emphasize her pain and—in the last
view—her exposure and helplessness. The legs so elegantly crossed in her
sessions with Tony here tighten in pain and shame. She is outraged when
the rapist is freed on a technicality—then again when she finds him Employee of the Month.

Despite his name, Jesus Rossi represents another world than Jennifer's.
Where the episode emphasizes Richard's careful preparation of a special
chicken dinner, Rossi works in one fast-food chain and is arrested in another. Both pale beside the New Vesuvio restaurant where Tony's gang
holds their better meetings. But Rossi's savagery connects both worlds.

In the episode's last scene, Melfi fights off the temptation to tell Tony
what happened to her. He would deliver a justice that the law failed to
provide. "What," Tony asks, "I mean, you wanna say something?" Melfi
is sorely tempted to unleash Tony on Jesus (!) Rossi. But she chooses silence,

to respect the ideal of law and order. This contrasts to the *omertà* of Tony's world, silence outside/against the law. In a hard close-up the episode ends on her climactic "No."

The central issue is Melfi's wavering faith in legal control, the benchmark of civilization. Here they discuss the "traffic accident" that injured her:

MELFI: You can't control everything that happens.
TONY: But you can get pissed off.
MELFI: And then what? You lose control?

Her rape reveals how fragile our civilization is. The act itself is savage. So is its aftermath. Melfi, Richard (her ex-husband, now back in her life), and their son Jason all lose their faith in justice. They want to take the law into their own hands. This desire increases when the rapist is freed because a misplaced evidence kit violated the chain of custody. On the blind scales of Justice that procedural violation outweighed Melfi's.

The rape shivers Melfi's relationship with Richard. She senses that he blames her for the rape, for ignoring his advice not to go alone at night to the parking lot. In return, she blames him for distracting her on the phone just before the rape: "You and your fuckin' hard-on about my patient [Tony]." And: "You should have seen your face when you heard the fuckin' shitbag who raped me had an Italian name." Richard's self-esteem is so weak that he cannot bear the idea of a countryman's transgression. Because of his anger at the Italian-American stereotype he cannot accept any Italian-American guilt.

Before the rape, the danger in Melfi's dealing with Tony was one of Richard's two preoccupations. Like her therapist, Dr. Kupferberg, Richard urged her to refer him to a behavioral therapist. Richard's second preoccupation is with the media's representation of Italian-Americans, which is a widespread concern about *The Sopranos* itself. For Melfi, Italian-Americans are "an advertisement for The American Experiment. We did great." But Richard is adamant: "Hollywood tries to give these sociopaths the tragic grandeur of Al Pacino." That, of course, Silvio changes to comedy.

The rape provokes vicious impulses in the two educated Italian-Americans who feel slandered by the gangster stereotype. Richard would kill Rossi but "they'd put me in jail, that's how messed up things are." Essentially, the good doctor Richard is now in Tony's camp, lacking only the courage to take the law into his own hands. Melfi's intellectual (well, at least deconstructionist) son Jason slips immediately into savagery: "I'm gonna kill those motherfuckers"—a colloquialism truer here than normally—"A bunch of animals running wild and they're winning." This is the Jason who was embarrassed when his mother fumed at the woman smoking in the restaurant (II, 11).

The psychoanalytic Melfi discovers her desire for Soprano justice in a dream. When her arm is stuck in an Acme Cola vending machine, whose operative coin is raw macaroni, Jesus Rossi comes to rape her again. This time he is attacked by a vicious Rottweiler, which at first threatened Melfi. As she tells Kupferberg, the breed descended from the Romans' guard dog, with hulking shoulders and brute power—the image of Tony. The dream restores the relief and safety that she lost in the rape.

Acknowledging she's been "charmed by a sociopath," Melfi is persuaded to pass Tony on to a behavioral therapist. But after her rape, when Tony agrees, she blurts out "No." Perhaps her experience and frustration have given her a visceral understanding of him. Or she may need to stay connected to his power, for assurance if not deployment.

Accordingly, there is no civility in Melfi's language. "The justice system is fucked up, Elliot," she tells her therapist. Richard is spending $300 an hour for a lawyer to investigate the dropped charges "while that Employee of the Month cocksucker is back on the street and who's going to stop him, you?" Though she "won't break the social compact," Melfi assures Elliot, she takes immense "satisfaction in knowing I could have that asshole squashed like a bug if I wanted." Gangster films provide their audience with a vicarious appreciation of illegal justice (as Chase observes on the Season One DVD interview). So we share Melfi's pleasure at that thought— and probably hope she will overcome her scruples and sic Tony after Rossi.

That temptation swells in the last scene, after she breaks down and is consoled by Tony. In the episode's last word—"No"—she suppresses it. If this elegant psychiatrist cannot control her anger then that other great experiment—civilization—will also have failed. So, rejecting Tony's reflex of consolation, she urgently detaches herself: "Go. Sit over there. Don't do this. Go. . . . It's just my knee."

Jennifer Melfi's attack is paralleled by Janice's assault by the Russian thugs sent to retrieve Svetlana's "pathetic leg" (as Irina correctly mispronounces "prosthetic"). After Jennifer recognizes her freed rapist and spills her drink, we cut to Janice struggling with the chords for "I can't get no satisfaction."

Though Janice is far more negative and less innocent than Jennifer and all she suffers is a few broken ribs and the loss of those record sales, their cases connect. The Russians' "justice" confirms the danger of the vigilante. The different cases of Jennifer and Janice and our very different estimations of the women and their predicaments complicate any simple view of illegal justice.

Janice is not enhanced when her assault makes her a Born Again Christian, because she is obviously self-unaware and faddist. Before "the man I loved died," she says, "I was functioning at a very high level." Now that she has hit bottom, "it's odd, I feel Born Again in the Lord." Tony lists her previous conversions. Janice's religion is a hollow parody of Jennifer's faith in civilization.

As usual, the comic language replays the serious concerns. Melfi's increasingly violent language conveys the tension between civility and brutishness (or, *Civilization v. Its Real Contents)*. More comical is this restaurant exchange:

RALPHIE: I'm the guy who's dating your mom.
JACKIE: 'Dating'?
RALPHIE: Don't get fuckin' filthy about it!

The language in this series may be of unprecedented vulgarity for television, but it often has a poetic wit and it constantly embodies the tension between the free and the forbidden. These wiseguys speak as they live—like unchained maladies.

So, too, the barrage of jokes about Johnny Sack's fat wife are curtailed when he enters. The Fat Woman jokes—funny in a puerile way—would normally confirm the Boys Club atmosphere of the Bada Bing/ Satriale's. In context, however, their brutalism is on the same spectrum as the Russians' assault of Janice and Rossi's rape of Melfi.

The jokes against Ginny Sack are qualitatively different and worse than the "Fat Fuck" sobriquets given Pussy and Bobby. Cruel, superior, and misogynous, the Fat Woman jokes express the disrespect that enables the violence against women. When Johnny interrupts those jokes, their viciousness contrasts to his dignity and warm authority. Our sympathy shifts further when we learn (in III, 8) that Ginny used to be "some hoofer" and now needs therapy for her physical condition.

In any case, the violent context undermines the traditional humor. What in another episode might have seemed harmless bawdry here occurs on the spectrum that leads to Janice's assault and Jennifer's rape. Similarly, Furio's pornographic magazine is quietly contrasted to the broken Melfi's *New*

Yorker. This humor makes a case for rather wider "behavior modification" than just Tony's.

There is no language in the end-credit song this time, Daniel Lanois's "Fisherman's Daughter." After Melfi's "No" has recovered a more honorable code of silence than the gangsters' *omertà,* we get a wordless blues.

The two women's assaults overshadow the activities in Tony's business world. But there are other Employees of the Month. To control the impetuous Ralphie and to maintain order, Tony makes Gigi captain of the Aprile family. Tony's attempts to keep Jackie from the criminal world are thwarted by the kid's laziness (He drops out of Rutgers) and his eagerness to work for Chris and Ralphie. Though Jackie wet his pants as the getaway driver, Chris still endorses him (perhaps because he remembers his similar embarrassment when he was beaten).

For all its seriousness, the episode still ripples with lighter ironies. The FBI hears Tony kiss Chris: "I love you. You're a good boy." The unerringly wrong FBI agents try to identify "Lord Fuckpants," Chris's one-off reference to Jackie. Tony's anxieties about Johnny Sack's ominous moving to Jersey reflect in Silvio's comment about another breakdown of civilized order, the fatal soccer stampede in Zimbabwe: "Unassigned seating, always a problem." The episode introduces Ralphie's infatuation with *Gladiator* (Ridley Scott, 2000): "What we do in life echoes through eternity." However comical, that quote is our last word on Rossi's, Ralphie's, Jackie's, and Janice's action—and on Melfi's silence.

■ The name of Melfi's detective, Piersol, may allude to baseballer Jim Piersall, whose memoir *Fear Strikes Out* was the subject of Tony's school book review (III, 2). The allusion contrasts Melfi's courage to Janice's religiosity in responses to fears.

■ In a comic version of contrasting cultures, Furio tells Ralphie that Pope jokes "don't translate" in Italy. Of course, it is rather a question of faith than of language.

III, 5:   Another Toothpick

Written by Terence Winter. Directed by Jack Bender.

Carmela joins Tony's therapy session, with little success. When a black cop gives Tony a speeding ticket, he has him demoted. Carmela's Uncle Febbie dies of cancer. Minor hood Mustang Sally brutishly assaults an Aprile gang member, then calls on his godfather, Bobby Baccala Sr., for help. The old man dies in a car crash after whacking him. Uncle Junior reveals he has stomach cancer. Artie admits he loves Adriana, plans a partnership with Tony, and pushes Charmaine toward divorce.

While the intermingling of weakness and power is a running concern throughout the series, here it moves front and center. In this episode, success and failure are inextricable. Tony, Artie, and Uncle Junior assert their authority—despite their mortal impotence. The paradox is caught in Ralphie's quotation from his beloved *Gladiator:* "In this world or the next, I shall have revenge." We postulate "the next world" because we know our powers and effect are so limited in this one.

The episode's title is what Livia remarked whenever someone died of cancer. As Janice and Tony over wine contemplate Uncle Junior's cancer, she explains that in the face of futility black comedy gives us the illusion of control: "You say the most horrible shit you can think of in the face of tragedy." In that spirit Ralphie jokes about the crony in a coma: "Look at the bright side. He wasn't that smart to begin with." Ralphie is called heartless—by the men who proceed to eat the patient's box of chocolates.

The opening scene in Dr. Melfi's office seems to continue the silence from the previous close, until the pan reveals Carmela's presence. She says she is frustrated with Melfi's inability to help Tony. Feeling targeted, Carmela suggests he carries unresolved guilts. Sticking his "dick into anything with a pulse" could be "a root cause." Tony still transfers blame. When Melfi observes, "You're both very angry," he wheels upon her: "You must've been at the top of your fuckin' class." Later, Janice may sense another source of Tony's guilt when she asks what really happened to Pussy. Tony spurns her invitation to pray with her.

In the story of the cop Wilmore—a man who is bigger than Tony and with more will and moral fiber—Tony's power brings him more guilt. After flashing his Policeman's Benevolent card and offering dinner for the cop and his wife do not cancel Tony's speeding ticket, he gets Assemblyman Zellman to do it. Wilmore is demoted to the Property Room and loses his overtime. Tony has second thoughts when he finds Wilmore working as a junior clerk in a garden statuary store.

Zellman assures him that Wilmore deserves demotion. He is a "rabble rouser" with mental problems (that is, unwillingness to be bribed). Tony may feel some sympathy—or even empathy—for the wound-up trouble-maker. But he feels validated when a black hood steals Meadow's 10-speed bike. Tony rejects Meadow's argument that black crime is an economic and class issue, not racial. When Zellman offers to cancel Wilmore's punishment, Tony decides: "Fuck him. He deserves what he got."

When they next meet at the store Wilmore declines Tony's charity—more firmly than Beansie. Having flexed his power over Wilmore, Tony is reduced by his conscience. In the last shot, as Tony walks away, he shrinks among the garden statues, which are as macho/phallic as the gangsters' cigars but less flattering.

Artie lives out a similar frustration in the face of success. His flourishing restaurant and Tony's offer of a packaged food business cannot assuage his suffering over Adriana. His joy from a profitable night is deflated when she quits her job. His waspish teasing provokes Christopher to threaten him with a fork. Tony shifts from rough anger at Artie's baiting Chris to affectionate sympathy after Artie says he loves Adriana. Consoling him, Tony kisses Artie's bald head, a reminder that the older man's quest is hopeless—even if he does wear an earring. Having pushed Charmaine to leave him, Artie is spurned by Adriana at her "retirement" dinner.

In contrast, 68-year-old Bobby Baccala Sr., who coughs relentlessly and red from his lung cancer, snatches one last success from the smoking jaws of death. Baccala is a surprise guest at Febbie's funeral. First, as Mustang Sally's godfather (no film allusion intended), he approves Tony's move against the hood. When Baccala seems the only person who can get to him he eagerly accepts the contract. It's the feeble old man's last shot at authority. This murder gives him "something to live for." There is more honor in Baccala's taking the job than in the upstart Jackie's and the irreverent Ralphie's offers.

After finishing the messy job, Bobby celebrates by lighting up a cigarette in the kitchen. With America's "Sister Golden Hair" on the car radio, he enjoys another to the phrase "I just can't live without you," despite his machine-gun cough. Stooping for his bloodied atomizer he blacks out and has his fatal crash, to the lyric "just can't make it." The car radio music implacably reflects an old hero's pathetic end—or a pathetic man's heroic end. Old Bobby is at once dignified and pathetic in his last hit. But that's the human condition here: a success and a failure in the same moment. Bobby Sr. knows what Charmaine tries to teach Artie: "Be happy in thine own self."

Uncle Junior is not. His cancer makes him more belligerent than usual. He is uncharacteristically humorless at Febbie's funeral, snapping at innocent observations. He rejects Bobby Jr.'s sadness about his dying father: "All this goddam morbidity." Having promised to spare old Bobby the assignment ("I'm still the boss of this family"), he saves face by telling Bobby Jr. he decided not to tell Tony to cancel it: "Some things are a matter of duty."

When he hears of old Baccala's death Uncle Junior runs amok. He hoped Bobby Sr. would die of cancer, not a car accident, so that the "comes in threes" would exclude Junior. This superstition is also articulated in Janice's Catholicism. Bobby Jr. doesn't understand Uncle Junior until he explains why he won't attend Baccala's funeral: "You selfish fuck, I can't go because I'm sick. I've got cancer." The opening insult to the orphaned Bobby qualifies under Janice's "the most horrible shit you can think of in the face of tragedy."

Or, as Tony describes those old-timers, "the more hard-assed their attitude the more they can suppress their feelings." Uncle Junior tries to keep his cancer secret, but such a fact will out. Tony immediately tells Janice and Junior himself has to tell Bobby Jr. As Uncle Junior and Artie demonstrate, and as Dr. Melfi has been telling Tony, strong feelings will make their own release, often in the violence of action or language.

Two statements emerge from the movie Junior is watching on TV when Bobby Jr. leaves for his father's funeral. The first is the standard Soprano response to a death: "But what can you do?" In the second Frank Sinatra's character rushes off with "Lady, I missed the boat a long time ago." That's the human condition.

On the other hand, as if to remind us there is a sympathetic God out there, Meadow unwittingly takes the FBI's painstakingly bugged lamp away to her college dorm. She's of the Old School, too: the new-fangled halogen gives her a headache.

III, 6: University

Written by Terence Winter and Salvatore Stabile. Directed by Allen Coulter.

Tony is unwillingly drawn into the life of one of the Bing dancers, Tracee. When she is killed by her pimp/lover, Ralphie, though he is "a made guy" the enraged Tony beats him up. Meadow is troubled by her roommate Caitlin's morbid hyper-sensitivity. Noah introduces Meadow to his father, then breaks up with her.

This powerful episode extends the critique of male power and cruelty from III, 4, where Melfi's rape went unpunished. The show intercuts two stories about young women completing their education. Meadow's college experience includes a neurotically obsessive woman, roommate Caitlin, and the hot-and-cold loving of the self-serving Noah. Meanwhile, the 20-year-old pole-dancer Tracee learns the dangerous folly of her romantic naiveté and her hot-and-cold Ralphie, who kills her.

This episode is framed by the pole-dancers' song, "Livin' on a Thin Line" by The Kinks. The ballad states that stories of past wars don't mean much anymore. Heroic sagas are "all the lies we were told." At the end it leaves us "livin' on a thin line," wondering "What are we supposed to do?" In this episode, even the idealists—like Noah Tannenbaum—are severely compromised.

The Kinks's wisdom notwithstanding, Ralphie foolishly plays at the heroic style of *Gladiator*. In the first Friday-night Executive Club party at the Bing, Ralphie enters high on (among other things) that movie's rhetoric: "I have come to reclaim Rome for my people" and the more prophetic "You are all dead men." He attacks doorman Georgie with a pool-cue spear and then a chain, injuring ("It was an accident.") his eye. At the Sopranos' dinner, Ralphie says he would have been an architect if he hadn't had to drop out of high school to raise his siblings. Despite Tony's skeptical smile, Ralph sees himself an empire-builder, after the glory of Rome. He's so committed to *Gladiator* that he ridicules Chris's recommendation, (the far superior) *Spartacus* (Stanley Kubrick, 1960). But all that emperor Ralphie rules is Tracee, his whore, whom he destroys.

To his later regret, Tony rejects Tracee's attempts at friendship. He refuses the date and walnut bread she baked to thank him for suggesting she take her son to a doctor. He spurns her after Ralphie's ruckus interrupts Tony's blowjob and again when she comes naked to show him her—new dental braces (which Silvio has funded instead of the usual breast implants). When she confides her pregnancy Tony recommends she abort, because of Ralphie's unreliability.

But Tracy finds no support in her world. Avuncular Silvio drags her back to work from Ralphie's apartment, where she has been sick, slaps her, and insists, "Until you pay what you owe, that shaved twat of yours belongs to me." Ralphie's laugh at her abuse flows over into Rosalie's dinner for Tony, Silvio and their wives.

At the end Ralphie attacks Tracee for insulting him in front of his friends. First he feeds her romantic fantasy, promising to help her have her baby and to get a little house for them. Her hopes thus raised, he dashes them. When she resists he goes at her viciously. Fired by her taunting— "That makes you feel good? You feel like a man?"—he kills her in a painfully prolonged beating. He walks away with a cold "Look at you now," then tells the gang she fell down and hurt herself.

Tony tells Dr. Melfi and Carmela that he is troubled by the death of "a young man" who worked for him. It was "a work-related deat'." In Tony's Jersey English, Tracee's death is indeed a debt. He missed several opportunities to help her.

Meadow's roommate Caitlin is as helpless as Tracee. Her initial NYC party craze has brought her down. "I have nowhere to go," she apologizes, when she returns to find Noah and Meadow on the bed. Caitlin is freaked out by *Freaks* (Noah is correct: Tod Browning, 1932). Growing up in an Oklahoma small town has not prepared her for people who find amusement in others' pain, or for a bag lady who wears newspaper underwear. "I think I miss my ferrets." As self-destructive as Tracee, Caitlin compulsively plucks out her hair.

Though Noah at first seems sensitive toward Caitlin, he abandons her after her blathering results in his writing a C-essay. Noah lets his lawyer father file a restraint order against her. This erases Meadow's earlier impression that Noah was "sweet. Most guys wouldn't give a shit." He doesn't either. In contrast, Meadow cares enough to take along her Exacto-knife when she leaves Caitlin to go upstairs to Noah.

When Meadow—impressed but not intimidated—meets Noah's high-roller father at a posh restaurant, she translates her father's waste management to "Environmental clean-up." In his dealing with Tracee Tony fails to live up to that. On Noah's social ladder—exemplified by his father's dinner—"Everybody's Jumpin' " (The Dave Brubeck Quartet). When Noah says his father is "in the business" (III, 2), he means show business, as if only that business matters. As an entertainment lawyer he's on the other side from Tony. As in entertainment "the business" subsumes everything from law and PR to the actual production, Tony's "business" subsumes all its variously respectable fronts. Again, the legal and illegal worlds reflect each other.

After Meadow's first lovemaking with Noah she is joyful when she comes home to Carmela and Tony the next morning. Comfortable in her new maturity, Meadow proposes that she and Carmela recapture her youth by going to see the new Eloise movie scheduled for Christmas release. This contrasts to I, 1, where she spurned her mother's invitation to their annual

New York trip, with tea at the Plaza Hotel under Eloise's portrait. Meadow's new sense of experience allows her to return to that innocence. The cut to the Bada Bing pole dancers reminds us she is still far from her father's world.

Meadow is unprepared for the way Noah breaks up with her. As they study together in the library, he simply states that he doesn't want to see her any more, because she's too negative: "You have this underlying cynicism about everything." He then returns to his book. The show does not idealize Meadow's black/Jewish lover. Though Tony is wrong to have opposed the boy, he proves to be as arrogant, exploitative and misogynous as the boys at the Bada Bing. Back home Meadow conceals her upset in the adolescent's belligerent anger ("Isn't there anything to eat in this house?"), at which Tony and Carmela exchange a knowing glance.

By interweaving the stories of Meadow, Caitlin and Tracee, the episode explicitly connects the worlds of the haves and the have-nots, across a range of female sensitivity and vulnerabilty. Tracee's proud new braces pathetically parallel Meadow's cavalier attitude toward her dental appointment. The scene-bridge of Ralphie's callous laughter contrasts Tracee's bondage to Silvio with the Dante/Aprile/Soprano plenty. Carmela's anecdote about an empty milk carton is a complacent parody of poverty. Caitlin's comfortable small-town upbringing and Meadow's affluence are opposite antitheses to Tracee's life of abuse.

The editing confirms these parallels. In successive shots Tracee and Meadow walk to their respective doors. We cut from the bag lady's newspaper undies to Paulie's wad of bills, from Tracee forced to fellate a cop to Caitlin raising her head from a pillow. From Meadow's snuggling in bed with her mother, discussing Noah, we cut to Tracee desperately asking Tony for advice about her pregnancy. After Tracee's murder we cut from the dark ravine behind the Bada Bing to Meadow's sunny campus. The point is that Meadow's world—the haves—draws its advantage, money, and strength from the exploitation in Tracee's world—the have-nots. Tony's "taste" from Ralphie's pimping of Tracee supports Meadow's college.

The episode ends with the Bing's eye-patched doorman Georgie admitting a new student into the Executive Club. Here the registration fee is "$50 plus a blowjob later." Even more chilling, the other dancers know what happened to Tracee but they're cowed to *omertà*, too. They live on a thinner line than the rest of us.

III, 7:   Second Opinion

Written by Lawrence Konner. Directed by Tim Van Patten.

Though Uncle Junior's cancer surgery is successful his surgeon recommends a second operation for malignant residue. After Tony urges him to seek "a second opinion," he opts for chemotherapy instead. Christopher's probation creates tensions with Paulie. Meadow's dean at Columbia takes Carmela to lunch to solicit a donation toward the new Students Center. After meeting alone with Dr. Melfi Carmela has a session with one of Melfi's old teachers. He recommends she leave Tony.

There are several "second opinions" in this episode. Usually that is recommended because even an expert can be wrong. After all, Chris and Paulie both err on their women's shoe sizes. AJ is glad he took his parents' "second opinion" and took the school trip to Washington, D.C.—because the hotel had some cool video games.

Matters of the heart especially invite an additional perspective. Where Meadow thinks that in Noah she lost "a wonderful man because of Dad," we might advise that she was well rid of the self-serving and self-righteous twit—notwithstanding his film scholarship. More discreetly, Meadow declines Carmela's invitation to express her view of her parents' marriage.

The "second opinion" also suggests human inconsistency. Thus Chris can be irate that in his 2 a.m. check, Paulie sniffs Adriana's panties, and yet betray her himself. As Paulie notes his premature adultery, "You're not even married yet, you're dipping into whores already?" Paulie agrees to respect the sanctity of Chris's marriage to Adriana: "As of her wedding day, anything that touches her pussy is off limits." As Tony admits, Paulie "can be a little quirky."

The only literal "second opinion" involves Uncle Junior's medical situation. This is the sense in which Melfi used the term re: her failed starter (I, 6). Tony suggests talking to another doctor before continuing with the surgery-happy Dr. John ("Cut, zip, over and out") Kennedy. Uncle Junior's devotion to that surgeon derives from his worship of the deceased president of the same name. As for the prosecution of Hoffa and his Teamsters, "That was the brother." This episode abounds with such hairline moral distinctions (e.g., the sanctity of marriage, above and below).

Dr. Mehta recommends the chemo, even though it may not avoid further surgery. The consensus board also recommends this, but only after Dr. Kennedy petulantly withdraws: "Mehta? . . . The last thing I need is to operate with that little shit looking over my shoulder." Apparently, you don't have to be a gangster to be profane, high-handed, self-serving, racist and undependable.

Normally "second opinions" are viewed less favorably in Tony's world, because they undermine the clear lines of authority. Tony smashes Angie's car with a baseball bat because, having spent his money on a Cadillac, she complained to Carmela that she needs $1,200 for her poodle's operation. "If you have a problem bring it to me, not Carmela." Similarly, Paulie threatens Chris if he ever again takes "any shit between us" to Tony.

To ease the atmosphere Paulie buys a fish that sings "YMCA" for the Bing office. That's another, unwitting "second opinion." Earlier Tony was so upset by the Bing fish that sang Annie Lennox's "Take Me to the River" that he smashed it on Georgie, still showing his wounds from Ralphie's equally irrational assault. Tony associates the song with Pussy, who now sings with the fishes instead of to the Feds. Ralphie's violence in the previous episode is disturbingly echoed in Tony's attack on Georgie and in Chris's attack on Adriana (when she recalls fellating Penn—of Penn and Teller—"the big one"—in an Atlantic City washroom). The context provides a "second opinion" on all these characters.

Sometimes Tony is enhanced by a "second opinion." When Carmela's mother bad mouths him after a disrupted Sunday dinner, Carmela reminds her parents of the behind-the-scenes help he has given them: "I earn it, you two get a free pass." Her mother's constant criticism of Tony again recalls *GoodFellas*, where the hero's wife (Lorraine Bracco, as it happens, pre-Melfi) is similarly torn between her unreliable husband and her critical mother.

Despite Uncle Junior's adoration, Dr. Kennedy does not answer Junior's phone calls until Tony and Furio confront him on the golf course, offer him a titanium club, and threateningly back him into the water trap: "Show that man the respect he deserves. Answer his phone calls." Dr. Kennedy drops in on Uncle Junior's treatment, compliments his doctor, and leaves his home number to call if he ever needs him (echoing Tony's earlier promise of help). In dealing with Dr. Kennedy, Tony's repellent criminal ways are attractively effective.

The most dramatic "second opinion" comes from the therapist whom Melfi recommends to Carmela. The white-bearded Dr. Krakower is a moral traditionalist, in complete contrast to the non-judgmental Melfi. Her airy modern office contrasts to the book-lined room in his home, with a glowing fireplace and a Freud-like (if not Freudian) clutter of personal objects and mementos. Melfi's therapist, Dr. Kupferberg, also leans toward the suspect modern, with large abstract paintings behind him and her (II, 9). Where Melfi recommends self-help books, Krakower prescribes Dostoyevsky's *Crime and Punishment*. In contrast to Melfi's intermittent marriage to Richard, this doctor has been married for 31 years. His Jewish respect for the sanctity of marriage matches Carmela's (not to mention Tony's, Christopher's and Paulie's) Catholic.

After Melfi's liberalism, her teacher's advice sweeps through like an Old Testament prophet's rage: "A depressed criminal, prone to anger, serially unfaithful, is that your definition of 'a good man'?" He implicitly criticizes Melfi's tolerance: "Many patients want to be excused for their current predicament because of events that occurred in their childhood. That's what psychiatry has become in America. Visit any shopping mall or ethnic pride parade to witness the results." Tony's whores "are probably the least of his misdeeds."

Dr. Krakower advises Carmela to follow her initial impulse "and consider leaving" Tony. Otherwise she will never feel good about herself or escape the guilt and shame of being his "enabler," if not his "accomplice." When she cites Father Phil's advice to "Work with him to make him a better man," the Old Shrink cogently replies: "How's that going?" Sensible virtue can also be pragmatic. Dr. Krakower's conclusion is devastating: "I'm not charging you because I won't take blood money. You shouldn't either. One thing you can't say—that you haven't been told." It is not that Melfi is wrong. The traditionalist—genuinely of the Old School—is more substantial. He speaks with moral heft.

When Junior is irked by Dr. Kennedy's neglect, Bobby consoles him: "What are you going to do? These doctors—it's not like on TV." As it happens, we see them on TV, albeit in a show that's not like what's usually on TV, not just for including Junior's barf but for the complexity and ambivalence of its moral vision.

At the heart of this episode is the antithesis of the two Dr. K's. Kennedy is the ultra-modern doctor of science, hustling stock deals between his brisk surgeries and his leisurely golf, who is self-serving and corrupt even when he falls back on principle. Krakower is the old-fashioned moralist, modest, selfless, who stands on the literature of spiritual awareness and moral responsibility.

At the end of the episode Tony finds Carmela curled asleep on the sofa in daylight. Having retreated from divorce, she has asserted herself against him in another way, by committing to a $50,000 donation to Columbia, when Tony approved only five. Dean Ross—a second-generation Italian-American, a bobbed Rossetti, also from New Jersey—and his "Development" project Tony has dismissed as "those Morningside Heights gangsters." At first Tony won't pay: "I know too much about extortion." But when Tony finds Carmela depressed he submits to her shakedown, for Meadow's "protection" at Columbia. Carmela will continue to take the "blood money." If Columbia University courts it, why shouldn't she?

When she and Tony walk away in the last shot, Carmela is cocooned in her heart-covered blanket. It is a parody of feeling warmed by love. In the foreground, two candlesticks form a profane altar that honors the blood money—and now and then puts it to respectable use. In another secular parallel to lost idealism, the song over the credits—Nils Lofgren's "Black Books"—reminisces about tender moments, a lost love gone because of "too many different needs to satisfy." "She wants new shoulders to cry on, New back seats to lie on," and "She always gets her way." The song plays over Carmela's troubled solitude when she waits outside Meadow's room, then at the end. There are second opinions on Carmela, too. One has her a corrupted idealist, the other a virtuous pragmatic. But, as David Chase remarks of her hospital scene with Tony in I, i, Carmela "made a deal with the devil" (Season One DVD, disc four).

When Tony coerces Dr. Kennedy to accept the titanium golf club, the doctor backs down from his principled refusal of a gift: "Well, I could use a little extra distance." "Who couldn't?" Tony agrees. This episode is about keeping one's distance from corruption (for example, Tony). Angie, Meadow, Dean Ross, Uncle Junior, Chris and Adriana, Carmela and her parents, and now Dr. Kennedy—all profit from Tony's corruption. Only Dr. Krakower keeps a morally proper distance—which is utterly to reject him and his money. When Carmela paraphrases his advice as defining her border and keeping "a certain distance," he corrects her. That mealy-mouth advice she got from her priest. Dr. Krakower requires the total rejection of Tony and his money—however charming and helpful they might respectively be. When Dr. Kennedy accepts Tony's gift he is caught in his water trap.

III, 8: He Is Risen

Written by Todd Kessler. Directed by Allen Coulter.

After Ralphie snubs Tony, Tony has Carmela cancel their Thanksgiving invitation to Rosalie and Ralphie. Johnny Sack persuades Ralphie to apologize. When the stressed captain Gigi has a fatal heart attack on the toilet, Tony makes Ralphie captain. Meanwhile, Meadow and Jackie Aprile Jr. start courting when Jackie gives her Ecstasy (the drug). Tony starts an affair with one of Melfi's patients, a Mercedes-Benz salesperson named Gloria.

As the title suggests, this episode originally ran on Easter Sunday. At Tony's Thanksgiving dinner, when Janice's new boyfriend, Aaron, snaps out of his narcolepsy to meet Jackie, Aaron's instinctive greeting is "Have you heard the good news? He is risen." Aaron himself periodically rises, only to sink back into sleep. This line provides the episode's unifying metaphor.

There are a variety of "rises" here, of which only Aaron's is Easterly. The most bathetic is Jackie's romancing of Meadow. On their first night together his "rise" ("I can't stop now") is thwarted when Meadow passes out from excessive tequila and the prophylactically named Ecstasy. At the end, after Meadow crashes his car, she asks to go to his place. As in his Uncle Richie's courtship of Janice, Jackie's interest in Meadow is shaded by his opportunity to rise in her father's gang. Tony's power also requires Jackie treat Meadow with extra care and respect, but the boy falls short.

Rosalie, Janice, and (more reservedly) Carmela are eager for this union. It would serve Tony's undertaking to care for his old boss's son. But despite their parents' encouragement, the teenagers are attracted to each other. Jackie's casual attitude toward both college and integrity prove him more interested in the Family than in the family connection. This "rise" begins his downfall. Jackie's interest in men's fashion design is like Chris's earlier dreams of Hollywood. Jackie doesn't want to do anything but "to be Hugo Boss."

The most obvious "rise" is the advent of Rosalie Aprile's new live-in boyfriend. Ralphie's tap on the construction industry gives him a new prominence—and a dangerous self-importance. As a "made" colleague, he is properly angered that Tony slapped him in public—"Rules are rules. Otherwise, what—fuckin' anarchy"—even though he was wrong to murder his whore, Tracee. Ralphie is equally at odds with Tony in mentoring Jackie, offering to provide him with Ecstasy and in a later episode giving him a gun.

In Tony's charge—"He showed disrespect for the Bing"—he places the club ahead of Tracee, suppressing his rueful sentiment. The same order is found in Ralphie's apology: "I disrespected the Bing—and the girl." Even Johnny Sack shares this misogyny: "But she was a whore, Tony." It is to Tony's credit that he feels so troubled about Tracee's death. When he and Ralphie finally meet the song behind them is "Ghost Riders in the Sky," as if Tracee were a spectral presence.

For most of the episode Ralphie chafes against Tony, even asking Johnny Sack about switching families. In their reconciliation, Ralphie is awkward and Tony rigid. His authority cannot let Ralphie go unpunished. But because Ralphie is such a good earner, Tony decides—despite having refused to do so—to promote him to captain. This resolution is prompted by Tony's reading of Sun Tzu's *The Art of War*. Tony finds this medieval Oriental text better on strategy than the "Prince Machiavelli," whose *Cliff's Notes* he has crammed.

In his own resurrection Tony is moved to express his loving concern to Meadow, when her approach with the cake reminds him of the murdered Tracee. Tony sees the parallel between the two women that was implied by the narrative organization of episode III, 6. More broadly, Tony is now so comfortable in his sessions with Dr. Melfi that he chats up one of her patients, Gloria Trillo, when Melfi has double-booked them.

The Mercedes saleswoman is beautiful, apparently poised, witty, strong, and independent, so it is no surprise to see Tony interested in her. Both fib about why they see Melfi. Tony claims to be trying to stop smoking (perhaps a fair metaphor for the Hell-bent), while the more innocent Gloria claims to be criminal: "Serial murderer—I murdered seven relationships." In a pointed coincidence, Uncle Junior remembers her father as a stonemason who had seven daughters. Though Gloria presumably referred to her romantic life, the number confirms the inescapability of family influence.

The episode follows Tony's developing interest in Gloria from their meeting to their consummation. In contrast to the series' opening shot, in this one Tony sits comfortably (though formally) beside the woman on Melfi's waiting room couch. He seems to stand shyly in the background, almost boyish, when Melfi leads Gloria into her office and closes the door on Tony, who has watched them depart. When Carmela mentions the

Meadow-Jackie possibility, Tony is distracted by the Mercedes commercial on television. Not only does Carmela encourage him to buy one, the ad's "Here's how you'll get your thrills" anticipates Uncle Junior's advice: "Take what pleasures you can."

Tony's test-drive with/of Gloria concludes with the camera drawing back discreetly from the tryst, showing Tony's boat (the ever-phallic *Stugots)* on the left and Gloria's Mercedes on the right, parked face-to-face like lovers. The image is of complementary transports of delight, shadowed by betrayal and truancy. This naval encounter and Ralphie's new captaincy share the pretense of submission in the closing song, Kasey Chambers's "The Captain": "You be the captain, I'll be no one."

Finally, Melfi seems on the rise as well, recovering from her rape and its aftermath. She calmly declines Tony's offer to walk her to her car after their after-hours appointment, even though—as she tells her therapist, Elliot— "I almost fell in his arms crying." She complains to Elliot about her whining, unreasonable patient, Gloria, and Melfi's sense that the therapist needs the help she is giving others. Elliot properly praises her strength of will through her terrible trauma.

One brief scene establishes the normalization of the gangsters' life. The black Reverend James arrives to receive his parish's share of the truckload of turkeys Christopher has hijacked. Hesh arrives, concerned about the stories about Ralphie's disrespect for Tony. The tangle of professional and personal betrayals is played out against the background of Thanksgiving, both as an appreciation of life's blessing and as a family event.

Finally, there are two lighter forms of resurrection. One is the running gag about leftover turkey sandwiches—starting at Tony's Thanksgiving dinner itself. The other is the urban resurrection that our heroes are planning to exploit, the huge New Jersey mall construction project. At the center of the Esplanade is the Newark Museum of Science and Trucking, which neatly combines the public and the private interests afoot.

■ Perhaps the only major character in this episode who does not "rise" is the stressed, constipated Gigi Cestore, who dies on the toilet. In the next scene Uncle Junior works up a contrary despair: "I don't give a shit anymore. . . . Everything goes through me." *The Sopranos* abounds with such paronomastic irony.

III, 9:   The Telltale Moozadell

Written by Michael Imperioli. Directed by Daniel Attias.

Carmela enjoys her family's birthday gifts. Christopher makes Adriana manager of the club that Rocco lost on football bets. AJ is punished for being part of a group that vandalized the school swimming pool. Jackie advances his position with Meadow but incurs Tony's paternal ire. Tony and Gloria arouse Dr. Melfi's suspicions.

The two dominant metaphors in this episode are gifts and fucking oneself. They may be related. The mix is even present in the film Tony is watching on TV: *It's a Gift* (1934) is the W. C. Fields classic about domestic afflictions.

With regard to the former, Carmela's birthday gifts are a sapphire ring from Tony, a DVD of *The Matrix* from AJ ("Right up her alley," Tony sarcastically observes), and from Meadow a daylong session at a Soho spa, purchased along with a session for Meadow on Carmela's credit card. Tony brings Gloria a present but impresses her more when he meets her at the zoo. Tony gives Jackie money (strings definitely attached) to buy dessert on his dinner date with Meadow. Tony even tips Dr. Melfi, overriding her refusal, when he pays his monthly bill.

Christopher "gives" Adriana The Lollipop Club, but only to run it; he and Furio remain the silent partners, with a secondary role left the owner/loser, Rocco. Jackie "gives" a friend's friend the illusion that he has secured his Ecstasy sales at that club in return for a kickback. The time Jackie lavishes on the Sopranos—cleaning out their garage, coaching AJ in defensive football—is equally self-serving, to impress Meadow and her parents. Courting Jackie's favor, Ralphie gives him a .38 pistol.

All these "gifts" are motivated by self-service. Though some gifts (AJ's, Meadow's, Jackie's) are more obviously selfish than others, all the gifts serve the giver's interests at least as much as the recipient's. AJ transparently rationalizes when he says he didn't wrap Carmela's gift because "it's wasteful to the environment." That's a falser front than Tony's Waste Management.

The second metaphor is introduced when Paulie, watching a nature TV show with Tony, remarks that because a snake combines both sexes, snakes reproduce spontaneously. That's why untrustworthy people are called snakes: "How can you trust a guy who can literally go fuck themselves?" This truth overrides even the Bible: "Snakes were fuckin' themselves long before Adam and Eve showed up." At the zoo, Gloria and Tony have sex in the snake house.

What joins these metaphors is the idea that people who serve themselves end up screwing themselves. Rocco loses his club because he bet over his head, not with it. Jackie starts on a very slippery slope when he courts Tony's interest by dating Meadow but fails his promises. He averts Tony's discovery at the Bing, but is caught at the casino. Worse, Jackie starts acting like a Godfather (film allusion intended) when, with minion Dino behind him to end the meeting, he agrees to ask his "associate," Christopher, to allow his friend's Ecstasy sales in the club.

When Jackie tells Tony he got an A in his literature paper, he omits that it was the essay Meadow gave him on Edgar Allan Poe. "I never should have taken 'The Literature of Obsession' " course, he tells her. In fact, he needs to learn from that course, to gain perspective on his own obsessions. So the shortcut of Meadow's gift is not in his best interests. When Tony and Jackie hug and kiss at their first parting, they look like twins in their matching black leather bomber jackets. But Jackie aspires to become like Tony, not what Tony wants for his daughter. Jackie lacks the character to grow out of the "gifts" of his family background (the advantages of which Ralphie spoke in III, 6).

The burgeoning romance between Gloria and Tony also serves both metaphors. That is, it is both a gift and self-destructive. Both lovers are so exhilarated that Dr. Melfi senses they are lying to her. Tony seems suspicious when he quotes Gloria's philosophy (another dubious "gift"): "Buddha preached joyful participation in the sorrows of the world." His second-hand Buddhism too easily justifies the neurotic lovers' self-indulgence. Tony does not cite culture well. He hears *Aida* as I EAT HER?

Gloria is especially vulnerable, having tried to commit suicide when her last relationship ended. Now she turns self-righteous when Melfi mentions hearing a man's voice when Gloria cancelled her appointment (That was *Stugots* Tony): "I don't pay you to be under your surveillance." In a similarly defensive response, Tony snaps "What the fuck does she know?" at Jeannie Cuzamano's name for Mercedes-Benz sportscars: "Midlife-Crisis-Mobiles." The adulterer doth protest too much, methinks, especially having just told Carmela he didn't buy a Mercedes because he felt like a douche bag in it.

Rosalie's romance with Ralphie also seems a mixed blessing. At lunch Carmela encourages Rosalie to "hold on to" Ralphie, as if he were not the murderous sociopath who promises her son Ecstasy and provides a .38. The gangster wives see the irony in their marriages surviving that of hardworking, responsible Artie Bucco. But Carmela's explanation—"You can push a man only so far"—undermines her own pretense, that she stays with Tony to make him a better person. In one shot she looks past his kiss to her new sapphire ring. Later Tony looks past Gloria's kiss to see if anyone sees them. In both cases the commitment of the kiss is compromised.

The school's relaxed response to AJ's delinquency is another example of a dangerous gift. After Tony has taken a hard line with his son—"Your football career—down the drain!"—the school suspends his punishment. This scene comes right after Jackie assures his troubled friend that "Chris and me are associates. You got nothing to worry about." The parallel defines the school as also self-serving. The coach contends: "It would be against [AJ's] best interest—and the team's—to sever his relationship" with the football team.

The teacher's "The Wall of Pride: What kind of animals . . ." recalls Carmela's "What kind of animal smokes marijuana at his own confirmation?" (II, 7). After a lawsuit ended detentions, the school may echo the parents' indignation but leaves all punishment to them. The teacher concludes with a hollow threat: AJ will be expelled if he commits just one more violation of the school code. Unless, presumably, the freshman football team still needs him. The school does AJ no favor by declining to take a hard stance. That gift screws him.

In all this flawed humanity, Aaron cites the Lord as the reason he will not drink alcohol. But when Tony cites Jesus's wine Janice responds: "He was Jesus, Tone. You can't make comparisons." The cocaine residue Tony brushes off her nose suggests Janice has accepted her human fallibility and admires the half-dead Aaron's proximity to God. The characters in this episode fall far short of Jesus—and use human imperfection to justify self-indulgence.

■ This episode features Carmela's favorite song, Andrea Bocelli's "Con Te Partiro," at her birthday party. It is also heard in II, 1, and 4.

III, 10:   To Save Us All from Satan's Power

Written by Robin Green and Mitchell Burgess. Directed by Jack Bender.

Under the rush and tensions of approaching Christmas, Tony remembers some gang meetings around Christmas, 1995, when Pussy's mysterious behavior seems to have augured his betrayal. The beautified, free Charmaine continues to work at Artie's restaurant and tells Tony she does not want the gang there. Jackie courts Meadow even after Tony beats him up. Meadow has a disconcerting Christmas gift for Tony.

Like Scrooge in that other seasonal classic, Dickens's *A Christmas Carol*, Tony is haunted by the spirit of Christmas past. In particular—1995, when O. J. Simpson's civil suit dominated the TV news, Tony had hair, and Big Pussy went to Boca to set up a sit-down to reconcile Uncle Junior and Boss Jackie Aprile, whose truck Junior had hijacked. The latter detail casts new light on the Season One episodes when Chris and Brendan robbed trucks under Junior's protection, and he appealed to Boss Jackie for justice.

The memories drip irony. In the first flashback, Jackie tells Pussy "You need money, come to me." Tony urges Pussy not to sell heroin: "Too risky." "I always wanted a house by the ocean," Pussy muses, "Maybe in another life." Pussy missed the sit-down, suspiciously, and that—Tony now realizes—was when the FBI "flipped" him. When Pussy arrived in the Santa suit for the children's party, he was already wearing a wire for the FBI. That's why he tried to talk business and angrily broke the jukebox when he was interrupted. With unknowing prescience, Silvio greeted him with his imitation of Pacino identifying his treacherous brother in *The Godfather Part II:* "It was you, Fredo."

Memories of Pussy give Silvio a nightmare about stolen cheese in the Bing and the dead rat—Pussy—on the floor beneath the sequined costumes. The latter image was set up in the previous episode, when Silvio complained about the problems of running a strip club beyond all the glitz and the glamour.

Of course, they don't make Santas like they used to. In Pussy's absence, Bobby Baccala is coerced into playing Santa, despite protesting "I can't. I'm shy." Bobby's suspicion that one little boy is on his second visit provokes the kid's "Fuck you, Santa." Bobby can't "Ho ho ho." At episode end, the gang agrees that Pussy was a great Santa. But as Paulie concludes (in non-Yule imagery), "I loved that cocksucker like a brother and he fucked me in the ass. . . . The world don't run on love. He was a rat bastard. . . . In the end, fuck Santa Claus." A Santa can smile, and smile, and be a traitor. But so can a husband, as Tony, Silvio, and Paulie compare what they gave their *goomahs* for Christmas.

In more devotional preparation for Christmas, Janice and her Born Again Aaron work on what he calls their "great motherjumping lyric" about Jesus's stain-cleaning blood. "Like Ajax?" Janice wonders. Even their sacred reeks of the profane, especially in Aaron's "motherjumping." Eschewing wine, they drink a jug of grape juice. Janice insists she is sincere in her new faith. Though she and Aaron do not sleep together any more, Christianity is "the fastest-growing marketing sector in the music business today." The episode includes traditional Christmas music as well, for example, Alvin and The Chipmunks' "Christmas Don't Be Late," The Drifters's "White Christmas," and Eartha Kitt's "Santa Baby."

In this comedy of the unholy, in which the O. J. Simpson trial defines the time, Janice is moved to genuine emotion when the television news reports her Russian assailant found severely beaten under Santa's sleigh in a store window display. She guesses who put him there. Waking Aaron from the salad, she announces: "What's missing from the song is the brother concept." Aaron rises to a cliché: "You mean, 'He ain't heavy'?" Janice cries: "Sometimes we don't see our loved ones." Tony's assault on the Russian raises Janice briefly into Yuletide joy.

Of course, Tony's violence was not completely in the Christmas spirit of brotherly love for Janice. Primarily, he had to preserve his own authority. Had he let the assault on his sister pass, he would have lost major face. He did what he had to do.

When Charmaine accuses Tony of making Artie "a friggin' mess," Tony sweeps Chris and Silvio off to a new club, where he finds Jackie under a lapdancer. In the men's room Tony beats him up for his looseness and hypocrisy—and finds his gun. "You bottomed out," he says, leaving him crumpled on the floor from a kneed groin. When Jackie brings the Sopranos the Apriles' Christmas gifts, Tony privately admits he hasn't decided what to do with him yet: "You bullshit me and you betray my daughter." The next episode disproves Jackie's dedication on the locket he gives Meadow: "I will always be true."

Carmela understandably doubts Tony's claim that when he was out all night he was "the monogamy poster boy." With Gloria holidaying in Morocco, he is almost faithful. But now Carmela—haunted by Tony's high school romance—thinks Charmaine is beautifying herself for him. When Tony gives Carmela the $50,000 sapphire bracelet to match her necklace and earrings, she glows with love regained.

To Tony's grateful surprise, Meadow also beams at him—"It's Christmas"—and innocently presents her gift that she wants to see on his desk. The wall-mounted fish turns to sing at him accusingly: "Take me to the river, Drop me in the water. . . ." Despite this symbolic resurrection of Pussy, Tony musters a grateful smile and a kiss for his daughter. Even from his house in the ocean Pussy does not stay silent.

In different ways, all the characters fulfill Melfi's observation. "The pressures we put ourselves under" at Christmas make her call the time "Stressmess." After all, the gang's annual Christmas party for the neighborhood children began in a cognate hypocrisy. Johnny-Boy launched it to ease the resentment when the beloved old Satriale killed himself after Johnny-Boy took over his store. The basic Christmas tradition here is the false front of community. The end credits have a more hopeful song: "Jesus told me, Everything is going to be alright." But then, He never had to live through a family/Family Christmas.

■ In a secular parallel to Janice's stain-removal song, Tony uses the Russian gangster boss to launder $250,000 of personal money in this episode and $200,000 in the next. Clearly, this series is post–Cold War as well as postmodernist.

III, 11:   Pine Barrens

Written by Terence Winter (story by Tim Van Patten and Terence Winter). Directed by Steve Buscemi.

Gloria storms off *The Stugots* after Tony admits fibbing about Irina's phone call. Paulie and Christopher, collecting Silvio's gambling debt from the Russian hood Valery, end up beating him to presumed death. In the frozen wastes of Pine Barrens, South Jersey, they bungle his premature burial and he escapes. They almost freeze to death before Tony and Bobby rescue them. Meadow discovers Jackie's shallowness and infidelity.

This black comedy demystifies the Family. Each of the three plots exposes the illusions of honor and effectiveness both in family and Family life. Here everyone is, in Irina's term, "broken up."

The failed execution of Valery and his chase through the snowy forest are a homage to the Coens' *Miller's Crossing* (1990) and *Fargo* (1996). Our heroes' bungling undercuts the gangsters' pretense to effectiveness. Paulie goes from ordering the "satin finish" on his nails to shivering in the shelter of an abandoned septic tank cleaner's truck, eating frozen packets of catsup and relish, and hoarding his Tic-Tacs. Chris is concussed and Paulie freezing with a shoe lost in the snow. They threaten to kill each other, Chris pulling his gun to break Paulie's stranglehold. Their squabbling and mutual suspicion and Paulie's indignation at having to collect a debt for the sick Silvio deflate their vaunted fraternity. But in the end, Christopher supports Paulie's story.

The arrogance and xenophobia in Paulie's treatment of Valery—with his sneering jokes at Russian technology, overcrowding, rubles, the Cuban missile threat—are destroyed by the indomitable victim's escape. Valery chews his way through the duct tape, overcomes the two armed gunsels, and escapes even after he is shot, apparently in the head. Though he's only wearing what Paulie calls "pajamas" Valery is more comfortable in the frigid wild than his jacketed assailants: "I wash my balls in ice water. This is warm!" The comedy of Bobby Bacala's hunting uniform parallels the epic survival skills of the underdressed Valery.

Paulie's inadequacy is reflected in his confusion. On his crackling cellphone Tony tells him Valery was a commando in the Russian Ministry of the Interior and he killed sixteen Chechins. This Paulie reports to Chris as an interior decorator who killed sixteen Czechoslovakians. As Chris has been haunted by his killing of the Czech Emil, the mistake adds to the nightmarishness of his experience.

Their problem begins when Paulie smashes Valery's universal remote control. For the rest of the episode Paulie struggles to regain control over Valery. He ultimately needs Tony to rescue him from the wilds. Their inconsistent cell-phone connection dramatizes the problems of their remote control, as Tony is continually called away from his family and from Gloria.

Paulie acknowledges he "fucked up," but he clearly resents Tony's criticism. He ends frozen, disheveled, humiliated, and ominously sullen. The question is whether the Russian boss Stava will prove more loyal to Valery, who is "like a brother" to him and who saved his life or, preferring his profitable arrangement with Tony, will excuse his friend's abuse. But Tony makes it clear that Paulie will bear full responsibility for any consequences of Valery's assault and escape.

Meanwhile, Meadow loses her romantic delusions about Jackie. He can contribute only three-letter words to their Scrabble game—"poo," "ass," "the"—and he thinks "oblique" is Spanish. Having told Tony he flunked out of Rutgers, he still lets Meadow think he's at school, though—in defense of his vocabulary—"not an English major." Even after she catches him lying to her and with another woman, Meadow resists her friends' conclusion that he's a "drip" and a jerk: "It's all my fault. I shouldn't have pressured him."

That young couple promised the one oasis of idealism and virtue in the Sopranos' world. But instead of following his dead father's character, Jackie emulates his Uncle Richie, the creep who sought advancement by marrying into the Sopranos. So Jackie complains to his "date" not that he lost his love but that he alienated "Tony Soprano's daughter." Jackie might have transcended the Soprano/Aprile ethos through the idealistic Meadow, but he lacks the moral will.

In their session with Melfi, Tony and Carmela reveal a new openness and harmony. But this marital peace is another illusion because—as Tony admits—it is based on his illicit happiness with Gloria. "As much as I love my wife, being with Gloria makes me happier than all your Prozac and your therapy bullshit combined." His adultery makes him a better husband and a better father, he avows. As in the other two plots, the illusion of harmony and loyalty is punctured by the characters' dishonesty and self-indulgence.

Even the Gloria relationship is brittle. In two scenes she attacks him for his unreliability: "If I wanted to be treated like shit I'd get married." The Moroccan gown she gives him creates an illusion he is at home in her apartment. That ends when he braves her barrage of steak and crockery to rescue Chris and Paulie.

Tony's last session with Melfi is introduced with a close-up of her waiting room statue, the Woman that unsettled Tony in the pilot episode's first shot. Tony tells Melfi that Gloria puzzles him: "Why does everything have to be so hard?" Melfi suggests that Tony is drawn to women like Irina and Gloria—depressive, unstable, impossible to please—because they are like his mother. In a phrase, for whatever fields our heroes are pining, they are barons of the barren.

And whatever happened to Comrade Valery? We don't know. One of this show's virtues is that it leaves some loose ends untied.

- Director Steve Buscemi is an extremely effective actor in such films as *Miller's Crossing, Billy Bathgate, Barton Fink, Reservoir Dogs, Hudsucker Proxy, Pulp Fiction, Dead Man, Fargo, Kansas City, The Big Lebowski,* and *Ghost World*. He directed the films *What Happened to Pete, Trees Lounge,* and *Animal Factory*, as well as episodes of *Oz* and *Homicide*.

III, 12: *Amour Fou*

Written by Frank Renzulli. Directed by Tim Van Patten.

Fearing she has ovarian cancer or is pregnant, Carmela wants to straighten out her life. She seeks counsel from a priest doing a Ph.D. in Psychology. Tony flees Gloria's tantrums, returns, then breaks off for good when he learns she introduced herself to Carmela. Taking his cue from Ralphie's nostalgia and his courage from crack, Jackie jumpstarts his career by robbing a card game. One player is killed, Furio wounded, and Jackie identified. Tony knows what his Captain Ralphie will selfishly need to do about Jackie.

"*L'amour fou*" is how Dr. Melfi identifies the Tony-Gloria affair, with its intensity and wildness—"crazy love, all-consuming"—after Tony has ended it the first time. But the term applies more broadly across this episode. It covers both the intense emotion in Jusepe di Rebera's painting, "The Mystical Marriage of St. Catherine," and Carmela's weeping at the sight of it: "She's so at peace. Beautiful. Innocent. Gorgeous little baby. Come on, let's go eat." At the other extreme, it applies to Jackie's overriding determination to be "made."

In contrast stands the stability of a loving marriage. Dr. Melfi is certain that Tony would never leave Carmela. "Despite your mothering," Carmela was his one good choice in all his relationships with women. And "In spite of everything, you're a very conventional man." Gloria's insulting Carmela—for her homemaking and jewelry—drives Tony to his first violence against her. Her threat to tell Carmela and Meadow of their affair makes him want to kill her. To ensure that she won't, Tony sends Patsy Parisi on a test-drive with Gloria. On a country road Patsy pulls a gun and warns that if she approaches Tony or his family again he will kill her: "My face is the last face you'll see. Not Tony's. It won't be cinematic." Thus Patsy inures Gloria against romantic thoughts of Tony killing her (as she begged him to, under his throttle).

For all his passion, Tony does prove himself the "hard, cold captain of industry type." Though he and Gloria drive each other into rage as well as ardor, in the crunch Tony proves cool. He stops short of killing Gloria when he first wants to. In dispatching Patsy he both defuses the Fatal Romance and measures his response. He shows the same strength when he refuses to let Christopher whack Jackie after the kid robbed and shot at him and wounded Furio. Though Chris charges him with hypocrisy in protecting Jackie, Tony insists he will make his own decision, not accept Chris's. Besides, "Every person you whack, you risk exposure." In an angry clutch that recalls his last scene with Gloria, Tony demands Chris's respect more than his love.

When Ralphie, as expected, comes to see Tony about the missing Jackie, Tony delivers a clinic in management style. As Ralphie is living with Jackie's mother and is nakedly ambitious, and as Jackie is still called Jackie Jr. long after the gang boss's death, Tony is in a very sensitive situation. It's further complicated by Tony's excessive response to Ralphie's murder of Tracee and by Tony having promised Jackie Sr. to look out for his son. Ralphie's strategy is to take the lead in defining the seriousness of Jackie's transgression, then concluding, as if reluctantly: "I want to give the kid a pass." Rather than argue, Tony advises Ralphie to go with his instincts.

However, as Tony elaborates his support for whatever Ralphie, as Captain, decides to do, he plants the seeds that will change Ralphie's mind. Tony is confident Ralphie will be able to handle what Chris and Furio would think of that "pass"—and if not, maybe they do not matter. "Who cares what shit they say, they don't have the balls to say to your face?" True, "The kid disrespected you," but "They don't have to live with your commitments." No one can say it was Ralphie's fault: "You took this kid under your wing. You schooled him the best you could." Then Tony returns Ralphie's .38 that he took from Jackie around Christmas.

By the time Ralphie steps into the clear bright day—the neon Satriale pig-head grinning over his shoulder, as in Chris's murder of Emil—he knows that his own reputation requires him to whack his lover's son.

The Tony Soprano Management Manual must be in the works somewhere.

Ralphie is a bad manager. First, he gives his young charges an unfocused directive: "Three fifty gets you a hello. Watching your back's gonna require a little more initiative." He encourages their foolhardiness with Jackie's father's example: "He wanted it. So he stepped up and took it." Ralphie brags about his own youth, when he, Tony, Silvio, and Jackie Aprile were all small-scale hoods, until Jackie proved his balls—"big as an Irish broad's ass"—by robbing a wheel's card game. Only a case of the clap kept Ralphie from joining that historic escapade. He ends his lecture with an insulting directive—"Rinse your plates before putting them in the dishwasher so they won't clog"—that fires Jackie to prove his manhood at Ralphie's expense. Jackie suggests Ralphie is a latent homosexual, both to bolster his own confidence and to assuage his feelings about his mother's lover. As the Dr. Fried commercial stresses, the entire episode is based on anxiety about potency. The boys want to be men.

Jackie Jr.'s attempt to match his father's "balls" fails. His robbery plays out as a comedy of impotence. His and Dino's first resolve is derailed by Sharon Stone's famous pubic flash in *Basic Instinct* (Paul Verhoeven, 1992) on TV. They're pussies after all. In the event, Furio is wounded so high in the leg as to threaten his manhood. For his safe treatment, Tony calls Dr. Fried, his private(s) doctor, away from taping a commercial for his treatment of erectile dysfunction. Conversely, when Tony sets Ralphie to deal with Jackie, instead of letting Chris assume the risk, Tony prefers method over macho.

As Tony has learned, Gloria and Ralphie are dangerous because they don't play by the rules. Tony initially misread Gloria as strong, independent, not the basket case Melfi knew and tried to counsel. The darkness he saw was in Gloria's eyes—like a Spanish princess in "one of those paintings by Goyim" (that is, *Gentiles,* for *Goya*)—not in the "bottomless black hole" that makes her like Livia. Melfi later defines both women by the "selfishness, incessant self-regard" that "passed for love." Both women kept Tony off-balance by their unpredictable, shifting demands, compelling him always "to try to please her, to try to win her love."

Though she doesn't have the most dramatic scenes in this episode, Carmela and her values may be its primary focus. The opening scene starts with a close-up on her purse and Tony's gift, her green sapphire ring, then broadens to show her striding among the sculptures at the Brooklyn Museum. This recalls the sculpture frame in the waiting room outside her first solo visit to Melfi. Appearing large when the focus is on her wealth/ style/baggage, she is reduced by the cultural and religious context. In the museum, she is defined as vulnerable, physically by her non-menstrual spotting and emotionally when a painting moves her to tears. Later she cries at a dog food commercial that waxes lyrical about the animal's protectiveness. Its brand name, Pedigree, may point to her arriviste life.

Where Dr. Krakower advised she leave Tony, the black priest here insists: "You made a sacred vow. Divorce is out of the question." She should define an area of comfort and self-respect in her marriage and to live within that, foregoing "those things that are without it"—the archaism may be moral as well as linguistic. "Learn to live on what the good part earns" may be a moral compromise but given Tony's laundering system that distinction is impracticable. The priest's glib pragmatism is essentially what the lunching women conclude: Hilary Clinton is "a role model for us all" because she spun all her husband's "negative shit" into gold.

Dean Martin's "Return to me. . . . Hurry home to my heart" plays over several scenes of domestic reconciliation. We hear it early, then again when Rosalie agonizes for news about Jackie, then when Tony returns home, where Carmela recasts her escape in terms of selling real estate and bakes lemon snaps for the church sale. We last hear it when Patsy Parisi lugs the groceries to his car, pausing to assure his wife on his cellular. He drives away, another killer presented as a warm-hearted and supportive husband.

For all her craziness, Gloria is pathetically alone. She feels bereft at banishment from her sister's children. She is bitterly envious of Carmela's children and husband. Gloria is doubly hurt when Tony comes to her office to break up with her and her colleague wants to switch shifts so he can take his kid to the Raffi concert. Patsy and Tony both enjoy the family life she craves but cannot achieve.

Those men's domestic scenes contrast to Gloria's black and testily driven solitude and to Jackie's failure to have through Meadow escaped his origins. Gloria is right when she says Tony has "a fuckin' dream life compared to mine"—but she denies her responsibility for it. The end-credits song—The Lost Boys' "Affection"—speaks for all the episode's lovers and leavers: "Gimme some affection, Why is it so hard? . . . Don't trust no stranger. You should know better." That is the "favorite" song Gloria turns up on the radio during a frolic with Tony. It haunts her at the end.

III, 13: Army of One

Written by David Chase and Lawrence Konner. Directed by John Patterson.

Ralphie finally has Jackie killed, renewing Meadow's doubts about her family. AJ and a friend are expelled for cheating on their geometry mid-term. Affected by Jackie's death, Carmela is finally persuaded to send AJ to a military school, but his panic attack saves him. Uncle

Junior is freed from house arrest. Paulie's discontent with Anthony grows when he loses his arbitration with Ralphie. The FBI assigns an undercover agent to befriend Adriana.

The third season's conclusion focuses on the tension between genetic compulsion and individual responsibility. What latitude does a person have in which to change?

The title refers to the individual strength that the military school aims to develop through its collective enterprise: "Here the higher good is the good of the corps," not the individual student's. The public school system confuses children with "too many options." In his interview with AJ the Major offers "a blueprint for total self-discipline that will take you through your whole life." He tells the parents that the regimentation is less of a factor than the mentoring in small classes and the faculty's involvement in the students' dorm life.

Paradoxically, the military school's values and methods closely parallel the gang's. Even the Major stretches his discipline, when he smokes during his interview with Tony and Carmela—albeit at an open window. There is some truth to Carmela's concern that a military school would "train him to become a professional killer." As Jackie Jr. proves, AJ could learn that at home.

Tony blames AJ's panic attack on "that putrid, rotten, fuckin' Soprano gene." Dr. Melfi disagrees: "It's a slight tic in his fight/flight response. . . . When you blame your gene you're blaming yourself." Tony admits no responsibility for Jackie's whack, but says he failed as a guide. Tony says he failed him, but "what the fuck are you gonna do, well, today?"

Any tragic dimension in young Jackie's death is deflated by Uncle Junior's recollection: "The kid was always a dumb fuck" who almost drowned in three inches of water at the penguin pond. Jackie can't learn chess from the little black girl whose father is hiding him. As the latter suggests: "You shoulda played that out. That's the only way you're gonna learn." Compared to the little black girl in the projects, Jackie is a failure less by his situation than by his will. His obviously bright host underscores Jackie's wasted advantage.

In another example of someone transcending her origin, the FBI casts a close-cropped mousey clerk as the brassy big-haired moll who will inveigle herself into Adriana's confidence. If that transformation seems implausible, remember what Woody Allen did with the waif Mia Farrow in *Broadway Danny Rose* (1984).

Meadow breaks down at Jackie's death because he is the first mortality her age she has known. His bell tolls for her. When she doubts that Jackie was killed dealing drugs, Carmela rejects her pointed suspicion. Meadow like so many others seeks to blame "bogeymen with Italian names." Meadow reacts differently when Jackie's sister cites the stupidity of his criminal ambition. She has a clearer sense of their families' power than Meadow's naïve insistence that their families only occasionally dealt with the Mafia. The Family's hollow valor is undercut by the windy rhetoric Ralphie hears over the Super Bowl coverage.

Meadow is torn. With Carmela, she acknowledges Jackie's lack of parental guidance but she denies her parents' "excuse to get intrusive and controlling" in AJ's and her life. When, after Jackie's burial, Uncle Junior enraptures the restaurant crowd with his song about "an ungrateful heart," Meadow drinks too much, starts to throw bread-balls at him, and then runs away from Tony. "This is such bullshit," she cries, and narrowly escapes the traffic. Meadow is clearly uncertain about her own and her family's identity. She can't hold to her earlier resolve—Tony's advice in II, 13: "You have to max out the good times with the people you love."

As for AJ, Tony tells Melfi the boy "would never make it" in his business. Typically, AJ's flustered excuse for cheating on the test is that the other boy peed first and that made AJ need to, too. Both boys are dumb enough to score a suspicious 96 percent on the test of which they stole a preview, then fall for the old DNA identification bluff. The teacher offers their Witness Protection Program: "If you cooperate now it will be easier later." AJ would probably be well served by the military school, with its 5:30 A.M. to 10 P.M. schedule and no television. He might learn more plausible alibis.

Tony is toughening toward all his "sons." He walks away from Chris's apology and reaffirmation of his love. He rejects Jackie's call: "Talk to your stepfather. Let him help you." His anger toward AJ is only briefly relieved by affection and compliments, such as how good he looks in his military uniform. As in the previous episode, the Dr. Fried commercial reflects on Tony's attempt to make AJ a man—though the uniform makes AJ "feel like a total jerk-off."

More ominously, Tony alienates Paulie. Partly to reward Ralphie for having offed Jackie, Tony settles Paulie's $50,000 claim against Ralphie for $12,000. Paulie is further embittered because now he can not leave his mother in Green Grove. When Paulie's mother uses the Livia line—"My son lets me live in a place like this"—it is out of gratitude: "He's such a good boy." She does better by her gangster son than by the doctor.

Uncle Junior's song at the reception warms the conclusion. It shows his resolve "to stop and smell the roses" (a felicitous variant on Tony's "stop and smell the gorilla shit" in III, 9). The scene is satisfying in part because it surfaces our extra-textual knowledge that the actor, Dominic Chianese, is an accomplished lounge singer. Also, it provides a different kind of summary canvas than the earlier two seasons' conclusions: close-ups of the individuals responding pensive and moved to Uncle Junior's earnest singing. In contrast to Janice's self-promoting funeral music disc, Uncle Junior personifies the Old Country values and sentiments here. He provokes tears from Bobby, Patsy, and Johnny Sack, and prompts Artie to hold Charmaine even as he casts a baleful eye on Adriana kissing Chris. Meadow's and AJ's silliness only confirms Uncle Junior's dignity.

At the end other singers and three other songs are overlaid, as if to broaden the cultural context in which we see but don't hear Uncle Junior sing. By this abstraction we are pushed out of the scene. In the last shot we are above and behind Tony, Carmela, and AJ. After all its complex identification, the season ends by detaching us from the family and returning us to a perspective of objective judgment.

The third season plants some possible seeds for the fourth. In the central family, Meadow has lost her moorings. How will she define her identity? So, too, AJ, for as Tony asks Melfi, "We can't send him to that place. How're we gonna save this kid?"

Among the Family tensions, Ralphie has Janice snuggling up to him when he jokes at the funeral reception, boding to blossom into another Richie. Worse, Paulie turns away from Tony, complaining to Johnny Sack and committing to Carmine. He told Uncle Junior "Tony fundamentally doesn't respect the elderly." Then, of course, where's Valery? Christopher, too, has been distanced from Tony and his indiscreet Adriana exposed to the FBI. As the Super Bowl Game reduces the crowd at Jackie's funeral, it is clear that the old center does not hold. Or as Patsy Parisi (III, 12) tells the sick Gloria in transit: "It's over, *kapeesh?*"

Season Four

IV, 1: For All Debts Public and Private

Written by David Chase. Directed by Allen Coulter.

As Uncle Junior's RICO trial approaches he learns that Dr. Schreck's nurse is an FBI undercover agent, while "Danielle" infiltrates via Adriana. In jail, Paulie phones Johnny Sack for support not coming from Tony. Tony uses his Uncle's predicament to rally his capos to correct "the zero growth in this Family's receipts." Planning to protect himself by depending more on Christopher, Tony lets him kill the cop who murdered Chris's father. Janice seduces Ralphie at a Sunday family dinner.

Two cultural allusions provide this episode's core. The first is the rap song that frames the action: "World Destruction" by Afrika Bambaata and John Lydon (aka Johnny Rotten, erstwhile Sex Pistol). "This is a world destruction, your life ain't nothing," the song purrs, "The human race is becoming a disgrace." Then, presumably to lighten the tone: "Is it a nuclear war? / What are you asking for?" Clearly the song is part of the show's response to the September 11, 2001, terrorist attack on the Pentagon and the World Trade Center. (Out of respect, the shot of the Twin Towers was unobtrusively removed from the opening montage.)

In the second allusion, as Tony digs into a consoling sundae, he watches Dean Martin sing "My Rifle, Pony, and Me," in *Rio Bravo*, the 1959 Howard Hawks movie, on TV. The ironies in this reference show *The Sopranos* has not lost any of its brilliance. For one thing, here as in his "Return to Me" (III, 12) Dino represents Tony's Old School ethos. The song's theme of male self-sufficiency reflects on Tony's bluff confidence, until Carmela interrupts with her financial concerns. Moreover, as the song begins over Chris injecting heroin between his toes, this "shooting horse" (as in I, 10) gives new meaning to Dino's rifle, pony and self. The sun "sinking in the West" could be Tony's adoptive "son" Christopher, sinking under his shooting and horse.

The song is ironic even in its original context. The point of *Rio Bravo* is that sheriff John Wayne is a rugged independent but he needs the help of a woman, a kid, an irritating old cripple, and a struggling drunk to survive the siege. The song alludes both to Tony's false security and to the FBI siege of his Family. Finally, director Hawks intended *Rio Bravo* as a rebuttal to the classic *High Noon*, arguing that Gary Cooper's Will Kane was out of character when he scurried around for help, instead of assuming his duty. Hawks confirms Tony's choice of the strong, silent Cooper as model for American manhood.

The season opener begins and ends with breakfast scenes. In the first Carmela reads about an Italian court ruling that "Influence peddling is not a crime." As a sociologist testified, "This is our version of the Protestant ethic"—omitting the distasteful "work." A government official accepted 88 pounds of fish to expedite a trial (bribing with the fishes?). David Chase reminds his AIDA critics that there is some factual basis to the representation of Italian criminals.

In the last scene Christopher's mother finds him in her kitchen, studying photos of the father he has just avenged, and reveals another family's desolation. She lacks the peanut butter to make Chris's comfort food. Livia-like, she implicitly blames her son for her lonely widowhood: "Did I saddle you with a stepfather?" The ONE DAY AT A TIME sticker on her fridge declares her a recovering alcoholic. Chris covers it with the $20 bill he took from the cop he killed.

Rather than take heart from Carmela's news report, Tony yearns for his ducks (I,1). When he comes out for his local daily he waddles ducklike back. He's disappointed when a movement in the poolside shrubbery turns out to be a squirrel. Later he squirrels cash away under the duck food. Tony craves his ducks but gets the rodent squirrel instead, not just in nature but in himself.

Christopher's murder of Detective Lt. Barry Haydu recalls his murder of Emil (I, 1). Instead of the gangster film stars and pig-heads behind him, here a *Magnum PI* TV episode obliquely comments: "Police? In a Ferrari?" After a reference to a planted gun, Chris poses his victim as a suicide. The TV parody suggests Chris is still role-playing. But Chris remains Chris. He stoops to steal the cop's watch, weapon, and badge. The cop's last $20 contrasts to Tony's piles of hundreds, suggesting that crime didn't pay for this corrupt cop. Chris's vengeance is undermined further when Tony corrects the legend that his father was bringing Chris a crib when he was killed: "It was a bunch of TV trays. Could've been a crib just as easily." Tony's instruction, "Kill the dome light," recalls Othello's "Put out the light, and then put out the light."

This murder affirms Tony's family values. He sets it up to tighten his hold on Chris. Avenging his real father binds Chris to this false one, as Chris's loyalty oaths in later episodes prove, and makes Tony even more his father surrogate than the "made" ritual. By the way, we have only Tony's word that Haydu is that killer; we don't need Chris's certainty.

That cynical reflection coheres with this episode's prevailing sadness. As Bobby explains, "Mom really went downhill after the World Trade Center." Dr. Melfi explains Tony's depression: "A lot of people are feeling vulnerable." As usual, Tony takes his edginess out on Georgie, beating him up for not conserving ice. Meadow and AJ sulk about their whacked lover and private school, respectively. Paulie is in jail—a broken light on his pilgrimage to Dean Martin's birthplace (see above) found him with a gun connected to an unsolved murder—but he has the *stugots* to commandeer the jail phone and TV.

Chris also thinks Tony has "a hard on" for him, paradoxically suggesting a negative interest. In his insecurity he shoots heroin daily, though assuring Adriana "He can depend on me." But Tony is grooming him in order to avoid the high profile gangster's usual fate—"Dead or in the can." Instead, "You trust only blood." Chris "got his act together, the kid," he assures Melfi.

In similar delusion, when Chris notices a Chevy tailing them Tony laughs off the suspicion: "A couple nuns. Might be undercover Feds but I doubt it." In fact, the gang *is* undermined by two undercover FBI women. Dr. Schreck's nurse is a black Gloria, whose cheeky style and face attract Tony. He is also charmed by Adriana's new friend, "Danielle Ciccolella" (FBI agent Deborah Ciccerone). Janice's flirting with Ralphie disturbs both his Rosalie Aprile and Tony, who dreads a replay of the Richie Aprile fiasco (Season II). Carmela's mother undercuts her husband's motorcycle story by reminding him he was beaten up by hoods. Tony confides in Dr. Melfi because "I trust you—a little." But the episode bristles with betraying women.

Ominously, Carmela evinces a romantic interest in Furio. She primps in the stove reflection and is disappointed when Chris, not Furio, comes for Tony. Oblivious, Tony assures Melfi "Things are good. Especially with Carmela." Her insecurity increases when she spots Angie Bonpensiero distributing samples of kielbasa (an ethnic as well as a class betrayal) in a supermarket. As Carmela ominously concludes, regarding family finances, "Everything comes to an end."

Especially Tony's good intentions. Tony skips a workout because it's too cold out, then digs into a large ice cream with whipped cream on top. Instead of Bobby's steak and fries, he orders "scrambled eggs, no oil, tomato slices," but adds a steak sandwich. His susceptibility to the two agents parallels Uncle Junior's pathetic flirtation with his doctor's "young cooze." Yet Tony criticizes him: "How could you fall for that flirty shit?" We're alerted by the "Detecto" brand on the foregrounded scales. Uncle Junior is humiliated: "Time was my instincts would never have failed me like that. . . . I'm an old man, Anthony. An old man that's going to trial. There's much else to say about me?" He seems living proof that "Everything comes to an end."

As usual our heroes hide behind lofty principles. Angry at his legal costs, Uncle Junior plays environmentalist: "An entire forest in the northwest must have given its life for the Xerox paper just for this one fuckin' trial." A sit-down could have passed one page around to everyone. Tony spurs Christopher by citing his father's loyalty: "straight up." Though he refused to help his uncle, Tony cites the Family head's needs—"on trial for his life"—in his pep talk to his captains: "Crack some fuckin' heads. Create some earners out there." When Tony buys Uncle Junior's vacant garage for $100,000, ostensibly to help his legal bills, it's because his Assemblyman Zellman has noted its soaring land value.

Nonetheless, Tony feels trapped. He can't legitimize his money, as Carmela asks, because he's outside the system: "We don't have those Enrontype connections." That corporate scandal confirms that the *Sopranos* underworld mirrors rampant capitalism. "Since time immemorial" Tony says, there have only been two kinds of "recession-proof business," which Silvio identifies, smooth as a pimp, "Certain aspects of show business and our thing." Yet after 9/11 even the mob's "thing" has been hit. Fortunately, as Zellman assures him, "Who's going to quibble with patriotic entrepreneurism?"

Tony seems trapped, smarter than his colleagues but below respectable society, like the stock-savvy Cusamanos. That may be the point of his comic exchange when Bobby remarks that Quasimodo predicted 9/11. No, it was Nostradamus, Tony corrects him: "Nostradamus and Notre Dame—it's two different things altogether." Still, Bobby fixates on the coincidence that Quasimodo was a hunchback and Notre Dame has a quarterback and halfbacks. "You never pondered that? The back thing with Notre Dame?" More unsettlingly, boss Carmine corrects Tony on his cook-out garb: "A don doesn't wear shorts."

The episode closes with a full-screen close-up of President Andrew Jackson's eye (on Chris's ill-gotten $20 bill). This may suggest the Fed spying (e.g., "Danielle"), especially as this Jackson is not the Stonewall of Tony's ethic. Andrew Jackson's just and decent politician is now rare. He emblematizes the old populism to which Christopher pretended when he first sought redistribution of wealth. But since becoming made, Chris represents the corruption and oppressive institutional wealth that Old Hickory opposed. The allusion represents Chris yet undercuts him. Moreover, as the father of the Democrat party, Jackson's eye may be a baleful witness to the 2002 Republican government's political and economic disappointment. In context, the climactic emphasis on money reminds us that the currency for paying off all the titular debts public and private is loyalty and trust. In these there are creeping signs of bankruptcy.

IV, 2:   No Show

Written by David Chase and Terence Winter. Directed by John Patterson.

When Tony makes Chris acting capo over Paulie's crew, Patsy Parisi and Paulie's nephew, Little Paulie Germani, feel bypassed and Silvio "marginalized." Tony scolds Chris for stealing fiber optic cable from the construction job the boys are already skimming for paid "no show" and "no work" carpenter jobs. But Silvio approves Patsy's theft of a trailer of imported floor tiles. Chris drives "Danielle" away. When the FBI try to "turn" Adriana she vomits on the table. At home, Tony opposes Janice's affair with Ralphie and Meadow's plans for a year in Europe. After a heated showdown Meadow returns to Columbia.

At Columbia Meadow registers in a philosophy course, "Morality, Self and Society," which unlike more popular courses still has space. The title posits the Self between the proverbial rock—Morality—and the hard place—Society. In this episode various characters struggle to sustain their self-respect, *sans* moral foundation in an antipathetic society. As relationships crumble, characters find their assumed fealties were false. So the title, "no show," refers not only to the payroll scam but to relationships that have been stripped of their "show" or pretense.

The episode assumes a pervasive world unrest. A TV set reports riots in Korea as Meadow resists control: "What is this, Afghanistan?" Even the FBI agents are unsettled. The opening scene discovers "Danielle" and her agent husband, a handsome young couple with a baby boy, their bedroom dominated by the cell phone dedicated to her undercover operation. Paralleling the gang's politics, her husband later hopes "This reorganization of the Bureau could be good for both of us." FBI agents Harris and Cubitoso both feel "Danielle's" allure, the Bureau Chief even dreaming about her. The gangster community is so disturbed that here the bartender (Artie) complains to the customer (Tony) about his divorce costs and problems. In these troubled times Artie recognizes an occasional customer (Jack Massarone) by the dish he complained about (the sacciatelli).

In jail Paulie feels abandoned: Nobody has called his mother. He is provoked when Little Paulie reports Tony's killing in real estate (off Uncle Junior's garage) and Ralphie's mean joke: Johnny Sack's wife "had a 95-pound mole surgically removed from her ass." Like his Biblical namesake, the Pharisee, Paulie is converting to a new boss.

At Chris's promotion Silvio also seems to become alienated, despite having stated "We trust there will be no ill will." Silvio sensitively rejects Chris's quip: "The first thing I'm doing is getting wings in my hair"—à la Paulie. Silvio conveys his disappointment to Tony as Patsy's. He approves the tile theft while trying to repair a golf trophy with dried out Krazy Glue, an emblem for Tony's irreparable oversights. When Tony exacts his payoff Silvio sullenly seals their difference as "a misunderstanding."

Chris continues to fall short of Tony's confidence. As Chris complains to Adriana, "I owe this guy a lot, but he's a fuckin' jerk sometimes. Like he never heard of a learning curve." Chris further endangers the Esplanade scam when he and Patsy fight on the site. When Chris pulls a gun, a black worker starts to call the police but Patsy attacks him ("Ralph Bunche over here?") with a pipe. Chris accuses Patsy of having rifled Adriana's underwear drawer; in fact, it was Paulie (III,7). Guardedly, Chris suggests he's advancing to Tony's position: "Carmela ain't gonna be first lady forever." The new leader turns on others—Adriana, Patsy—the very terms Tony used to correct him: "Think!" "Use your head!" "The big picture."

Despite his drug use and folly, Chris does have the leader's saving instinct. Suspicious about "Danielle," he concludes she's a lesbian. Adriana entrusts her with the secret of her abortion, not the secret Danielle invites when she says a previous lover "was connected or something." The club in which Adriana and Danielle meet is papered with giant eyes, recalling President Jackson's eye (IV, 1). When Chris tries to initiate three-way sex, Danielle leaves and Adriana chooses to believe Chris's claim that Danielle invited him. "She's trying to fuck us up, Adriana," he falsely but correctly contends.

This undercover ploy thwarted, the FBI confront Adriana directly, demanding information as Chris rises through the ranks. If she doesn't cooperate, "Danielle's" tapes could get Adriana 25 years in jail for cocaine possession. On bail she'd have to tell Tony why she brought an FBI agent into his home (IV, 1). Shocked, Adriana clings to the minutiae of her betrayal: "Is your name even Danielle?" Before she can "sing" she pukes, spattering "Danielle" and the Harry Winston diamond bracelet—"with more karats than Bugs Bunny"—with which Chris marked his promotion. The episode closes with a long shot of the Soprano bathroom, Carmela soaking in tub left and Tony "abluting" at sink right. They enjoy a brief, precarious sanitation, with Adriana's decision still looming undeclared over them. The shot is taken from so far away that it's apparently a theatrical set, not the Soprano home. It summarizes the posing that characterizes their world.

That quiet bathroom close is a relief from Tony's "Peaceful Acres" scenes. When he questions Janice's affair with Ralphie, Janice charges Tony is "just like Ma, with your condescension and your sabotage." "My happiness really drives you crazy, doesn't it, Tony?" As Tony explains his interest, "I had to haul your last boyfriend out of the kitchen in a Hefty bag." His poetic license omits her narcoleptic Christian and her go-all-night youth. Meanwhile, Ralphie's selfish interest in Janice is parodied in his one-sided basketball game with Vito Spatafore. After Janice flings Ralphie's Ralph Lauren "style" at Tony, Ralphie shoots a toenail ("schrapnel") at her in bed.

In the main domestic tension, Meadow has wasted the summer on her melancholy over Jackie Jr. and plans to suspend college for a year in Europe. She uses her new knowledge to assert her independence from Carmela. Citing Henry James on "the restorative nature of travel," she may be on shaky ground. Tell Daisy Miller. But as Dr. Melfi observes, though Meadow has been regressing that summer, it's striking that at 19 she wanted to stay close to home.

Unfortunately, Melfi's wisdom and character are not matched in the adolescent psychologist whom she recommends for Meadow. Dr. Wendi Kobler is so laid back she encourages Meadow's self-indulgence, encourages the free use of tranquilizers, and digs for dirt about Jackie's drugs, Tony's real job and the possibility that Tony and even Carmela molested Meadow. Where Melfi sits erect Wendi lolls like on a hookah. "Perhaps they should examine their own needs to have you stay in school," the truly adolescent counselor opines. Drinking and doing a joint are fine "so long as you didn't deliberately purge." As a consultant to the University of Barcelona, she offers to get Meadow into that "hot school." Compared to Wendi, Melfi's counsel seems above reproach, though she has also advised that "With today's pharmacology no one needs to suffer with feelings of pain and depression" (I, 1). The unprofessional, faddish Kobler confirms the episode's sense of disintegration. Even in therapy, the center does not hold.

Arguing over Meadow's year abroad, Tony goes through three phases. (1) "What the fuck's in Europe?" Carmela's reply—"Experience. Real life. Art."—confirms Tony's suspicions: "I knew all this constant harping on art was gonna cause trouble." (2) Tony will let her go, to thwart her oppositional stance. "The college of hard knocks is what she needs." And if she should marry an Italian boy—"There's Furio, what's so wrong with him?" As we have again caught Carmela primping for Furio's arrival, and Meadow's friend Misty dissolves over him, Tony's confidence is misplaced. When Misty calls Carmela "Mrs. Sope" she may foreshadow a soap opera adventure. (3) When Tony finally supports Carmela's ban he and his daughter go face-to-face.

Carmela's reason—"Just getting what you want is for babies, not adults."—can't cool this heat. Meadow begins with sarcasm—"the pivotal role of the work ethic in this family"—then erupts in inarticulable frustration, anger and loss: "Listen to Mr. Mob Boss. All this fucking pussyfooting around, all these years. . . . As if you could talk honestly for three fucking seconds." Though Tony reminds her of his attempts to save Jackie Jr., she runs out crying, set for Europe.

To her credit, Meadow evaded her therapist and stuck to her family line: "There's no such thing as a Mafia." Now, even when Meadow seems to have left for Europe, she proves the confidence that Tony expresses to Melfi: "She loves me. I know that. Since she was a tiny baby." While all the apparent friendships and fealties dissolve around them, beneath the father's and daughter's rage persists their love. Tony could say to Meadow what Chris falsely assured Adriana: "What we have is stronger than any of that shit." On that love Meadow safely sets her Self, regardless of her father's suspect Morality and their rejection by Society. With that she can stay the course.

IV, 3: Christopher

Written by Michael Imperioli and Maria Laurino. Directed by Tim Van Patten.

When the New Jersey Council of Indian Affairs plan to disrupt the annual Columbus Day Parade Silvio rouses his colleagues to fight the Indians. From jail Paulie turns the bosses against Tony for not sharing his real estate profits and Johnny Sack against Ralphie for his Ginny joke. Ralphie leaves Rosalie Aprile for Janice, but she throws him out. Janice is deeply touched by Bobby Baccala's open emotion when his wife Karen is killed in a car accident.

This episode's title, "Christopher," has both explicit and implicit point (beyond the fact "Chris Moltisanti," Michael Imperioli, co-wrote it). Its explicit reference is to Christopher Columbus, whose national memorial day is attacked by Indian protest groups as emblematic of "the genocide of America's native people." The implicit effect is to remind us of the Christopher-Adriana-FBI subplot which, so intense in the previous episode, is suspended here. There's a close-up on Adriana when Carmela refers to another two-faced woman and Adriana suggests Furio should "lose his ponytail" but no hint how Adriana will deal with her FBI ultimatum.

The episode's focus on ethnic identity confronts the vociferous complaints from Italian-American (and Italian-Canadian) pressure groups that *The Sopranos* reduces the Italian community to the gangster stereotype. The response is three-pronged: (i) an explicit statement of the positive side of Italian-American culture; (ii) an affirmation of individual over group responsibility; and (iii) a reminder that "melting pot America" is composed of various ethnic communities whose bristling at historic slights—perceived or real—threatens the nation's unity. As Patsy objects, "Some fuckin' balls, bad-mouthing America, especially now." Here internecine betrayals turn into ethnic warfare.

For the positive image Father Phil sponsors a luncheon lecture on "Italian-American Women and Pride." Montclair State College Professor Longo-Murphy applauds the "proud, strong, beautiful women" for preserving their traditions while becoming the "new Italian-American women." Despite their flair and sophistication "America still sees us as pizza makers and Mama Leones." "If they say 'John Gotti' you tell them

'Rudolph Guiliani.' " The professor would reply to one stereotype with another, albeit higher class: "Our grandmothers may have dressed in black but we're in Moscino and Armani." Instead of smelly cheese and cold wine "We're from the land of aromatic asiago and supple Barolo." She urges her audience to flaunt "the other side of Italian-American culture, the educated, wage-earning, law-abiding side, because isn't that who we truly are?" A Princeton study shows that 74 percent of Americans associate Italian-Americans with organized crime "because of the way the media depict us." But she doubts the sample in the Fairleigh Dickinson survey that found Americans dismiss those representations as fictional. Even this pacific event proves divisive. Gabriella Dante criticizes Father Phil for letting Carmela, the parish's prime supporter, be humiliated "at the hands of an outsider" (that fractious clannishness again).

Gabriella's husband, Silvio, calls the Indians' protest "anti-Italian discrimination"—after the boys have ridiculed the Native American stereotype. "Columbus Day is a day of Italian pride, it's our holiday and they want to take it away." He reminds Tony that gangster Joe Colombo founded the first Italian anti-defamation group. For Silvio, "This battle's gonna be won on the PR level. Hearts and minds. They manipulate your image—Columbus. We manipulate theirs." So Ralphie threatens Professor Redclay with the public revelation that the Indians' "poster boy," Iron Eyes Cody (a Hollywood supporting player of the 1950s) was really a second-generation Sicilian from Louisiana. Redclay's TA/girlfriend assures him that "Cody was definitely native American and totally environmentalist." Despite Redclay's initial upset, the rumor is taken in stride: "It's like knowing James Caan isn't Italian." At the demonstration, Artie is typically first out of the car and first back in, cowering from a water bag.

After Assemblyman Zellman and Chief Douglas Smith can't cancel the Indian protest, Tony has a genuine breakthrough in understanding. People should not seek their identity, gratification or excuse in their clan identification. People act and should be judged as individuals. He scolds Silvio for proscribing himself as Italian: "All the good things you got in your life, did they come to you because you were Calabrese?" No, he got them because of how smart he was and what he did (to Tony not mutually exclusive). Tony's "self-esteem" does not depend on Columbus, The Godfather, or Chef Boyardee. Ethnic identity is unrelated to the gang's activity and success. Hiding behind or flaunting an ethnic identity is irresponsible. This rebuts the contention that The Sopranos equates Italian and Gangster. Tony's model, "the strong silent type," Gary Cooper "did what he had to do" without complaining that "his people got fucked over." This recalls

Livia dismissing psychology as "what people do when they are looking for someone to blame for their life."

Further denying the Italian=Gangster equation, here even the noble Native American community has its corruption. For Tony's free day in his casino's High Rollers Room, Chief Doug Smith exacts a favor: a week of Frankie Valli. The coerced gig echoes the Corleones' Vegas deployment of Johnny Fontane. Chief Smith admits having passed for white until his "racial awakening," when he accepted his grandmother's mother's being quarter Indian—in time to cash in on the Native American casino industry, Tony notes. Conversely, Maggie Donner, activist Redclay's assistant, claims to be one eighth Italian, her ancestor having been a Pony Soldier, or at least "a violinist [!] attached to the 7th Cavalry." There's always room for a fiddle in these ethnic cash-ins.

This episode blurs away the line between the Indian and Italian. Hesh cites the persecuted Jew's empathy for the Indian. As a conscientious Neopolitan, Furio rejects Christopher Columbus for being a Genoan. The Northern Italians always had the money and power: "Even today they put up their nose at us like we were peasants. [spit] I hate the north." That Furio has to explain this pecking order to his Italian-American colleagues recalls how remote they are from their Italian roots (II, 4).

This episode's America is a nation divided by its ethnic communities' hyper-sensitivity and belligerence. Supporting the Indians, AJ's history teacher contends that today Columbus would stand trial, alongside the Yugoslavian dictator Slobodan Milosovic, for slavery and genocide. But for Tony, "In this house Christopher Columbus is a hero. End of story."

Two moments demonstrate the warring groups' self-centeredness. In his initial sympathy to the Indians, Hesh notes the white men's "gift" of smallpox-infested blankets. But he turns against them when the Cuban Reuben (a Jewish name) declares that "Christopher Columbus was no better than Hitler." Hesh considers such "trivializing" of The Holocaust as "covert anti-semitism," orders his long-standing friend off his property, then suggests a native contact to stop the demonstration. A similar reversal happens on the TV panel discussion. The black man initially supports the Italians but shifts when the Italian appropriates a term from the black slave experience: his ancestors' "middle passage" to America. In both cases the politics shift because of self-centered sensitivities. As a curt phone conversation between Carmela and Corrado demonstrates, it is easy to "villain-ize" someone by ignoring their perspective.

Taking a god's eye view on the divided citizenry, two high angle shots suggest "What fools these mortals be." The opening shot, from behind the

Satriale's pig-head, shows the gangsters schmoozing and seething. The parallel looks down on an Indian-Italian skirmish. Large issues seem petty when characters fix on minutiae. Thus Johnny Sack graphically rejects Ralphie's cash graduation gift to his nurse daughter and Marty Schwartz nags that his granddaughter's Bat Mitzvah gift, a bubble jet printer, doesn't work. As Uncle Junior's trial begins he bothers his lawyer with complaints about his fees.

Janice's therapist provides the cure for this national schizophrenia. As Janice blames her parents for discouraging her art, Dr. Shaw suggests Janice chose Richie and Ralphie as lovers to prove something to her dominant "figure of authority," her brother. "The work is to make new choices that have nothing to do with old patterns." That advice pertains to America's fractious ethnicities as well as to Janice's snake pit psyche.

Though Dr. Shaw seems slightly wiser than Meadow's therapist (IV, 2), she naïvely believes Janice's performance of Injured Innocence. In the two negative shrinks Chase denies any easy source of reliable guidance, wisdom, and responsibility. We're on our own. Also, as these therapists are more negative versions of Melfi's non-judgmentalism, they reflect upon her approach. In Melfi's only scene here, her ex-husband turns on the news report of the riot in Columbus Park, then beats a cerebral retreat from the ethnic politics he once fervidly espoused: This "tragedy . . . could be scored with Albinoni's *Adagio*." But Tony's independent escape from ethnic paranoia suggests Melfi has had some success.

Janice finds her path out of darkness in Bobby Baccala. She is so profoundly moved by his devotion to his dead wife that she feels unworthy to be in his presence. Still, she sets out to seduce him. Dr. Shaw advises Janice break up with Ralphie, to "level with" him "with the compassion and respect you're famous for." She does—attacking him for not taking his shoes off in her house and throwing him down the stairs (her "leveling").

Though Janice was already nervous when Ralphie announced he left Rosalie, their relationship is still surprising. In their sex Janice calls him "slut," "bitch," and "cunt," while sodomizing him with a vibrator. In parody, the Schwab TV commercial has a kindly old family doctor remark how his patient after 30 years still hates the thermometer; the lovers' sadomasochism may mirror the current stock market scandals. This sex scene is a reversal for the man who so abused his whore Tracee (III, 6) and for a woman who is always the victim. As Richie held a gun to her head during sex, sometimes unloaded, the men's homonymous names seem to equate them. Ralphie may carry more guilt than he lets on—or he needs some guilt for erotic pleasure. He leaves Rosalie for "No more guilt . . .

just sex." In contrast, Tony wrestles with his guilt to clear a healthier life, albeit within his professional boundaries.

In dignified contrast stand Bobby Baccala's naked grief and remorse when his wife dies. Karen is going to her dentist for a "new crown" when she's killed and canonized. Bobby sobs uncontrollably at her funeral. "My sweet love," he calls her, "My sweet Karen, my sweet girl." Usually a figure of comic simplicity, dismissed by Tony's "lazy fuck," forced to fail as Santa (III, 10), and looking ludicrous when he rescues Chris and Paulie (III, 11), here Bobby reveals profoundly human value. His family love makes Bobby an uncompromised Big Pussy. Gabriella recalls the men ridiculing Bobby for being the only one without a goomah. Now that he has lost his wife he's ashamed that his last thoughts were anger that she wanted him to buy the steaks and eggplants when he was tired and caught in the traffic jam caused by her accident. The death restores his priorities. This loss and regret make the political issues seem petty.

■ Life follows art. New York Mayor Michael Bloomberg invited *Sopranos*'s stars Lorraine Bracco and Dominic Chianese to march with him in the Columbus Day parade. When William Fugazy, president of the Coalition of Italo-American Associations, claimed the show "denigrates Italian culture," Mayor Bloomberg cited both actors' stellar reputations in the arts and community. His predecessor Rudy Guiliani supported Mayor Bloomberg's invitation but parade organizers banned the actors. The mayor skipped the parade and took his guests for lunch—to an Italian restaurant in the Bronx.

IV, 4: The Weight

Written by Terence Winter. Directed by Jack Bender.

Angry at Ginny's insult, Johnny Sack attacks Ralphie's crew member, Donny. Carmine implicitly permits Tony to have his good friend Johnny killed, to protect his captain Ralphie. Johnny's rage is assuaged when he catches Ginny furtively eating chocolates. When he cancels his hit on Ralphie he saves his own life. Meanwhile Tony worries about Meadow's volunteering at the campus Law Center to provide legal help for "the indigenous and disenfranchised." At Furio's house-warming, his folk dance draws Carmela closer.

As the title suggests, little things swell into a disproportionate burden. After all, Ginny Sack used to be a hoofer and ballet teacher before child-bearing left her with a huge weight problem. Ralphie's joke about her having a 95-pound mole removed from her rump (IV, 2) weighs heavily first on Johnny, then on his relations with Tony and boss Carmine. For relief from this pressure, Johnny urinates on Donny K. ("Let me buy you a drink"), then the old hood promises to eliminate Johnny "as silent as a mouse pissing on cotton."

Johnny's anger threatens the multi-million dollar Esplanade scam. "Either name the price or get the fuck over it," Carmine urges, but Johnny insists Ralphie should be whacked. "If he were drownin' I'd throw him a cinder block," Tony admits weightily, but as Ralphie's boss he has to protect him. Conversely, Tony offers Johnny "Ralph on a platter" if he reveals his source. With the burden of choice, Tony opts to have his 20-year friend Johnny whacked instead. Carmine's approval is implicit and self-protective: "I appreciate your thoughts." He twice states "I didn't say nothing," to avoid any later load of responsibility.

Johnny's burden is honorable. He deeply loves Ginny: "I never had a problem with Ginny's weight. To me she's beautiful. Rubenesque. That woman is my life. To think that she's being mocked?" In the Benito One bar, Johnny is tormented by seeing Ralphie's man Donny K. laughing and by hearing his own guy talk about his hot date, a dancer who greeted him in a *Cats* suit. Even the name of the bar connotes macho belligerence. The combination drives Johnny mad. Pleading his case to the captains, Johnny stresses the offense to his and his wife's honor, especially since "We bend more rules than the Catholic Church." But Carmine has a narrow sense of honor: "Ralph slept with Ginny?" Johnny can forgive Ralphie when he discovers Ginny has not been fighting her weight problem as valiantly as she claimed. When Johnny turns back to discover her, his car-radio's song is warning, "Johnny, don't go." Conversely, it may argue for his supporting her despite her bulky frailty.

Even as he escapes with his life, Ralphie bears out Johnny's description: "a two-faced fucking prick." He says he dumped Janice when she wanted to sodomize him with a dildo. He at first denies his Ginny joke, then admits it, then breaks Tony's instruction and apologizes to Johnny for something he claims not to have said. Ralphie joins his assassin in the elevator just as the cell-phone call cancels the hit, but Ralphie leaves aggressive: "What's your fuckin' problem?" Ralphie was the man's problem/mission and remains his own burden.

The metaphor of weight pervades the episode. As Uncle Junior watches *Who Wants to be a Millionaire?* it's "the fifth question and the poor prick's lost all his lifelines," i.e., is sinking. Carmela's financial cousin Brian advises them: "Liquidity is the real concern"—as Ginny wishes her too, too solid flesh would melt. Bent under his boredom, AJ resents accompanying Carmela to Furio's and locks Bobby Baccala's small son in the garage. Off-camera, Donny K.'s permanent nerve damage leaves him a burden on his mother, hardly lightened by Johnny's promise to send her "something nice."

The theme subtly colors the minor plots. Furio has his own burden, when a Pakistani neighbor opposes his plan to convert his garage into a guest house for his parents' visit. To whack Johnny, Silvio and Chris contract aged killers with genetic blindness. Their burden is compounded by the plethora of Jesuses in their home. The volume of icons cuts two ways: it underscores the absence of such faith in the more upscale homes and it points to the abyss between this profuse profession of faith and the occupants' real profession, contract killing. The head hitman is nicknamed DiMaggio because of his different strength with a bat. The burden of 9/11 is varied in Meadow's first client, a young Moslem man who was beaten with sticks for the "severe immorality" of possessing a picture of Britney Spears, and when the gang adopts the Taliban strategy of disposable, one-use cell phones.

Meanwhile, Dr. Melfi pursues her own demons with Dr. Elliot Kupferberg. Now that her "well adjusted" son Jason suffers "epic drift—no focus, no drive," and may drop out of college, she feels fraudulent for having counselled Tony about Meadow. Jason has barely spoken to his father since Melfi's rape. "Jason may be feeling guilty himself, Jen. He's powerless to avenge you and resents his father for the same shortcomings." Another burden may be Jason's Senior Year: "There's something about the light at the end of that tunnel that can be very frightening." Later Elliot describes his burden of fear from a parking garage exchange with "this big Bluto-sort of guy"—Tony—who walked threateningly in front of his car. Melfi should not keep blaming herself for the rape, because "Parking garages are not inherently dangerous places." When Elliot's gender-bent daughter, Saskia, brings Meadow into the Legal Aid program and Elliot unknowingly encounters Tony the snare around the Sopranos seems tighter.

Meadow joins Legal Aid to make her undergraduate program more than "an audition for grad school." Tony applauds her helping people but warns her not to be "a sucker," helping "the indigenous types who got plenty of money to buy crack and gamble and all that shit." Tony seems still bothered by the Indians' attack on Columbus Day and his shakedown by Chief Smith (IV, 3). Though Meadow may still resent his treatment of

Noah, there is a palpable lightness and warmth in her bantering with her dad: "Believe it or not, the world doesn't revolve around you."

Carmela's new burden is knowing her love for Furio. At the house-warming Tony urges her to dance with Furio while he chats with Silvio and Chris. The folk dance is a courting ritual that apparently works. Earlier, Carmela is touched by Furio's sadness when the smell of olives reminds him of his happiest time, when he worked with his "hands in the dirt, the hot sun," in Naples, tending a rich man's olives. Now he plans to grow vegetables and grapes to make his own wine. His warm roots contrast to Tony's remoteness from nature and the natural.

After their financial discussion with Brian, Tony and Carmela accuse each other of equating love with money. This echoes Johnny's indignation when Carmine tries to mollify him by fining Ralphie: "Is it all about money?" For Carmela, "When you ignore me, Tony, when you trivialize things that are important to me . . . it makes me feel unloved." The scene closes with a long shot of them sitting at opposite ends of the kitchen table, Tony eating, Carmela "consolidating some bills," in their separate recesses. The closing love scene bridges that gap—only partially.

Tony—touched by Johnny's ardor for Ginny and relieved both that he does not to have to kill him and that his wife is no Ginny Sack—brings Carmela a Saks size Small cocktail dress and a dozen red roses. Even as she responds to his caresses she seems distracted. Two different forms of music are used here. First, the heavy-breath silence is broken by Furio's Italian music, but it's traced to Meadow's room. The record turned off, the next music is non-diegetic, i.e., not originating in the scene. It suggests that mentally Carmela is back in her house-warming dance with Furio. Meadow can turn off the record but Carmela can't turn off Furio's music. Carmela appears troubled, wide-eyed and detached, under Tony's hairy bulk. She is under both the present weight of her husband and the absent weight of her memories of Furio. Vapors can weigh heavily.

IV, 5:   Pie-O-My

Written by Robin Green and Mitchell Burgess. Directed by Henry J. Bronchtein.

To qualify for a racing license Ralph keeps his race-horse, Pie-O-My, in his maid's name. Tony finds himself sentimentally attached to the horse, especially after his strategy wins a taste of her $40,000 winnings. Tony frustrates Carmela's plans for financial security. To win Bobby Baccala, Janice outlasts JoJo Palmice and exhorts him to do Junior's assignment. After the FBI tell Adriana her Uncle Richie and Big Pussy are not in the Witness Protection Program, she coaxes Chris to move to California, but he won't: "What I owe [Tony], I would follow that man into hell." The unpaid vet refuses to treat Pie-O-My, so Tony rushes out in a cold and stormy night to pay him and to comfort the stricken steed.

Tony's accountant, Alan Ginsberg, warns Tony off the Life Insurance Trust that Carmela wanted, because "that type of trust is irrevocable" in the event of divorce. "We don't want to get locked in," Tony passes on to Carmela. In this episode's theme, every trust is rather temporary, partial, indeed quite revocable. As Uncle Junior remarks, indignant that Bobby was in mourning instead of doing his strong-arm work, "Each of us is alone in the fuckin' universe." Of course, Junior is a few concepts short of Existentialism. On trial for his life, he worries about what his driver Murph is wearing to court and the court cartoonist's poor likeness of him. Junior gives the court cartoonist the intimidating glare a wiseguy might better turn upon a juror.

Their financial arguments widen the breach between Carmela and Tony. She sulks despite his flowers and concessions. By the time Tony okays the medical stock it has split. Though Tony opens an investment account with Brian, he withholds the Life Insurance Trust. When he tells Carmela he "gave" her two out of three, she is insulted that he thinks he is giving his mate something that's not hers. If not "alone in the fuckin' universe," she is locked out of her marriage. His financial fear Carmela might leave him pushes her away. Nor is she mollified by Tony's track winnings: "You bought a racehorse? . . . It followed you home?"

Ironically, Tony's financial defensiveness lies behind his first winning strategy for Pie-O-My: "Maybe you should try holding her back. Save something for the finish." Though Tony wouldn't own a horse—"It's an animal. It's a commitment."—he's quickly attached to Pie-O-My. He scowls when Ralph instructs his trainer: "Tell the midget not to be shy with the whip." ("If only his mother had taken that advice," Hesh adds, anent Ralphie.) Where Tony urges "Come on, baby," Ralphie yells "Run, you fuckin' nag"—when the horse is winning. Proving Cousin Brian over his head in the Soprano investment world, he mistakenly bets on Pie-O-My only to show.

Overall the name "Pie-O-My" suggests an exuberant celebration—as in "My oh my!" The "pie" suggests sharing, as in "pieces of the pie," as well as reflecting Tony's constant noshing. The name twists "Of my pie." The emphatic "my" echoes Tony's increasing possessiveness. After briefly declining Ralphie's first offer of a "taste," after the second win Tony keeps his hand out till Ralphie unpeels enough. Ralphie's gesture hardens into Tony's extortion. So, too, his threatening thanks to the vet: "Here's your fuckin' money. You better hope she's gonna be all right." In effect, Tony has made himself Ralph's partner in the horse, so he asks about "our girl." "Our?" Ralphie replies. Tony suggests "we switch" her horseshoes to titanium.

Ralphie is quick to exploit Tony's sentiments. He has his maid roust Tony out of bed to pay the vet. Ralphie rails against the vet, "These guys. No compassion for the fuckin' animals whatsoever." In the last scene, Tony lights up a stogey, caresses and calms the stricken horse, and is joined by the stable's mascot goat. In this touching manger, three afflicted animals gather against the outside storm. Recalling Tony's ducks, here nature provides a community and trust unavailable in society. Tony embraces Pie-O-My because the horse seems his only contact who is not out to exploit, deceive or betray him. Animals don't revoke a trust.

The episode closes on the *Rio Bravo* song Tony caught on TV (IV, 1). Now Dean Martin's song, "My Rifle, Pony, and Me," evokes the original film's ironic pretence to independence. The true horse outweighs the heroin. When young Ricky Nelson joins old Dino at the end the song evokes the film's besieged community.

The antithesis to Pie-O-My is Adriana's Crazy Horse club. In the first scene she imagines Tony and Silvio plotting retribution for feeding the FBI, even though No Soap Radio sing "It's not about you, you, you." The tilt of the shots suggests her paranoid distortion. Newly sensitized by the FBI, Adriana notes the telephone-book beating of the incontinent Giovanni, mysterious conversations in her office, Chris's unknown whereabouts and stashing his pistol above her detergents.

When the FBI replaces "Danielle" with Robyn Sanseverino, changing jockeys in midstream, Adriana is so confused that she cries when her betrayer walks away. Adriana was initially upset to see her: "Eat shit, Danielle, or whatever the fuck your name is." Now Adriana is pathetically alone. Christopher laughs when she falls off her broken chair—in the Livia tradition of loving family memories. At home Chris rejects her "negative shit": "If you love me, stir my eggs, OK?" Against the FBI's warnings she marshals false bravado: "Tony would never let anything happen to Christopher. He's his nephew. He loves him." The FBI's knowledge of her club use by the mob prompts her to report Patsy's suit scam. When Inspector Harris asks "See? How hard was that?" the image tells us: Harris is in *soft* focus in the foreground, Adriana *hard* in the back. When she shoots heroin, the FBI drive her into Christopher's self-destruction.

As a self-serving callous manipulator Janice is a thoroughbred apart. She uses racetrack binoculars to spy on Bobby. Beside the defeated Adriana and the sulking Carmela, Janice shows the will and strength to come from behind the pack. However touched by Bobby's marital love, Janice remains irrevocably untrustworthy, elbowing out JoJo and advancing Bobby in Uncle Junior's crew.

When JoJo assures the mourning Bobby, "Like the president says, we have to keep going. The family has to eat," Janice solicitously asks JoJo about her son's Ritalin: "The way they medicate kids today. It's the answer to everything. And then they wonder why teenagers get hooked on drugs." Janice deploys Carmela's prize lasagna against the other women's casseroles, hijacks JoJo's chicken massala for Junior, and especially plans to get Bobby over saving Karen's last ziti. Janice nags Bobby back to action: "My uncle loves you. He needs you. . . . So you're gonna do what needs to be done. Aren't you!" She tells Uncle Junior that her father predicted "Some day Bobby will be [Corrado's] lynchpin." But Junior sees through her. When her father died Bobby was still just a head waiter, he reminds her. He tells the naïve Bobby Carmela made Janice's impressive lasagna.

But the show allows no uncontaminated virtue. Bobby has won a healthy respect since his Karen's death—"I loved her so much. I thank God for every day we had together." But his virtue shows two faultlines. First, his sentimental connection to Corrado crumbles: "Uncle Junior's been so good to me and I'm letting him down. Aw, fuck him. He only thinks of himself, the selfish old fuck." The second is Bobby's threat to a union leader over an upcoming election. Bobby pretends to be the victim: "I got kids that depend on me, like you. If I thought I wasted my votes on him, I might just as well put a bullet in my head. Here, here and here." Just when we thought we could trust this poor gull—a lovable lug more sinned against than sinning—he proves as vicious as the rest. When it comes to divvying up the pie, our trust even in Bobby Baccala has been revoked.

IV, 6:   Everybody Hurts

Written by Michael Imperioli. Directed by Steve Buscemi.

Tony tells a stoned Christopher he will direct his orders through him. AJ wins wealthy Devin with his family's criminal allure. After learning that Gloria killed herself, Tony extends himself to prove he's not "a toxic person." But Artie Bucco defeats Tony's good will. First, he tries to borrow $50,000 from Ralphie, instead of from Tony, to lend to his beautiful new French hostess's brother. After the Frenchman reneges on his loan, Artie attempts suicide, to Tony's disgust.

In the ambiguous title, "hurts" can be transitive as well as intransitive. That is, everyone feels pain and everyone can cause pain. Pain seems inescapable in relationships. The afflicted afflict others. As our Waste Management Consultant asks Artie, then Janice, "What the fuck am I, a toxic person or something?" He fears he is what he does. Like the "hurt," the "toxic person" both contains poison and poisons others. Hence AJ's attempt to explain Tony's work as "recycling," not garbage.

Being sensitive means suffering. Tony's relief at being free from Gloria turns into guilt when he learns that shortly after he left her she hanged herself. So, too, Carmela, worried about Furio's loneliness, arranges a blind date with hygienist Jessica, then feels discomfited and jealous when he embraces Jessica at dinner. "She's a romantic one, this one," Furio reports, "She's gonna clean my teeth for me."

The ambivalence of a close relationship recurs when Tony takes Janice to a fine dinner, briefly suspending their constant antagonism. She bristles at his mention of her relationship with Bobby. Similarly, as Tony explains Christopher's promotion: "Syl, Paulie—one thing they're not. They're not my blood." Chris's blood makes him Tony's right-hand man (as Michael Corleone appoints his illegitimate nephew Vincent in *The Godfather Part III*). But as Chris's blood is increasingly contaminated with heroin, he represents Tony's vulnerability as much as his power.

Tony is implicated in the Mercedes salesman's explanation of Gloria's suicide: "I got the impression she wasn't very lucky with men." Her "suicide note" turns out to be a classified ad to sell her wolf stole. The animal reference feeds Tony's concern that he may be inhuman. He has the coarseness to qualify: He swigs his Armagnac from the bottle as he leaves Artie, ignoring the ceremony of a "snifter, nice cigar." Yet Tony wants to transcend his family's nature, emblematized by Janice slurping "God, I love marrow!" She compares Livia's bone-love to "half-price day at the liposuction clinic."

Janice eating *osso bucco* at Artie Bucco's restaurant foreshadows Tony's exploitation of his good friend. The chef is on his menu. Ralphie even calls Artie "Chef Osso Bucco." In the show's familiar mingling of meat, sex and violence, Tony's unbridled hunger is about to consume his friend Artie, even as he helps him. After Tony saves him, Artie compares Tony to a hawk that "sees a little field mouse moving around in the cornfield from a mile up," then pounces. He accuses Tony of foreseeing and exploiting his predicament. For bailing him out, Tony gets Artie to cancel his $6,000 tab, yet Furio—not likely be put off with "It's business. It's a risk."—will extract Jean Philippe's $50,000 debt. As the Sopranos do business they run no risk. Artie realizes Tony's "worst case scenario, I eat for free." Tony profits even from generously saving Artie. With Melfi Tony worries that he may have a hawk's compulsive intuition. For even at his most humane, Tony is a predator.

When Tony confronts Melfi about Gloria, he moves from grim humor— "How's Gloria Trillo? She still hangin' around?"—to fury: "Why the fuck didn't you help her?" As quickly, Tony turns his anger back upon himself: "She reached out for me to care and I wasn't there for her." When he first confronts, Artie, Tony's "reach" shows he has Gloria on his mind: "Artie, you need a favor. What did I do you don't reach out to me?" Janice picks up on Tony's need: "We can go at it pretty good, but you always seem to reach out when it counts." To make amends, he gives Carmela her Life Insurance Trust and wins cousin Brian's repeated "You're a great guy!" Even Tony's generosity is delimited by his career. Brian's deal on hot suits evokes the classic gangster film convention, where the gunsel is initiated with spiffy new clothes. The closing song bemoans Tony's failure: "I've been trying to make you love me."

The Artie plot recalls the Dave Scatino bankruptcy (II, 6, ff.), for Artie, Dave, and Tony were high-school chums. After his clear warnings, Tony ruined Dave's life when he could not repay his debt. Ralphie denies Artie his loan because "If you don't pay me back, I ain't gonna be able to hurt you." Ralphie seems concerned about lost pleasure as much as money. Tony's generosity costs Artie more.

Like Don Vito in the first scene of *The Godfather*, Tony scolds Artie for not coming to him first. Before trying to kill himself, Artie phones Tony with a last-gasp apology: "I love you and I'm sorry I let you down." Though Tony saves Artie's life he remains selfish: "Suppose I come over to your house and I find you dead. How am I supposed to feel?" In his last scene with the recovering Artie, Tony shifts from genuine care—"Can't you come talk to me? Hey, I'm your friend."—to anger: "You fuckin' suicide. You're disgraceful."

The episode also depicts the danger of vanity. Meadow is less sensible than proud when she brings her naïve kid brother into the South Bronx (where he might be mugged by Robert Iler's buddies) to see her Friday night volunteer work. If she seems mature for refusing AJ her room—"The greatest cultural center in the world, and you came here for sex?"—she's also showing off her superiority. She recommends a reading by a friend's novelist sister. Equally smug, Devin and AJ feel for the less fortunate, like the math teacher's son who lives in a house without a dining room.

AJ can't live up to his friends' *Godfather* expectations. As for the Sopranos' attack dogs, "she was hit by a car." When AJ tries to find his dad's office at the Bada Bing, he directs them to the bathetic Satriale's. "It looks really clandestine," Devin says, trying to salvage some thrill; the others compare it to Don Vito's front, Genco Imports. The teenagers' attraction to badness is a counterpoise to Tony's new attempts at goodness.

Under the same temptation, Artie disastrously emulates the loan sharks he has been feeding, to Charmaine's disgust. Though he needs $10,000 for his daughter's orthodontics, he borrows $50,000 to lend to Jean-Philippe for $7,500, for the North American distribution rights for Armagnac. Besotted with his French hostess, Elodi, Artie disdains Charmaine as "not remotely" French—then ambitiously plunges into ruin. Artie makes such a bad bad guy that the defaulter beats *him* up. This after Artie rehearsed his routine—after de Niro's famous "You talkin' to me?" scene in *Taxi Driver*—before a mirror wall. Artie is so over his head he aspires to Scorsese, not *The Godfather*. His pretence is deflated when in the next scene Chris examines his stoned eye in a similar mirror, while another junkie vomits. Rhyming actions suggest Artie's project is doomed from the outset. He flirts with Elodi by tugging her earring: "Little pitchers have big ears." Later her brother bloodily rips off Artie's earring. Thus Artie—who tried to step up to the gangster's table, to become one of the big eaters—ends up eaten.

AJ's girlfriend reminds us that crime is not the only path to extreme wealth and social power. As their name implies, the divorced Pilsbury family has real dough. When we compare her father's wall of late-Picasso paintings to Carmela's prized $3,000 Lladro, the legal fortune far outweighs that for which the Sopranos have—if not sold—at least mortgaged their soul. Disappointed that the Sopranos don't live in a Corleone compound—as she does—Devin dismisses wealth, insisting she likes AJ for himself.

The women in Tony's dreams here personify the ambivalence of virtue, by which everybody hurts. Like the nurturing Isabella (I, 12) and the kindred spirit Annalisa (II, 4), his dream women are a projection of the mother he didn't have. In the dream that persuaded him to marry Carmela, the woman in a blue dress represents salvation. As his grandfather taught: "If you've got a good wife, you're a millionaire." Now Gloria in the black dress represents death. Her scarf slices him when she walks to the stove. She offers Tony a choice between seeing her throat wound and her sex, i.e., between the intimacies of pain and pleasure, death and love.

While everyone here hurts, Tony seems especially vulnerable. He pathetically misplaces his trust in Chris. Having seen Chris try to slap himself out of his stupor, we expect their doom if he is "gonna take this family into the 21st Century." For the Sopranos don't have the Egyptians' cooperative community, generations of craftsmanship, and "level of organization" that built the pyramids extolled in the opening scene TV documentary. The stoned Chris and Adriana and garbage-gobbling Cosette are oblivious to it all.

Closer to heart, Tony teases Carmela's matchmaking for Furio—"My little *Hello, Dolly!*"—unaware that her feelings may provoke her Good-bye, Tony. However sobering Tony's experience with Gloria, Artie's phone call finds him in bed with Miss Reykjavik. Artie's disintegration shakes Tony out of his guilt over Gloria: "One suicide is bad enough. But two? They can go fuck themselves. I made a donation to the suicide hotline in her name. That's it." Rediscovering the pain of commitment reseals Tony's callous veneer. Not for him Dr. Melfi's professional responsibilities: "I give my patients everything I've got. And when something like this happens, I'm devastated."

IV, 7: Watching Too Much Television

Written by Terence Winter and Nick Santora. Directed by John Patterson.

Tony's pay off can't salve Paulie's resentment following his jail term. After Adriana learns from TV that a wife can't be forced to testify against her husband, she urges Christopher to marry. He is enraged to learn she may be sterile, but relents. Brian prompts Tony and Ralphie to scam Federal Department of Housing and Urban Development funds. When Assemblyman Zellman reveals his affair with Irina, Tony at first approves but later whips Zellman with his belt.

The unifying theme of this episode is the spectrum of lies we tell each other and ourselves. Indeed "fibs" could be the answer to Paulie's opening line: "Whaddya hear? Whaddya say?" The title may imply that the more TV we ingest (present company excepted) the more lies we have on which to misconstrue reality.

One form of lying is withheld information. Christopher is furious that Adriana did not reveal her possible sterility: "Jesus fuckin' Christ. How could you lie to me like that?" Even after he returns: "I'm not happy that you lied to me." Zellman apologizes for not having told Tony earlier about Irina. Tony says he earlier exploded at Dr. Melfi (IV, 6) because she failed to tell him about Gloria's suicide: "You lied to me. . . . You withheld information about a very sensitive subject." In that "lie" Melfi was being professionally responsible.

Another lie is the hit-and-run innuendo, at which Paulie proves as adept as Livia. After reporting Tony's HUD scam to Johnny Sack, Paulie insists "this shit don't leave the table." Completing the ritual, Johnny replies "I'm hurt that you even have to ask."

The whole HUD scheme is a web of lies. Penis doctor Fried is the frontman, who buys the derelict houses with Tony's money, then resells them at almost tripled value to the black non-profit housing project fronted by Zellman's college activist friend Maurice. He applies for redevelopment mortgages the government guarantees. The money secured, the houses are abandoned—after Tony has pillaged their pipes, sconces and mantelpieces. He and Ralphie share ten times the $60,000 that Zellman and Maurice each get. When Brian first explains the possible scam, the camera retreats to a silent, exterior long-shot, so we don't hear how the grant applicants renege, just their initial pretence. At the payoff Ralphie expresses his greed as sympathy: "There's plenty more where that came from. A lot of poor families need affordable housing in Newark."

Tony lies to himself and to AJ when he drives through the slum to show him the church his ancestors helped build. For all Tony's principles, he's sapping funds dedicated to low-cost housing for the homeless. This scam undercuts his respect for the Italians who "gave a shit" about Newark. "This neighborhood used to be beautiful," because they did not abandon the community or their church. He lauds his forefathers for not seeking hand-outs. But after cashing in Tony toasts the federal government—for the progressive program he's perverting.

The corrupt trio—Jewish assemblyman, black social reformer, and Italian gangster—betray those Italian-Americans' ideals. Rationalizing their action, Zellman and Maurice recall how they ended up corrupt. Idealists slid into self-service. "When I think about when we started out," Zellman muses. Maurice recalls their anti-drug programs and voter drives, but "Over the years, it's like shovelling shit against the tide. . . . Yeah, you cut corners, but you help out. Do the best you can. . . . What are we supposed to be, the only honest men? . . . C'mon, let's get something to eat." Both men cite the current crisis to justify their corruption. Maurice explains his non-profit company's "hard times:" since 9/11 there are more competing charities. As Tony rationalizes robbing the taxpayers: They'll pay "for airport security. See how well that's doing. Give me a fuckin' break." Zellman is touched when a little black boy asks him: "Is there gonna be a nice house here now?" With the little girl whose father is shot in clearing the crack house, the boy represents the future our heroes are robbing.

Passing on the responsibility to evict the squatters is another form of lie. Wanting to appear uninvolved, Tony requires Zellman do it, then Zellman suggests Maurice mobilize his gang outreach program. When a black gang shoot up the tenement, all three schemers are false innocents. Similarly, Tony exercises his new detachment by leaving the steam room before Ralphie firms up the gang's deal with Zellman and Maurice.

Adriana's TV legal education provides another form of falsehood— pop misinformation. If one show teaches Adriana that a wife cannot be forced to testify against her husband, another asserts she can. A volunteer lawyer breaks the tie, against Adriana's interests. In contrast, there is a refreshing candor in the FBI agents' lunch debate whether to encourage her marriage plans. Chris is "a great catch": "Tall, dark and sociopathic." When they opt for Cupid ("They have our blessing.") the agents openly pursue their own interests, intending the bountiful bride to "sing" after her wedding.

As Adriana evolves from troubled mistress into blushing bride, her romance is increasingly shadowed by falsehood. With FBI agent Robyn in the greeting card shop, Adriana's sentimentality is exaggerated by the Hallmark setting. Her wedding joy seems another white lie, once her practical reason for marrying—to evade the FBI—collapses. Then there's Christopher's bitter rejection: "You knew you were damaged goods and you never fuckin' told me? . . . I don't have a son, the Moltisanti name dies."

Though Adriana relishes "seeing how much people give us," at her shower she's disappointed by the domestic gifts. Domestica threatens to turn her into the Carmela she dreads becoming, with her "stretch marks and houseful of kids" (I, 10). Her Cuisinart is shadowed by Gabriella's "I can't count how many cheese melts I've made for Silvio in that thing." And Carmela has already shifted the wedding ceremony from Las Vegas to *chez* Soprano. "It's a sacrament. . . . We'll decorate the whole house in 'mums' "—an unwitting reminder of Adriana's inability to become one. Still, these falsehoods prevent another: "Vegas? And get married by an Elvis impersonator?"

In contrast to the others' self-deception, Furio acknowledges and controls his love for Carmela. Tony in the steambath, Furio looks wistfully at Carmela's photo and phones her, on the pretence of having left behind his sunglasses (stashed in his glove compartment). When he next comes for Tony, Furio declines her invitation to coffee, claiming a troubled motor: "I need to keep my foot on the gas pedal." Translation: Outside the car he's riding the brake. This little white lie controls the troubling truth of his feelings for Carmela. As Carmela has not acknowledged hers, she can't exercise Furio's control. She feels troubled by Furio's coolness here, hard upon cousin Brian's new crookedness.

Clean-cut Brian's conversion shows how pervasive the duplicity is. Brian, after all, assumed that Paulie's welcome party marked his return "from college." Paulie's coming-out party proves Brian's, too, as he laps a topless dancer's bosom and awakens pantless on the Bada Bing stage. For innocently suggesting how HUD could be exploited—"Sometimes there's money in shit"—Brian scores a $15,000 Patek watch from Tony. Now Brian fibs to Carmela, pretending to borrow Tony's power drill. With no self-reflection he claims to be "sinking some anchors for a wall mirror." Brian is becoming another of the gang's legitimate anchors, like Dr. Fried. Ironically, Carmela involved Brian to legitimize enough family income to justify her complying with Tony's life. She is resisting Dr. Kracower's counsel (III, 7) for the easier advice of the academic priest.

Tony still tries to deceive Dr. Melfi: "I did exercise impulse control. And I have been controlling my anger." After the previous episode's attack, Melfi won't allow physical threats: "You loomed. You threw my tissue holder." Though a few weeks late, she insists they confront the issue, rather than accept his apology of flowers. Melfi demands the same respect he proudly showed the slum crack-heads when he forebore to return their attack. But Tony's restraint may have been more self-defending discretion than self-restraining valor. With AJ beside him and the crack-head's pistol in his face, Tony's new impulse control was his old survival instinct.

The Irina subplot exposes Tony's hair-trigger anger. His attack on Zellman erases the previous episode hopes that Tony might change from Gloria's tragic end. He seems generous when he wishes Zellman and Irina well: "You're both adults. Enjoy yourself." More sentimentally: "Frankly, I'm glad to have her off my payroll." His problem begins when he's driving along to "Hey, girl, I'd be in trouble if you left me now." At "I don't know where to look for love," he weeps and turns into Irina's where he erupts. After he belts Zellman, Tony brushes Irina's cheek, then leaves immediately, suggesting less love/lust for Irina than indignation at her lover. Tony may feel indignant that the corrupt politico has violated Tony's possession: "All the girls in New Jersey and you had to fuck this one?" Or if, as Tony initially assured Zellman, "The heart also wants what the dick wants," it wants even more what some more respectable dick wants. Cowering, Zellman pleads "Calm down. . . . We can talk about what's bothering you." Melfi also encouraged Tony to verbalize his anger, but here his action speaks more honestly than words.

The language that tells the deepest truths is art, in this case, song. For example, what "truth" lies in the fact that killer Paulie's favorite song is Sinatra's "Nancy With the Laughing Face," the *paisan* god's hymn to his baby daughter? Paulie is shooting solo pool when he advises Christopher to stay single as long as possible: "Marriage and our thing don't gibe." He's Silvio's example—as Uncle Junior is Tony's—of the horrible fate that awaits Chris if he does not marry. But we glimpsed Paulie's attempt at family life, with a mistress and her two children (II, 9). Now his solitude leaves him increasingly bitter. Perhaps his favorite song indulges a paternal warmth that his professional resolve has cost him, a loss that he denies.

"Tony's song" in this episode is the Chi-Lites's "Oh, Girl," piped into the steam-bath dressing room, where Tony and Maurice connect over the 30-year-old memories of this pop song from their high-school glow. Whatever the gap between the white mobster and the disillusioned black activist, this song is a bond, their shared experience. Indeed, Tony impresses Maurice when he corrects Maurice's assumption about the group's recording label: Brunswick, Tony insists, not Roulette. His knowledge shows respect. When the song returns on Tony's car radio, the lyrics stir Tony's loneliness. In addition, like Zellman's and Maurice's recollection of their more idealistic days, this song sets Tony's current corruption against his more innocent school days. For all the characters here, the promises of youth are their cruelest lie.

IV, 8:   Mergers and Acquisitions

Written by Lawrence Konner. Directed by Daniel Attias.

At his father's funeral in Naples, Furio admits his love for Carmela; an Italian TV cook's ponytail prompts her reverie. Tony is drawn into an affair with Ralphie's girl, Valentina La Paz. Carmela robs Tony's bin for private investments. To ease his mother's social exclusion at the Green Grove Seniors' Residence, Paulie has a ninth grade chum, Charles, now a high school principal, beaten up.

Within the title's focus on business partnerships, this episode surveys various forms of fidelity. Adriana confronts Ralphie's rudeness with her mother's advice: "You can tell everything about a man by the way he treats women." Fidelity is the respect for bonds. This episode provides a spectrum of such bonds from the faithfully served to the betrayed. If, as Furio says, "cancer don't respect nothing," the unfaithful's disrespect is the cancer of the time.

Apt for a high fidelity show, this has pertinent music. Twice Carmela hears Italian music, in the restaurant thinking about Furio, and at home, watching *Mario Eats Italy* and remembering Furio's touch when they danced. She hums his Italian song in the shower. The bagpipes on their new entertainment unit isolate Carmela and Tony as much as their cold silence later. Tony sings "We don't need no thought control" in the shower, while he considers freeing Valentina from Ralphie. Taking her cue from that and the TV discussion of women excluded from their husbands' finances, Carmela loots his stash.

The most touching fidelity is Paulie's devotion to his mother, despite his usual twist. Concerned for her, Paulie asks if Furio's father wears a colostomy bag. When Cookie Cirillo excludes Nucci Gualtieri because "We're a set group," Paulie pressures her son to soften her. Paulie has to excuse protecting his own mother: "For all the bad I did, . . . she always had my back." Charles's wife speaks for the broken-armed son, threatening to move Cookie to the Salvation Army home if she doesn't welcome Nucci. But as the social director tells Paulie, his mother "will have to accept responsibility for her own behavior." She cries a lot, omits her teeth, tattles on others, and has trouble making friends. Paulie's forceful service may not solve her problems. Even fidelity has its limits. In the context of the title, having acquired the Green Grove spot for his mother, Paulie now must negotiate her merging into that community.

Tony's scenes bristle with minor fidelities and major betrayals. Christopher fumbles to serve him, writing orders on his pillowcase. As for Brian, Tony's new pal: "What doesn't this kid know about money? You know, I trust him 1000 percent"—a proportion closer to Tony's usury than to Brian's math. When Rosalie admits that her Jackie left her uninformed and under-funded, Carmela grows insecure: "Tony pulls people into his circle. . . . I don't know what to think." Chase provides a clue: In the next shot the rear end of a horse crosses the foreground.

Tony figures in the major infidelities. After their one-afternoon stand, Tony deflects Valentina's ardor. He enjoys their initial merger but won't close the acquisition. Valentina questions his noble motives: "You got morals all of a sudden? . . . Some dago macho rules about you don't fuck your friend's girlfriend?" It's not ethics but distaste for Ralphie: "I don't like to go where Ralph Cifaretto has been." This revulsion is deeper than for Zellman occupying his Irina. Tony accepts Valentina only after she has left Ralphie and Tony is persuaded that Ralphie has not been where in Valentina Tony would go: "He doesn't fuck me. He's some kind of freak or something."

That is, rather than merge with his latest acquisition, Ralphie wants her to drip hot wax on his genitals before he goes off to masturbate or "to rub his cock raw with a cheese grater." Silvio nibbles baby mozzarella balls while trying to remember why Ralphie killed Tracee: She insulted his manhood. Finally Valentina leaves him, rather than lose face in some undefined foreplay with a leather mask. From Janice's revelation that Ralphie neither can nor wants to "get hard" in the normal way, Chase cuts to Tony rolling off Valentina, exulting in their normalcy. Nonetheless, in Ralphie's first scene here he dismisses the others as "Fuckin' sick, all of youse." He claims to love Valentina: "I've never been fucked so long, so good. I may have to marry her."

Janice respects her intimacy with Ralphie: "You're asking me to betray confidences. . . . Three thousand dollars!" Then she details what we've seen: "He bottoms from the top . . . He has to control things but he pretends he doesn't." That also describes Tony's new management techniques. Dribbling administrative slick, Tony tells Silvio and Christopher he's "trying to free myself up to do a little global thinking." He pumps Janice about Ralph because "I got my reasons. Managerial." He plays executive golf with his oily lawyer Malvoin.

Tony and Valentina engage over commissioning one of her gallery artists to paint Tony's horse. The merger develops under the guise of this acquisition, when they stop for sex. Both in the photo and in Valentina's sex life Tony wants himself included and Ralphie "cropped out." When Tony rejects her—"It's not going to happen. . . . For one thing, I already took his horse."—Valentina slaps him. She infers his rhyme of horse and whore and won't be Ralphie's possession. That's the point of the artist's mistake, Pie-O-*Mine*.

Valentina has the black "*Goyim* princess" looks, aggressive intelligence, professional respectability, and sexy manipulativeness that drew Tony to Gloria. Her juvenile mischief—maneuvering Ralphie into horseshit, loosening the cap on Tony's saltshaker—appeals to Tony's childish humor. When Tony plays a trick on Carmela she angrily reminds him that his honeymoon promise not to do that "is one promise I would like you to keep." His mischief is a miniature of his infidelity. But Tony doesn't see the Gloria in Valentina. When Melfi explains the "textbook masochist" Ralphie's perversity, she attributes the sexual release from "receiving pain, being humiliated" to his possibly having had "a controlling, punishing mother." Instead of recognizing another Livia, Tony fumbles about Ralphie rejecting "penissary contact with her Volvo." This Freudian slop recalls Gloria, the Mercedes seller. Tony remains in denial: "Is everything about everybody really about their mothers?"

When Carmela detects Tony's new affair she begins to overcome her fidelity. To Rosalie she repeats her impatience with the *goomah* tradition. In a supper club Ralphie brings Valentina while Tony is with Miss Reykjavik, who explains that "minding your p's and q's" originally referred to handling ones pints and quarts of ale. That is, manners are a social convention to control self-indulgence. To Melfi Tony regrets that the gang has drifted from the old tradition of Friday nights out with the *goomahs*, Saturdays with the wives (as we learned from *GoodFellas*). To Carmela Tony's infidelity requires she "steal" his money for her own investment. Chase justifies Carmela with one cut. Tony discovers her theft right after he tells Valentina, "I just had to get my head into a place where I felt I could really commit, to lavish all the care on you that you should have."

As Uncle Maurizio consoles Furio, his father "lived a full life. He had lots of women. That's the best you can hope for." But he advises Furio to "stay away" from his don's wife: "Are you fucking crazy? . . . The only way you could have her is if you killed the man." That Furio knows. He and Carmela are torn between their love for each other and their respective duties to Tony, as his boss and her husband. In fact, the episode is framed by Carmela serving her men coffee. The first she gives Furio, "with lots of milk and sugar. It's more comforting that way." He notes her soft touch on his shoulder. In the last, Carmela rises to make Tony a dutiful decaff.

In the episode's ominous end Tony, circling the mystery of his lost money, asks AJ if he or the pool guy has been in the backyard. When Carmela repeatedly asks Tony if there's something he wants to talk about, she seems poised to admit what she did and why. But Tony retreats, unaware that his infidelity is provoking Carmela's. The couple's chilled silence is emphasized by the absence of music. But the lyrics over the end-credits—sung in Gloria's/Valentina's sexy brass—diagnose their marriage: "When this battle is over, Who will wear the crown? Will it be you? Will it be me? Who will wear the crown?" Here the crown suggests both the cuckold's horns and the regal authority that prevents Tony from confronting Carmela.

This low-key episode heats up only when Paulie's goons chase the principal through his school. In effect, Paulie fights for his mother while Tony lets his marriage wilt. Tony's lack of fidelity also contrasts to Harrison Ford's in the film, *The Fugitive*, on the new TV, where the hero saves himself by tracking down his wife's murderer.

IV, 9: Whoever Did This

Written by Robin Green and Mitchell Burgess. Directed by Tim Van Patten.

Eager to serve the pretty TV reporter, Uncle Junior is knocked down by a boom mike outside the courthouse and emerges disoriented. Junior pretends to be mentally unfit to stand trial. While Ralphie is soaking in his tub, Justin, his 12-year-old son from a previous marriage, suffers accidental brain damage. Ralphie's grief changes his character. But Tony concludes Ralphie killed Pie-O-My in a stable fire, for the insurance. Tony kills him, then summons the stoned Christopher to hide the body.

In the Sopranos' (under)world sensitivity makes one vulnerable. Consider the two senior citizens, Nucci Gualtieri insecure in Green Grove and Corrado Soprano on trial for his life. Having deduced that Paulie reported his

Ginny joke to Johnny Sack, Ralphie phones Nucci in the middle of the night. He claims to be "Mike Hunt, Beaver Falls," a Pennsylvania cop, reporting that her son has been arrested for fellating a cub scout and with a gerbil in his *anus horribilis*, for whose extraction he requires her insurance number. Sniffing Paulie's soft spot for his mother, Ralphie exploits her instability.

Tony pounces on the doctor's suggestion Uncle Junior's accident may have nudged him into dementia or Alzheimer's. An obliging nurse attends him fulltime and he rehearses plausible confusion. Corrado's concern about his loss of dignity Tony dismisses as "just a good, clean way out." At the end, when Corrado steps out in his pyjamas for the morning paper, he spots the FBI watch, strolls to the neighbor's house, and asks for ice cream. Returned home, he blames his nurse for not bringing in the paper. As she is party to the scam, Corrado may be genuinely confused. He seems awry when he complains his trial caused him to miss The Early Bird Special dinner. Real or affected, he will exploit his own vulnerability as well as others'.

Another exploited vulnerability is Tony's profit on Artie's lost loan. Carmela tells Rosalie that the two men are obviously at odds but Tony won't say why. When Svetlana brings Nurse Branca to care for Corrado, Janice apologizes for her earlier cruelty (III, 3) then cries at her rebuff—to impress Bobby. Even that gentle hood shows his cold hand. At Uncle Junior's concern that his dementia claim might fail, he promises "We'll go after a juror."

In an unexploited vulnerability, Rosalie rejects Ralphie's distraught marriage proposal, despite her sympathy. Corrado's lawyer is off to Ireland to watch his daughter address the Irish parliament on abortion issues. Good and evil, idealism and pragmatism, coincide. So do honesty and duplicity, when Chase cuts from Rosalie assuring Ralphie that Justin is "going to be fine" to her telling Carmela "He's going to be a vegetable." As that lunch scene ends, Carmela waves and smiles to Artie, having just dissed him. Here discretion is the better part of honesty.

The central vulnerabilities are Tony's (as usual) and Ralphie's (dramatically new). The latter provides the episode's emotional roller coaster. After brutally teasing Nucci, Ralphie evokes sympathy by his emotional response to his son's brain damage. The usually irreverent wag seems transformed when he weeps in front of Tony ("I'm a different man. My poor baby. My little boy"), when he apologizes to Rosalie for not having understood her grief at losing Jackie Jr. (on his commanded hit, in III, 13), and when he donates a $20,000 annual scholarship in Jackie Jr.'s name at Rutgers. As the arrogant joker bewails his irresponsibility and makes amends for his failures, Ralphie becomes astonishingly human and vulnerable—for a cocky sado-masochist.

For Ralphie the best Father Phil, the popular culture priest, can do is steal a line from the Rolling Stones' "Sympathy for the Devil": "Were you there when Jesus Christ had his moment of doubt and pain?" Despite his assurances that "God understands . . . God has a plan for all of us . . . God is merciful. He doesn't punish people. . . . God loves him very much. Your job is you. To get yourself right with God," the priest is supercilious and insensitive to Ralphie at his most helpless and human. This episode gives us a surprising sympathy for the devil, Ralphie.

Perhaps Father Phil thinks he's quoting gospel, not the Rolling Stones, for the allusion resonates beyond his awareness. Ralph, too, is "a man of wealth and [albeit perverse] taste," stealing souls and faith, whose spirit has attended epic violence and injustice. In his world, too, "Every cop is a criminal, every sinner a saint." The song assures us that in Lucifer's world "heads is tails." Chase's gives Father Phil this Rolling Stones line as he gave Paulie's priest the *Godfather* line in II, 9, to secularize them. The priest speaks the devil's line—to the show's most satanic character.

Humanizing Ralphie complicates our response to his murder. For despite his new vulnerability, Ralphie is Ralphie. He veers from his responsibility for Justin's accident to blaming his ex-wife, Ronnie, for buying the bow and arrows. Then he blames Justin's weeping playmate. When Tony grabs Ralphie by the throat to subdue him—"It was an accident, alright? Just kids."—he foreshadows his fatal choke. Ralphie's arrogance outlives him on his answering machine: "With my schedule I cannot look up phone numbers."

Though he has his own shiv to hone, Paulie is unconvinced by Ralphie's "alligator tears. . . . You forget the thousand incidents with that guy?" Paulie would kill him for abusing his mother: "With all respect, T. There's a line in the sand with respect to mothers." That won't sway Livia's son: "This is a business." Then he kills him in a personal rage.

Tony intuits Ralphie burned the stable from how coolly he receives the news, his complaints about Pie-O-My's colic and bleak racing prospects, and his glee at the $200,000 insurance: "The horse was no fuckin' good." Carmela is touched by Tony's feelings when he introduces his "Lady Pie": "She busts her heart to win." But to Ralphie she's just "a fuckin' animal . . . a fuckin' horse. What are you, a vegetarian?"

As it happens, Pie-O-My was introduced quietly in "Columbus" (IV, 3), but was lost in the drama of Hesh's quarrel with Reuben. Ralphie buys her from Hesh immediately after Rosalie charges him with insensitivity: "Do you have any idea what it feels like? Do you? It's not just stuff. It's death. It's pain." The nexus of Rosalie's son's death, Ralph's responsibility for it, his leaving her, and his buying Pie-O-My returns six episodes later.

When Tony suspects arson, Ralphie asks "What sick fuck would do something like that on purpose?" Perhaps recalling how he similarly deflected Artie's suspicion ("Am I that fuckin' stupid?"—I, 3), Tony identifies the sickest fuck he knows. Tony conflates the burning of Pie-O-My with Ralph's murder of his whore Tracee (III, 6): "She was a beautiful, innocent creature. What did she ever do to you? You fuckin' killed her." His repeated "You killed her" connects both occasions when Tony breaks the code and attacks the made Ralph. Considering Ralph's behavior with Janice, Valentina, Rosalie, Tracee and Pie-O-My, his macho murder is a defence of the feminine. Aptly, it happens in the kitchen and paradoxically, while Ralphie is scrambling Tony some eggs.

But there is nothing heroic in the mortal combat. Ralph knees Tony in the groin, attacks him with a pot, a hot frying pan, a knife and a toaster, and sprays his eyes with Raid insecticide before Tony prevails. This fight bloodies and brutalizes Tony more than eliminating the rat Peters (I, 5) or Pussy (II, 13) did. This murder is personal, not the boss keeping order. However justifiable, Ralphie's killing is unbridled vengeance.

The gory aftermath should heighten our disgust. Chris hacks off the head and hands in the bathtub and drops them in Ralphie's bowling ball bag for separate burial. He's disturbed only when Ralphie's toupee comes off in his hand, another falseness. In a grisly irony, Chris dismembers Ralphie in the bathtub where he luxuriated when he should have been attending his son's visit. As Ralphie's humanization and cleansing begin and end in that bathtub, it blackly reflects Father Phil's prayer for him: "Wash away all my guilt. From my sin cleanse me."

For all this black comedy, the murder violates our moral code. And the gang's order, as even the stoned Christopher points out: "People could take it the wrong way. . . . Like it could happen to them. Without the protection of the boss." As a "made" man Ralphie should have been as immune to Tony's murder as to his assault (III, 6). Tony may increase his vulnerability by entrusting this most dangerous secret to his weakest aide, for Christopher has just shot up on horse when Tony summons him and may be—from the FBI's hold on Adriana—Tony's biggest heel, Achilles or otherwise.

At the end Tony stands under his own judgement: "If you can quote the rules you can fuckin' obey them."

Tony also has a more positive vulnerability. When he tells Ralphie of his affair with Valentina he puts himself into Zellman's position (IV, 7). Ralphie pats Tony's cheek affectionately and hugs him. Would that he had lucked into marrying a Carmela instead of his "miserable twat" Ronnie. Respecting his boss's wife might undercut his acceptance of his boss's new mistress, but normal values don't apply here. From Tony's advice—"Go see Pie. Take your mind off."—and his admission about Valentina may spring Ralphie's plan to kill Pie-O-My. If Ralph feels toward Tony what Tony felt toward Zellman and worries what secrets Valentina may divulge, how better to punish Tony than by killing "his" beloved horse. For Ralphie, "You can't argue with the fuckin' logic of it."

There is an emotional whallop when Tony looks under the blanket at the charred horse, that suffered through the fire, then watches it dragged away by the tractor. Her buddy, the goat, is foregrounded as a reminder of their animal community.

After the murder Christopher and Tony relax in front of *The Last Time I Saw Paris* (1954) on TV. Richard Brooks' adaptation of F. Scott Fitzgerald stories about dashed romance reflects on Tony. Charlie (Van Johnson) falls in love with and marries a Gloria/Valentina type of dark, needy beauty Helen (Elizabeth Taylor). In the present clip she has reformed into a responsible wife but he has turned unfaithful, drunk and disillusioned. When he refuses to let her in from the winter she catches a fatal cold. Later her sister Marion (Donna Reed) refuses to let him have his young daughter, because— still hurt that he chose Helen over her—she wants to deprive him of what he loves most. Her motive confirms Ralph's. The clip evokes Tony's betrayed wife, a mercurial love, and the loss of his private treasure. As Tony eats peanut butter off a knife, he projects his own sinister innocence. After all the splendid Italian meals we've seen here and Tony's compulsive noshing, this eating shows him stripped of all ceremony, taste, community, warmth, manners, civility—the bare forked appetite.

Nonethelss, Pie-O-My was—just "a fuckin' horse." More movingly, Tony and Carmela are affected by Justin's tragedy. AJ is ambushed by parental love when he comes down for breakfast. Carmela provides French toast and Tony encourages him not to be worried about his weight (*contra.* his earlier criticism). After Tony teases him about his blonde girlfriend, AJ stuggles to escape his bearish hug. Tony can only express his love for his son through this rough-house manner. In their silent glances Tony and

Carmela express a wellspring of love for their son and relief that they have not suffered Ralphie's loss. Tony's warmth toward AJ in this scene sets up his generosity in the next: "It could happen to anybody, Ralph." Justin's accident focuses the characters on children and their vulnerability. Paulie's continuing rage at Ralphie is excused by Silvio and Tony in parallel terms: "He's got no fuckin' conception" and "He's got no kids. You can't expect him to understand."

In the closing scene Tony wakes up alone in the Bada Bing, abandoned by his business "son," Christopher. Though Tony carefully showered and changed before sleeping, he awakens shaken and sullied. His Bada Bing t-shirt recalls his earlier complaint that Ralphie "disrespected the Bing" when he killed Tracee there. Tony studies himself in the dressing room mirror, among the pictures of the Bing girls, including (unemphasized) Tracee. As in the series' first shot the brute is framed by the feminine. The episode closes with two men facing the bright morning in an ambiguous mental and moral condition. Uncle Junior plays with his FBI observers, pretending to a dementia that may well be true, while Tony, awakening from a very dark night, walks alone into the blinding day. In very different ways, both men have made themselves vulnerable by their own power.

IV, 10: The Strong Silent Type

Written by Terence Winter, Robin Green and Mitchell Burgess.
Directed by Alan Taylor.

With his heroin use out of control, Christopher accidentally kills Adriana's dog and is robbed by drug dealers. A formal "intervention" by his family and friends erupts in his assault. Tony insists Chris go into rehab. Tony blames the New York Family for Ralphie's disappearance and refuses to share his HUD profits. Still trying to prove he's not "obnoxious" ("a toxic person"), Tony tells Dr. Melfi he's "the sad clown," gives Ralphie's ex-wife a plump envelope of cash, and is disappointed when Svetlana refuses to extend a quickie into an affair. While Furio keeps his pained distance from Carmela, she finally acknowledges her love for him.

In the opening scene Christopher shoots up in front of a *Little Rascals* TV episode in which: "Somebody's going to get something that he ain't expecting. . . . Look out, here he comes." An ape carries off a child, as Chris feeds the monkey on his back. The marauding mini-Kong is a comic embodiment of Tony's animal nature that has recurred since I, 1 ended with "God help the beast in me." When Chris sits on Cosette, the animal threat turns out to be human. The TV clip also parodies Tony's image as lovable rascal.

The "he" who comes in the next scene is not Furio, for whom Carmela expectantly primps, but Benny, his substitute driver. Furio becomes the threat Tony "ain't expecting." Carmela is disappointed that Furio does not bring her a gift from Italy, though his good-luck key ring for AJ, miniature Dante for "Maedo," and uncle's wine for the grownups amply express his warmth. He makes amends with the sweet gift of vinegar. Carmela is so distracted she roasts the turkey without first removing the giblets. She defends Furio's wine against Tony's complaint about the broken cork. She makes up reasons to visit Furio—e.g., her interior design—but drags AJ along and hides behind Martha Stewart: "Wait till you see how a mirrored backsplash can amplify your home." Though she hasn't slept with him, she tells Rosalie, her love for Furio is "real. We communicate. He looks at me like I'm beautiful. He thinks I'm interesting when I talk." Carmela lives for their fleeting moments together and fears Furio is her last hope for joy.

Furio prefers to wait for Tony in the car, rather than suffer Carmela's bittersweet company. When he cabs from the airport details Americanize him: Old Glorys everywhere, along with such new ones as Burger King, a Heaven is a Spa, and his incomprehensible Arab driver. Later Furio leaves Tony with Svetlana to go "watch the Bloomberg"—the financial TV channel, but also an homage to the NY mayor.

Furio tells Carmela that his visit home was a disappointment: "It was no so nice. I don't belong there no more. Something change. Maybe me. . . . I'm like a visitor in my own town. Life went on without me. There is nothing there for me now. . . . It feel strange to live [or 'leave'] here also. Maybe I should never have come to America." Carmela's setup, Jessica, is no girlfriend: "There is no communication. Like there is with some people, you know what I mean?" In their most intimate conversation, their real communication lies beyond their words, in their comfort. But AJ interrupts before Furio can explain that he returned to America for Carmela.

Unaware of the threat to his marriage, Tony objects that Carmela cut her hair without consulting him. He believes Furio is crying over his father's death, not love for Carmela: "Alright, but you gotta get over it." In his false security Tony has a date with Valentina plus an afternoon romp with Svetlana.

In equivalent Family tensions, his gunsels suspect Tony killed Ralphie over a horse. Albert Barese says Silvio would be in line "to pull his fuckin' plug" if he did. (Chase cuts to Justin, plugged in at the hospital.). Patsy's warning—"If it can happen to him it can happen to any of us."—carries special force, as Tony had Patsy's twin killed (III, 1). It's Patsy Tony has clear up his personal problems, silencing Gloria (III, 12) and keeping watch on Christopher here.

Tony still poses with Dr. Melfi: "I got to be the sad clown. For my friends. My family. The brave front." This was his original pretence (I, 1), "laughing on the outside, crying on the inside." But Melfi denies it: "I've never seen it . . . Your response to sadness is usually rage, not humour." She reminds him of his violent temper, compulsive eating and denial: "You've caused much suffering yourself, haven't you?" Everybody hurts. Tony rejects that "touchy-feely Freudian bullshit." Surveying Ralphie's son's suffering, his beloved Chris's heroin addiction, and "this 9/11 shit, I dunno, this shit that's going on everywhere, it's like some fuckin' asshole's stuck on the whole human race." Conflating icons, he sometimes feels "like the Reverend Rodney King Jr., you know, why can't we all just get along?" The episode shows Tony upsetting personal and work relationships left and right, but he denies responsibility: "My wife prays to God. What kind of God does this shit?"

Tony hides his guilt in his animal sympathy. He flees his Pie-O-My painting, then orders it burned. When Paulie hangs it in his own home, with Tony repainted as a Napoleonic soldier, Tony seems set to relive his torment by the Bada Bing's and Meadow's singing fish after he killed Pussy (III, 10). Melfi sensibly responds: "It's sad that you've lost something that you love. But that being said, it is a horse." Tony hasn't "grieved in this way for people." To Melfi, his pain at losing Pie-O-My recalls his ducks (I, 1). In the family "intervention" for Chris, Tony is most disturbed about Adriana's dog's death: "You killed little Cosette? I ought to suffocate you, you little prick." Tony knows "what it's like to lose a pet"—whether the ducks, the horse, a dog, Irina, or imminently, Carmela. Animals give and take the unconditional love denied in his power-based human relationships.

In cognate terms Uncle Junior advises Tony to kill Chris: "A dog you love catches rabies, you put it out of its misery." But Tony opts for Chris's rehab: "You're my nephew and I love you. . . . Anybody else would've had their fuckin' intervention right through the back of their head."

Even Tony's love is guilt-edged: "You and me, we're close. We've done a lot of things for each other," most recently, Ralphie. Equating selfdestructors, Chase cuts from Tony's libertine enjoyment of Svetlana to Chris's admission into rehab. Paradoxically, the very restrictive institution— no phone calls, no chocolates, no caffeine—is named Eleuthera (i.e., freedom) House ("A place for new beginnings"). Of course, those restrictions are calculated to develop freedom from drugs. Not freed from his literary delusions, however, Chris plans to publish a journal under his pen name.

Chris's family intervention turns into black comedy. When Chris insults Tony, Paulie jumps him, goaded by Chris's mother: "Smack some goddam sense into him." "My own mother," Chris responds, "Fuck you, you fuckin' whore." So much for the "non-judgmental confrontation—a carefrontation." In contrast to Carmela's civilized "intervention" with Father Phil (I, 13), here Chris's mother evokes Livia's bitter strength and Chris, despite having avenged his father, is a less than dutiful son. Chris is hospitalized with a hairline skull fracture, ostensibly having fallen from the kitchen counter while "spraying for ants"—Tony's guilty memory of Ralphie's Raid. The scene reminds us how far Tony's world is from the possibility of therapy.

Tony keeps looking for love in all the wrong places. He drifts into a relationship with Svetlana, Irina's one-legged cousin. First Tony is impressed that Svetlana is developing her own Web site. Her absent fiancé Bill is "a lucky man," because she carries on with her life regardless of her disability. Indeed, she doesn't even think of her leg as an excuse: "There are worse things." Even *sans* prosthesis, she's so independent she can drive herself to drink. Tony notes her smile and caresses her cheek, her face delicate in his paw. Tony now sees Svetlana as Furio sees Carmela: a beauty with substance. Svetlana deflects Tony's compliments: "That's the whole purpose of people like me, to inspire people like you." But she acknowledges Tony's "many positive qualities": "You're big and strong and full of life." After sex she declines an affair: "You're a nice guy. But I got my own problems. I don't want all the time to prop you up." Branca's early return interrupts this intimacy as AJ did Carmela's with Furio.

Free from the sad clown's indulgent self-pity, Svetlana has the spirit and industry Tony admires in his forefathers. She diagnoses modern Americans: "You expect nothing bad ever to happen, when the rest of the world expects only bad to happen. And they're not disappointed. . . . You have everything and still you complain. . . . You've got too much time to think about yourself." In stopping at their quickie, Svetlana distinguishes herself from Tony's needy, manipulating women who exploit him. Putting on her face, Valentina responds to Tony's gloom over Justin and Christopher with

"I think I'm going to have the medallions of veal." The one-legged Russian, strong and independent, would rather enjoy and dump Tony than be ensnared in her hold on him.

In the montage that concludes the episode Chase parallels the solitudes of Tony and his two looming nemeses. To varying degrees the three men lack Svetlana's self-sufficiency. Melancholy Furio listens alone to an Italian love song (the only song in the episode). While dependent Tony nukes Carmela's rigatoni, Furio makes himself linguini from scratch—with the Old School Italian's self-sufficiency. After Furio grates his parmesan and pours a wine, Tony pours himself a milk (All-American boy or for an ulcer). The boys are having dinner together—alone. The intercutting proposes a community of isolated men, with unspoken conflicts between them. That is visualized when Paulie turns on the baseball game with his Napoleonic Tony showing off Pie-O-My behind him. The revision reduces Tony's genuine emotion to cliché. The military drums continue through the end-credits, beneath the surface of lonely male pleasure threatening war.

IV, 11: Calling All Cars

Written by David Chase, Robin Green, Mitchell Burgess, and David Flebotte. Directed by Tim Van Patten.

Though troubled by Ralphie's murder and Svetlana's rejection, Tony quits Dr. Melfi's treatment. He asks Carmine's son to help in his conflict with Carmine and Johnny Sack. Janice exploits Bobby's children's grief to inveigle him. Uncle Junior is ruled competent to stand trial, despite his apparent disintegration.

Tony's two dreams frame the episode. In the first Carmela is driving Tony in his father's stuffy Cadillac, with Ralphie beside her. A turquoise caterpillar on his pate turns into a black butterfly. Gloria beside Tony in the back seat offers a test drive, then changes into Svetlana. The opening bars of Smokey Robinson's "The Tears of a Clown" on the car radio recall Tony's "sad clown" (IV, 10). The opening shot, a crucifix on the rear-view mirror, supports Melfi's suggestion that the dream expresses Tony's troubled conscience. He wants "to square with Carmela" his girlfriends. As Johnny-Boy would never be driven by a woman, Tony still lives in his father's shadow. Carmela is driving him "no place. We never seemed to get anywhere. Kinda like this therapy."

In the second dream Ralphie brings Tony to a large old house, where Tony turns into his respected forefathers, in work clothes, suspenders, cloth cap in hand: "I'm here for the masoner job. . . . Me no speaka da English." The shadowy female on the stairs may be Death, Gloria, Livia (like his father's invisible shadow in the first dream Caddy), the ghost of lost aspirations—or all of the above. Her enigma counters the sensuous precision of the beautiful leg that starts the dream. Both images reiterate the ambivalent mystery of the Feminine, before which Tony has squirmed since the series' first shot (I, i). After Ralphie progressed from colorful creep to airy spirit in the first dream, here Tony regresses. In both dreams, Tony confronts his moral compromise in deeply disturbing images.

After waking, Tony stumbles sweating and panting into a hellishly red hotel bathroom. Out in the bright morning, he looks at the turquoise ocean and hears on a radio the Beach Boys' upbeat "Surfin' USA," on which the episode ends. After Tony's panic attack, the lyrics taunt the "immigrant" outsider, who could never crack even Cusamano's country club, with an All-American buoyancy beyond him: "We'll be planning our route, that we'll be taking real soon. We'll be waxing our surfboard. . . . Everybody's gone surfin', Surfin' USA." As a summons to carefree pleasure, the song contrasts to the emergency alarm of the episode's title, "Calling all cars." Melfi uses the phrase jocularly when she tells Dr. Kupferberg's answering machine, "Guess who's no longer a patient of mine." As she does not call his emergency number, she may be the only major character in this episode who is *not* crying for help.

The idea of surfing the ocean may also reflect Tony's decision no longer to probe his subconscious. At the start of the first session here Tony is silent, withdrawn, angry that "four fuckin' years" of Melfi's therapy have (obviously) not helped his "impulse control." After turning aside a Carmine affront—"I'm not gonna go fuckin' ballistic"—he explodes at a car horn. In the session he ridicules his association of meat, sexuality and violence: "Oh, my mother would come when she saw a pot roast."

In the second session, he acknowledges that his new "fuckin' self-knowledge" gave him "some leadership strategies," but he remains "a miserable prick. I've said that since day one." His "such a fuckin' prick" is as false as his "sad clown" pretence. Tony's self-criticism is never honest. Conflating his last two flings, he briefly claims *he* ended the affair with Svetlana: "Broke a woman's heart. Told her I couldn't see her no more." His Freudian slip—"I had to cut off her leg—I mean our affair"— proves his everyday psychopathology even as he rejects therapy. Tony refuses Melfi's proposal to commence "the real work. . . . We can delve into who you are and what you're really after in your very brief time on earth."

Instead of "changing . . . finding a way out," Tony retreats to his sexual strategies. He lightly offers Melfi the diamond horseshoe pin he claims always to give girlfriends when he leaves them, cowardly. Again his self-criticism is false. He usually gives his women (Carmela, Gloria) jewelry to keep them, not to see them off. The pin he gave Svetlana is the one Valentina rejected; he gave none to Gloria or Irina. Otherwise the horseshoe is both a memento of his Pie-O-My and a secular totem, like the opening shot crucifix, another sentimental rear-view mirror. It reveals his ambivalence toward the feminine. Earlier, he told Melfi that if he had spent his therapy money on a Ferrarri instead "At least I would've got a blow-job out of *that*," then evades Melfi's follow-up. Just as he disdains dream analysis, he expresses a suppressed desire that an earlier dream defined. Tony departs Melfi with a jaunty *"Adios,"* a kiss, and a handshake. After this formal affection Tony leaves Melfi standing alone in a wide high angle shot. Like two similar shots in their first session here, it defines the gap Tony's evasion has always cut between them.

Svetlana phones as Tony is listening to another song of guilt/denial, "I Shot the Sheriff (but I did not shoot the deputy)." As pragmatic and selfish as Tony, she doubts that she deserves the diamond pin but "I'm going to keep it. Don't worry, diamond like this?" She dismisses their pleasure as her spoiled Americans should learn to deal with their pain: "These things happen, then life goes on." Tony is more affliction than blessing.

Sadder cries for help come from the Baccalas. In his mourning, Bobby buries a fourteenth-anniversary cake at his wife's grave. He visits the site daily: "That's what I miss the most. Talking to her." In his children's struggle, Bobby Jr. tries to strengthen his younger sister—"There's no such thing as ghosts"—then hides to cry under his comforter. At Carmela's Sunday family dinner, AJ avoids the orphans, then exceeds his earlier cruelty (IV, 4) by terrifying them with a séance. Sensitive Bobby is forgiving: "Part of growing up. Don't worry about it."

"Stuck at Platonic" with Bobby, Janice shakes him out of his "morbid clinging." At first, he refuses to pay the funeral house because they "put on 15 extra pounds" preparing Karen for burial. Continuing the show's collocation of meat, eroticism and trauma, Janice says Bobby likes his steak "still moving." She complains that Bobby didn't tell her that she was bringing dinner on his anniversary night: "The sides alone were over $30." On a movie date, Janice's generosity cracks:

JANICE: She's dead. I'm here.
BOBBY: Shut the fuck up.
JANICE: You shut the fuck up.

Finally, Janice exploits the children's superstition. As Vlad 666, aka Rising Damp, which combines Dracula, Satan, and a household's disintegrating foundation, she eerily E-mails Bobby Jr. directions to the ouija board. The children's upset persuades Bobby that his grieving is "bad for them. It's unwholesome." As Janice assures him, "The dead have nothing to say to us. It's all narcissism that makes us think they even care." Janice, the ultimate narcissist, takes control when Bobby agrees to eat Karen's last ziti. In a wordless, candlelit dinner Janice wolfs and Bobby nibbles her rival's last remnant. As she told the kids, "It's a sin to waste good food." As Junior depends on Bobby to suborn a juror, Bobby is rising (damp?) in the organization. Janice runs him with her mother's cold power.

And so to the minor figures' calls for help. Vic the Appraiser is first beaten up for serving Tony, then by his goons for staying away. In an echo of past viciousness (II, 3), the crippled Beansie is summoned to arrange Tony's Miami Beach meeting with Little Carmine. Carmine and Johnny Sack, demanding 40 percent of Tony's HUD profits because "we share Zellman," disdain Tony's compromise offer of 5.5.

In Little Carmine Tony finds a pretentious parody of himself. Little Carmine also smokes a cigar but wears a white suit, not Tony's costly casuals. With Tony's easy knowledge, he speaks of the French King Lewis and his castle at Ver-sales. Little Carmine emulates the Corleones' rhetoric: "I appreciate the respect you show me by coming down here and reaching out to me at this time." Tony is slightly less arch: "If the proper response is not forthcoming in a business-like time frame—my next move will not be further conversation."

But Little Carmine feels more secure than Tony: "Do you know how long it's been since I was afraid of my father?" When Tony carefully calls Johnny Sack "always usually a voice of moderation," Little Carmine is more accurate: "True, he's a pragmatist. But he's also a greedy mother-fucker." Tony plans to tell Johnny Sack of the meeting, unaware that Johnny is conspiring with Carmine and tempting Paulie with the idea of replacing Tony. Against that unknown conspiracy, Tony shifts suspicion about Ralphie's situation: "Maybe you can tell me." With his false security and dismissing Dr. Melfi, Tony proves unaware of his emerging emergency, "calling all cars."

IV, 12:   Eloise

Written by Terence Winter. Directed by James Hayman.

Bobby selects which juror to intimidate. Tony's dispute with Carmine escalates. Paulie robs and murders one of his mother's friends. As Furio's feelings for Carmela deepen he impulsively flees to Italy. Meadow invites her family to Sunday dinner and Carmela for their traditional Eloise tea at the Plaza Hotel, but Carmela explodes their comfort.

"Eloise" is Kay Thompson's 1950s' fictional heroine, a six-year-old who lives independently atop the Plaza Hotel, with money and plane tickets (but no interference) from her mother. This fantasy is an innocent parallel to the Sopranos' liberty. "Eloise" has been a barometer for Meadow's closeness with Carmela. In I, 1, angry Meadow rejected their annual tea as childish. In III, 6, Meadow proposed the tea, flushed (via Noah's seduction) with her new womanhood. Here the tea should confirm Meadow's adult comfort with her mother, but Carmela denies that.

Meadow hoped to clear up whatever upset Carmela at her family dinner, when Carmela argued against the homosexual subtext in Melville's novella *Billy Budd*. Despite Meadow's overture, Carmela snaps at her daughter's advice and treats her as a child. Despite her formal white gloves, Carmela's attack is gloves off, leaving Meadow feeling belittled. This explodes their earlier closeness, when Meadow confided "I keep waiting for [Finn] to say he loves me and he hasn't" and Carmela replied from her experience: "Some men have to move at their own pace, Med." Sensing Carmela resents her love, Meadow calls her "Mrs. Danvers," the villain of Daphne DuMaurier's *Rebecca*, who turns her mistress's memory against the widower's new love.

Though the episode's title points to the feminine values of sensitivity and care, this episode focuses on their smothering antithesis, macho power. This tension is implicit in the prosecutor's opening words: "Ladies and gentleman . . . Corrado Soprano is not some harmless old man but a killer who orders up murder like you or I order up coffee." It's implicit when Colin but not Alessandra laughs at Tony's dentist joke about Meadow's protective Finn: "If anyone bothers her he'll knock their teeth out. Then he can put them back in." It's explicit when AJ's proud flatulence drives Meadow away and, in the next scene, Paulie kills Mrs. Matrone.

In the Sunday argument, Carmela contends that *Billy Budd* is about "an innocent sailor being picked on by an evil boss." Her naive reading is based on the Peter Ustinov movie but is more influenced by Tony having just told her Furio has returned to Naples, presumably to avoid confronting *his* evil boss. The song over the closing credits, Annie Lennox's "Little Bird," expresses a woman's frustrated dreams of escape: "I wish that I could be that bird, / And fly away from here." Furio is Carmela's version of Tony's lost ducks.

As Carmela confides in Rosalie, she has lost her chance to escape her narrow marriage. Coming out of church, when Carmela learns Furio listed his house, "I felt like someone punched me in the stomach. I almost threw up the sacrament." When she visits Furio's vacant house, the shot starts with a close-up of Carmela outside the window. As the camera tracks back through the empty rooms, Carmela shrinks boxed into the background and the empty rooms express her void.

Though Carmela tells Tony "She hates my guts," she seems to resent her daughter's blossoming. Amplifying her frustration, Meadow's subversive reading of *Billy Budd*, supported by her superior education and friends, affronts Carmela's oddly conventional morality. Her grief prevents her from enjoying Meadow's praise from her flat-mate's mother, her impressive lover, Finn, and even Tony. In the last scene he congratulates Carmela on the "wonderful . . . smart, beautiful, independent woman that you created. Isn't that what you dreamed about?" "Yes," she replies, as they lie in bed, with her back to Tony and her eyes wide open. As she has been watching *How to Marry a Millionaire*, the 1953 romantic comedy starring Marilyn Monroe, Lauren Bacall, and Betty Grable, she has lost her wide-screen dream that Furio would sweep her away into a passionate love. Carmela's realized dream (Meadow) pales before her lost one (Furio). In a parallel delusion, Paulie reminds his mother that Richard Kiley stared at her all through his performance of "The Impossible Dream" in the Broadway *Don Quixote*.

For his part, Tony shows some new sensitivity, *sans* Melfi. Misreading Carmela's tension and her haircut, he offers a spontaneous cruise. Though he's pleased that Finn is not living with Meadow, the dentistry student is Tony's dream come true. His fantasy nurturer, Isabella (I, 12), studied dental surgery and a Finn is a pole away from a Mafiosa. At Meadow's Tony shows a genial comfort. Though he's embarrassed by AJ's reference to "fags" Tony is paternally disappointed that her male flat-mate is hetero. His joke smoothes over Carmela's argument: "Must be a gay book. Billy Bud's the ship's florist, no?"

AJ also imposes his personal experience on Melville: the novella shows "how mean humans can be to each other, especially when living under crammed conditions." He's even more straight than his mother: "Why would an officer care if a sailor is handsome or not?" AJ probably won't fare much better with his teacher Mr. Wiggler's (!) next assignment, Thomas Mann's *Death in Venice*, another novel of fatally suppressed homosexuality.

As touching as his closing conversation with Carmela is Tony's chat with Meadow about her mother's "going through a tough time right now." The staircase setting suggests a new leveling in their relationship, as he reveals his therapy and marital counseling. "On some level she may feel unfulfilled. Switch on Rosie O'Donnell, that's all these women bitch about. A little of that is probably my fault. Anyway, it's an epidemic, right?" Meadow has deduced Carmela's source of grief from AJ's callow reports on Carmela and Furio, but she lets pass Tony's explanation, menopause. If Carmela is suffering from "change of life," it's because Furio's departure prevents it.

Tony remains associated with brute phallicism. When his goons draw an erection over the gondola in Carmine's restaurant mural, that elegant boat becomes Tony's coarse *Stugots*. Carmine's retaliatory closure of the Esplanade site is announced with the wheeling of the Giant Rat, apparently a Philadelphia tradition for union closures. Carmine "rats on" Tony—and his own partnership in the scam. At the casino, Furio coldly watches Tony nuzzling and dancing with a blonde whore and rejects the one who invites him. His disgust increases when Brian, a new convert to Tony's corruption, stumbles along, whoring and puking. Brian hums the helicopter theme—from the wrong Coppola movie, *Apocalypse Now*. When Furio joins Tony to piss against the powerful winds of the helicopter that the casino has provided to fly its big losers ($15K) home, it's an image of phallic arrogance. The incident realizes the casino manager's joke about a customer's "I gotta leak in the sink." Feeling stained by this life, Furio jumps on Tony, throttling him. But he checks his urge to push Tony into the propeller. When Furio explains, "You're standing too close," he masks his new moral awareness as more respectable homophobia.

Not killing Tony suggests that Furio's love for Carmela has made him want to stop being like him. So he returns to Italy. He earlier managed to tell Carmela that she is "a very special woman"—to which she responded with the suggestive "Have you thought about flooring yet?" They agree to "a date"—to choose floor tiles for his mother's guest house. They beam and glow at each other. Her fresh scones are "like the smell of heaven" to him, but he foregoes their taste. In contrast, Tony takes one and discards it after a bite. Furio walks away from their quarrel over Tony's cruise. When Tony complains "She can be a moody bitch," Furio defends her: "She's probably worried for her mother." Insensitive, Tony storms off because Carmela isn't concerned that "one of my key guys disappeared to Naples, for Christ's sake."

Paulie is a parody of filial devotion. After Minn involves his mother in a car accident, he offers to drive the three old women to *The Producers*, Mel Brooks's popular play where, *inter alia*, a crook seduces little old ladies. Paulie limits his generosity to gas and parking, making the other women pay for their dinners. In a parody of the myth of the nurturing mother, the old women scramble for the buns, crackers and sugar at the restaurant, "for my son," the high school principal's mother claims. Paulie allots his mother some rolls from Minn's doggy bag.

When he hears Minn keeps her cash under her bed, this model son shows his colors. To recover Tony's grace Paulie robs Minn. She tries to phone his mother to tell on him. After she knees his groin he straddles and smothers her. Paulie's action is matricidal, the posture incestuous, and the incident an explicit image of male force smothering the vulnerable female. We're reminded a son can be as monstrous as a mother. Though Minn is unlikable, her murder is as offensive as the Russians' attack on Janice (III, 4). In that anti-sentimental spirit, gentle Bobby Baccala picks a family man as the weak spot on Junior's jury. His goons intimidate him by paying for his son's chocolate bars, recalling Mahaffey's ice cream threat (I, 1). An American flag behind the frightened juror questions American justice.

In their secret meeting, Johnny Sack's "pragmatic" comments about Carmine—"Yes, he's very healthy. Thank God. Call me."—license Tony to whack the senior boss. The scene reverses Carmine's tacit permission for Tony to whack Johnny (IV, 4). But as Paulie discovers, Johnny is untrustworthy. For all Johnny's promises, Carmine has never heard of Paulie and offers Tony's turncoat no support. After the vandalizing of the restaurant Johnny advises Carmine that "We have to break [Tony's] back."

Tony and Carmine are both unyielding. Carmine loses money, too, when he closes down the Esplanade site, but he refuses to give in to Tony's will or to Little Carmine's attempt to end the "total deb'-acle." Despite his own misfit language—"He's an old-fashioned guy, Pop. Very allegorical."—Little Carmine calls Tony "a pose-oor." A reaction shot reveals Little Carmine's hurt when his father remembers first meeting Tony: "Decisive as he is, I would've been proud to call him my son." Of course, it's that decisiveness that makes both men inflexible. We remember Little Carmine as a traffic danger (II, 11), which may be why he was assigned to Palm Beach (as the Corleones banished hapless Fredo to Las Vegas).

To Carmine, the Soprano "Family" is no more than "a glorified crew," the male power's alternative to the bright, young, domestic "crew" Meadow invites her family for Sunday dinner to meet. That rhyme suggests that Meadow has—alone, so far—transcended her Soprano roots and found values and relationships beyond Carmine's "crew."

IV, 13:   Whitecaps

Written by Robin Green, Burgess Mitchell and David Chase.
Directed by John Patterson.

Tony charms his family by deciding to buy a seaside house, "White-caps." But when Irina reports his affairs Carmela demands a divorce. Carmine settles his dispute after Tony puts out a contract on him. Corrado's hung jury causes the judge to declare a mistrial. Chris returns from rehab renewed.

The Season Four conclusion is primarily about broken agreements or trusts. Some are minor, like the Chinese take-out omitting a dish and Vito hustling Adriana with colleague Chris in rehab. Chris violates his 12-Step Program when, rather than apologize to all he offended, he takes Tony's advice and lets "sleeping dogs lie." (Irina invalidates this strategy.) Others are life and death. When Chris cancels the hit on Carmine, he pays his "trustworthy" hoods their fee, then kills them, recovering the money. Despite all this contractual uncertainty, Tony broadens Carmela's real estate principle: "More is lost by indecision than by wrong decision."

In this moral seascape even long-standing commitments crumble. After Carmine accepts Tony's terms, even as the mobsters hug, their word is empty. Carmine is "healthy as a fuckin' rhino," Johnny assures him, and Tony amens: "You just stay that way." But Johnny still wants him killed and feels betrayed by Tony's refusal. To Tony's "John, I still consider you a dear, dear friend," Johnny glares with revulsion. Paulie, Tony's traitor, claims he was serving Tony's interests. In this episode there is no honor among killers.

Nor in real estate. Sniffing more security in Tony's offer, Whitecaps owner Alan Sapinsly bullies his first buyer into cancelling the deal: "I spent ten years as a litigator. Buy this property, I'll make your life a misery. I'll tort you into the poorhouse." But when Tony wants out Al refuses to cancel the agreement, or to return the $200K deposit. Deposits "hold parties to agreements." "We have a signed contract," he reminds Tony, echoing his reply to his first buyer: "I'm aware we have a contract in place, Dr. Kim."

This Jewish lawyer resembles our Italian gangster. His wife Trish is another Carmela, in appearance, sense, warmth, and long-suffering duty. Al has Tony's profanity, homophobia and threats. Rejecting Tony's withdrawal, Al says "You and your wife could be back together in a month, leaving A.S. here fucked in the ass." He dismisses Tony as "Fuckin' gangster asshole!" Al is also an Equal Opportunity racist, from "The *Stugots*? Fuckin' *goombah* trash!" to dismissing his wife's scruples with "Rabbi." When Tony has his *Stugots* anchored on Al's waterfront to blare Dean Martin's Las Vegas act through the night, he seems the more civilized. Like a bonded wiseguy, Al initially urges Tony to "meet perfunctorily" with all the major divorce lawyers so that none could work for Carmela.

Corrado's trial also involves betrayal. Bobby's threatened juror stands alone against the others' unanimous conviction. Later, he is rebuffed when he asks another juror to call when her new grandchild is born. She rejects his family sentiment, which exposed him to the gangsters' pressure. Instead of appreciating Bobby's success, Corrado orders him to stop snuggling Janice to fetch Murf's payment. Their dancing to "I Got You, Babe" reminds us Bobby has been "had" by Janice. Corrado denies Bobby the Janice warning he gave Richie (II, 11).

In another broken promise, Chris avoids marriage plans and "isn't sure anymore he could be a good father, after killing [Adriana's] dog." Given his concerns about her sterility, his excuse rings false. This premarital tension extends into Johnny Sack's uncharacteristic anger at Ginny and the climactic shattering of the Soprano marriage.

This split provides some of this show's most remarkable acting and complexity, with insights comparable to Ingmar Bergman's *Scenes from a Marriage* (1973). Before Chase had Ralphie killed, he humanized him with his son's tragedy. Here Tony's domestic generosity deepens his loss. Tony buys Whitecaps to keep the family together after the kids grow up and away. AJ has mentioned his love for the ocean (IV, 7). This sentiment intensifies Tony's loss. Hence the tragic emptiness of his promise to his kids: "You'll inherit this." By episode's end, they have only the shards of their family. Carmela's "You're full of surprises" proves as prophetic as Tony's earlier "Me to know, you to find out," which refers to their surprise trip to

Whitecaps but also encapsulates his years of secret adultery. If Whitecaps is "like the Kennedy compound" so is the family's humiliation by betrayals. Their family dream—"When we was piss poor this was the biggest caviar wish we could come up with"—is destroyed by Carmela's nightmare: one of Tony's goomahs reaches into her home. To Carmela's rue—"You were my guy. You could be so sweet. Nobody could make me laugh like you."—he responds: "You knew the deal." The gangster's wife must tolerate his gumahs. To Tony, Carmela broke their marital vows of unilateral infidelity.

But their split results from manifold betrayals. For Tony it began with his assault that left Zellman feeling diminished in Irina's eyes and impotent. Abandoned, the drunk Irina phones Carmela: "Tony loves me, you know. . . . If it wasn't for his kids you'd be out on the street." If Irina is "shit," she muses, where does that leave Carmela "in the pecking order." Irina learned of her cousin's matinee with Tony through Branca's betrayal of Svetlana's trust. There is no *omerta* among adulterers or other caregivers.

For Carmela the split began when she realized (IV, 12) that Meadow has matured and fulfilled her mother's dream. Meadow's moral responsibility transcends her Soprano roots. Carmela could reverse Irina's claim: It was because of her kids that Carmela did not throw Tony out. With Meadow grown, Carmela can finally act on Dr. Krakower's prescription (III, 7) that she escape Tony's pecking order. Our third Dr. K. confirms the latter's relevance here, as Dr. Kim's heated business negotiation on his way into surgery recalls Dr. Kennedy (III, 7).

Svetlana offers Tony cold comfort: "Divorce hard for kids. After this they don't trust. I'm child of divorce." But she assures him: "Take care. You're stronger. You'll be all right." That anticipates Carmela's last advice, "Be careful." More like Irina, Paulie advises Tony to throw Carmela out of his house.

Like Furio's departure (IV, 12), Irina's news visibly hits Carmela like a punch in the stomach. She feels especially betrayed because she knew Svetlana as Livia's caregiver. They discussed Livia's alopecia and bowel movements and shared vodka at her death. "You have made a fool of me for years with your whores," Carmela begins, but the familiar caregiver and Irina's intrusion are too much. Under Tony's weight she declares, "I don't love you anymore, Tony. . . . You're not sleeping in my bed. The thought of it makes me fucking sick."

Carmela moves through rage, fear of madness, hatred, to seething calm. Tony goes from surprise, through "innocence" (the "Who, me? shit" Carmela defined for Father Phil in I, 13), to promises for forgiveness, to bitter resignation, anger and his rebounding hatred. Her climactic attack is admitting, "For the last year I have been dreaming and fantasizing, and in love with Furio. . . . He made me feel like I mattered." Tony counters with Svetlana's advantage. She has suffered and emerged strong and independent, while Carmela is comfortable and materialistic. With Svetlana he could converse, while Carmela only complained. Carmela rejects this defence: "Were you best friends with [all the other strippers and cocktail waitresses] too? You fuckin' hypocrite." Tony can't fool Carmela anymore: "I know you better than anyone. That's why you hate me." The rage turns violent. After her first, "Don't you ever touch me again," Carmela taunts him (like Gloria): "You want to hit me, go ahead." Tony slams her to the wall and table. Told about Furio, he punches holes in the wall beside her head.

Tony won't let his new marital vulnerability soften him. He accepts Carmine's and Artie's sympathy but drives his hard bargain and complains the pasta is "not *al dente.*" He phones Dr. Melfi but hangs up. Muscling back home he commandeers the giant screen and righteously eats out of a jar of Guiltless Gourmet dip. His family lost, he feeds his appetite, compulsive and guiltless. The image also shows how far Tony has fallen from the grace of Carmela's generous meals.

Both parents respect their children's needs. Tony defends Carmela, slipping AJ cash for gifts to apologize for the boy's disrespect. Meadow having deduced her mother's love for Furio, Carmela assures her she was never unfaithful to Tony and refuses to cultivate her daughter's knowledge of Tony's betrayals. When Tony moves to the Plaza, his illusion of freedom plays against the women's Eloise bond.

Both children reel under the news. Meadow flees in sympathy for Carmela: "Jesus, how could you eat shit from him for all these years?" But later she runs to share Tony's embrace of AJ. Less conflicted AJ provides the male parallel: "Well, you don't have to put up with her shit anymore," and tries to escape Carmela's discipline to Tony's camp. Despite sensing that her family's good times were "all predicated on bullshit," Meadow used to feel superior to her "friends who had these fucked-up divorced parents." She anticipated rearing her own children to enjoy their family reunions (Tony's vision for Whitecaps). In her grief Meadow recalls her particular anger—"God, isn't there anything to eat in this house?"—after Noah dumped her (III, 6). This memory shows she regrets her insensitivity but also her experience of male betrayal. So Chris's hood hides his score from his ex's child-support claims.

In counterpoint to these broken trusts and moral chaos, Chase provides an aesthetic order, a surface of rhyming shots and phrases that suggests the possibility of coherence. He cuts from the trial's Allen Charge (instructions to a hung jury) to Alan's firm charge of the lost deposit. The real-estate agent Virginia Lupo rhymes with the lupus that Dr. Cusamano rejects as Carmela's illness. Svetlana's butting out with her cane parallels Adriana's lovely legged butting at the FBI agent's car. This Have is more vulnerable than the Have-not, for if Adriana brings down Chris she would prove, like Svetlana, her lover's "most expensive piece of ass."

So, too, the irony of the bosses' settings. Johnny and Tony plot Carmine's killing in an office-supplies store, as if murder and betrayal were Staples necessities. They last meet in a dark alley, as if stopping a murder were shadier than planning one. The conciliatory sit-down with Carmine is at a park chess table, where the men maneuver strategically. Though Chris's former heroin suppliers call their contract "Wop whackin' time," they're offended at the "stereotypin' shit" when he wants Carmine's murder to seem a carjack.

As the marriage ends. the Season Four conclusion recalls the first season. Where I, 1, opened with Tony behind a female sculpture at Melfi's office, in this opening Carmela is foregrounded in Dr. Cusamano's office, with Tony fidgeting in soft focus behind. The emphasis has shifted from Tony's health to Carmela's. Tony throws back Carmela's charge at his MRI (I, 1) that he will go to hell when he dies. Floating in his pool, Tony recalls the opening-episode ducks, which portended losing his family. The seasons also ends antithetically. In I, 13, the family enjoyed a warm refuge from the storm and Tony toasted their happy times and their children's future families. Here, that promise is lost. Season One closed confirming the family contract; Season Four on its end.

The last shot is Tony's *Stugots,* which extorted his deposit. When its paint fumes prevent his sleeping on it, he seeks rest in Whitecaps, at Satriale's, then back home. The site of his wanderlust becomes homelessness. His manhood rings as trivial as Dino's boozy ragging, "I Love Vegas." Despite its apparent triumph, Tony's *Stugots* has crashed him in white waters. For the end credits, the brash Martin song gives way to Richard Rogers's melancholy "I Have Dreamed." Tony's dream is dashed when Carmela awakens.

Season Five

V, 1: Two Tonys

Written by David Chase and Terence Winter.
Directed by Tim Van Patten.

Some old mafiosi are released from prison, having served their 20-year sentences. Tony is worried about a black bear prowling around his former home. Having ended his therapy, he courts Dr. Melfi. The animosity between Paulie and Christopher erupts and is resolved. Carmine's stroke renews Johnny Sack's resentment for Tony.

The episode's unifying theme is the struggle for authority, at home, at work or, in relationships. In the opening montage, Tony's emptiness is imaged in his former home. In the cold autumn, we see leaves blowing along the back deck, his abandoned barbecue, compost pit, and patio furniture. The leaves in the pool bespeak neglect and desolation. The house quivers in the pool, then stands stark against the cold sky. The local daily waits in the driveway, but Meadow drives over it in her Mustang convertible as she collects AJ for the "traditional" Sunday family dinner—chez Janice and Bobby Baccalieri.

Although Janice can for the first time say, "It's my house, Tony," she still has no authority. When she calls the men to dinner, they stay, feet up, at the TV. Bobby delays her request for ice. With her Sunday dinner of charred roast and canned clam chowder, Janice can't match Carmela's meals. "Your mother didn't send anything?" she asks Meadow, disappointed. Like Tony, Janice still expects Carmela's family service. Uncomfortable as a bear in her new role, Janice rummages through the garbage for her lost wedding ring.

The struggles for authority continue *chez* Soprano too. Tony strolls in and out and commands the fridge, swigging orange juice from the container. Tony and Carmela snipe as if they lived together. Carmela charges that Tony is "trying to make my life now as hard on me financially as possible." So he bribes the children with Meadow's convertible and AJ's $5,000 set of drums, to disrupt the harmony they have with their mother. But Tony won't replace her coffee machine, which, like the marriage, suffers from a corroded heating element.

The black bear contrasts with the ducks that visited Tony's pool in I, l. Aptly, the bear is drawn by Tony's duck food. Where the ducks foreshadowed Tony's loss of his family, the bear is an emblem of his solitary savagery. Tony has shifted from victim to cause of his family's disintegration. He jokes that he is half stalking Melfi. When he sees Carmela exchange smiles with a fish-and-game officer, he reasserts his authority first by offering a bribe (declined), then by suggesting the man is gay ("a little light in the Timberlands"). Out of guilt, Tony offers Carmela extra money to move into a hotel, but when she refuses to disrupt AJ's routine, he retracts it. To salve his conscience, he assigns two guards, Benny Fazio and Little Paulie Germani, with their AK-47s. As usual, no Tony gift is string-free: he pumps Benny for information about Carmela's visitors and phone calls. In the last shot, Tony, having replaced Benny on the night watch, smokes his big cigar with a loaded AK-47 erect in his lap. With his strut of gun and stogie, his manly presence makes the house as desolate as it was at his opening absence.

With Tony gone, his children assert more independence. AJ bristles at Carmela's orders. When she gamely sings, "It's so nice to have a man around the house," he mutters "You should've thought about that before." But the bear pierces his sullen maturity: "Mommy! Help! Mommy! Mom! Mommy!" Plucky Carmela scares the bear off with the tools of her profession, pots and pans. As Meadow, too, blames Carmela, she collects AJ by honking, not going in. With her filthy car and the "Bichu Rap" (by Thierry "Titi" Robin) on her radio, she flouts her family style.

Even without a wife, Tony invents excuses to leave his *goomah,* Valentina. Her sandwich can only delay his departure. Whether his "Got an overseas call coming at home" is a lie or a reference to his contract on Furio in Italy, Tony is false to her. His glimpse of *The Prince of Tides* (Barbra Streisand, 1991) redirects his romance. He approves of patient Nick Nolte: "You [women] expect a man to be a tower of strength, and then, when it turns out he has a few weaknesses and some insecurities, what do you do? You turn around and . . . betray him." At therapist

Streisand's "So you feel your mother betrayed you," Tony smiles in recognition. After Nolte's "Goddamn shrink. Her questions are making me as dizzy as her perfume," Tony resolves to court Melfi, ignoring Valentina below.

Minor scenes replay these major authority struggles. Over her ironing board Adriana presses Christopher to assert his rights in the gang: "If you get the extra responsibilities, you should get the benefits too." He needs her $400 of pocket money to pick up the tab for "the guys' " Friday dinner with their *goomahs*. Deferring to office decorum, Tony obeys when Dr. Melfi requests that he stop kissing her. And Feech LaManna regales his old cronies with the story about how, on his first day in prison, he established his authority by beating up the biggest black man in the mess.

When Christopher and Paulie laugh about their misadventures with the Russian ("Pine Barrens," III, 11), their self-deprecation switches into mutual blame. Paulie feels displaced by Chris: "Always playing that blood relation card. Tony's little favorite." Christopher challenges the tradition that the junior must pay for the group dinners. After Paulie flashily pays the first bill, $860, he demands that Chris repay him. Then he delights in running up Chris's next bill, ordering untouched "Lion-ease potatoes," "shrimp fuckin' cocktails" for all, and a bottle of bubbly for three "skags" nearby.

This argument between earned and unearned authority is only resolved by an "outside threat." When their waiter—an earnest chap trying to support his family—questions Christopher's $16 tip on a $1,184 tab, Chris throws a brick at his head and Paulie shoots him. "That's my money, Paulie," Christopher reminds him, conscientiously. When this inexcusable murder restores the gangsters' friendship, it exposes the emptiness of their code. Paulie's philosophy, "Life's too short, Chrissie. You can't waste it fighting with your friends," is a gloss over murderous selfishness. So, too, is Chris's righteousness the next morning over his self-help book on alcoholism, *My Search for Bill W.*, by Mel B.

When Tony courts Dr. Melfi, she initially refuses because of their "previous clinical relationship." Undermining this resolve, she has Tony's old dream where in mid-sex his *goomah* transforms into Melfi. Denying this temptation, she assures Dr. Kupferberg that her initial attraction to the "dangerous alpha male" dissolved from the ugliness she found in his nature. When Tony books a session to meet her, we see through his claim that "this is the place where we have been most honest with each other.

That's the way I liked it." Melfi seems to have adopted Tony's self-deception even as she rejects him.

Melfi draws on her professional authority to clinically deflect Tony's romantic interest. She explains his desire for "not just the smart things you say" but also her skin, mouth, and eyes as projection. She may be projecting her attraction to his physicality onto him. He reverts to an inapt cliché: "Forget the way Tony Soprano makes his way in the world. That's how he feeds his children. There's two Tonys. You've never seen the other one. That's the one I want to show you." The Tony she has seen is the private one, the fleetingly sensitive, vulnerable one, not—except for his explosions—his Mob face. In fact, there is only one Tony: the selfish brute who can sometimes make nice, briefly.

Tony plays with this strategy when Johnny Sack regrets not killing Carmine: "You want an apology? A fuckin' Whitman's Sampler, what?" The image parallels Tony's Streisand-inspired gift to Melfi: a bouquet of roses with a large jug of Tide detergent, from her Prince of Tide. Of course, Tony did not come clean with her, and he promoted her other client Gloria's fatal duplicity. Feech reflects Tony's pretence of a tough who plays gentle. Warned not to "step on any toes" when he resumes "the game," Feech assures Tony, "I'm Fred Astaire."

When Tony coaxes Melfi to explain her rejection, she is gentle: "It's just something I'm not going to do, and I would like you to respect my decision. . . . And try to feel that I know what's not right for me." Though she did not judge him when he was her patient, "in a personal relationship I don't think I could sit silent" at his values, his falseness, his disrespect for women and for people, and his use or threat of force. Tony hardly assuages her concern when he slams out with "Fuck you! You're a fucking cunt."

Tony confides in Silvio that he's in love with "a fuckin' broad. . . . It's the real deal, I think," but she wants to keep it platonic. Tony's "real deal" is still completely selfish. Hence the disconnect when he asks, "Why can't I do something that's just for me for a change?" In fact, Tony never does anything that's not primarily for himself, as even his gifts here demonstrate. As Dr. Kupferberg warns, Tony is "unpracticed at not getting what he wants."

Indeed, the title's "Two Tonys" may refer not to any alternative self but to the tough mirror provided in Feech. He and Tony are both Old

School bosses determined to rebound from defeat. "I'm Old School. I don't believe in separation shit or divorce," Tony reminds Carmela. Christopher must "pay till I tell you you don't have to pay anymore," because "it's tradition . . . a sign of respect." But Feech deflates his Old School class when he notes that the biggest change during his 20 years away is "broads shaving their bushes. I went over to Silvio's. Like girl scouts over there."

That Old School authority is parodied by the radio station motto "Atlantic City loves its oldies on Oldies 98.3"—which segues into Freda Payne's "Band of Gold": "Now that you've gone . . . / All that's left of the dream I hold / Is a band of gold." The song provides a romantic version of the Old School's lost ideals. When the TV news titles the old gangsters' release "The Class of '04" (with some sarcasm around "class"), the alumni reference evokes those crucial episodes "College" (I, 5) and "University" (III, 6). The news story introduces characters who will figure prominently in this season: Angelo Garepe, Phil Leotardo, and especially Tony's beloved ("I miss the shit out of him") cousin, Tony Blundetto, who would better fit the "Two Tonys" of the present title.

The Old School Tony also resents the fact that "Carmela was going after some fuckin' immigrant"—denying both his own sponsorship of the virtuous (and explicitly Old School) Furio and his own infidelities. Indeed, Carmela's having made Furio coffee may explain why Tony won't replace her coffeemaker. When Tony says of Furio, "If certain people see him, he's a dead man," he may rather be defining himself and his cronies in their spiritless death-in-life.

The episode's framing song, Emmylou Harris's "Heaven Only Knows," defines its ethos: "Every night, it's the same / I feel your heart turn cold as rain, / And know that you'll be gone again." The rain that falls outside Carmine's hospital room confirms the characters' autumnal desolation. Perhaps the song especially speaks for the women: "Heaven only ever sees / How love's made a fool of me / I guess that's how it's meant to be / But Heaven only knows." Especially Carmela and Melfi: "I don't know who's right or wrong / But all we had is dead and gone / So why you keep me hanging on / Heaven only knows." Tony's knowing is hardly of Heaven. In his closing shot as night guard of his family's home, he pretends to responsibility and sacrifice—as always, on his own terms. As a brute of threatening appetite, Tony is the bear.

V, 2: The Rat Pack

Written by Alan Taylor. Directed by Matthew Weiner.

To celebrate the opening of the gang's cash cow, the Museum of Science and Trucking, Jack Massarone gives Tony a painting of the Rat Pack: Sammy Davis Jr., Dean Martin, and Frank Sinatra, when they sang at the Sands in Las Vegas. However, Massarone and gang veteran Raymond Curto are "singing" to the FBI. Tony's close cousin, Tony Blundetto ("Tony B."), is released from prison but plans to go straight as a licensed massage therapist. Carmela's movie club watch and discuss the American Film Institute's list of the greatest American films.

The Rat Pack are the models of the Sopranos' macho bonding and delinquency. "They had some times," Tony tells Jack, with the sexual gesture of his thrust fist. In the painting the marginalized (one-eyed black Jew) Davis and the icon of cool, Martin, are linked by the powerful Chairman of the Board, Sinatra. Of course, Martin and Sinatra songs are prominent throughout the series. Sinatra is deified as the New Jersey Italian-American success who never lost touch with his people (e.g., the Mafia). We often see his emphatic mug-shot poster in Tony's Bada Bing office. The Soprano gang aspire to the Pack's self-indulgence, making their own laws and enjoying their pocket of male loyalty against the square world.

In the Pack's spirit, Massarone articulates the male bond against women: "So they go through labor. Big deal. Try a prostate exam." Hence the compulsive amount of male hugging in this episode—though Tony has an additional reason when he frisks Massarone for a wire. As Tony admits, in his postseparation "mind-set" his womanizing is less fun sans cheating. For all his baiting, Tony complains that Carmela "goes from zero to bitch anytime I show any warmth." The operative term is his false "show."

Massarone's treachery makes the gift scene ironic. The setting, the Napoleon Diner, forebodes Tony's Waterloo rather than power, and recalls his general's costume in Paulie's Pie-O-My painting (which resurfaces in V, 13). The sad jukebox song, Roy Orbison's "Crying," contrasts to the upbeat "Smile, smile, smile" of Dean Martin's "Power Your Face with Sunshine" at Tony B.'s welcome party. When Tony calls the picture the rare piece of "modern art" that he likes, he doesn't know where it's coming from, neither its genre (traditional kitsch) nor its motivation (to mask Massarone's betrayal). When Massarone is exposed, Tony throws the painting off the Pulaski Skyway into the river. As an emblem of corrupt loyalty, it follows Tony's police source Vin Makasian (I, 11) to sleep with the fishes. As usual here, the macho ethic proves false.

Despite the Rat Pack's camaraderie, the episode begins and ends with betrayals. First Massarone tapes his conversation with Tony. When the police question a suspicious car outside the restaurant, we assume the law have spotted Massarone's hoods. On the contrary, a bought cop has caught the feds listening to Massarone's wire and will expose him. At the end of the episode, Adriana finally benefits from her collaboration with the FBI. After her maid of honor flirts with Christopher, Adriana tells Sanseverino that Tina is embezzling her boss. As Tina herself advised, "Sometimes you just gotta take care of yourself, you know?"

The Pack's power lies behind Uncle Junior's confidence in his freed colleagues: "The Class of 2004. Old rats on a new ship." In fact, the gang's rats are the Feds' turncoats, abandoning their sinking ship. Though Curto and Massarone are more dangerous FBI informants than Adriana, even they show no moral motives. Curto corrects a transcript—"It's 'crack fuckin' heads,' not 'legs' " (from Tony's pep talk in IV, 1)—but his primary interest is getting paid: reimbursement for the shirt on which Ralphie spilled coffee, and a raise to cover his son's MS treatment. Ralphie's stain suggests how slow the FBI works.

Tony feels betrayed when Tony B. opts out of crime. His virtue validates Uncle Junior's verdict—"a fucking weirdo, if you ask me"—and recasts Livia's old reply to Tony's request for a brother: "What's wrong with your cousin Tony?" What's "wrong" is his desire to live right. These verbal ironies remind us of the gang's inverse values. When Tony says Tony B. "is back now—for good," the "good" refers to his reform as well as his permanence—albeit temporary.

"If I've got a shot at staying out and putting shit together I should take it." In taking the noncriminal shot, Tony B. leaves the Family to recover his family. He is disappointed when his ex-wife and twins aren't at the party. His lost daughter Kelly's name is tattooed on his left arm; he blames his absence for her delinquency. In his sentiment, responsibility, and good nature, Tony B. seems a model alternative to Tony S., like the good-brother, bad-brother center in Chase's favorite. *The Public Enemy.*

This episode's dramatic irony deepens as the season progresses. For example, when Tony B. speculates—"If things had gone different way back when, who knows?"—Tony S.'s thoughtfulness turns out to be his guilt for having missed the heist that sent his cousin to jail. Scolding Tony B. will encourage his fatal freelance. Tony is already ambivalent toward Tony B. when Christopher suggests his cousin whack Massarone: "What the fuck's the matter with you? The man is trying to go straight. Don't you give a fuck about your cousin? . . . Fuck him. The guy's fuckin' useless to me." Later Chris will chafe at the two Tonys' ridicule of his own attempts to "go straight" re drugs, and he will resent his cousin's promotion.

Tony is so stressed he senses betrayal both in Massarone's compliment—"Have you lost a little weight?"—and in Tony B's insults—"Boy, are you fat!" Tony B.'s parody of Jackie Gleason's aristocratic fool, Reginald Van Gleason III, along with his '70s white Travolta suit, shows how anachronistic his jail sentence has left him. As Tony scolds, "Things have changed here. I'm the boss of this fuckin' family. . . . You don't make fun of me. Got it?" Still, in his late-night loneliness Tony phones Tony B.—on his gift cellular, which trills the delusion "We are the champions." But even as Tony tries to smooth over their differences, he snaps at Tony B. for saying "You're the boss" on the phone. As Silvio explains, "Tony's got his own process."

When Carmine dies, he is heralded as "a great man"—for having "invented point shaving" on a college basketball game (CCNY vs. Kentucky, 1951). The bond breaks at the funeral, when Carmine Jr. rejects Ginny Sack's fundamentalist Catholicism. Johnny's indignation—"Fucking Little Carmine. And after what? Five years in Florida fixing wet T-shirt contests"—is undercut by his sitting uptight and smoking in an open toilet stall. Though Uncle Junior wants his ashes left "on a mantelpiece, surrounded by family," he sees life as the old children's game: "Crack the Whip. You run around like an idiot, holding hands as tight as you can. Then someone let's go and you're next." The game denies the pack's loyalty, for these rats let go. The returned Feech is clearly playing that game. When he gives Tony B. cash for his new start, Tony suspects him of gathering subversive support and will have him "let go" (V, 4).

The FBI are another form of Rat Pack, mainly males maneuvering for power. The boss is ardent to learn "how they penetrated the anonymous jury system"—not from any commitment to justice but because he "fucked up his six-figure future" when Junior wasn't convicted. In a brusque attempt to "share" with Adriana, Agent Sanseverino reveals how her marriage ended. When "we were trying to get pregnant," her FBI husband "climbed right over me"—but to a promotion—and "jumped a pay grade without me." Nonetheless, she assures Adriana that "nowhere but the FBI is the line clearer between the good guys and the bad guys, and you're with the good guys now." Though both FBI cars provide refuge from the rain, Adriana doesn't share Sanseverino's "comfort from knowing you're trying to do the right thing by helping your government." "I'm being ripped apart here snitching on people," Adriana notes. "For what? What do I get out of it?" Tina's bust, finally, and her own release (V, 12).

Whereas Sanseverino acts for justice and a bigger salary and Adriana out of desperation, Tony's values are based on the male loyalty articulated in the History TV interview with a bomb survivor: "All your life you gotta remember what one guy did because he thought it was his job to do, and he took a shot for you." From this ethic, Tony B. will, however involuntarily, take a shot to save Tony's authority (V, 13).

In *The Sopranos,* moral codes have a selfish rather than ethical basis. Massarone's topic for the museum opening, "Challenges of Contemporary Urban Development," speaks for the Soprano family dilemmas, for they have made the dishonorable their code of honor. Their religion is not felt. To hang his painting of the Vegas gods, Tony drops two Jesus pictures from the mantelpiece. At Carmine's funeral, Phil Leotardo tells an irreligious joke—Jesus leans down from the cross to tell Peter, "I can see your house from here"—that trivializes the idea of a watching, saving Christ.

Carmela's Rat Pack is her movie club. The gang's women collect in mutual support against their problem men. For, as Tina forces Christopher to admit, men like women who talk like whores, who feed their fantasies, and who betray each other instead of gathering against them. On movie night, unlike their spouses (II, 4), the women are attentive to the opening FBI warning about copyright. Still, they sustain their men's code of *omerta*. As Rosalie explains, Angie Bonpensiero is banished because her Big Pussy betrayed the gang: "What kind of person does that? . . . I mean, at least Judas didn't go into any Apostle Protection Program. He hung himself. He knew what he did." Their closeness aggravates Adriana's alienation for feeding the FBI: "I'm not what you think." She wants to tell them "what's driving me crazy," but instead—and prophetically—she runs out, falls, and is suddenly gone.

The movie club's first movie, *Citizen Kane* (Orson Welles, 1941), reflects upon the whole episode. As Carmela reads Leonard Maltin, *Citizen Kane* is the Rat Pack—or even *The Sopranos*—of movies, because it "broke all the rules and invented new ones." The women's responses are telling. Squealer Adriana says, "The sled, huh? He shoulda told somebody." As Silvio's wife, Gabriella, notes, Kane had everything, but "he died alone with nothing and nobody." "Good. The prick," opines objective Carmela. Rosalie, who lost a husband, son, and ex-lover Ralphie to the Mob, doesn't like the movie because Kane is "conceited." Unwittingly, Janice proves the most insightful when she reports, "Six months and Bobby still hasn't found my rosebud." For the film's "Rosebud" connotes more than Charles Foster Kane's sled. Director Orson Welles had heard that "rosebud" was the term William Randolph Hearst, the film's model, used for his mistress Marion Davies's genitalia. Over even such sophisticated film analysis, the senior group member, Donna Parisi, prefers gossip.

Like Kane and his first wife, when Carmela and Tony find themselves briefly alone at Tony B.'s party, they have nothing to say to each other. Kane's selfishness parallels Tony's theft of the home viewing equipment, which prevents the women's enjoyment of *Casablanca* (Michael Curtiz, 1942), and his hope to work out a separation agreement without lawyers, "like adults." Perhaps Tony had a subconscious reason to keep the women from *Casablanca*. Its selfish hero, Rick (Humphrey Bogart), reforms when he insists on himself making the personal sacrifice for democracy, instead of accepting the woman's (Ingrid Bergman's) offer.

The women fall silent at the prospect of next week's number three AFI-ranked film, *The Godfather*. Even the bonding women remain mired in their men's mythology. For the Soprano rat packs, there is no escape from their killing codes, not in the AFI's hits list, not in the FBI's, and—as Massarone finds, with a golf-club cover jammed into the mouth that squealed—most certainly not in the gang's. The NO TRESPASSING sign that opens and closes *Citizen Kane* is also this rat pack's warning to their own members and to their women, as much as it is to outsiders, to respect their unforgiving codes.

V, 3:   Where's Johnny?

Written by Michael Caleo. Directed by John Patterson.

Johnny Sack and Carmine Jr. fight over the New York operation. Paulie defends his Aunt Mary's gardener, Sal Vitro, when Feech mus-

cles in on his territory. Janice assumes Livia's mantle to taunt Tony
and alienates Bobby's children. Uncle Junior's insults infuriate Tony
until he learns the old man has been suffering infarcts, small strokes
that affect the mind and memory.

The theme of this bleak episode is isolation. The characters crave connection but are either too emotionally paralyzed or too selfish to achieve it.
The last shot is a close-up on Uncle Junior weeping, unable to answer
Tony's question: Why can he only repeat "something mean? Why not
something good? . . . Don't you love me?" Uncle Junior can't say he loves
Tony, not because he doesn't, but because he is too self-absorbed—in his
fear of death, his disintegrating mind, frustration—to reach out. He can
only snipe. When two cops respectfully bring him home, he thanks them
with "Go shit in your hat."

In his insecurity, Uncle Junior thinks an episode of the HBO stablemate
Curb Your Enthusiasm shows him (Larry David) and Bobby (Larry's
agent) at Junior's trial. His search for Johnny-Boy is an attempt to recover
a lost family connection. Having lost his authority, he thrice insists that
Tony "never had the makings of a varsity athlete." Tony is so insecure that
the petty gibe hurts more than he admits: "It's undermining. And it's the
kind of thing I'm teaching my kids not to do." Tony repeats, "He's fuckin'
dead to me," until he learns about his uncle's condition. Tony and Junior
need to connect, but their self-absorption prevents it.

As Tony remarks, "This family stuff, these Sunday dinners, they're important, Janice." But angered by Junior's insult, he vows never to come
again. After Uncle Junior sneers at Tony's sensitivity—"a hothouse
flower"—the camera holds on Bobby's two children, another generation
of hothouse flowers that Janice denies nourishment.

From that need, Tony invites Artie to move into Livia's house with him:
"We're like brothers. How long we gonna hold a grudge?" Livia divided
them by telling Artie that Tony burned down the Vesuvio. Now the
"brothers" reunite under her roof. This fraternal offer unsettles Artie
when Tony offers to save him 70 percent on his linen costs, for Artie has
learned the price of Tony's generosity (IV, 6).

In another family defense (cp IV, 8), Paulie restores his Aunt Mary's
gardener Salvatore Vitro's lawn route, which he has worked for 26 years.
After Feech beats up Sal, Paulie—motivated by his tape of Sun Tzu, *The*

Art of War, recommended by Tony—assaults Feech's men. But Paulie's generosity mainly serves himself. He keeps half the $1,000 compensation Tony orders for Sal's broken arm, and levies "a token. I dunno, a couple percent" on his future earnings. Sal ends up reduced to half his former territory, with his son pulled out of college to help, and having to do Johnny Sack's large and Tony's small lawns for free. Paulie's glare freezes any complaint.

As Artie and Sal have learned, even these men's generosity exploits their friends. Their lavish greetings are false celebrations. "There he is," echoes through the episode, for Tony's "Mister Clean" (Tony B.), Paulie's "The King of Breadsticks" (Feech), and "Salvatore My Dolly" and "Salvatore my boy" (Sal Vitro). Paulie's salutes make Sal his possession ("*my* Dolly," "*my* boy").

In this feeding chain, even powerful people are vulnerable. Paulie resents Tony skimming his and Feech's scam, retroactively. Uncle Junior is helpless when he wanders off alone. The police find him in his pyjamas and slippers hiding behind a recycling bin in Newark. So, too, when the "Lady Shylock" Lorraine sweeps into a bar to coerce her payoff, she is instantly made helpless. Leotardo forces her to pay up to Johnny Sack instead of to Carmine Junior. Though Johnny rejects her excesses— "Never enough body count for Lorraine"—his motive is greed.

Lorraine plunges from bravado to self-debasement. Under Leotardo's gun she begs for her life, offering to fellate him and his men. With the show's macho prejudice in the politics of oral sex (cp I, 9: "Boca"), Phil suggests Lorraine's muscular bodyguard taught her how. (Lorraine insults her man, too: "Jason, men are talking here.") She's saved when Leotardo shoots her through a phone book and the bullet stops at her *r*'s (*sic*). In Paulie's term, she is "rehabullet-ated." Similarly, Janice erupts when Tony recalls her "blowing roadies" in her hippie days, a suggestion that also perturbs Bobby.

Lorraine's abuse supports Janice's new sympathy for what Livia suffered in this corrupt man's world. "It's less and less a mystery why she was the way she was . . . ungrateful husband, selfish kids." But even Janice's sympathy is selfish. For the Sunday dinner she brings a few pastas from the Vesuvio and waits for sister Barbara's veal and chicken entrées. Bobby catches his children insulting his new wife, but not her provocation. She dumps Bobby Jr.'s milk snack with a basilisk (i.e., like Paulie's) glare. Assuring the boy's further humiliation, she tells Tony and a smirking AJ that Bobby Jr is bed-wetting again. Nonetheless, like Livia, Janice declares herself the victim.

Applying the domestic need for connection to the Family problems, Tony proposes that Johnny Sack, Carmine Junior, and Angelo Garepe form a triumvirate, "like Caesar" (as in I, 6) to share the major decisions. Though this would prevent a bloody war, Johnny's egotism won't admit a partner. Angelo's fear, "There's a lot of potential for bloodshed," will be borne out when he is whacked. Ever self-serving, mediator Tony plans to "pick up any crumbs from the fallout."

Tony counsels partnership in the domestic as well as business plots. With Bobby, who spent 40 minutes, Tony addresses "caring" in both contexts. He needs Bobby to care for Uncle Junior, but he will try to find a way "to take care of" Bobby with more rewarding work. In parallel conciliations, Tony advises "Look, Bobby, marriage—or any partnership, for that matter—is a give-and-take," and "There's fuckin' compromises in life, Paulie." Similarly, Tony needs Christopher, even though his intrusion provokes Johnny Sack.

What's uncompromised is the constant threat of violence. Even on probation, the convivial Feech keeps a short fuse. After a luxurious lunch with Tony B. he pauses to break Sal's arm. His interview with Paulie begins with hugs, hardens—"What's yours is yours, Paulie, but what ain't is anybody else's"—and ends in an angry expulsion.

Adriana's car scene with FBI agent Sanseverino replays the tension between isolation and connection. Their sessions parody the relationship between "sisters." When Adriana explains Tony's relationship to his "nephew" Christopher—tenuously via Carmela and tortuously through Livia—arbitrary links between the remote show the need for connection.

In the parallel next scene, an old black whore chats up Uncle Junior. By offering "a half-and-half in your backseat," she tries to revive an old form of connection—like his search for Johnny-Boy. For all her friendly pretence to know Junior, the close-up shows her predatory nature. Similarly, in the black church hall the children get questionable lessons from a huckster (coercive strategies to sell their Turkish taffy) and from Junior's ejection (how to treat the elderly and infirm).

Some victims are innocent. Sal is coaxed out of going to the police by Paulie's ostensibly friendly intervention. Because of her love for Christopher, Adriana faces the contrary pressures of Tony's world and the FBI. Neurologist Dr. Harry Winer treats Uncle Junior, but "the last thing I wanted to do is get into the middle of a family squabble." The hapless Artie takes the punch Janice aimed at Tony.

Then Tony turns on Bobby: "You want more responsibility? Start by controlling your wife." With *Godfather* machismo, Tony reduces Bobby to Fredo. As in his first marriage, Bobby is the character of fidelity and love. He takes his children to church, to Janice's disdain, and he defends her: "She's prone to depression, frankly. Not that I have any regrets." When Uncle Junior disappears, Bobby is more concerned than his relatives. "Sometimes I think I love Junior more than you do," he tells Janice.

As usual this season, the title—an allusion to Johnny Carson's *Tonight Show* intro ("Here's Johnny!") and its demonic inflection in *The Shining* (Stanley Kubrick, 1980)—points two ways. Domestically, it underscores the futility of Uncle Junior's quest for his dead brother, i.e., the lost familial closeness. In business, it refers to Johnny Sack's isolating ambition. In both contexts the tone is ominous, confirmed by the soundtrack's throb and by the general darkness. In the closing scene Uncle Junior muses over a TV documentary: "These prairie dogs, they'll sleep during the day." In this episode the characters are frozen in the daylong darkness of their insularity. They seem taunted by the Henry James quote that starts an Anthony Robbins infomercial: "It's time to start living the life you've imagined." For their perverse values severely narrow their sense of what their life could be.

V, 4:   All Happy Families

Written by Toni Kalem. Directed by Rodrigo Garcia.

In the unhappy Family, Johnny Sack has Lorraine and her bodyguard Jason killed, and he supports Feech's theft of expensive cars from Dr. Fried's daughter's wedding. Tony gets Feech back in jail by framing him with flat-screen TVs. Carmela sends her uncontrollable AJ to live with Tony.

This episode is emphatically rooted in current political issues. America's engagement (with Britain and other allies) in Iraq was a compelling concern in 2004, when the season first aired. But references originally clear will likely recede when the show engages future viewers. For them, the particular political context will probably be subordinated to the gangster archetypes and the characters' personal interplay. Still, America's international character should remain a theme of this episode.

When Rusty Millio exhorts Little Carmine— "We go all out, we steamroll right over John, and I predict the guys on the street in Brooklyn and Queens, they'll welcome us as fuckin' heroes. It'll be easy"—he explicitly evokes the American government's naive prediction of how Iraqis would greet the overthrow of Saddam Hussein. Then the doomed Feech tries to divert the parole officer by joking that his garage is "where I make my weapons of mass destruction"—the disproved rationale for the American-British invasion of Iraq. Feech's desperate joke fails to ward off the inspector's "invasion." AJ's school counselor, Wegler, catches the day's panic rhetoric when he warns that "we're rapidly approaching crisis mode here with these grades."

These references to America's engagement in Iraq go beyond the drama's earlier post-9/11 atmosphere, where Bobby observed, "Mom really went downhill after the World Trade Center," and Melfi, "A lot of people are feeling vulnerable" (IV, 1). The Iraq parallels make the Sopranos an emblem of America's character on the international stage. This follows Francis Ford Coppola's example, where the three *Godfather* films expanded the gangster's signification from American business to American politics, and finally to the international Catholic Church. The political framework heightens two themes. One is Tony's new diplomacy, which gets Feech re-jailed but not bushwhacked. The other is the expression of American materialism through brand names, which recalls the debate about whether America entered Iraq as Freedom Fighter or as Oil Mogul.

This episode is characterized by Tony's quiet diplomacy—however uneven. His gift of a bathrobe, bath products, and a letter is his apology for having called Melfi a "cunt." Even his soft soap sends her back to her therapist. Dr. Kupferberg reads the obvious: the gesture is Tony's "ablution—a desire to cleanse himself of the deed." More likely, Tony still imagines her showering. Though he continues to insult Carmela, he scolds AJ for his rudeness and throttles him for swearing at her. Tony has his own quiet diplomacy.

Or as Carmela complains, "I get to be the prison warden over here while you indulge him." Concerned about AJ's low grades and lower college prospects, Tony buys AJ the "carrot" or "motivational tool" of an SUV, which AJ may not drive until he has raised his grades to C. In a quiet example of America's distribution of wealth, AJ's new "tank" contrasts to his SAT tutor's rattletrap. In the opening scene, AJ drives in and out of the family driveway, expressing both his restlessness and the fact that he's driving on the spot, not getting anywhere, not even in a circle. At the end, Carmela's fantasy of young AJ in his soapbox recalls the happier time when she could imagine him getting somewhere on his own.

AJ's indulgence further divides the family. He breaks the terms on which Carmela lets him stay in New York after a rock concert. He doesn't go to Meadow's and instead gets stoned. Waking up with his eyebrows shaved, he loses yet more face from having been glued to the carpet. After a fatal student car accident, Carmela's worry overrides her anger. But after his filial "Fuck you!" and Tony's forgiving AJ's "few beers," she rejects their "bullshit." Realizing that "my pathetic need to compete with [Tony] clouded my judgment," she banishes him to Tony. Bonding, the men— Artie, Tony B., Tony, and AJ—fart over their chicken wings in front of the TV.

This episode bristles with brand names—the Dr. Hauschka organic cleansers, the SUV with "the Nissan triple safety philosophy," the high-price German cars stolen from the Jewish wedding, the stolen Phillips 50-inch plasma flat screens, even Silvio's complaint about his poker deal: "This hand's from thalidomide" (a disastrous fertility drug). Christopher lures Feech with his gift of a Canale suit and the comparison of Georgia with New Zealand peaches. Brand goods are both Tony's way to buy people and everyone's grasp for status. One wedding guest's gloat—"Now who's a genius for keeping his Regal?"—is a shallow reason to prefer American over German. And Dr. Fried complains that the "wedding planner" is now an "environment and event coordinator."

Even universities are reduced to brand names. As Carmela assures Wegler, "He's a good father. Don't get me wrong. Our daughter's at Columbia. My friends tell me I'm a snob about this college business." Here everyone is. Colleges are classified as either accessible or "reach." In Wegler's cynical advice, a Mississippi summer course on the blues compensates for the applicant's lack either of minority status or of community service. Dr. Fried is irked that to get his daughter into the *New York Times* "Featured Couple of the Week," her Harvard law degree "means bubkes" (Yiddish: "nothing"). AJ is keen to use his ADD to circumvent the SAT requirement. Brand name schools and products and pedagogical jargon are like Carmela's and Wegler's marriage mistakes, "some notion of escaping the quotidian."

Tony resents Feech making him a brand name, with his sardonic "Godfather" and "Don Antonio." *Godfather* imitations have debased the currency. From Tony's excuse—"He's old. How do you think that feels?"—Chase cuts to a Botox flyer that Carmela is (needlessly) considering. When Chris starts Feech's downfall, he finds him enjoying wine and peaches on his New Jersey porch. The scene draws on the decline from Don Vito's gentle death in his garden with his grandson (*The Godfather*) to Michael Corleone's desolate end (*Godfather III*). Feech's peaches evoke the Corleones' ominous oranges.

When Feech tries on the Canale jacket, he says, "I look better than Sinatra." In his last scene with Tony, Sinatra's mug-shot poster between them augurs Feech's arrest. It also relates to the episode's casting of some brand name characters. A relatively minor crooning Frankie, Frankie Valli, plays Carmine's bellicose *consiglieri* Rusty Millio. Rock star David Lee Roth (who recalls writing off his condom expenses), retired Giants linebacker Lawrence Taylor ("Sir Lawrence of Meadowlands"), and TV producer Bernie Brillstein (the Santa figure) play themselves at the first big poker game. The "Alan Ginsberg" is not *the* Alan Ginsberg. For the show, as for its characters, there is a cachet in associating with celebrities.

After all, Tony's aura was what first attracted Carmela. Wegler reads her well when he recommends Flaubert's *Madame Bovary,* "almost the perfect novel . . . about bourgeois loneliness, emptiness," further distinguished by the *Sopranos'* mix of tragedy and comedy. It addresses both Carmela's alienation in her marriage and her need to extend her mental territory. So she stops by "Borders on my way home" for the book. Carmela is a Borders woman, not an Amazon. Also, Bovary bankrupted her husband by trying to fill her void with shopping. Reflecting on the volume of emptiness, Tony's SUV interrupts AJ's question about the number of zeroes in a googel. Earlier, a subjective shot of Tony B. surveying Tony's mansion and then staked by Feech at the executive card game attributes his later decline to Bovarian discontent.

When Tony rejects AJ's therapy with his brand-name manliness—"Whatever happened to Gary Cooper, the strong, silent type?" (since I, 1)—he cites an *image* of character. A *Honeymooners* clip on TV expresses Tony's fluster (at getting AJ) through Ralph Kramden's quiz-show panic. This deflates Tony's "strong, silent" man. In the Happy Families' brand-name world, both their security and their satisfaction are illusory. Anodynes don't work deep.

Tony is sobered by Carmela's remark that he has no friends, just "flunkies" who laugh at his jokes and flatter him in fear. His power bought them as it first wowed her. The boys' overenthusiastic laughter at his joke—combining an accountant with a giant jet aircraft gets a Boring 747—reveals his friends to be false, and Feech resentful. Feech is in soft focus behind the laughing Silvio, Paulie, and Vito. But when Tony recalls the incident, his pan picks out Feech in sharp focus, grimacing at Tony's popularity and perhaps taking Tony's "Boring" personally. The combination of the friends' sycophancy and Feech's chill prompts the latter's dispatch. Though Tony is not "runnin' a fuckin' popularity contest here," his Richie Aprile experience has taught him to nip antagonists in the bud. That lesson may have been augmented by President Bush's new policy of preemptive defense against terrorism.

If the title points to the tensions in even happy families, it also reminds us of their variable bonds. For not returning his power drill (a pretence in IV, 7), Tony demotes Brian from his partner back to Carmela's cousin. Sisters are supposed to cover for their brothers, Tony reminds Carmela after Meadow lies about AJ's visit. Paulie's laughter at Tony's joke softens his sinister toast: "Always got his eye on the big picture." That was how Artie described Tony's predatory instinct (IV, 6).

Though the Jewish wedding is a warm celebration by a considerably extended family, Dr. Fried regrets that his accomplished daughter is marrying a TV puppeteer. Someone else will pull her strings, after her father "had to sedate my own little girl at her wedding." When his guests are robbed, Dr. Fried is disappointed that his friendship with Tony seems as "fuckin' *gornisht*" (Yiddish: "nothing") as his current standing among his friends. Like Carmela, Dr. Fried has drawn upon the gangster's brand-name security.

Of course, as Tony embarrassingly joked at the card game, his working and gambling "friendship" with Fried did not get him invited to the wedding. The joke—"I didn't get my invitation"—assumes Tony has forgotten that the Italian gangster and the Jewish penile implant specialist are not as close as they pretend to be. Fried's embarrassment is Tony's "gotcha!" Yet Fried rushes to the Bada Bing to report the car thefts, especially to retrieve the Mercedes "fucking SL 55 convertible" for which the friend's brother had to wait "a motherfucking year." The two ethnics speak the same language across an unbridgeable class gap.

In the Family spirit, Tony respects that Feech granted him and Jackie Aprile "a pass" when they made their name by robbing his card game (the feat Jackie Jr. emulates in III, 12). Silvio attributes Feech's magnanimity to Johnny-Boy's having "so many friends." When Feech's return to jail follows the baseball commentator's "end of the inning," we're reminded that these hardball gangsters make a game of everything. They deal out death by their own rules. And life, as Tony took a hand in Tony B.'s twin sons by smuggling his cousin's sperm out of prison to impregnate his wife ("It was the least I could do"). As the twins argue over who first poked the other's eye, they are already miniature gangsters—or stooges.

Lorraine and Jason are murdered to a bubblegum pop song by Edison Lighthouse: "Love grows where my Rosemary goes / And nobody knows like me." But in his loveless world Johnny has Lorraine killed for submitting to her ex-lover Carmine's authority. There's no rosemary for remembrance here. The disparity between the perky song and the murders intensifies the season's bleakness.

Similarly, Meadow and Finn neck in front of *Frida* (Julie Taymor, 2002) on television. The film's subject, Frida Kahlo, is an artist of both highbrow achievement and popular recognition, a creative, independent woman. She suffered both physical pain and a lover, Diego Rivera, as "magnetic, larger-than-life," and abusive as Tony. The allusion reflects Meadow's family situation, her more sophisticated interests (cp. Carmela's literary inexperience), yet also her thwarted ambition, as Finn's engagement prevents her from focusing on the film.

In the last image Carmela brings home groceries and a plant. The house looks emptied—as if Tony has sucked out more than the home entertainment system. In this subjective shot Carmela senses that her home is hollow, in the sense of T. S. Eliot's *The Hollow Men* (1925), where the stuffing is valueless. Her home seems emptied not just of her family but of any substance—and she has yet to sink into her *Bovary*. As the camera withdraws from behind her, she stands faceless, alone, an image of the human condition stripped of illusions of community and material support. The hollow mansion summarizes all families of such shallow happiness.

Of course, the episode's title comes from the famous opening sentence in Leo Tolstoy's cognate novel, *Anna Karenina*: "All happy families are alike; each unhappy family is unhappy in its own way." Here lives are individuated by their unhappiness, by how their experience separates them from the glossy appearance of contentment. As well, the episode scrutinizes the values that America went to war to promote in the name of capitalist democracy. As a result of the divisions both within and between former ally nations over the war in Iraq, there were no happy families in the international community, and each had its own particular split and concerns. While in 2004 the episode's families could be nations, future viewers may restore its address to the domestic.

V, 5: Irregular Around the Margins

Written by Robin Green and Mitchell Burgess.
Directed by Alan Coulter.

Tony returns to Dr. Melfi to deal with his attraction to Andrea. A late-night driving accident prompts rumors that Adriana was fellating him. Tony confronts Christopher's anger and restores the appearance of family unity. Adriana refuses the FBI request to bug the Crazy Horse bar.

The title is Tony's term for his cancerous moles. Here the physical represents the characters' mental or moral afflictions. Adriana's irritable bowel syndrome means "on top of it all I'm a head case" (implying both psychosomatic problems and the "head" as a colloquialism for *toilet*). Tony's forehead skin cancer is among "the things that run through your head." These irregular margins are dangerous, possibly fatal. On the other hand, Dr. Melfi praises Tony's "milestone" when he came "to talk about this impulse, instead of just acting on it without thinking." In her advice to "establish limits or boundaries" with Adriana, to resist temptation, regular margins are healthy.

The dangerous margins involve two kinds of fray. First, frayed nerves are clearly the cause of Adriana's IBS, whatever her given excuses. Out of jealousy Christopher attacks Vito, beats up and expels Adriana, shoots up Tony's new SUV, and even draws on his F/family head. Pushed, Tony pulls a gun on him: "Either you tell me now that you can take it into your heart that I never did this shit, or we've come as far as we can together." Unless Chris accepts the smooth border on their relationship, Tony will kill him.

Surprisingly, Paulie appears to defend his rival. He implies that Chris was not threatening Tony: "He must've known the gun was empty. Look what he pumped into your car." But acquitting him by an empty gun reconvicts him for shooting up Tony's vehicle. Fortunately, Tony B. intercedes, then draws on his "pre-board massage therapist" savvy to help the ER doctor prove that Adriana was upright on impact, i.e., was not fellating Tony. As we will later learn (V, 13), Tony B. may see his own fate when Tony holds a gun to his "nephew's" head.

For all his new control, Tony is also fraying. He snorts cocaine, despite his disdain for druggies. After four seasons of sneering at "degenerate fuckin' gamblers," here Tony bets thousands on baseball games and plays darts with Adriana for "a sawbuck a game, to make it interesting." The characters also have minor addictions, like Tony's confidence in brand names. He claims his Escalade (so close to his aborted Escapade) saved their lives, when it rather endangered them by rolling from a raccoon. After her near-fatal accident, Adriana tells Chris, "I thought I'd die in there without a cigarette."

The second "fray" is violated borders. When Meadow meets her "coked up" father at the Crazy Horse, she wants to go elsewhere. Both are embarrassed at their territorial overlap. Tony marks out his authority when he peels off Carmela's "allowance." Against the Adriana rumor, Tony asks Carmela to help him "put a good face on this thing. For the sake of the kids. For the family." As in the stormy night dinner at the end of I, 13, the (here extended) family dine at Artie's restaurant together, weathering the storm of rumors and recovering their *image* of family harmony. They smooth out the irregular border. Vito comes over to salute Tony and to make peace with Christopher. In the last shot Tony studies Carmela's poise under the pressure, whether cynically or admiringly, perhaps reevaluating the woman he lost. Despite all the frayed ends, Carmela gives the family a neat profile.

We know that image is false. The fake front also appears lightly. When Adriana tells Tony of her stomach problems, her bare midriff exposes what is embarrassing her. Her jeans, whether slashed or extra-pocketed, also hide and reveal her IBS anxieties. At Carmela's, Tony bites an apple, then puts it back in the bowl for her still life drawing. Both the broken apple and his license in her kitchen are false fronts. Agent Sanseverino's sympathy proves false when she mimics Adriana at the FBI meeting: "We really don't know [Tony]. He listens."

Metaphoric loose ends also appear in Adriana's and Tony's afflictions. Their intimacy starts with their medical secrets. In Tony's skin cancer, an unruly cell grows out of control and requires radical excision. That parallels his various business challenges from Richie and Ralphie through Uncle Junior, Jackie Jr., and Feech. Typically, Tony is more aware of the threats around him than of internal threats.

Adriana's more literal loose end is her irritable bowel syndrome. She ends her first session with Agent Sanseverino because of her pressing "number two." Tony calls her real affliction, Chris, "my Number Two." Tony reminds him of his place by telling him to dump the dog excrement Tony scraped from his shoe. Adriana used "number two" for Christopher's panic excretion in "Meadowlands" (I, 4). The term suggests Adriana's childlike nature, coherent with her wistful view of Tony as "such a good father. I wish my dad had been like that." The IBS and its moral tenor seem to e catching: Livia had it all her life, and here Tony B. rushes to Tony's toilet after reporting Chris's rampage. But Tony B.'s condition is mild. Though consistent with Steve Buscemi's film persona as an eccentric, here it's Tony B.'s healthy virtue and responsibility that make him freakish.

Also true to form, Christopher is insensitive to Adriana's suffering. When his aunt had bowel cancer, he assures her, "her whole asshole rotted out." The image unites Tony's cancer, Adriana's bowels, and their link, the rotting Christopher. Tony mimics Chris's "constipated owl look." Chris is more concerned with his toothache than with Adriana's diarrhea. When she blames her stress on the war and the Middle East, he extends the previous episode's political context by citing President Bush's assurance: "We're gonna mop up the floor with the whole fuckin' world. The whole world's gonna be under our control, so what are you worked up about?" In this context, her doctor's euphemism, GI, conflates her gastrointestinitis with the U.S. soldiers.

As usual, the script is remarkably cohesive. The SUV accident is set up by Adriana's "I'm so scared I'm going to have an accident" (from her IBS) and by Tony and Meadow's mutual warning about drinking and driving. Eager to be vulnerable, he suggests Adriana set him up with "Danielle," her first FBI agent. When Adriana says she drowned at a picnic, another traitor theoretically sleeps with the fishes. Right after Tony tells Melfi he wants to start a new family with Adriana, to "do it right this time," Adriana recalls his ducks, which prompted Tony's initial anxiety. The cut suggests Tony would always lose his family because of his irredeemable nature. But unlike Carmela, Adriana would not put up with infidelity. In her troubled mind, she is grateful for Chris's beating, because had she found him with another woman she would have killed him.

As in Lorraine Calluzo's humiliation (V, 3) Adriana's servitude is imaged as fellatio. First she rejects Sanseverino's hint of Tony's interest: "I am not going to blow this guy for your sick purposes." But for her own. . . . When she stoops for the dropped darts, she finds herself at Tony's crotch. Sensing their spark, he urges, "Come on. Get up." The rumor begins almost innocently, with Adriana's "severe blow to the head." But the metaphor grows, until Uncle Junior gleefully reports that Tony "came all over the sun visor." Similarly, the cause of the accident swells from the raccoon into a deer. With that malicious momentum, Vito claims that Adriana came on to him when Christopher was in rehab. At the time, of course, Adriana told Sanseverino of Vito's unwelcome pursuit. The rumors are another malignant growth, with irregular margins.

Christopher has grounds to suspect Tony: "Everybody knows you been the biggest fuckin' cooze hound around the last four or five years. Your midlife crisis. You'd fuck a catcher's mitt." Chris loses his moral advantage when his assault makes Adriana his catcher's mitt. But the scandal shows Tony how low even his admirers consider him. For Chris he recycles his Artie Bucco defense: "What kinda fuckin' animal do you think I am, huh? The thought never entered my mind." And to Carmela: "Am I that horrible? Really?" Her silence assents. When Tony realizes his kids believe their father would have sex with his "nephew's fiancée," he insists on the family dinner to project "the good face."

Even as Tony reviews his family's damage, he tells Melfi "I might as well have fucked her. Thanks." Because of his newfound virtue, he suffered the infamy without the sex. Tony's only value is utility. Similarly, for Chris, whatever the truth, people now view him as "Joe Jerkoff." Whatever Tony's growth, he can't shake old habits. Even as he admits to Carmela, "I know I haven't been a fuckin' saint," he unfairly accuses her.

The episode that began with Adriana's rough-edge rock group closes with the lofty arc of opera, Luba Orgonasova singing *"Chi' il bel sogno di doretta."* In Puccini's *La Rondine (The Swallow)* a wealthy Parisian's mistress loves a young innocent but has the moral humility to renounce him. Only in Doretta's beautiful dream can love trump such social imperatives: "Who cares for wealth / If at last happiness flourishes!" The lower-case but higher-class soprano frames the family's pretense with a formal grandeur and order to which they can only pretend. Even the highly artificial art of opera is more real than their life.

V, 6: Sentimental Education

Written by Matthew Weiner. Directed by Peter Bogdanovich.

After a fight with Tony, AJ returns to live with Carmela. Tony B. passes his massage therapy exam and accepts his laundry boss Kim's partnership in a clinic, to be run by Kim's beautiful daughter, Amanda. When Tony B. finds a drug dealer's $12,000, his girlfriend, Gwen, advises he invest it in the business. Instead, he blows $11,600 on fancy clothes, toys for his sons, and gambling. He cracks, beats up Kim, and rejoins Tony's gang. Carmela's affair with school counselor Bob Wegler ends when he accuses her of using him to help AJ.

In all three plotlines, the characters find they have absorbed too much of Tony Soprano's ethic to escape him. That sad discovery constitutes their coming-of-age. As Carmela tells her father, "Whatever I say, whatever I do, because I was married to a man like Tony my motives will always be called into question." "Well," he responds, then walks away, as if in assent. Clearly, Carmela has learned from Tony to deny responsibility. Given his antisentimental education, perhaps the whole family is represented by the song over the end credits, Etta James's "The Blues Is My Business": "I got a heart full of trouble. . . . Blues is my business and business is good."

In a light version of self-disrespect, AJ's T-shirt proclaims him TRASH. A quarrel over breakfast cereal leads to Tony's throttle and AJ's implausible threat: "One of these days I'll kick your fuckin' ass." But what "demoralized" Tony is AJ's threat to call in the authorities: "Violence? You're lucky you didn't get my shoe up your ass." To return to Carmela, AJ accepts her "nonnegotiable ground rules," which include involving her more in his life, dedication to school, and no swearing: "After 16 years of uninterrupted potty mouth from you people, I get slammed?" AJ is the third-generation Soprano to claim to be an innocent victim.

After defending AJ's essay on *Animal Farm* against plagiarism charges, Carmela learns that he bought an essay on *Lord of the Flies,* on which his English grade and college admission hopes depend. Both allegories on human savagery are more pertinent to his situation than Wegler's sexual readings of *Billy Budd* and *Death in Venice* (IV, 12). Although English teacher Fiske's judgment and principles appear to be correct, he proves Carmela's suspicion of prejudice: "So, what does it mean to the kid who really breaks his ass in here if Fredo Corleone can get a C because you asked?" His *Godfather* citation lacks the Sopranos' reverence, but Fiske respects the Wegler offer that can't be refused.

Carmela's affair begins when Wegler pretentiously gives her "a first edition, well, Modern Library's first edition," of *Madame Bovary*, then lauds her looks and unpretentiousness. His "first edition" is as fatuous as Carmela's "What a wonderful thing to have in the den." As he summarizes the heroine, "Outside nothing happens. But inside she has these extremes of boredom and exhilaration."

To distance us from Wegler and his courting tool, *Bovary*, the episode title privileges another Flaubert novel, *Sentimental Education: The History of a Young Man* (1869). The title summons up the 18th-century novel of sentiment, which valorized strict morality, honor, and an open emotionalism. Flaubert, like Jane Austen, challenged the genre's excesses. In both novels, Flaubert demonstrated how literary and social fictions can distort the reader's emotional life. If Flaubert's characters seem anachronistic for constantly analyzing their surprising feelings, they point to the hollowness of the Soprano characters' self-unawareness and focus on material pleasures. The Penguin edition of the 12th-century "Heloise" in Wegler's bathroom shows how far Carmela has moved from her Eloise retreats with Meadow (I, 1; III, 6; IV, 12)—and how little. For as Madame Bovary draws her hungers from romantic fiction and Wegler his pedagogic model from Abelard, Carmela still finds her life models in the pervasive pop culture.

When Carmela leaves him frustrated because she's obsessing with AJ's cheating and "the laws of the church," Wegler directs Fiske to give AJ a C for an essay 90 percent based on Cliffs Notes, which is where Carmela finds her advice. Wegler's guilt increases when Carmela rewards him with sexual eagerness: "Every time I think about putting the arm on Tom Fiske, I want to poke my eyes out with a knitting needle." Wegler counters her Bovary with his Oedipus in horror at discovering his bedmate's motherhood. He suggests they take a "time-out" because "I think you're a user, Carmela. Maybe you saw an opportunity in me and you took what you needed." As Artie Bucco defined Tony's predatory instinct, Wegler concludes, "You strong-armed me using the only weapon you have, your pussy."

Bob is both wrong and right. Carmela has genuinely been excited by him. She tells Father Phil that, despite being "remorseful and confused," she has "been walking around on a cloud like Maria in *West Side Story*." Tony interrupts her dreamily peeling a carrot to "Over the Mountain" (Across the Sea), by Johnnie and Joe, which catches her adolescent fervor. But she has not consciously been using Bob for AJ's benefit. On the other hand, as we saw when Carmela pressured Joan Cusamano to write Meadow a college recommendation (II, 8), she has a flair for coercion. When Wegler says, "I just thought you should know how I feel," her response justifies his suspicion: "Fuck you. You better watch yourself." That's a Tony threat.

In terms of sexual exploitation, Wegler may be more guilty than Carmela. When he renews his dinner invitation in his office, he looms over her from his desk, drawing force from his influence on her son's future. As he spent an hour choosing his wardrobe, he is as calculating as she is. She wears a plunging neckline in his office and a transparent skirt for their first dinner date. He first kisses her when she says she feels "like some teenager." Wegler may be looking for an uneducated woman with whom he can have a legal version of the romance between teacher Abelard and pupil Heloise. But he and Carmela—with their separate motives—lack the castrated monk's and the nun's devotion. For Wegler, "Their passion burns on through these incredible letters for the rest of their lives." For judgmental Father Phil, their story "ends badly."

Wegler's pressure on the English teacher, a far more blatant abuse of his power, comes entirely on his own, at neither Carmela's request nor promise. When he doubts Tony "would break his son's teacher's legs," he misses the greater threat: that he will on his own adopt the Soprano bullying. Carmela catalyzes the Tony in her Bob.

After their first sex, Carmela worries about sleeping with the photo of Tony, AJ, and their large (sleeping?) fish, so she stashes a pistol under his pillow. Fearing her husband's retribution, she is equally oppressed by her church's moral strictures, again embodied by Father Phil. After their earlier relationship (I, 5; I, 13), the priest clearly resents her sexual satisfaction with another man. Over Carmela's gift lunch, he is cold and supercilious, despite her compliment: "The funny thing is, I was sure he was gay. He sort of reminded me of you. He's intellectual. You know what I mean." Maliciously, Father Phil wants to include Tony in their discussion of her affair. He refuses to "absolve you of a sin you're going to continue to commit." He doesn't even try to answer her questions: "Why am I the only one held to any standards?" Why would God "put the need there" if He didn't intend her to respond to it? As Carmela defends her natural appetites, Father Phil dumbly watches the extra pepper spice up his pasta.

Father Phil is smug and insensitive: "Will [Bob] be here beyond the here and now?" For all his ostensible superiority, Father Phil applies Tony's Old School male authority: "You took a vow. You both did. For your penance I want you to do something kind for Tony." Failing that, she should pray for him. When Father Phil slams the confessional window, Carmela proves strong enough to resist his religious proscription—or too weak to resist temptation. The jury is hung. With new strength, she tells Tony and AJ to work out their differences and sets stiff terms for AJ's return.

The third victim of the Soprano hold, Tony B., loses his valorous battle to go straight. Given the Flaubert title, Tony B. is the episode's central character, a provincial antihero trying to rise through the contradictions and hypocrisies of a troubled, tumultuous times. First Kim blames him for the theft of the Kim South Side Laundry truck: "Why you fuck me like this? . . . I no forget you professional criminal." If he didn't need Tony's support against the union, "I show you the window." As is, Kim flashes his gun. When Kim realizes the thieves acted for his cousin on the North Side, the Korean family recalls the North-South Italian animosity that Furio expressed (IV, 3). Tony B. can't escape family turf wars, even as Kim's clinic offers, "You, me, my daughter, we make the big success journey." When Tony B. takes his sons away from their homework to smash the walls, his paternal indulgence also suggests his slipping discipline.

Tony B. is ruined by his inability to handle his *good* luck. His certification rewards his doing "two years of medical school" on his own. But his $12,000 windfall adds the pressures of drinking and gambling to his day shift and night labor at his clinic. Hence Silvio's two-edged coinage: "From now on, anytime somebody steps in a pile of shit—it's gonna be called a 'Blundetto.'" His new wealth turns to excrement when it revives his taste for the gangster's luxury.

The "doubly blessed" Tony B. also loses his girlfriend, whom he met on the prison Internet and whose support helped him pass his board exam.

"I'm so fucking sick of your gambling and complaining," Gwen admits. Tony B. cracks at Kim's encouragement: "So, partner, we open in three days." When he attacks Kim, the qualified massage therapist throws out his own back, showing a weakened spine. This scene ends with a close-up of one of the spa's exotic fish fatally flipping on the floor. The "straight" Soprano is out of his element, a fish out of water.

Tony B. opens the episode lugging heavy bags of soiled laundry, just before his truck is stolen. When the episode ends on alternating close-ups of the two Tonys, the Soprano quagmire has pulled back in another victim who tried to escape. Tony B.'s sentimental education is completed. His problem is not "the fuckin' prejudice against ex-cons" but his own weakness. Tony is understanding: "It's hard doing business with strangers." That restates Carmela's rationalization to Wegler: "How could asking someone you're with for help be using them? That's what people do." That's certainly what Tony does and what Wegler is properly ashamed of doing.

In a comic replay of the Soprano "education," Paulie waxes philosophical: "Tell me this. Why do pissing, shitting, and fucking all happen within a two-inch radius?" The newly sage Chris replies, "Everybody asks that, Paulie. There's no answer for it." But indulgent Vito has one: "They're all sources of pleasure, though." Christopher's postrecovery wisdom is ludicrous: "Fear knocked on the door. Faith answered. There was no-one there." And to Tony B.: "Other people's definitions of you—sometimes they're more about making themselves feel better. *You* gotta define yourself." However the new, improved Christopher defines himself, he remains a corrupt dolt. When Tony B.'s redefinition fails, he reverts to Soprano. So, too, Carmela follows Tony's example when she exploits her lover, admits that "sneaking around is half the fun," and blames Tony for the consequences of her action.

The projection of blame is replayed in the theme of prejudice, as people demonize the different. Kim is prejudiced against the ex-con, until he sees in Tony B. his own Korean diligence and ambition. That is, Kim redefines Tony B. as himself. Thrilled that Kim "sees something in me," Tony B. looks beyond their differences to the bond between the immigrant and the ex-con, both victims of prejudice. When he cracks, Tony B. is specifically irritated by his boss's mispronunciation. When their language difference overrules their partnership, he has his excuse to explode. Paulie blurs disparate Others together when he confuses the 1940s Japanese with the

2004 Koreans: "A word to the wise. Remember Pearl Harbor." Hence, too, the derigueur jokes about Koreans eating dogs and Tony's assumption that English teachers Wegler and Fiske must be homosexuals. As Tony reminds Carmela, she hated homosexuals until she "got a couple friends who're baloney smokers." From his old anxiety around meat, Tony detects his wife's attempt to transcend him: "Since when do you eat duck?"

V, 7: In Camelot

Written by Terence Winter. Directed by Steve Buscemi.

Uncle Junior uses funerals to escape going "stir-crazy" from house arrest. At Johnny-Boy's grave, Tony meets Fran Felstein, his father's old mistress. He negotiates her promised share of the midget auto racetrack. Tony uncovers more childhood traumas, including losing his dog Tippy and at 16 backing his father's lie when Johnny-Boy spent the night of Livia's miscarriage with Fran. Christopher encourages his rehab partner's gambling, which drives JT back to drugs and bankruptcy.

As the title suggests, the season's halfway episode explores the false nostalgia that glosses over betrayals and despair, on the national as well as personal fronts. This pivotal episode undercuts the characters' and the culture's rationalizations of their conduct as tradition or old-school values.

In the first scene, Tony and Janice spar about their history of conflict ("That shit about roadies?"). In the last, Tony, behind his cigar smoke, contemplates his exaggeration of Fran's affair with President John F. Kennedy, turning a one-night stand into a major relationship. From the Bada Bing, Tony prefers the delusion of glamour in a tenuous connection to the Kennedy Camelot. The big band number over the end credits is Jackie Gleason's TV theme, "Melancholy Serenade," more nostalgic than Etta James's conclusion to the previous episode. The music derives from Fran's memory of Gleason at JFK's party—and Tony B.'s mimicry.

Uncle Junior has lawyer Malvoin exaggerate relationships to justify his release to attend Italian funerals. The one with bagpipes proves the strain. Junior refuses to visit his brother's grave: "Five hours they let me out for these funerals, I'm gonna spend it bein' maudlin? It's a beautiful day." At the funerals he veers from inappropriate merriment, eating and singing, to excessive grief. When Father Phil reflects on the loving 70-year marriage of Niccolo and Concetta. Junior cries for himself, not them: "Aw, this fuckin' shit, what's the point? I can't take it anymore." Junior is "so fuckin' blue. . . . My life was only debt. I'm living in a grave." The "debt" is the "death" every life inevitably pays.

On the other hand, Junior romanticizes his unrequited ardor for Fran: "I loved that woman. She was the reason I never married. . . . She never knew my feelings. . . . For years I suffered in silence." But she remembers him as "practically a stalker," pestering her with phone calls. "I always had a hunch he told Livia about me and Johnny." A romantic illusion hides a betrayal, in this case betraying the betrayer.

When Tony finds Fran at Johnny-Boy's grave, still faithful in her fashion, she gives Tony what she gave his father, a love, support, and warmth that Livia couldn't: "Johnny was very proud of you. You were very special to him." Locked in her own world, she has risible problems hearing: "Do I know you?" "Oh, no, no, you're not annoying me." "What's this?" becomes "Catsup?" "Too vain" for a hearing aid, she lives in the isolation of the deaf—and the nostalgic. When Tony secures her $150,000, she buys expensive new shoes and dresses but doesn't pay her overdue phone bill. Her self-indulgence recalls Tony asking Melfi, "Why can't I do something that's just for me, for a change?" (V, 1).

Fran clings to her illusion of Camelot, even flirting with Tony ("Tell me about your women"). She shows him her JFK–monogrammed hanky: "We had a little thing. March. '61. Right before the Bay of Pigs." As she remembers JFK's line, she had to stay "in the interests of national security" so he could ensure she wasn't "working for the Russians." That one-night stand was a heady experience for a woman Tony immediately remembers as "The lady from Bamburgers. From the fur department." It sustains her still. When she dons Tony's JFK captain's hat and sings Marilyn Monroe's "Happy Birthday, Mr. President," Tony is discomfited, because he can enjoy only his fantasies, not hers. Her hanky relic preserves her imprint, not the president's.

The Kennedy Camelot has already been demystified by revelations of Jack's womanizing, illness, and dishonesty. Yet Fran cultivates the myth, which Tony amplifies for his buddies. In his version Fran had a three-year relationship with the president, he often brought her to the White House when his wife was away, and "For a while there, Jackie Kennedy thought the marriage was over." From his unsatisfying life amid the pole dancers, Tony seeks refuge even in an exposed myth. Tony's escape into mythology parallels Junior's into funerals—and is ultimately as unsuccessful, when reality impinges.

Tony's dog Tippy evokes more rue. The boy was told the dog was sent to the country to recover from worms, but Janice claims he was gassed. She marvels that Tony—"so cynical about everything else"—could be so naive about his dog. Now Tony learns that Johnny-Boy gave the dog to Fran's son, Bruce. Tony is more disturbed at having shared his dog with Fran than his father. As the shaggy dog story deepens Tony's feelings of loss, a William Wegman dog calendar disturbs his sex with Valentina.

Melfi urges him to stop resenting Livia: "You need to forgive her and move on." But he won't forgive her—"She made my father give away my dog"—despite his unease for supporting his father's betrayal. Tony supported Johnny-Boy's lie—that he couldn't come to the hospital because he took Tony to the Yankees game and a broken timing belt kept them from getting home—when in fact Tony was watching *Cannon* alone and, unlike Cannon, could not draw his father home from Fran. Now Tony can't accept Melfi's criticism of his father: "Is there any blame on his part? The man you emulate? The lies, the betrayals with all those women?" For to condemn Johnny-Boy's marital style would be to condemn his own. To avert responsibility, the adulterer blames the wife for driving her husband to other women. Johnny-Boy's lie remains Tony's excuse.

Tony seems disturbed by Fran's references to Livia: "She was a handsome woman, your mother. Not sexy, exactly, but statuesque." And how she conflates her passions for Johnny-Boy and for JFK: "That's something your mother never understood. When you're married—to a powerful man—you damn well better make him feel . . . powerful." Pathetically, Fran still glows from having made JFK feel powerful one night. In a New Year's Eve photo, Livia was "dressed like a refugee." Unable to defend Livia, Tony jokes away her death: "At least she didn't suffer. She made all of us suffer instead." He is more disturbed that Fran kept smoking through Johnny-Boy's emphysema.

The demystifying continues. Tony's bond with Hesh is shaken when he learns that Hesh denied him and Fran Johnny-Boy's share in the racetrack. Though Jewish herself, Fran remembers Hesh as "a whoremaster. And cheap. . . . He screwed me out of my retirement money." After Johnny's death, Hesh sent her only $500. He recalls that she always rubbed him the wrong way but denies any jealousy: "She was a little pale for my taste." Unlike the conventionally prejudiced (V, 6), Hesh embraces the difference of some Other.

The Camelot illusion is undercut by two subplots of hardball debt collection. When Phil Leotardo avoids paying his share of the racetrack sale, Tony chases his car into a bus. The thieves' honor is as mythical as courtly love. The Tony-Phil tension starts with an echo of actor Frank Vincent's (Leotardo) role in *GoodFellas*. "You got some balls, kid. I'll give you that," he tells Tony. Bristling at the "kid," Tony snaps, "You'll give me what I tell you to give me." The older man's provocation recalls the Vincent character Billy Batts's fatal exchange with the Joe Pesci character in *GoodFellas*. The connection between the two roles will be resumed in V, 11.

In the second collection, Christopher supports his rehab friend J.T. Dolan, a television writer—therefore a confessed "douche bag"—against alcohol and drugs but exploits his gambling. JT can't utter the word "addicting" here: "There's something about that excitement that's so—." After introducing JT to the Executive Game, Chris covers his $57,000 debt at two percent weekly interest, compounded, then pressures repayment more harshly than Tony did with his school chum Dave Scatino (Season II). Christopher has the cheek to recast his usury as therapy: "This is your problem. I will not fuckin' enable you." Like Tony's therapy, Chris's reform provides a new vocabulary but not responsibility.

The deluded JT pins his hopes on landing a job with Dick Wolf—whose *Law & Order* show and spin-offs are a police alternative to David Chase's franchise. Christopher claims the high ground, dismissing a *That's Life* episode as a "fake guinea fest for Paul Sorvino . . . totally unrealistic." Sorvino, of course, established his credentials as the solid boss in *GoodFellas*. Chris dismisses JT's screenwriting ambition: "I got out of that business because people fuck you over." But then Christopher and Little Paulie savagely beat JT when he misses his first payment. Chris takes JT's European sports car at book value ($17,000) and forces him to pawn his laptop and his Emmy. For the latter, the pawnbroker offers $15: "If it was an Oscar, maybe I could give you something. Or an Academy Award. But TV?" Though this may be an HBO gibe at network TV, the television show's joke about television's reputation counters the characters' delusions of glory.

Having driven JT back to heroin, Christopher warmly sees him off: "I'll see you when you get out of rehab. We'll figure out the rest of the payments. You can do it, man. I have faith in you. There's no chemical solution to a spiritual problem." Chris's support is as false as Camelot, too. For all his pontificating, Chris has ruined JT in the guise of supporting him—and shows no sense of his responsibility. In the same vein, Janice betrays her duty toward Bobby's kids. They like her now because "I leave them completely free to do whatever they want. How else are they gonna learn from their mistakes?"

In this episode, one distinctive editing device is the deceptive transition. Junior inaptly (and ineptly) sings *Volare* at a funeral, but the applause is for JT's introduction at the addicts' circle. From JT's promise of "a moral inventory," Chase cuts to Tony's session with Melfi. He contrasts Chris's visit with the broken JT to Tony's constructive therapy. From Chris drinking a Coke, he cuts to Fran and Tony having cocktails. An element missing in one scene crops up in the next. In these transitions, the illusion hides an incomplete reality—as myths like the Kennedy Camelot or the Mafia's Old School integrity do.

But then, perhaps the entire episode happens, as the title says, "In Camelot." For as is the custom in nostalgia, future generations may well locate their lost ideal in our present disenchantment. They will add what is missing. However bad our times, they will become someone's "good old days," not because they were, but because they will be needed to provide that enabling, consoling myth.

V, 8: Marco Polo

Written by Michael Imperioli. Directed by John Patterson.

Johnny Sack persuades Tony to pay Phil Leotardo's car repair costs. Though Tony wants to stay out of the New York dispute, Tony B. secretly accepts Carmine's contract to avenge the murder of Lorraine Caluzzo. After Hugo's 75th birthday party, Carmela and Tony make love.

This episode's dominant theme is possessions and the decadence of envy. That's why *La dolce vita* (Federico Fellini, 1960)—*The Sweet Life*—is the Italian movie Uncle Junior sleeps through on TV. In the first scene, Carmine Jr. gives Angelo Garepe and Jerry Basile each Whirlpool washers as he shows off his new mansion, with special pride in his "trompay loil" painting. As the trompe l'oeil genre cultivates the illusion of materiality, it is a useful metaphor for misleading materialism.

After sinking Carmine's boat, "My Funny Valentine," Johnny Sack shows Tony his $100,000 Maserati that's more than he can comfortably drive and less than his wife can stuff herself into. But "she loves it"—as a status symbol, presumably, not for her transport. Given his devotion to Ginny (IV, 3–4), the car signals Johnny's new selfishness.

When Tony pressures Angie Bonpensiero to keep down the costs on Leotardo's car, he, like Johnny, is insensitive to the woman. Though Leotardo leaves her in tears, Angie is harried from the outset. She is grateful to Tony for letting her assume Pussy's shop. Her struggle to put her kids through college is a far cry from the indulgent Angie of Season III. But her pathetic urgency asking Tony to "please say hello" to Carmela suggests that her work consumes her life. Tony takes unattractive pleasure in pressuring Angie: "You want to be a woman in business, then do what the situation calls for. . . . It's your call." Because he resents Carmela's demands on him, he would stick Angie with the $2,000 cost of Leotardo's new seat.

Tony has to pay Phil's car repair costs because Leotardo's son-in-law, a broker, let his car insurance lapse "looking for a better rate." In a rare turnabout, their responsibility is passed on to Tony. The hunger for ever-better deals also feeds the Johnny-Carmine conflict, engulfing Tony B. and squeezing Angie Bonpensiero between Tony's demand for economy and Leotardo's complaints. In the same spirit, the shot of broken Sal Vitro doing Johnny's lawn gratis reminds us of the exploitation that provides the bosses' luxuries.

Hugo's 75th birthday party replays the theme of possessions and envy in several forms, especially in his pile of presents. Tony's gift of a prize Baretta rifle "made my father's year," Carmela says, and revives both her affection for Tony's generosity and her attendant moral compromise. Auguring her return, she fetches his beer and defends him against her mother's snobbery.

There is even a false "ownership" of the decision that Tony should not attend. He tells Carmela and Tony B. that on his own he decided not to. When Hugo insists she invite him, Tony's coyness adds to her pressure and reasserts his power. He shows up late, twirling his sausages insouciantly, still cock even of the banished walk. In another false pretense, Uncle Junior spoils Hugo's surprise out of pique that he was not invited. He blames his house arrest for his not coming. "What are we, kids?" Junior says, as he childishly spoils the surprise. Here these characters pretend to a position/power they don't have.

The question is: Who owns the party, the guest or the hosts? Carmela's mother prefers Tony absent—"Why put us—and people—in an uncomfortable situation?"—and assumes that Carmela agrees. But Hugo "won't come if the man of the house isn't there." When he thanks Tony publicly "for having us all at your home," Carmela doesn't recognize the slap, because even she still feels that Tony belongs there. When she's drawn back to Tony's wealth, her independence dissolves into the house Tony reclaims, "manning the grill, playing the host."

Later Carmela realizes that her mother's opposition was not in sympathy but to prevent Tony from embarrassing her before her diplomat friends. Of course, the drunk Hugo should be more embarrassing than Tony's sausages. In any case, the Fegoles—he a retired "assistant to the ambassador to the Vatican"—are pretentious twits, as evidenced by their Christmas card—five pages of name-dropping—and Russ's party-poop remark that Baretta doesn't export its best models. But as Carmela properly condemns her mother's "closet self-loathing," she reverts to being Tony's enabler, compromising her own self-respect.

In another cameo of familial embarrassment, Chris implicitly criticizes his mother's drinking. On the wagon, Christopher resents either his mother or Adriana enjoying what he can't. This is an especially righteous form of envy. To scriptwriter Imperioli's credit, actor Imperioli's only line is "Goddamn," in response to her "I didn't have a drop."

Though Hugo has always loved Tony, his endorsement here may also reflect his concern to leave Carmela protected, especially after his fall from her roof. That tile repair would have been Tony's job. In V, 6, handy Hugo told Carmela, "If you had a man here, you wouldn't have to call me," but he did not make a case for Tony. Now he does, as if his accident reminded him of his mortality. As Junior and Hugo both repeat, "At our age it's enough of a surprise every day that we get up in the morning."

By insisting that Tony attend, Hugo in effect joins Tony and AJ as the males throw Carmela back into the old swim of things. After all, Hugo's "If you had a man here . . ." only echoes AJ's "You should've thought about that before" (V, 1). All the Soprano men think Carmela needs Tony around the house. When Tony and AJ throw her fully dressed into the pool, they violate her even within the party context. More explicit is Tony's persistence to seduce her, though the underwater shots imply that both their subconscious impulses take control.

The cut from the party to the brothel creates a telling ambiguity. After Tony rises from the sleeping Carmela, the hall shot initially implies other bedroom activity *chez* Soprano. We then find it's a brothel. That cut puts Tony's reclaim of Carmela into the context of the whorehouse, where men pay to use women. Though the cut takes us to a contrasting space, it underscores the moral compromise in Carmela's surrender to Tony's finances.

Tony B. also links the Soprano mansion and the brothel. Because he envies Tony's affluence, he accepts Carmine's contract to kill Joey Peeps, despite their comradely exchange at Angie's body shop. The Faces' song "Bad 'n' Ruin" connects the scene where Tony B. asks Tony for more rewarding work—"I'm a team player. Charley Hustle"—and the scene where he kills Joey for Carmine's side. The lyrics point to Tony B.'s reversion to crime: "And I'll find my way back home/ Back home bad 'n' ruin. . . . Mother, you won't recognize me now."

Preparing for Tony B.'s fatal freelance, he envies Carmela her mansion and pool, then encumbers her with his twins. At the party, bored and bitter, he films the excess of Tony's gut and Carmela's stripe-slacked rump, then feels like "a slave" when she summons him to help carry Hugo. When his Jason steals AJ's Atlanta Olympics medals, Tony B. donates both boys' Gameboys to the Salvation Army. As Dr. Krakower criticized Carmela (III, 7), Tony B. declares the brother Justin "just as bad as he is, 'cause you didn't stop him." His greed and indignation revived, Tony B. shoots Joe Peeps outside the brothel, then limps away, his foot run over by the victim's car. The limp gives Tony B. the Oedipal reference of Wegler's urge to blind himself in horror at his transgression with Carmela (V, 6). As Tony's cousin, his action will likely cause more serious tensions than even a 75-year-old's surprise birthday party.

All that said, however, *The Sopranos* is too subtle to settle on such an obvious theme as the dangers of materialism, whether trompe l'oeil or moral. Another level of genuine emotion balances the theme of possessions. That is to say, there is an alternative reading for the evidence above.

Despite all the tensions, here the Soprano family begins to recover. When Hugo stands up to his wife and daughter to involve Tony, the henpecked patriarch begins to restore the family order. At the party Tony is again a force. In addition to cooking the meats—a salutary advance from his cold-cut phobia (I, 1)—he renews the family's pleasure in each other. He teases Meadow on his lap, with Finn a comfortable, healthy mate (unlike predecessors Noah and Jackie Jr.). AJ is at his least surly, smoothly squiring his Devin, accepting his mother's rules, and even providing a romantic model for his parents. In parallel vignettes, Tony and Carmela share smiles at seeing Hugo and Mary kiss, and Tony B. is chilled when Tony's ease with Meadow evokes his lost Kelly.

To Carmela, Tony's Baretta, however sinister a gift, shows her husband once again doing the right thing at the right time—and for her father. Even the boys' dunking Carmela over her protest can be read as family fun, a bracing normalcy. Carmela's spirited defense of Tony against her mother is not only moral compromise but respect for his openness. Earlier, Carmela rejected her mother's silly rationalization that leaving Tony luckily "spared" her the misery of outliving her mate. The family's joy is recovered by Carmela's hard work and her boys' playfulness. Whatever else, their material luxury also betokens their generosity, success, and closeness. When Artie sleeps alone poolside through Tony's seduction of Carmela and through the night, he has yet to awaken to the realization of the importance of family. Perhaps because his Charmaine is at such a remove from Tony, Artie does not dive back in.

The poolside party recalls the one that concluded I, 1. Where the first forebodes the dissolution of Tony's family, here his intimacy with Carmela augurs its recovery. But this episode extends beyond the pool romance to Tony B.'s double murder and limp. The positive and negative ramifications provide an uncertain balance.

The episode title refers to the game of tag played in the pool, before Tony and Carmela find themselves alone. This water Polo is a far cry from the Italian hero who brought back unbelievable riches and tales from a more exotic Camelot. Perhaps the title undercuts the pretensions of the Fegoles and Carmela's mother and Tony B.'s ambition to exceed Tony's authority. In any case, as the game involves people trying to connect through calls from each other, it suggests the emotional need behind and served by material exchanges.

V, 9:   Unidentified Black Males

Written by Matthew Weiner and Terence Winter.
Directed by Tim Van Patten.

Tony's panic attacks return when he suspects that Tony B. may have killed Joey Peeps. To allay Johnny Sack's suspicion, Tony gives his cousin an alibi. Chris resents Tony B.'s promotion with a profitable casino. While Carmela is frustrated in her divorce plans, Meadow and Finn resolve their differences by getting engaged.

Several characters use the title's "unidentified black males" to evade their own responsibility. A construction site assault is blamed on "a couple niggers walkin' that way": "Oh yeah. Those two guys." To Melfi, Tony repeats his lie that an assault by two black men—"a bunch of mulignans . . . fuckin' jigaboo cocksuckin' motherfuckers"—kept him from the heist that sent Tony B. to jail. Tony B. blames his Joey Peeps foot injury on an attack by two black men. Characters project their own failings, guilt, and fears on some Other. Self-deceiving Meadow relays the fiction that Jackie Aprile Jr. "was killed by drug dealers. African-Americans."

Blaming others seems a ritual part of the boys' games. Indeed, Feech calls their business "the game" (V, 1), before he imposes his personal rules. Tony's panic attack grows out of his verbal tussle with Johnny Sack during golf. Vito's homosexuality is a surprise because he has been projecting— however implausibly—a macho sports image. He first engages Finn in man-talk about baseball, then forces a date for a Yankees game. Vito played one-on-one basketball with kinky Ralph (IV, 2).

The episode is framed with the men's selfish summer pleasure. In the first shot, an extension cord enables the two Tonys to watch a baseball telecast outside. In the last, Carmela's emotion at Meadow's engagement news is complicated by Tony, blissfully splashing in her pool. In both scenes, the men extend their personal territory, as the wild animal marks out his turf in the *Never Cry Wolf* (Carroll Ballard, 1983) clip on TV.

Finally, Tony tells Melfi the truth, as he struggles to breathe: "Black guys, my ass. I had a fight with my mother, and I had a fuckin' panic attack." Despite his face-saving lie, "He went to Nam and I was 4-F. And that's how our friends look at it." While that incident ruined Tony B.'s life—at least his marriage, family, and career—it launched Tony's "success." Paradoxically, Tony's present power dates back to that moment of vulnerability. Because it saved him, he prefers to deny it. To emphasize Tony's softness, his quarrel began when Livia criticized Carmela for being late with yarn for baby Meadow's booties. Tony is not proud of his feminine side: "I'm just a fuckin' robot to my own pussy-assed weakness." Where Melfi likens his self-exploration to childbirth, Tony insists "Trust me—it's like taking a shit."

In both Melfi scenes, two small female bronzes appear on the window ledge behind her, an echo of the large bronze in the drama's first shot (I, 1). The dancer on the left catches Tony's sprightliness as he reports his night with Carmela and his shrewd promotion of Tony B.. With both he seems cavalier. He left Carmela asleep to prevent "mixed signals." With Tony B. "I put a very good piece of manpower to work." The contemplative seated woman appears on the right when Tony confesses why he missed the robbery. The bronzes are an emblem of the feminine mystery he confronts both around and in his own nature.

This mystery becomes Tony's one persistent guilt. With only one exception, Tony has controlled his regret over failed responsibilities, such as Gloria's suicide or his impatience with AJ. Now we learn he has one lasting guilt—for abandoning Tony B. to his bust and jailing. But as Tony B.'s arrest was not caused by Tony's absence, he feels guilty for having shown his feminine side in defending Carmela and fainting. Tony feels guilty of sensitivity.

The sensitivity that Tony denies, Finn exemplifies, for better or worse. As he plans his professional life, he rejects his "solidly unsentimental" photographs. His conscience won't let him take a job away from a minority. But as he and Meadow argue about their summer options, their mutual deference prevents a decision, whether it's to go to California—

MEADOW: Do you want me to come out [west]?
FINN: Do you want to?
—or just to a movie:
FINN: What do you want to see?
MEADOW: You say.

FINN: No, you.

Nor does their college vocabulary ensure understanding. Finn is neither clear nor reassuring when he contends: "There was no abundant functionality in my taking out my suitcase." Finally, his proposal seems prompted less by love than by battle fatigue:

FINN: Why don't we just get married?

MEADOW: Married?

FINN: Let's get engaged.

MEADOW: Really? Why are you saying that now?

FINN: I can't think. It's too late. It's just something I feel very strongly.

His emotional impulse cuts through their rational miasma. Even then, he quickly retreats from "married" to "engaged." Perhaps even the New Man Finn has something of Old School Tony's fear of a no-loophole commitment.

Of course, Finn's virtue, education and character make him a helpless naïf among the Sopranos. To teach him, Meadow adopts Tony's rationalization of the gangsters' codes: "They bring certain modes of conflict resolution from all the way back to the old country," to defend against the corrupt order. Given that academic language, her accusing Finn of anthropological detachment is another case of the pot calling the kettle an unidentified black.

Tony's generous embrace of Finn begins with the construction job at $20 an hour—"Holy shit, how's that even possible?"—at which he learns not to work. For the latter, the more crudely seductive Vito claims credit. Finn suffers what Tony called "mixed signals." Once "Uncle Paulie" hears that Finn is Meadow's friend, instead of having to wash the turd off Paulie's tires, he gets a fistful of dollars to spend on her. When Finn pays for dinner, Tony attacks, "You're lucky you don't get your head handed to you." To Tony, that generosity is an encroachment on his power. Until the boy has his own family, Tony rules: "You eat—I pay." Outside Tony apologizes: "Listen. I didn't mean to bite your head off."

The given "head" references lead us to the motif of oral sex. It lurks in the homonymous name of Felicia, in the student "oral surgeon," and in Meadow's "blowing off" re dental school and the law center. The image of Vito blowing himself with a ridiculously small fan is a visual pun. The men's ambivalence over oral sex—prizing it but disdainful of its provider—points to the larger theme of homophobia, a fear of that particular "mixed signal," male softness. On the construction site, the lads' bantering erupts into a vicious attack. "Well, you oughta know, sweetie," one man replies to the other's charge, that his girlfriend's moustache would be like "kissing a fireman." Nauseated by the fight, Finn is comforted by Felicia. Meadow says the attacker Gene Pontecorvo is "so sweet," but to Finn he was "like an animal." Nor does she accept Finn's fear of Vito: "Vito Spatafore is a married man, Finn. I seriously doubt he wants to kill you." "Well, maybe he wants to fuck me and then kill me." After the site assault, Finn is wisely reluctant either to suggest who would win a Tyson-Ali fight or to date Vito.

Finn's nightmare begins when he comes upon Vito fellating a security guard. After Finn urinates, he finds Vito waiting outside with a menacing baseball date: "Don't pull that 'aw shucks' shit with me. You're fuckin' going." When Vito warns, "I don't like to miss the national anthem," Finn is uncertain what kind of stand-up guy to expect. Understandably, he considers flying to California "until this thing with Vito blows over."

Vito has seemed heterosexual, given recent references to his wife, Adriana's complaints of his pursuit, and his bragging of hers. Here he laughs along with both the homophobic joke and Pontecorvo's attack: "I knew that was coming." His homosexual aspect seems well hidden from an antagonistic male society. Indeed, its elaborate rejection may function like the blame on unidentified black males, to hide guilt. Especially in Tony's florid "a bunch of mulignans . . . fuckin' jigaboo cocksuckin' motherfuckers"—the laddies doth protest too much, mayhap?

Latent homosexuality may also color Johnny Sack's reminiscence about the murdered Joey Peeps: "I picked him out of the chorus. Schooled him those years he was my driver." Johnny's surprising feeling for his former driver may help explain the new sports car that excludes Ginny. These sexual motifs support the episode's primary themes, Tony's tension between being hard or soft and the characters projecting upon "unidentified black males" their own secret nature and guilt.

Their night of love (V, 8) revived Carmela's feelings, but Tony suppresses his. He phoned the next day, said it was nice, and sent her flowers. But when he drops off AJ without coming in to talk, the disappointed Carmela rationalizes: "Thank God. The last thing I needed was to talk to him now." Like the homophobes, Carmela hides her susceptibility behind denial. Tony hides his feelings when he tells Melfi the lovemaking was strictly for Carmela's sake: "The poor thing was starved for it, honestly.

I'm the only man she was ever with." That delusion reveals more swagger than sympathy.

More "mixed signals" abound when Carmela invites Tony to lunch—only to restate her intention to divorce him and to "aggressively pursue . . . an equitable distribution of our assets." Artie says, "I hope you brought your appetite"—mistaking his friends' hunger. In more mixed signals, Tony beckons Artie over, then sends him away twice. To Carmela he gives a very clear signal. Her mansion, "$500 shoes, and diamond rings" are due to his "fuckin' sweat": "You knew every step of the way exactly how it works." But he storms out with another mixed one: "You're entitled to shit. She's ready to order."

The mixed love and rage in Tony and Carmela's marriage and the proposal's resolution of Finn and Meadow's tension demonstrate what Felicia calls the wedding ring's "kind of, like, weird power." The marriage symbol can yoke antagonists as well as lovers. Here the joys of the boys of summer betray their women's isolation.

And their insecurity. Even the sensitive Finn unsettles Meadow with his suspicious suitcase. Despite this experience of romantic insecurity, Meadow remains unsympathetic to Carmela:

Meadow: Have you ever thought beyond being dependent on some man?

Carmela: It's so simple for you. . . . You have options. I have a lawyer.

On the contrary, Tony's maneuvering and reputation prevent her from getting either a lawyer or a forensic accountant. On Alan Sapinsky's advice (IV, 13), Tony has staked out his territory across the legal community, just as he reclaims his pleasure areas—the fridge, the pool—in Carmela's home. When the last lawyer rejects her because of his "full case load," she throws down her bag of groceries in frustration. The two bags she later brings home betoken the basic security for which she will resume the moral compromise of her marriage.

For now, perhaps the dominant "unidentified black male" is the black bear that rummages through Carmela's deck. The editing identifies him with Tony's bullying. The bear first appears just after a divorce lawyer demurs because of Tony's contact. The bear leaves after the lawyer proposes a colleague whom "your husband hasn't contaminated."

The gangsters' tough front admits glimpses of sensitivity. Hence the upset when Silvio has the headstone carved with the victim's nickname, Peeps, instead of Paparelli. And Chris fears that Tony B.'s promotion has reduced him from "number one cousin" to "dogshit in Tony's eye"—i.e., from Number One to Number Two (cp V, 5). There is even an element of sensitivity in how the relentless betrayers lie, whether to others or to themselves. Confronted over the Peeps contract, Tony B. lies to Tony quite candidly: "Even if I was [guilty], would you really want to know?" Carmela tells Meadow that Tony left with Artie the night of their fateful party. Tony lies to Johnny at Joey's funeral: "I'm sittin' here humbling myself out of friendship to you, John." Indeed, Tony openly counsels a politic hypocrisy: Johnny should shake his enemy Carmine Jr.'s hand. The brutes can use sensitivity.

Over the end credits Bobby Darin sings that romantic folk song where love can transcend all differences, "If I Were a Carpenter," an American equivalent to the Italian opera that sealed V, 5. Darin's earnest, Finn-ish naïveté is a counterpoise against the characters' projection of their own venality upon some outer blackness, and the various sad stages of romance portrayed by Meadow and Finn, Carmela and Tony, and Vito and the boys on the crew.

V, 10:   Cold Cuts

Written by Robin Green & Mitchell Burgess.
Directed by Mike Figgis.

Johnny Sack stiffs his partners on a shipment of Vespa scooters that he claims did not arrive. When retired wiseguy Uncle Pat Blundetto sells his upstate farm to developers, Tony dispatches Chris and Tony B. to dig up and dispose of three bodies buried there. After Janice is arrested for a soccer mom assault, Tony tests the success of her anger management classes.

As this episode digs up Chris's first kill, Emil (I, 1), and the Johnson brothers planted by Tony's father, its title revives the source of Tony's traumas, his association of meat with his father's violence. When Dr. Melfi defines depression as "rage turned inward," Tony concludes: "Revenge is like serving cold cuts." Melfi corrects him: "Revenge is a dish best served cold." The original Family heads acted genial while they plotted revenge, because anger "is bad for business. It clouds your judgment." The episode shows the high costs of Tony's "intolerance for frustration." His new girl-friend, a dermatology nurse, may get him skin treatment at half price, but Tony's real problem is what gets *under* his skin.

The episode's theme of anger management was prefigured in a short scene in the previous episode, where FBI agent Sanseverino tensely corrects her daughter. Where the FBI agent needs perfect anger management skills, the gangsters enjoy more leeway. So Johnny Sack is open about avenging Joey Peeps: "Lots of things didn't happen that seem like they happened. Your cousin didn't whack Joey, the Vespas didn't get into my hands." When Tony learns he may lose out on a heist of imported provolone, he responds exactly as he does to the news report of Janice's "soccer rage": "Motherfucker! [SMASH]." As the TV psychologist warns, "Certain indi-viduals are particularly prone to rage" at any frustration or inconvenience. The scammed objects—Vespa scooters and provolone—are like the gang-ster codes—Meadow's "modes of conflict resolution" (V, 9)—classic im-ports from Italy.

When Johnny Sack blames the Vespas' putative loss on "tightened se-curity at the ports. Al Qaeda," Melfi's diagnosis of Tony extends to West-ern civilization: "We live in a time of technological and spiritual crisis, but you think you're above it." When his frustration leads to an irrational violence, Tony may represent America's response to 9/11. He certainly suffers a new understanding here. Having so richly profited from lax U.S. port supervision, he is shaken to learn that only two percent of the six million containers that enter American ports each year are ever checked. At the prospect of terrorists or bombs being smuggled in, Tony realizes the national costs of his advantage: "Customs ain't so bad for us, but terrorismwise they're doin' nothing.'" His "but" should be "because." Tony's new sense of America's vulnerability overrides his happy exploita-tion of it. Now he feels endangered by the national cost of his license.

As Tony feeds his fear—"They got a nuclear bomb in a container and we're fuckin' dead"—he is irrationally infuriated by Georgie's agreement: "That's why ya gotta live for today." "We're talking about annihilation," Tony says. Because Georgie "can't even think about that," Tony attacks him, a blizzard of money blowing in the air. Georgie suffers permanent hearing loss. When Tony tries to buy him off, Paulie reports that Georgie has quit the Bada Bing and doesn't want Tony to visit.

Georgie proves the importance of even the occasional bit players across this drama. In Season 1, Tony pounded Georgie with the new telephone, ostensibly because he couldn't operate it, but really because Tony was frustrated about Livia (I, 2). Later Georgie is stabbed by Ralphie, flushed with his *Gladiator* image (III, 6). Here Tony attacks him from fear of terrorists. Why does Georgie stay at the Bada Bing this long? The job has perks. For the Friday night Executive Club, Georgie charges each girl $50 and a blow job (III, 6). He suffers his abuse in return for criminal rewards and—the trickle-down theory?—his own small scale of power. Georgie replays the moral compromise that all the major characters—with the bracing exception of Charmaine Bucco—show when they support, accept, or even just profit from Tony and his ways. In Georgie's case the worm finally turns. Paulie's conclusion bleakly equates criminality with the social norm: "These things happen, T. That's why I don't like to talk politics."

In a more dramatic—albeit temporary—transformation, Janice's soccer field violence forces her to take responsibility for the character she has blamed on her dog-eat-dog upbringing:

JANICE: That bitch is lucky I didn't kill her.

TONY: Well, we know that.

BOBBY: What?

Unaware that Janice whacked her fiancé, Richie (II, 12), Bobby consoles himself: "On the other hand, she called Sophia her daughter." But Janice's motherliness is dispelled by her tone of voice and the girl's fear:

JANICE: Now go to sleep.

SOPHIA: Are you going to punch me?

Sophia turns off her bedside light to ward off her visit. Janice's leonine defense of her stepdaughter only alienates her further.

After Bobbie insists Janice take anger management classes or "this with us ain't gonna work out," she takes group therapy. The director contends that anger is internal, not provoked. "*It* doesn't make you mad. *You* make you mad." Even here Janice is belligerent. When she attacks a black woman she seemed to support, the UPS driver delivers the summary: "This is fuckin' priceless." Another man's quote of a Bufferin commercial suggests America has institutionalized and commercialized anger. Nonetheless, the kinder, gentler Janice recovers the Baccalieri peace.

Though Tony appears to applaud Janice's new discipline, his gimlet eye refuses to accept her stability. After sarcastic respect—"Mahatma Gandi over here"—he baits her: "I wonder where Harpo's eating his Sunday dinner. . . . I wonder what's French-Canadian for 'I grew up without a

266 · THE SOPRANOS ON THE COUCH

mother.'" Though Janice takes a fork to him, it is Tony who revives Livia's malice when he undermines his sister. As Tony saunters away, laughing at her destruction, his boyish charm can't conceal his ugliness. He has no saving grace when, angry that Carmela has drained the pool to save the heating costs, his low-angle shot at the edge makes him a physical threat.

In Carmela's scene of anger management, when she encounters ex-lover Bob Wegler she blurts: "I'm going back to my husband." As she tells Rosalie, she didn't plan to say that and doesn't intend to return to Tony. The line was a reflex defense against either Wegler's criticism or his renewed interest. It reminds her of the comfort of using Tony's power, especially when she can't find a divorce lawyer "uncontaminated by [her] husband" (V, 9). Surprising even Carmela, her line prepares for her return. To suggest its effect on her, her walk away from Wegler slows into a freeze, then a wipe to the next scene. There Chris and Tony B. revive their boyhood summer joys at Uncle Pat's farm. Carmela recalls her lost power, the gangsters their innocence. As Chase hardly ever deploys old rhetoric like a freeze or a wipe, its use here is arresting.

In another cooling, Chris and Tony B. bond during their farm assignment. Chris needs to cool off: "Where's my Barney's underpants, with the ventilated cup? . . . I need Tony B. up there like I need a third nut." Chris also needs his Tinactin to cool his athlete's foot. As they unearth, pulverize, and make disappear three corpses, Chris and Tony B. talk out Chris's resentment. When Chris scapegoats Benny Fazio for his own complaints, he anticipates Benny's vicious beating on his behalf (V, 13).

Tony B. remembers Tony as "the funnest guy in the world," but now "He's got the world by the balls and he acts like everything's a fuckin' imposition." "Being at the top, he's isolated himself," Chris explains. When the philosophical Chris picks up Emil's skull, he regards it thoughtfully, then—no Hamlet, he—sacks and smashes it. There is anger even in Chris's non-angry action.

The cousins' camaraderie proves as brief as Janice's calm. Tony and Tony B. resume teasing Chris. He especially resents Tony's urging him to drink: "Sobriety is hard enough work without getting mocked over it." Earlier, when Chris tells Adriana his dissatisfaction with Tony, she renews her suggestion that they escape: "You're so unhappy. What if we left here? Went far away. And you went into something else." Chris still plans to be a writer (like Harry Hill). He assumes he would succeed as a male model, but (typically insecure about his manhood) he "wouldn't like the people." "I'm a soldier, Adriana. When are you going to understand that?"

As Tony recalls, Janice named her son Harpo after a Phoebe Snow song, forgoing even that Marxist spirit. Over the end credits, the Kinks provide the anthem for this episode: "I'm not gonna take it lyin' down. . . . I'm not like everybody else." The song expresses both the tradition of American individualism and the nation's anger at having been attacked. Both the characters and the culture run the risk of losing their cool. That would be the most damaging cut of all.

V, 11:   The Test Dream

Written by Matthew Weiner and David Chase.
Directed by Allen Coulter.

As Tony's *goomah* Valentina makes him a postcoital snack, her kimono catches fire. Tony rushes her to the hospital. He collects cash from an obviously perturbed Tony B., then registers at the Plaza hotel for a carefree night's sleep. After the Leotardo brothers kill Angelo Garepe, Tony B. kills Billy Leotardo and wounds Phil.

The 20-minute dream sequence pushes this popular series past complexity almost to enigma. As Tony's first extended nightmare (II, 13) revealed Big Pussy's treachery, this dream explores Tony's guilts and prepares him dutifully to kill Tony B. and to return to Carmela.

The revival of Tony's marriage derives from the episode's four bedroom scenes, two real, two dream. The episode opens on Tony's sex with Valentina, followed by her unpromising offer of food. Compared to Carmela's cuisine, Valentina's—Egg Beaters and Tabasco—feels Spartan. His "You're not gonna cook, are you?" turns ambiguous—like her argument for a tropical vacation in Antigua, where "the air is the same temperature as your body"—when she burns. At her "Is it so much to fuckin' ask for, a little attention?" her dressing gown bursts into flame. The flame is an emblem of her anger—provoked, repellent, and self-destructive—but it does get Tony's attention.

Tony has been planning to end this affair—she is "a constant pain in my ass"—but her trauma delays the break. This despite his "good news" that her hair will grow back and she won't need skin grafts or "the hyperbolic chamber," an apt malapropism for Tony's exaggerated support. For as usual, Tony hides his emotional withdrawal behind financial generosity: "I'm gonna take care of everything. The doctor bills, the wake, whatever." When Tony recalls Carmine's last remark before dying, a "burned-hair smell," this sexual relationship assumes his air of mortality.

Seeking more than sex, Tony contemplates an affair with Charmaine Bucco, who is not just beautiful and "in some ways a better cook than Artie," but a "licensed notary public." Tony associates her with a kind of—useful?—legality. "I'm thinking this is the kind of woman I need." Ignoring her obvious loathing, he phones her. When he can't speak, his subconscious inhibition seems wiser than his desire. After setting out his family photos (Tony with Meadow, the alienated AJ alone), he settles on a call girl. His prompting by the TV escort service ad ("Let them satisfy your every need") shows him susceptible to easy distraction. Two long shots of Tony eating emphasize his solitude amid the empty lavishness.

At the episode's close, Tony finds the intimacy he needs in his sunrise phone call to Carmela, to cancel his fishing trip with AJ. Tony seems to forget his worries about Tony B., as they chat about her evening out with Gabriella and Rosalie and the neighbors' barking dog. She knows about his Coach Molinaro dreams and Tony's recurring anxiety: "Were you unprepared as usual?" Tony's two sexual encounters, with Valentina and the Jade girl, lack the solace and intimacy of this phone chat with Carmela. And in so amenably accepting his wake-up call, Carmela moves closer to reconciliation.

Meanwhile, Tony is pushed away by Tony B.. His old cellmate Angelo is embarrassed to bring only part of his Joey Peeps payment: "Rusty, I think he bangs his wife in installments." The male characters' sex lives define their overall character. The joke and the scene show the closeness that will prompt Tony B.'s vengeance. When Tony visits him, both are isolated in their obsessions. Tony focuses on his woman problems—the burned Valentina, his unreliable Guatemalan housekeeper, Charmaine's allure—culminating in "Why the fuck does this shit always happen to me?" Like Janice and Livia, Tony declares himself the victim. Preoccupied with the Leotardos, Tony B. blames his tension on his twins. Both Tonys conceal their truer connections, to Carmela and to Angelo respectively. They don't connect even in their ritual hug.

The episode's title conflates test drive and dream. Literally, the dream involves Tony's being driven out to a contract on "our friend," Tony B., who Tony intuits will attack the Leotardos. The title draws together the "test drive" that began Tony's fatal affair with Gloria and the drive in the first dream in a parallel episode (IV, 11).

Here Gloria personifies the feminine consciousness and conscience. The dream Gloria has the character's wit and wisdom without her madness. Gloria and Tony's violent relationship is sanitized by Ralph Kramden's threats to his wife in *The Honeymooners,* but Tony's worries about Tony B. intrude: "My cousin does a mean Gleason." Gloria brought out the meanness in Tony. She reminds him that Livia, not she, threatened to fork out his eye, confirming Melfi's remark upon the women's similarity (III, 12). Their laughter assuages Tony's guilt for his lover's suicide.

Gloria enters by replacing Melfi in Tony's therapy session, then returns as an interviewer and an organizer in the crowd that criticizes Tony for failing to prevent Tony B.'s shooting Phil Leotardo. Though the dream's summary of Tony's greatest hits also resurrects Big Pussy, Richie Aprile, Patsy Parisi, Mikey Palmice, and Ralphie, Gloria's prominence makes the dream a test of Tony's ability to distinguish between his shallow and his significant needs for a woman.

Tony's dream blends his emotional and business concerns. From the Jade girl's offer of fellatio, Tony finds himself in bed with the dead Carmine, who says he misses his wife: "I'm all alone on the other side. It ain't right." The line conflates Tony's anxieties around connection, his need for Carmela, and his avoidance of the New York turf war. When the phone rings Carmine says, "If it's Him, tell Him you ain't seen me." Carmine's hiding from "the Man upstairs" reflects Tony's armor of evasions.

Coach Molinaro pierces through them: Tony failed by staying with the delinquents of his youth and by wasting his natural leadership gifts. When Tony pulls his gun to silence him, the clip falls out and the bullets melt on his fingers. This premature ejaculation coheres with Coach Molinaro ridiculing the gun as "a bigger dingus than the one God gave you." We recall Tony reclaiming his manliness around his house at the end of V, 1, with the AK-47 erect in his lap. In another image of impotence, when Tony meets would-be dentist Finn's parents, he spits out bloody teeth. The fiancé's imminent power weakens the father. When AJ supplants Finn, Tony projects onto the DeTrulios his son's prospect of failure.

Between the Carmine and Molinaro scenes, as the major characters remind Tony of his mission, various film and television allusions point to Tony's mediated personality and sometimes conflicting layers of self. When Gloria asks if he's "ready for what you have to do," she directs him to a TV image of them together in a car, along with the other men he already has "had to do." Hence, too, Coach Molinaro's disdain: "I see you on TV. Some show you put on. The five o'clock news." In the transition from "show" to "news," Tony moves from fiction to documentary, and is attributed layers of motive and pretense.

In Carmela's kitchen Tony finds TV "much more interesting" than his life. "It *is* your life," Carmela tells him. The sequence declares Tony both product and embodiment of American popular culture. As we have often noted, Tony personifies the American heroism defined especially by *The Public Enemy,* the Godfather trilogy, and *GoodFellas.* The clip of Alistair Sim's Scrooge awakening in time to reform in *A Christmas Carol* (Brian Desmond-Hurst, 1951) parallels Tony's present review of his transgressions, with the spirit of his Whackees Past. In both other cited films, *Chinatown* (Roman Polanski, 1974) and *High Noon* (Fred Zinneman, 1952), the heroes strive against networks of corruption.

That last clip recycles Tony's familiar ideal of stoic manhood, Gary Cooper, as he and Carmela leave for dinner with Finn's parents. Their meeting explores the characters' fluidity of character. Finn's parents are played somewhere between actor and role. The casting adds the actor's persona—the continuing identity that incorporates outside roles—to the character. Finn's mother is identified as actress Annette Bening, both in Tony's smug aside and in her own allusion to *Bugsy* (Barry Levinson, 1991), the film (about Jewish gangster Bugsy Siegel) in which she costarred and united with Warren Beatty. Finn's father is portrayed by John Heard, who played Vin Makasian, Tony's corrupt cop, in Season I. At the urinal with DeTrulio, Tony's "You don't do this anymore?" may acknowledge his sense of Heard's Makasian within his DeTrulio, the persona within the character.

Vin's close relationship with his Madam Debbie (I, 11) may lie behind DeTrulio's song, "Once, Twice, Three Times a Lady." Tony's selves lack the cohesion of the song's Lady. Finn's mother is unmoved by that serenade because her identification as Bening detaches her from her role as wife. When Heard asks if Tony will "be able to come through on the thing," Tony says, "I done my homework"—*The Valachi Papers.* Peter

Maas's bestseller about the first mafiosa to "sing" on his people is antithetical to Gary Cooper's strength of silence. That book also adds a sinister promise to DeTrulio's song: "The memory is all in my mind. / Now that we've come to the end of our rainbow, / There's something I must say out loud." Tony's subconscious bodes betrayal—perhaps just of Tony B., perhaps of the whole criminal operation. Whether that happens or not, his subconscious is undermining his conscious principles.

When Tony dreams of sex with Charmaine, Artie attends and advises, "She loves it when you rub her muzzle." This cuts to Tony aboard Pie-O-My in Carmela's living room. This elision of the one uncompromising woman with his idealized mare leads Tony to accept fidelity to Carmela. Leading off her "nonnegotiable conditions"—her term when she readmitted AJ (V, 6)—he will no longer ride the horse in her house. "Why?" he has to ask. "The smell, the shit all over the place." In an oneiric pun, Tony giving up his horse means giving up his whores. Indeed, the name of the escort agency, Jade, undercuts the exotic gem with a worn-out horse.

In the dream overall, Tony moves from Carmine's cold solitude to Molinaro's accusation: "You're not prepared!" and "I also told you, most likely you'd take the easy way out." From the call girl's oral offer of the easiest sex, Tony comes to realize he needs the most demanding, his marriage. Over the end credits, the Commodores repeat DeTrulio's song, "Three Times a Lady," which may now allude to Tony's three false alternatives to Carmela: the burned-out Valentina, the professional Jade, and the unattainable Charmaine.

In their telephone non-sex, Carmela observes that at Artie's "the veal was dry." But the Sopranos have been eating at the Buccos' for years. Their relationship goes back to high school, like Tony's with Carmela. The occasional disappointment does not end the relationship, nor provoke dining elsewhere. As Tony's dream here discovers, his marriage to Carmela is more nourishing and appetizing than his fast-food alternatives, like the call girl's takeout. His real ball-breaker is the Egg Beater Valentina (now toast), not the high-cal Carmela.

The dream's resonance of metaphor extends into the reality sequences. When Carmela muses, "Coach Mole . . . I wonder where he is now," the answer is implicit. The Mole must be in the ground, however he survives in Tony's conscience. Tony registers at the Plaza as "Mr. Petraglia," which harmonizes with the strangled *Petrullio*/Peters (I, 5), Gloria *Trillo,* and Finn *DeTrulio.* When Chris visits as "a Mr. Mantovani," the puppet pretends to be the master of the stringed instruments. As Mantovani was the Italian-American (of course) king of light orchestral music, his name also connects to Tony's dream confusion of Carmine's wife, Violet, with "violin."

When Angelo says his son Charlie, who "takes after his mother," is in "architectural salvage," the reference goes beyond Tony B.'s reminder of the *Sanford* (né *Steptoe*) *and Son* TV shows to this episode's overall thrust—Tony's attempt to salvage the architecture of his psyche, on the foundation of a good woman's support.

The actor's presence within the character, like Heard's and Bening's in Tony's dream, also operates in the "real" scene of Angelo's murder. When Frank Vincent, as Phil Leotardo, kills Angelo with shots into his car trunk, he reverses the murder of Billy Batts, Vincent's character in *GoodFellas*. Leotardo's trouble with Tony began with an earlier echo of Batts (V, 7). Moreover, the song over this murder scene is *Peanuts*, sung by the Four Seasons with Frankie Valli. In his role as Rusty, Valli contracted Tony B. to kill Joey Peeps. So Valli's presence in the song signifies his character's continuing implication here. Leotardo kills Angelo because of the Valli character's contract on Peeps.

In the same vein, we found Michael Imperioli's persona behind his character in "Legend of Tennessee Moltisanti" (I, 8). His Christopher shoots the bakery clerk the way Imperioli's character (Spider) was shot by Joe Pesci in *GoodFellas*. In all these cases, in the real scenes as in the dream, the actor's persona is part of his character. This relates to Tony as a personification of American popular culture, especially of the classical tradition of gangster movies. Also, at an existential level, human behavior is defined as an unstable layering of motive and action. Characters are defined by what they do, especially when that differs from what they claim, and their actions resonate across all their roles and lives.

Even the Plaza reality scenes seem dreamlike. Dr. Melfi passes unexplained through the lobby when Tony registers. He notices an odd wedding shoot, sans groom, and is offered service by a bellboy named Jesus. Portentously, Tony sees a figure leaving the empty hotel corridor, then steals the neighbor's *New York Times*. Tony watches the hotel's ad on TV as if to validate his being there. The last scene plays like Carmela's dream. Tony wakes her at 5:30 for a meandering conversation, with the barking dog and the couple's easy intimacy. In the last line, over a black screen

Tony asks, "Is it light where you are yet?" Carmela is the light to which he is reawakening to return—and he her overbearing darkness.

V, 12: Long Term Parking

Written by Terence Winter. Directed by Tim Van Patten.

After Adriana conceals a drug-related murder, the FBI threaten a 25-year jail term unless she brings Christopher to testify under the Witness Protection Program. When Adriana confesses to Christopher and urges their escape, he agrees, then changes his mind. To prevent war, Carmine Jr. ends his challenge to Johnny Sack. Johnny orders Tony to turn over Tony B. for killing Joey Peeps and Billy Leotardo. Under these looming clouds of peace, Carmela and Tony reconvene their marriage.

The central theme of this episode is the need to leave shifting allegiances for more stable commitments, i.e., "Long Term Parking." In particular, the characters are torn over family bonds. Phil Leotardo and Tony flash back to experiences with brother and cousin, respectively. Paralleling the gangsters, the FBI uses, then brushes aside the Long Branch police on the druggie's murder.

Of the shifting loyalties, Adriana proves the biggest victim. Letting a friend use her photocopier implicates her in a murder. Yet she excuses the killer, Matush: "He's not a bad person. He's very religious. . . . He prays, like, all the time. . . . He doesn't even do drugs anymore; he just deals. And every month he sends all his money home to his family . . . [in Pakistan]. His brother owns a prep school someplace, for young boys." Given Tony's new fear of Muslem extremism (V, 10), Matush's drug money may well support a terrorist training camp. Adriana would forgive what Tony fears, whether Matush or a singing Chris. In Chris's one unwitting insight: "She's got the world at her feet, and she walks around like impending doom." That's how he translates her offer of salvation.

As Agent Sanseverino warns, Adriana's double life "is what's costing you your insides." Though Adriana is cleared of polyps, she has ulcerated colitis. Silvio's advice—"Maybe you should be a vegan"—is wiser than it seems, given Tony's traumatic association of his father's violence with meat. Adriana suffers physically as well as emotionally from trying to sat-isfy both Chris's and the FBI's demands. As she parks with one, then the other, she needs to choose one side for long-term health. In this respect, Adriana replays Tony's marital movement begun in the previous episode.

Adriana's condition prompts excremental imagery. Chris calls her his "smelly Valentine" and quips, "They're gonna replace her colon with a semicolon." His reference to the song "Born to Run" is acidly about her condition, not about what she needs them to do. The scatology includes the FBI complaint "You've been giving us shit" and their excuse for not providing counsel: the public defenders are "backed up." The aptly named Matush allegedly sold laxative as coke. Tony B. regrets "leaving a real pile of shit in [Tony's] lap." And as Silvio considers Johnny's loss of pragma-tism, "Some people are better at being Number Twos."

Tony's "Number Two," Chris, is indignant at Tony's insults (V, 9) and losing his cigarette operation to Paulie. Swigging vodka, Chris is ready to leave Tony: "Fuck this piece of shit. I'm done. . . . Fuck family. Fuck loyalty. . . . That's the guy, Adriana. My uncle Tony. The guy I'm going to Hell for." But when Adriana is encouraged to confess her FBI involvement, Chris explodes, "We're dead. You know that? How could you fuckin' do this to us? I fuckin' loved you." After punching and choking her almost to death, he stops, cries, and they embrace. He agrees to leave with her, to switch from Tony to park long-term with the FBI.

Chris changes his mind when he goes to a service station for cigarettes. Though Adriana intuits the danger in Chris's going, she worries (obviously too late) that his smoking could lead him back to vodka. When he com-pares his $50,000 SUV to a working man's decrepit sedan, we infer Chris's thought: "There but for the grease of God—or the grace of Tony So-prano—go I." As Georgie put up with his abuse, Chris opts for the perks and betrays Adriana.

Tony lures Adriana with word that Chris tried to kill himself (a not inapt metaphor for the Tony/FBI choice). On Silvio's car radio, Shawn Smith's "Leaving California" taunts her: "If you ever want to get away from California / Maybe in another life you'd like to stay." Cut into Sil-vio's drive, Adriana imagines driving herself away from that life, with the red suitcase she left behind. Silvio's drive is her only possible escape. Prov-ing himself the "Barracuda" of Heart's opening song, Silvio drives into the woods and shoots her as she tries to crawl away, now unable even to run. When the last scene returns to the autumn forest, Adriana's murder shadows Carmela's real estate project, which signifies *her* failed escape from Tony. The same Shawn Smith closing song, "Wrapped in My Memory," links back to Adriana's failed escape and expresses our regret at losing her: "Before you started to fade / You gave me something to believe."

The episode's title—and presiding metaphor—derives from the scene where Chris throws away Adriana's filled suitcase and leaves her car in the long-term parking lot at the airport—for, as the airport recording intones, his "increased security." Having sacrificed his lover for his macho fraternity, Chris watches *The Three Amigos* (John Landis, 1986) mirthlessly on TV. When Tony punches and kicks him, ostensibly to stop his self-pity but mainly out of his own frustration, we may reevaluate Chris's choice for long-term parking.

From that macho perspective, when Silvio assures Adriana—"He's a strong kid, Chrissie. He's tough. Very resilient"—he refers not to Chris's recovery but to his having betrayed Adriana. To Silvio she is now just a "fuckin' cunt." With the excremental, this macho callousness pervades the dialogue. Paradoxically, Carmine Jr. wears a cowboy shirt when he decides to stop playing cowboy and to end the war. That is, his action transcends his image, role, or expectation. But rather than appreciate the peacemaking, Paulie declares, "I knew he'd cave. He's a fuckin' pussy, that kid." When Tony fears having to "get down on my knees" to Johnny, his dread is sexual, not religious.

Like Chris but not Georgie, Carmela lapses back into Tony's support. She and Tony resume their long-term parking, i.e., their marriage, on her two conditions. The first is that Tony abandon his short-term parking, his affairs. "If we do reconcile, that stuff wouldn't happen again," he offers, as if that goes without saying (as likely will he). He swears "on our children that my midlife crisis problems will no longer intrude on you anymore." Even that may promise discretion rather than fidelity.

As in Carmela's scene with Wegler (V, 10), the reconciliation helps Tony avert the burned Valentina. He detaches himself with his usual generosity—"the medical bills and the prescriptions, that's covered. Ad nauseum"—and sensitivity: "You're gonna look nice with short hair. . . . You'll heal up. You'll meet someone else." Then he leaves to take a phone call. *Infinitum* with Tony is *nauseum*. Earlier Tony told Adriana—perhaps to forestall their intimacy—that he and Carmela were considering reconciliation. Tony, like Carmela, finds their marriage convenient.

Having realized her financial dependency, Carmela's second demand is to have her own business, as "something else in [her] life." Tony provides $600,000 for a scenic acreage on which her father will build her a house to sell. This is how Carmela, upon Meadow's suggestion (V, 9), will provide for herself. But Carmela's new independence still rests entirely on two men, her father and her husband. Anyway, the house bodes tacky, given her father's regard for their architect's "Normandy châteaus up on Tisch Drive" (V, 13).

The marital reunion is more business than romance. Carmela and Tony seal it with a kiss as perfunctory as a handshake, then resume eating. Conversely, at home Tony advises AJ to drink his champagne slowly: "You're supposed to savor it. It's important in life." Tony's practice still doesn't match his pretense. The family bliss is shadowed by the W.C. Fields film Tony watches on television. In the clip from *It's a Gift* (Norman McLeod, 1934), a bitter satire of small-town American family life, the blind Mr. Muckle (Charles Sellon) begins to stumble through a hardware store shattering everything in sight. This film also figured in III, 9, which focused on the family's empty gift-giving.

At the "fuckin' weird" dinner with Carmela and AJ, Tony toasts his reunited family: "To the people I love. Nothing else matters." But Tony compromises this sentiment when Johnny Sack calls for Tony's beloved cousin Tony B. "on a fucking spit": "You either deliver that prick to my door or I will rain a shitstorm down on you and your family like you have never fucking seen." When Tony B. finally phones, Tony warns him not to come back and promises to look after his twin sons. This generosity bodes a matching set of Christophers. Finally, Tony tells Tony B. why he really missed the Betamax heist. "Now we're even," Tony concludes, as he prepares to betray him. Aptly, Silvio is working a stain remover on his jacket when Tony sets up the call trace. When Tony B. makes his last call, Tony is watching *The Great Caruso* (Richard Thorpe, 1951) on TV—as he prepares to "sing" to Johnny.

At their East River meeting, the new "King of New York" promises Tony they won't need such an undignified setting again. Tony agrees to turn his cousin in but asks to handle Tony B.'s killing himself. That denied, he asks that it be done quickly. But Johnny is uncompromising: "I choose not to. . . . Phil's going to do it and he'll do it his way." Prepared to betray his beloved cousin, Tony recoils from the prospect of torture. "You know what, John?" Tony smiles: "I'll give you undignified. Go fuck yourself.

And Phil and whoever. He's my fuckin' cousin." Over the Family's shifting allegiances, Tony chooses to park long-term with family—for now.

Of course, even the long-term parking establishment denies responsibility for the vehicle or its contents. The parker remains responsible, sometimes with only a delusion of security. As Adriana, Georgie, Christopher, Carmela, Wegler, Artie, Johnny Sack, and Tony park, they are responsible for the moral implications of their choice. In returning to Tony and the marriage, Carmela once again shrinks from Dr. Krakower's moral alert in the series' pivotal episode (III, 7). When Chris parks with Tony instead of Adriana, he commits himself to the tragedy imaged in his overly poetic excuse for being late: "The highway was jammed with broken heroes on a last-chance power drive."

V, 13: All Due Respect

Written by David Chase, Robin Green, and Mitchell Burgess.
Directed by John Patterson.

Tony and Carmela worry about AJ's torpor. Because Tony refuses to turn in Tony B., Johnny cuts the Sopranos out of the big provolone heist. Phil Leotardo hunts for Tony B. and Christopher and viciously beats Chris's driver Benny Fazio. As his gang resent his protecting his cousin, Tony executes Tony B. and recovers their support. As Tony and Johnny reconcile, the FBI arrest Johnny's operation.

In the fifth season finale, despite very dramatic actions the examination of leadership turns mock heroic. The theme is explicit in the History Channel documentary about Rommel that Tony watches over a bowl of ice cream and chocolate sauce (i.e., with un-Rommelian self-indulgence). The German general had "a sixth sense of sizing up the situation" and a genius for startling, spontaneous, and even obscure planning. "His men idolized him and had boundless faith in him." At least the latter Tony does not enjoy. Confiding his colleagues' concern, Silvio tells Tony (in admirable deadpan), "Frankly, you got a problem with authority," plus the deadly sin of pride. The insight reverses Tony's claim that Tony B. has "a problem with rage" and that Chris "keeps it all bottled up. Then they wonder when they get chemical dependencies." Of course, Tony's rage is a convincing argument for "keeping it bottled up." As Tony looks to historic heroes for his own virtues, he projects his own flaws upon others.

To his credit, Silvio squelches Christopher's complaints about Tony's "favoritism," but conveys to Tony the concerns of the "unhappy people out there." After Tony kills Tony B., Silvio tacitly expresses his support with a warm pat on Tony's shoulder as he leaves. The men's appreciation for Tony's sacrifice is expressed in Patsy's "Skip," in Bobby's warm look, coffee, and pastry ("Anytime, boss"), and in his parting "Take it easy, pal." Their unspoken feeling is the positive side of the male bond. On the other hand, before he acted Tony's critics included his closest aides, nephew Chris and brother-in-law Bobby, as well as Vito.

In a parallel to his scene with Silvio, Tony visits Paulie to address his "beefs" but is diverted by finding his painting with Pie-O-My. Paulie's defense—"You never come here no more. I didn't figure it would be a problem"—makes him seem like a rejected mistress, especially as he is steaming his suit. He denies any disrespect: "That's not a lawn jockey. It's a general." He has two explanations for adding the military uniform. Because his decor is not modern, he needed something more traditional. And he wanted to bring out Tony's inner leadership quality.

After Tony trashes it, the painting prompts him to go shoot Tony B.. It works in a paradoxical way. On the one hand, Tony's image as a powerful general evokes the traditional hero's need to subordinate his love to his duty. On the other, the painting's reminder of Tony's beloved horse revives his feminine side, his sentimentality—which he must again suppress. By killing his beloved Tony B. Tony expunges his guilt—ostensibly for having failed his cousin at the heist, but really for having revealed his feminine side. In killing Tony B. Tony again suppresses his own sensitivity. In any case, finding his inspiration in a Dumpster turns Tony's resolve and sacrifice mock heroic.

Over both rural scenes, Tony's murder of Tony B. and the FBI's arrest of Johnny, we hear Van Morrison's "Glad Tidings": "And we'll send you glad tidings from New York . . . And you'll visualize not taking any chances / But meet them halfway with love, peace and persuasion. . . . And they'll lay you down low and easy." The song's rhythm catches the pursuers' energy, but the lyrics ring ironic. The demands from and on Johnny Sack from New York are hardly glad tidings, and Tony hardly meets anyone "halfway with love, peace, and persuasion" or allows a "low and easy" final laying.

Acting by the code, Tony visits Christopher to determine what Adriana told the FBI. Tony B., he adds, "should be buried. It should be you that does it," both as family and to bury his own resentments. The macho code continues to demean Adriana. Christopher has no sense of her devotion: "She was willing to rat me out because she couldn't do five fuckin' years. I thought she loved me." Tony repeats Silvio's reduction (V, 12): "She's a cunt." When the two men hug, weeping, they seem to be the true "fuckin' stagmire" that Carmine feared (V, 12), a mire of macho bluster. In this vein, too, Tony assumes "event management" is "gay, isn't it?" The men's ambivalence toward women is encapsulated in Phil Leotardo's obscene assault on Chris's mother and his aide's restraint.

Earlier, Tony drops by Raymond's birthday party to address the gang's concern that he is protecting his cousin. Tony admits that Tony B.'s going "into business for himself" was "inexcusable," but as "we're talkin' torture," his protection is Family (not family) favoritism: "I'm offering him the same protection I'd offer any of you in the same situation." Tony's principle has echoed through the series: "We are a family, and even in this fucked-up day and age that means something." With his frontier spirit, he also expects them "to circle the wagons and support" Christopher.

But the gang's honor is false. We have just seen Raymond convey secret tapes to the feds (as in V, 2). He lives conflicting camaraderies, as from his "Say hello to Ike and the guys" at the FBI we cut to the gangsters celebrating his birthday. Johnny's arrest is due to a different snitch, Jimmy Petrille, who has delivered 18 years of evidence and even advised Johnny at Tony's sit-down with Phil (V, 12). Only the Sopranos aren't "singing."

Tony's rejection of torture proves prophetic in the context of America's engagement in Iraq. Though the show was produced before the Abu Ghraib prison scandal, the threat seems to spring from the headlines. Tony's position becomes a corrective to the national embarrassment. Similarly, his reply to Silvio approaches President Bush's call for international collaboration against terrorism: "This is the course I've chosen. And those of you that are not with me on it—well, that makes me sad. But it will be dealt with in time." Wisely, Tony's "well, that makes me sad" supplants the president's "are against us." Again, the Sopranos suggest America's response to its siege anxieties. Unlike Johnny Sack's rigidity (V, 12), Tony proves a flexible leader.

When Tony and Johnny later commiserate on the challenges of being in charge, they may also reflect America as the last remaining superpower.

As Tony scolded Silvio, "All due respect, you got no fuckin' idea what it's like to be Number One. Every decision you make affects every facet of every other fuckin' thing. It's too much to deal with almost. And in the end you're completely alone with it all." Right after Johnny cites that pressure, he is arrested.

In his own way, Uncle Junior shares Tony's anxiety over isolation. When Tony seeks his advice, he can't pierce the old man's concern with the fruit basket he has ordered for his lawyer Malvoin. Did he give the home or office address? "The man had a stroke. You want it to go to the wrong place? It's fruit. It'll rot." More than concern for his lawyer, Uncle Junior is excited that the stroke will postpone his retrial. Uncle Junior's "I'm fuckin' nonplussed with all this news" anticipates Tony's "I'm very confused. . . . It's my mess. All my choices were wrong."

Dr. Melfi proves more helpful when she counsels Tony to move beyond his "high-sentimentality mode" and deal with Tony B. as he must. As usual, Tony's objection proves her right: "Sentimentality mode? We were children together!" Of course, Tony's feelings for Tony B. are riddled with his denial of sentiment. He feels guilty for the softness that saved him from the doomed heist. Melfi unwittingly recommends that he commit murder. "Own your feelings," she advises, and do what you have to do, without guilt. In killing Tony B. Tony removes the living reminder of his own soft side.

Tony lies when he tells Melfi that AJ is off the starting football team because he is stressing his academics, "determined to get into a good school." When Carmela warns, "If he thinks he is getting into East Stroudsburg State, he is sadly mistaken," AJ's challenge falls far below Meadow's candidacy at Georgetown and Berkeley. AJ seems to be following his father's path to an easy, suspect career. After he and his friend make $600 from a house party, his "event planning" sounds like a gangster euphemism, e.g., "waste management." His father's son, AJ is excited to watch two boys fighting over an evaded admission fee. He also shows Tony's flexible legalism: "We're getting ripped off. You think it's like downloading music?" But as Tony consoles Carmela, "Well, I guess. . . . I dunno, he's fired up about something at least." The two lie atop the bedcovers, not touching, in joined isolations as they rationalize their son's future. When Carmela remarks that "poverty is a great motivator," she might have admitted that so is luxury.

In a lighter version of the leadership theme, Christopher complains to Carmela that when Adriana "left" him, she "broke my heart. . . . She stiffed me on the club. Never showed up for work. The place is rudderless." Carmela is herself a parody of domestic leadership, with her inapt responses to Adriana's disappearance. "There's other fish in the sea," she consoles Chris, unaware that Adriana has joined those sleeping with the fishes. With Tony, Carmela speculates that Adriana must have been "seeing somebody"—but she suspects a lover, not FBI agent Sanseverino.

These small ironies and large ignorances confirm this episode's mock heroic. More to the point, for all their similarity Tony is no Rommel and his campaign is neither the expansion of the German empire nor the defense of the free world. When the stakes are unstamped cigarette sales and a purloin of provolone, Tony is no *grand fromage*. Consoling the skull-fractured Benny, he promises that the Plumbers Union Health Plan will cover all his medical costs and his new post won't require him to beat up more people. Having been Tony's driver and Carmela's night guard (V, 1), Benny is a very sympathetic victim. Amid the drama of Johnny's arrest, poor Sal Vitro ("I'm the gardener!") is wrestled down, handcuffed, and his broken arm rehurt—a reminder of the gangsters' continuing damage to their victims.

So what respect is Tony's due? He has an ethical dilemma here. From our conventional viewpoint, Tony could have been the "nice cousin" Tony B.'s whore declares, and funded his escape to Italy. But for the Sopranos the execution has two justifications. First, the general saves his—albeit treacherous—soldier from torture. Second, the leader puts his responsibility to his organization ahead of his responsibility to a family member. As Tony concludes, "I paid enough, John. I paid a lot."

And yet. . . . And yet, aren't we taught that killing people is wrong? And that extrajudicial executions are vigilante madness, not justice? Increasing our sympathy for Tony B., we get close-ups on his shot face, his eyes open accusingly. After his admirable attempt to live straight, his studies are reduced to a whore's bonus: "Thanks for that massage. My toe doesn't hurt hardly at all now." And as Tony reminds Johnny, "You started this cycle of bloodshed when you whacked the girl Carmen used to fuck." (In V, 8, Angelo was more elegant: "Little Carmine went to school with her.") The captains' peace brings their soldiers no amnesty. Whether or not one accepts capital punishment, we have ample reason to reject Tony's rather rough justice—however sensitive and principled he presents himself. Here, as in the series as a whole, our judgment is tested rather than directed.

For a season climax, the plot delivers even more irony than wallop. Under the mixed blessing of Melfi's and Silvio's counsel, Tony proves his leadership by killing his most likable, virtuous, and capable F/family member. But when the FBI intervenes, it becomes clear that he did not have to. Johnny Sack's arrest makes Tony B.'s murder unnecessary. The deus ex machina of the FBI makes Tony's sacrifice a folly. For a hero of Tony's "bad eminence" cannot make a right decision. He is hopeless at event planning.

Extending the previous episode's autumn setting for Adriana's death and Carmela's deal, this one is framed with the frigid. It opens on Billy Leotardo's corpse in the morgue and closes on an exterior shot of Tony's home in winter. Tony lumbers through the snowy woods and creeks like Carmela's black bear. He stumbles home exhausted, his coat torn, reminiscent of Chris's and Paulie's absurd adventure in "Pine Barrens" (III, 11).

But contrary to his appearance, Tony is triumphant. As he is not named in the indictment against the Brooklyn operation, he was not sufficiently incriminated by Adriana or the other snitches. Tony has not just survived Johnny Sack but won—if surviving by self-destructive choices can be considered winning.

If not, then that implicit triumph is itself false. So Carmela's last words ring bathetic: "What happened to you? Your shoes are soaking wet." Tony's triumph, to some extent ethical and for the moment legal, is shadowed by the metaphor of winter and his feet of muddy clay. For his strictly pragmatic survival delays yet again his moral recovery. His ostensible triumph is another lost opportunity to salvage his moral architecture (V, 11).

Perhaps the central metaphor of the episode is not Tony as a savage bear but Silvio's quip at the shrouded Christopher: "Claude Rains." In James Whale's classic film *The Invisible Man* (1933), Rains establishes his character's invisibility by being completely covered in clothing. His material visibility implies his invisibility. He can appear only by being concealed. As in that paradox, Tony's survival signifies his failure, Carmela abandons her self-respecting character for the shameful security of her marriage, and Christopher fails as a man by abandoning Adriana in favor of his fraternity's code. All due respect, when they do what their code considers right, they are dead wrong.

Season Six

VI,1: Members Only

Written by Terence Winter. Directed by Tim Van Patten.

The building commission rejects Carmela's "spec[ulation] house" because her father used substandard lumber. While AJ fidgets through college, Meadow interviews for a law internship. Chris is back in AA, with a sponsor who is expert at forging documents, and Artie is happily back with Charmaine. With Johnny Sack in jail, Phil has been running his business. One of his hoods, Gerry Torciano, beats up Hesh and his son-in-law Ely for apparently encroaching on their Brooklyn territory. New parents Janice and Bobby nag Tony to move Uncle Junior into an assisted-living home. Junior sinks into dementia, feeling hounded by phone calls and money demands from Pussy Malanga (who was whacked in I, 1). In his paranoia, Uncle Junior shoots Tony in the chest. Tony crawls to the phone but is unable to respond to the 911 operator's query.

Against the spirituality of the William Burroughs incantation, three motifs emphasize the characters' absorption with the physical world. The most familiar motif is their focus on the body. After confirming Gene's bondage, Silvio passes a poster of two naked blonds hugging. And Meadow returns with a sexy dance for Finn. As Tony exults over sushi, since he stopped his antidepressants, "The bonefish is back in season."

Amid this spiritual interest, this episode associates the body with disorder, as in Silvio's joke: "If your nose runs and your feet smell, you're built upside down." This line encapsulates the characters' inverse priorities. In the opening scene, FBI agent Harris's vomit seems to respond to and proves his partner's quotation of H. L. Mencken: "Nobody ever went broke underestimating the taste of the American public." Harris picked up a parasite on an anti-terrorism assignment to Pakistan. "Get the fuck out," Tony blurts, nonpolitically, but the parasite may suggest America's is growing weak—politically and economically—from its Middle East excursion. Uncle Junior shares Harris's non-Sartrean "nausea."

Vito embodies abstemiousness when he proudly displays his reduced girth for a commercial photo. He lost weight by two-mile walks and taking hot water in lieu of coffee and his hot dog *sans* bun. Ralphie's marginal goon—who claimed to have been solicited by Adriana but who tried to seduce Finn—now fancies he might succeed Tony. Meanwhile, Tony weighs in at 280 pounds, even after shucking his shoes and pants. Although already bloated, he starts in on a new tray of sushi.

With Carmela, Tony gloats over his expensive sushi: "Forty dollars for a piece of food they just flew in first class. I'd say we're more than lucky." In contrast, over a business dinner, Tony complains about his hard life: "What the fuck is it? I can't catch a fuckin break." With the expensive sushi and Tony's new boat, imaginatively named *Stugotz II*, the couple's complacency sets them up for his fall *chez* Junior. Their sushi obsession also shows the couple transcending their past culture (Italian-American cuisine). Thus Agent Harris, however nauseous from Pakistan, comes to Satriale's for some real Italian meat. The cultural past rises again when Tony is shot while cooking pasta for Junior. The food scenes also confirm the primacy of the characters' physical appetites.

The second metaphor, vision, suggests the characters' focus on the visible, material order. Johnny Sack gets contact lenses so he won't look weak at his trial. Although he depends on his beloved fat wife, Ginny, now that she "has the weight of the world on her," he seems to have soured, grimacing at her photo. Johnny also deploys her brother who sells the expensive Armani sunglasses Tony and Silvio simply take. Gene's rich aunt Edie, having been married to Victor Borge's agent, like the return of Frankie Valli's character, Rusty Millio, recalls the continuum between show business and the mob, between the respectable and criminal orders, and between the starry false "show" and the sordid reality.

The third motif, housing, grows out of Carmela's "spec house." She took Tony back in return for his financing of her construction career. But her new independence is based on her husband's money and her father's construction acumen. "Bureaucratic bullshit," her father dismisses the inspector's concerns. "In my day they took a blind eye." His "took" for "turned" implies bribery. Like Carmela, her righteous father has not just benefited from but practiced Tony's corruption. He is smug at her criticism: "No good deed goes unpunished."

In variations on the housing theme, the Baccalas attend a preschool meeting to secure their 15-month-old baby's school prospects. In a mobile version, new cars emblematize the characters' success. Carmela flaunts her new Porsche Cayenne at Ginny after the strapped Sacrimonis have to sell Johnny's beloved Maserati. Carmela is dashed when Angie Bonpensiero shows off her new Corvette. Because where Tony gives Carmela a car, Angie earns hers in her body shop. Angie is no longer the "fucking shell since Pussy disappeared" (in I, 13). Carmella's callousness here marks a new nadir in her self-unawareness. She is also disappointed when Tony visits their new sushi place by himself: "It just felt nice to have something special—for us." Restaurants are another form of emblematic housing. The housing motif may explain the episode's title, which suggests exclusion from whatever shelter the character craves.

Gene Pontecorvo's home is torn by his tensions with his druggie teen son and his wife's, Deanne's, desire for a particular Florida dream house. She rejects her Jersey contemporary, but Gene insists: "Cathedral ceilings. You'll fall in love." He offers to buy a vacation place in Florida to which she could move before his promotion enables him to follow.

Indeed, Gene is plagued by two houses. Just as he wants to escape Tony's, Chris pulls him back in—to kill debtor Teddy Spirodakis. When Gene wipes the blood splotch from his cheek, he smears it on his map (his future course)—to the taunting song "Dreamin'." Like another Charmaine, Deanne calls Tony "a piece of shit," only she urges Gene to kill him. "His Master's Voice," she declares when Gene's phone rings, but it's his other master of house. The FBI summons him to meet at a dead end. The FBI won't release Gene either, having just lost their informer, Raymond Curto.

As Rusty Millio remarks over Curto's open coffin, "Stand up guys like that—they're a dying breed." Curto was rather prone to "singing" to the Feds and died just as he was going to implicate Tony. (Of course, Tony doesn't know when he "catches a fuckin break.")

Torn between his antithetic bosses and his wife's anger at not being able to leave, Gene hangs himself in his basement. First, he reviews beach holiday snaps, when his son was young and pure, then fondles the souvenir seashells from a simpler time. Gene's last spasm segues into Tony's last scene with Junior, with the—what else?—swing music of Artie Shaw.

Trying to recover a similar innocence, Bobby Baccalieri retreats from Janice suckling their infant to his childish hobby, a model train set that fills the garage. The new parents' unreliability ties Tony to Junior's care. Although Uncle Junior is losing his sense—as he does his dentures, his patience, and a banana—Tony refuses to move him out of his home: "Fuck assisted living. . . . Remember what they did to Ma?"

Tony's care for Junior, Dr. Melfi reads as his continuing denial that his mother had encouraged Junior to kill him. Tony also denies having tried to smother Livia: "I grabbed a pillow, but just to keep my hands occupied." The scene, in reality, was rather more violent. Because he feels guilty for putting Livia into a home, he keeps Junior in danger at home. Then Junior shoots him, hides the gun under his bed, and cowers in a closet, ignoring his loving nephew's cries for help.

Just before shooting Tony, Uncle Junior watches on TV the scene in *Paths of Glory* (Stanley Kubrick, 1957) where the hero, Dax (Kirk Douglas), is berated by a senior (but not superior) officer for his sentimentality and idealism. That may or may not have motivated Junior. Tony's shooting undercuts his advice to AJ: "I don't care how close you are, in the end your friends are gonna let you down. Family, they're the ones you can depend on."

Junior shooting Tony is a shock but it has been prepared for. His undoubted love for Tony has always had a violent potential. In Tony's first childhood flashback (I, 7), when Tony is distracted from their game of catch, Junior nails him, then shrugs as if helpless. Junior's paranoid visions of Pussy Malanga recall Christopher's nightmares of his victim Emil (e.g., I, 1, 8), Big Pussy's confession to Chris (I, 8), and Big Pussy's exposure and return in Tony's dreams.

The closing song compares the despair of love with physical discomfort. A headache you can lose in a day, but "comes love, nothing can be done." That physical despair segues into the end credits, where Burroughs's last two Souls—"*Khaibit,* the Shadow, Memory, your whole past conditioning from this and other lives" (i.e., earlier episodes) and *Sekhu,* the last remains—complete the spiritual framework. The characters' material successes may signify advancement but they connote failure because they joined the wrong housing. Paradoxically, the next episode—in which Tony's delirium provides a higher consciousness—is titled with a secular invitation, "Join the Club." Where VI, 1 frames the Sopranos' materialistic order against a spiritual incantation, VI, 2 frees Tony from his physical life.

VI, 2:   Join the Club
Written by David Chase. Directed by David Nutter.

In the hospital, Tony lies in a possibly fatal coma, with organ and brain damage. While his family tries to connect, Tony sees himself as a salesman trying to recover his identity after someone switched briefcases and wallets with him.

As VI, 1 closed on a high-angle close-up of Tony flat on Junior's kitchen floor, this episode opens with a high-angle, full-body shot of Tony flat on a hotel bed. When Tony moves through a business convention, we don't know whether this or the previous episode's conclusion will prove (á la the notorious *Dallas* TV series' finale) the dream. The bright lights from an overhead helicopter tracking some "perp" (i.e., a perpetrator or gangster) turn into the lights at Tony's intensive care surgery. Even in his alternative life, Tony feels chased by the law.

In his dream, Tony lives the civilian—or what Henry Hill in *GoodFellas* called "the schnook"—life. "Tom" Soprano used to sell patio furniture—an alternative career Tony once postulated to Dr. Melfi—but is now a star in "precision optics." The episode's X ray is into Tony's new insecurity: "I'm 46. Who am I? Where am I going?" "Join the club," his date responds. But this club is a non-club, the fragile identity and insecurity that normal mortals suffer when they don't have a gang boss's power. Tom's questions shake Tony out of his coma, as he tears out his tubes and repeats those questions. At the point of death, Tony asks the questions he evaded with Dr. Melfi.

As Tom Soprano, Tony has a wife on the phone like Carmela, a younger daughter like Meadow, who has just made the volleyball team, and a son absent and queasy ("He puked") like AJ. Having taken the wrong briefcase in the bar, Tom assumes the identity of Kevin Finnerty, a solar heating systems salesman from Phoenix. From Tony's ashes, the phoenix Tom rises as Kevin. A salesman's pun connects Finnerty and the Lexus Infinity, which of course Tony but not Tom could afford. With "Finnerty," Tony unfolds an infinity of possible selves and confusions. "Kevin" may be a guilty echo of the murdered Pussy's college son, Kevin. Tom has to assume Finnerty's identity to book a hotel room and a flight home. Using Finnerty's credit card leaves Tom worried about committing fraud. Tom may fidget like Tony, but he is without Tony's lack of conscience. Gandolfini gives Tom a softer voice and bearing and a more educated accent.

But even as Finnerty, Tom suffers Tony's trials. At first, he declines the other salesmen's invitation to dinner, but he relents when he notices a woman, a dark beauty like Melfi and Gloria, while "The Happy Organ" (Papa John Gordy's one hit) plays in the background. Rather than eat alone, Tony joins them for his "blackened grouper sandwich." After a long kiss, the woman rebuffs him: "This isn't going to happen. . . . I saw the look on your face when you got off the phone with your wife. . . . That's sweet." As Tom, Tony narrows the gap between his emotions and his actions. Although he is eager to betray his wife, his feelings protect him when they dissuade the dream woman. Even Tom's Carmela blames him for his predicament: "You're off in your own world. You're too distracted at work. This is partly your fault."

Although Tom is what Tony might have become had he eschewed the criminal life, he is still charged with dishonesty, albeit Tony's. Even in his fantasy, Tony cannot escape guilt, as when, in his fantasy of Isabella (I, 12), he imagined Carmela's excoriation. Tony is too corrupt even to imagine himself innocent. Here, two shaven Buddhists accuse "Kevin" of defrauding their monastery with inadequate heating. One says they are suing him. The other snaps, "Lose your arrogance" and slaps Tony's face. Big Tony's fight with the small Buddhist is a parody of his bullying life. When Tom shouts after the small monk, "He hit me. Don't let him go!" he reveals Tony's fear of his loss of power. Even as the TV crews converge on Tony's home and hospital, the dream Soprano has no clout, not even with hotel clerks.

As Tony's delirium builds upon his key dreams in earlier episodes, it grows cosmic. "My whole life's in that case," Tom says of his lost satchel. The convention locale, Costa Mesa (an echo of Casa Nostra), is "dead," the barkeep opines. The town looks like New York but the TV news reports a spreading brushfire. The hotel TV summarizes Tony's anxieties: "Are sin, disease and death real?"

The other characters define themselves by their response to Tony's mortal risk. His doctor is callous, for example, with his premature concerns about "degrees of brain damage—in the event he does survive," then declares Tony lucky to be in his "Level One trauma center." While Tony's younger sister, Barbara, provides comfort, Janice breezes in with a take-command authority: "I came by to help. Anything. . . . You both should get some rest." But when she sees Tony's open wound, the other women have to comfort her.

With Tony at risk, the gang skirmish for advantage. Chris squelches Paulie's plan to bring Tony a stereo, then delivers one himself. When Silvio fills in for Tony, Vito indiscreetly pitches for Gene's "sports book in Roseville" and blames Bobby for Tony having to baby-sit Junior. In contrast, Hesh is grateful Tony doesn't know about Gene's suicide. Silvio knows Tony caused it but prefers to blame "inoperable cancer or some shit." Vito stays closeted with his theory: "Maybe he was a homo and there was nobody he could talk to about it. That happens, too." For all his diet, Vito stuffs himself at Carmela's buffet and farts while watching the emblematic *The Invisible Man* (James Whale, 1933) on TV. For Vito, Junior "Marvin Gayed" Tony. When Paulie and Vito compete to drive AJ home, the unspoken issue is either Vito's predatory homosexuality (that frightened Finn in Season V) or their jockeying for Family position. Chris projects his Hollywood ambition onto Gene: "Who wouldn't like to take the easy way out?"

As she faces Tony's death, Carmela retracts her prediction (I, 1) that her husband will go to Hell. When she calls her curse "a sin and I will be judged for it," she recalls her more appropriate fear (III, 6) that she will be judged for enabling her killer husband. Now Tony is "a good father" who cares about his friends. "Yes, it's been rough between us. Our hearts get hardened against each other and I don't know why." Her memories of their early courtship include the first time Charmaine broke up with Artie, when she thought he tried to drown her by abandoning her to a tidal wave. That reverses their present dynamic, for Charmaine stabilizes Artie against Tony's tidal force. Now Carmela assures Tony that the doctors are confident because he is strong as a bull. "When you used to pick me up and throw me over your shoulder, my God, you used to get me so hot down there." Here, Tony is a force of nature, beyond conscience, and Carmela's poignancy softens his moral repugnance.

Close-ups reveal the tension between Carmela's perfect manicure and her care-ravaged face. She defends AJ against Rosalie's warning that she's spoiling him, while boys his age are dying in Iraq. But when she notes that Angie only phoned—"I guess she's very busy over there with her body shop"—Carmela still resents Angie's earned Corvette, which trumps her gift Porsche.

Meadow, lovingly attentive to her father, aggressively engages with his doctors. As she is skeptical about men, when Finn comes to support her, she notes a more selfish motive: "Dental school sucks." After Meadow reads Tony a Jacques Prevert poem—

Our father, which art in heaven,
Stay there
And we shall stay on earth
Which is sometimes so pretty.

—Chase cuts to the Sopranos' beautiful, vacant pool. The verse catches the family's tension between the orders of nature and grace and the moral costs of their lavish, unstable pleasure.

AJ is ambivalent about his father. He deploys several alibis—a stomach flu, laggard friends, homework, a newspaper interview—to avoid visiting. When he does, he enthuses over high-powered Shelbys and Mustangs, after having just lectured Meadow on the environmental responsibility of the hybrid Prius. Here, AJ is torn between his father's macho style and the age's new values. So, too, his most affectionate remark to his father: "You're my dad and I'm gonna put a bullet in [Uncle Junior's] fuckin mummy head."

With his long dark hair and pallid face, AJ seems Gothic; Paulie calls him Von Helsing, the pursuer of Count Dracula. But after Carmela thanks him for visiting, AJ admits he has flunked out of college. This additional burden on Carmela—"My God. With your father in a coma"—confirms Rosalie's diagnosis of AJ's—but also Carmela's—selfishness. For Carmela is more concerned about this new burden on her than about its effect on her son.

When Junior is tested for insanity, he raises his original suspicions about Tony: "If somebody shot my nephew it was him himself. He's a depression case." His despair parallels the dream Tom's discovery of the fact that he has Alzheimer's. "It's a death sentence." Tom tells the doctor he's not Finnerty but won't give his real name because soon he won't re-member it himself: "I'm lost."

When Christopher receives two outsider condolences, the parallel be-tween the FBI and the Muslim gangsters points to the Family's ambiguous position on terrorism. As Tony observed (long before the 2006 Dubai dock management controversy), the loose security on the docks rewards the gangsters but imperils the nation. Now Chris teases the FBI agents, citing Harris's "Diarrheastan" and the theft of a truckload of towels. "Towel heads," of course, derogates Sikhs, who to Chris are interchangeable with Muslims. But when the FBI solicits Christopher's help against terrorism—"If you ever heard of anything going down—Middle-Easterners, Paki-stanis—you'd be helping a lot if you picked up the phone"—he refuses, yet admits, "I take that terrorism shit seriously. And Tony? Don't even get him started."

In fact, Tony's first dream has Tom at a convention of military suppli-ers, where he is barred from a Colonel Collona's talk because he does not have his own ID. The receptionist's "It's a whole new world" refers to America's new security concerns. Tom "can't even get on a plane without a picture ID." Christopher's friendly exchange with the Arab druggies confirms the Sopranos' compromise. Although Ahmed and Muhammad enjoy their booze and the Bada Bing strippers, they still could be funda-mentalist terrorists. Or their sinister mien may derive from our ethnic profiling.

The episode closes on the dream Tom returning to his hotel room, kick-ing off his shoes, luxuriating in the free wiggle of his toes, and then picking up the phone to make a call—home? He puts the receiver back instead. Even as Tom, Tony is uncertain whether to return to his waking life or to move on to his celestial/infernal home. As the end-credit song confirms, "I can't hear you through the fog."

Tony's hospitalization echoes his earlier one after Junior's contract (I, 12). At both, Meadow is tensely solicitous and AJ scared silent. The Red Cross poster behind AJ and Meadow in the first waiting room looms im-plicitly over this one, too: SAFE FAMILIES. EVERYBODY NEEDS ONE. Here, Christopher hugs a weeping Carmela and holds Meadow's hand while she sleeps. Where the first attack released Silvio, Paulie, and Christopher's love for Tony, the second betrays selfish ambition. They have not seen the new light dawning on Tony.

VI, 3:   Mayham

Written by Matthew Weiner. Directed by Jack Bender.

Tony is "really fighting" for his life while he continues his Kevin Finnerty dream. On Vito's tip, Paulie robs a Colombian hideout, killing two and suffering a kneed groin, for a dishwasher full of laundered cash. Paulie reduces the rumored million to $750,000. He quarrels with Vito over the split and with Bobby over the late Gene's Roseville collection. As Vito and Silvio manoeuvre to succeed Tony, their pretensions put the "ham" in the "mayhem" of the headless crew. When AJ's insolence appears on the TV news, Carmela explodes at him. Tony's pulse stops but an electric shock snaps him back into consciousness.

In Tony's dance with death, the dream Tom pursues his look-alike Finnerty. At the Crystal Monastery, the senior monk advises, "To a certain extent all Caucasians look alike." The more cynical adds, "There's no fraud without a fairy tale." As Tom is "kind of worried about what I might have done," he asks the bartender, "Is it possible that I am Kevin Finnerty?" Again, even as an innocent schnook, Tony cannot imagine himself guiltless. Of course, the human condition is to bear some ineluctable sense of guilt, whether or not we believe there was ever an Eden.

Tracking Finnerty to a family reunion at a posh country club—The Inn at the Oaks—Tom is greeted as a Finnerty by Steve Buscemi. In the credits, Buscemi is "A Man" but he trails his association with Tony's cousin Tony Blundetto (whom Tony killed in V, 13). In this episode, Phil Leotardo rages at "that mother-fuckin animal Blundetto" for killing Phil's younger brother. As Vin Makasian re-appears in a dream (V, 11) as Finn's father, with Annette Benning (playing Annette Benning) playing Finn's mother, here Buscemi projects a character only semidetached from his earlier role. Semidetaching Buscemi from Blundetto alleviates Tony's guilt for his death. So, too, the shadowy woman departs the doorway before she registers as Livia.

In any case, the dream lures Tony from his coma into the afterlife. When Buscemi tries to take Finnerty's briefcase—"You can't bring business in there"—Tom clings: "My whole life was in that case." The man urges him into the bright, impressive mansion: "Your family's inside. . . . They're here to welcome you. . . . You're going home. . . . You need to let go. . . . There's nothing to be scared of. You can let it go." Tony's cousin's spectre is welcoming him into death.

Tom segues back into Tony when he is distracted by a young girl's voice from the trees: "Daddy. . . . Don't go, Daddy. We love you, Daddy. . . . Don't leave us." Her last "Daddy" becomes Meadow's "Don't leave us, Daddy. We love you," which brings Tony back to consciousness. Carmela's "He's still not out of the woods yet" evokes the oaks of his dream scene. The reviving trees recall the seminal ducks from I, 1, which signify the lost nature in which Tony found refuge from his family anxieties. By leaving the Finnertys, Tony prefers his real family over infinity.

Tony's spiritual dream draws on his waking life. Finnerty's monks reflect Tony's Asian doctors. One is even named Dr. Ba, after the Egyptian embodiment of the heart. The monks' vision of an afterlife—"One day we will all die and then we will be the same as that tree. There will be no you, no me"—parallels both Tony's division into Tom and Finnerty and his pull to The Inn at the Oaks. It is echoed in the Ojibwe saying on Tony's hospital bulletin board: "Sometimes I go about in pity for myself, and all the while, a great wind carries me across the sky."

In a bathetic replay of the theme, Chris's writer friend JT claims "prior reincarnation" as a drug addict. As Tony does in his dream, JT says writers "mythologize our inner narrative" because "we are all hung up on our hang-ups." Christopher coerces JT to pay off a new gambling debt by developing a screenplay for him, "about a wise guy with a big mouth and bigger dreams."

In Chris's "*Saw* meets *Godfather II*," a young wise guy is killed by his envious colleagues and cut into pieces. He reconstructs himself—"by science or the supernatural"—and with a cleaver on his stump he bloodily attacks his enemies, including "the cunt he was engaged to" who "was getting porked by his boss the night the hero was killed." In Chris's inner narrative, art follows his life. Little Carmine Lupertazzi, an experienced producer of nine features, including four in the estimable *South Beach Strumpet* series, invites the gang to invest in *Pork Store Killer* but Chris prefers the crisper title, *Cleaver*. The crew picks nits with either its factual basis or its implausibility. With unwitting reference to Tony, Carmine explains that in slasher films, "the maniac is almost always a supernatural force."

Otherwise, Chris and AJ show differing maturity. Chris confronts AJ's plan to kill Uncle Junior: "You can't go there. . . . Trust me, your dad does not want you to get involved." He would save AJ from Michael Corleone's vengeance, career, and doom. AJ bristles at Christopher's condescending head rub ("You little hothead, here") and is determined to avenge his father, even as he forgets to bring Carmela the sweater or coffee she requested. But as soon as Tony recovers, Chris pressures him to invest in his film: "All due respect, I think you owe me this, cause I came to you about Adriana."

The other crew members pursue their vanities. Faithful advisor Silvio preens as Acting Captain, urged by wife Gabrielle: "You have such strength in crisis." As he studies his mirror, she counsels, "It's the times that make the man, honey, not the other way around." Silvio reports that because he preferred the backstage advisory role, he declined Jackie Aprile's offer to precede Tony as Captain. His reference to "stepping up to the big C" shades the captaincy with Jackie's fatal cancer. Here, power is a fatal disease.

But now, Silvio finds it flattering as, with the presumed wisdom of Solomon, he gives Bobby temporary control of Eugene's territory, but with a 20% kick-up to Vito, thus gratifying neither. From his bathetic throne in the men's room, Silvio decides that Carmela should receive Tony's due from the Colombian take, $100,000 from each of Paulie and Vito. The pressures exacerbate Silvio's asthma until he, too, is hospitalized. Still hoping for promotion, he blames the spring flowers.

Although Vito flatters Silvio by calling him "Skip," he advertises his post-weight-loss health and he bonds with Tony's enemy, Phil Leotardo, to whose cousin Vito is married. Though he drowns his disappointment in a bag of small carrots, he still appears too large for Paulie's greeting, "Diary of a Thin Man," and for the John Travolta image Phil recalls from his cousin's wedding. Vito again flirts with Finn. Hailing him as Phineas Fogg he (1) flashes an unexpected erudition and (2) offers an *Around the World* experience, presumably in less than 80 days.

Like Vito and Silvio, Paulie mouths dedication to Tony and Carmela but privately chafes at paying her. As he prepares her $100,000, he bitterly clips grocery coupons. After Vito and Paulie pay her, she spots their gloom at Tony's recovery. As Christopher warned AJ, Silvio deflects Gabrielle's ambition with "Don't go there" and Phil stills Vito's reluctance to pay

Carmela with "Don't even go there." Their love for Tony stills their desire that he die.

Earlier, Paulie seemed to drive the comatose Tony to death with his chatter about his afflicted groin and general decay. His once muscular arms are now flabby, "Fuckin wrinkles like an old lady's cunt." As this physical imagery jars against Tony's exploration of his soul, the dream Tom pounds his hotel walls: "Will you please shut up in there!" Self-absorbed Paulie doesn't notice the alarms on Tony's machines

Although prompt to revive him, the medical staff behaves coldly professional, as in Dr. Plepler's advice to Carmela: "You're really going to have to recalibrate your expectations at this point." A nurse complains that Meadow dislodged his tubes. Another "ball buster" (Meadow speaks Soprano) allows Tony only one visitor at a time.

Having first declined Dr. Melfi's help—"I have plenty of people around to talk to"—Carmela turns to her after attacking AJ ("You're a cross to bear. That's all you are. To your father, to me, to everyone"). Meadow understands: "It had to happen. She's fried." In their session, Melfi's elegant heels contrast to Carmela's pigeon-toed loafers. At first, Carmela impersonalizes her concern: "Guns in the house—it's a societal concern." She gradually reveals self-doubt. Her children having "to face all those years of facading" made them all—Melfi supplies the word—"complicit" in Tony's crimes. Carmela can't lie to them anymore and she fears that if Tony recovers, she may not be able to tell him she loves him. On their second date, Tony brought her and her mother each a dozen roses and gave her father a $200 power drill. Now she wonders if she fell in love with Tony despite his suspicious, easy wealth or because of it. As Tony's plight has exposed the family's delusions, Melfi suggests "Clarity can't be a bad thing."

Tony's only waking words are his whispers to Carmela: "I'm dead, right?" Instead, he is reborn. Having experienced the alternative identity of the schnook Tom and the suspect Finnerty, Tony has a new awareness of life. While Carmela moistens his lips, over a rock version of "Over the Rainbow," Tony returns to his altered reality, his post-Oz Kansas. Perhaps Christopher foreshadows Tony's new awareness in his phrase for the advantage of his new "run at the movie business." He will "own the negative." However, even after the Sopranos have been jolted out of denial, Carmela puts down her $200,000 kickback, brushes her hands á la Pilate, and tells Tony, "I don't know how you do it." By now she does.

VI, 4: The Fleshy Part of the Thigh

Written by Diane Frolov and Andrew Schneider.
Directed by Alan Taylor.

As doctors seal Tony's open wound, evangelists Aaron Arkaway and Bob Brewster try to convert him. Jason Barone inherits his father's garbage company but, ignorant of the gang's involvement, agrees to sell it to Chuck Cinelli, who works for Johnny Sack. Tony won't give up his hold, vomits at Johnny's first offer, but accepts a compromise. When Paulie learns that his Aunt Dottie, a nun, was actually his mother he boycotts her funeral and disowns his adoptive mother, his Aunt Nucci. In his ward, Tony befriends a philosophic John Schwinn and rap star Da Lux, whose seven bullet wounds have increased his celebrity and sales. Da Lux's colleague Marvin hires Bobby to shoot him similarly, in order to help his career.

As the title suggests, the episode centers around the characters' vulnerability, where they wound. As rapper Marvin commissions a shot in the fleshy part of his thigh, Tony in his new values assumes a new vulnerability. But even safe spots may prove vulnerable. Marvin ends up shot in the ass, either because Bobby is not the "marksman" he claims to be or because Marvin produced only seven of Bobby's eight thousand dollar fee. Da Lux (a.k.a. Reginald G) proves that being hard pays better than being soft. When his post-shooting "street cred" makes up for his having held a job, the music scene's ethic proves as perverse as the gang's.

Tony retains some justifiable hardness. He marshals his carnal spirit against the evangelists, Janice's friend Aaron Arkaway and his partner Bob Brewster. With a WOMB IS GOD's placard, they defend a hospital pharmacist fired for refusing to fill a birth control prescription. The evangelists recommend prayer over morphine, but Tony worries about his access to Viagra: "What if someone decides it's wrong, God don't like it?" Carmela is delighted at this return to form: "What are you, a wise ass?" So, too, Tony repels the insurance company's Utilization Review Specialist's attempt to hasten him home: "Get out of my room, you sick cunt." After the Specialist refers to a paramedic's "wallet biopsy," Tony insists the paramedic, Rusty Diaz, give him the $2,000 that he may (or may not) have removed from Tony's wallet. Apparently innocent, the Spanish-American opts to pay protection if not a refund. With Tony back from the abyss, Carmela resumes her material concerns, suspecting Vito lightened his payment.

When Tony finally declines Diaz's $2,000 he shows he has softened. Vomiting at Johnny's first offer suggests he may be sickened by his past life. He accepts Johnny's second offer with a parody of spiritual generosity: "Truth be told, there's enough garbage for everybody." As he tells a nurse, "I've been feeling, I dunno, not myself. . . . My thoughts keep running away from me." Like an emblem of his obsolete self, the best Carmela can find for his interest in history is a picture book of dinosaurs.

Tony comes to believe we are all part of something bigger, which he learned from Finnerty's Buddhists and the Ojibwe quotation on his wall. As they watch a satellite fight on Da Lux's flat-screen TV, the patient John Schwinn contends that a profound unity underlies even conflict. People are like tornadoes, with only the appearance of separation. Even the battling boxers only appear to be "separate entities," because everything is connected, part of the same quantum field. Schwinn seems under the undue influence of the popular 2004 film *What the #$*! Do We (K)now!?* For all his philosophy, however, Schwinn is hospitalized for a sinus infection but loses his larynx to cancer. Still, he strikes a chord with Tony, in light of his new experience, and with Da Lux: "Everything is everything. I'm down with that." Significantly, the men embrace this spiritualism while enjoying a fight. In a parody of Tony's new depths, operating surgeon Plepler quips, "Omigod. . . . I just found Jimmy Hoffa."

The opening shot provides another example of Schwinn's unseen unity. Paulie emerges from behind an Oriental sea monster in front of a scuba shop. Later, Paulie will first bully and then cripple Jason Barone when Jason returns from rowing. The water motif connects the apparently antithetical: the naïve Jason who cruises calm surfaces and Paulie, a monster from the roiling deep.

In a more conventional uniting, Jason and Meadow show an immediate attraction. When Tony beams that she may become a doctor, Paulie proudly adds, "Or a lawyer." As he shares Tony's paternal pride in Meadow, Paulie ignores how dangerous an upright lawyer Meadow could be. In his pride, he must assume she would be his idea of a lawyer, like the protection boss he expected his priest to be (II, 9).

Here, even the boss's money has a soft fleshy side. For all his wealth, Tony depends on small contributions. On the Barone sale, Tony haggles to preserve his health insurance, his legitimizing W-2 (i.e., his annual income total for taxing), and his waste consultancy fee. He finally settles for 10 years of those benefits plus 12% of the sale price but gives up his weekly $2,000 skim.

Amid the new spirituality, Chase satirizes religious fundamentalism. The evangelists hope Tony will emulate the Watergate criminal Charles Colson, "a ruthless powerful man who thought he was above the law." For Pastor Bob, salvation includes "being saved from yourself while you're still alive." But Tony avoids evangelical smugness, as Schwinn rejects the false "duality between good and evil." Schwinn is so comfortable with his sinner friend that he jokes about having Tony put him out of his misery. His "whack" is a playful version of Bobby's contract on/with Marvin.

Pastor Bob assures Tony that evolution is Satan's plan to deny God. The world is six thousand years old and dinosaurs coexisted with man. "What?" Tony asks. "Like *The Flintstones?*" Chris provides a more pragmatic exegesis: "No way. T Rex in the Garden of Eden? Adam and Eve would be runnin' all the time, scared shitless. But the Bible says it was paradise." Where Tony finds the dinosaur's history makes man seem insignificant, Chris adds, "I don't feel that." His spiritual ignorance parallels the evangelicals' righteousness. When Hesh's daughter Bess defends the evangelicals as "great friends of the Jews, because Israel is the Holy Land," the worldlier Hesh adds somberly: "You wait."

Tony shows his new softness when he sees a little girl hospitalized with burns and when he deals with the episode's most innocent figure, the clean-cut ski instructor Jason Barone. Jason wonders why Tony, a "friend of the family," is the company's second-highest-paid employee but has no function. Tony cites their "different corporate culture." But Jason can't wriggle out of his agreement to sell the company to Chucky Cinelli without losing his mother's financial security. Initially, Tony, in his guise of a force of nature, dismisses Jason's plea for fairness: "Talk to the Katrina victims about 'fair.' "But Helen Barone brings Tony a home-made stuffed zucchini and pleads for her son: "If anyone has to pay for this let it be me." Mellowing, Tony promises her, "Nothing will happen to him. . . . You got my word." In this episode, Johnny Sack, Tony, and Paulie all selfishly complain about others' selfishness, but only Tony softens.

After Helen's plea for her son, Paulie leaves the room weeping at a devoted motherhood he never knew. Unlike Tony, here Paulie recovers from this softness to smash Jason's kneecap with a pipe and demand a monthly $4,000 skim secret from Tony.

In contrast to Tony's harmony, Paulie feels a new alienation because he was pole-axed by his Aunt Dottie's confession that she is his mother: "I was a bad girl." As a novitiate, she conceived him on a one-night stand with a soldier. Paulie is shaken: "I'm not who I am. It's like my whole life is . . . a big fuckin joke on me." Because his mother rejected him, he calls her "a fuckin whore" and hopes "she rots in hell." He even turns on his loving adoptive mother, Nucci: "I gave you a son's love. All under false pretences." Now he cuts her off altogether, stops paying for her $4,000 a month nursing home, and smashes the $2,000 flat-screen TV he gave her: "I was your meal ticket. . . . Your real children can start now. . . . You're on your own now. I never want to see you again." The love and warmth expressed in earlier episodes turns to anger.

Alienated, Paulie also rejects Schwinn's position: "You think you got family, but in the end—they fuck you too. . . . Each and every one of us, we're alone in the ring fighting for our lives." In fact, Paulie commits the familial betrayal with which he charges his real and adoptive mothers. In condemning them and in ignoring Tony to assault Jason, Paulie fulfils his own cynical prophecy. When he first pressures Jason on Tony's behalf, his impropriety registers in the antithetical religious song on the soundtrack, "The Three Bells," by the Browns. The discrepancy between the action and the music shows Paulie putting himself out of sync with the universe.

Essentially the episode contrasts two worldviews, as expressed by Tony and Paulie's dispositions. When Tony leaves the hospital, he takes his antagonistic sister's hand and exults: "Janice, I'm supposed to be dead. Now I'm alive. I'm the luckiest guy in the world. From now on every day is a gift." He abandons his impatience ("Everyone keeps telling me how lucky I am"). He even beams at Carmela: "Hey, Blondie. It's all you, you know, the reason I'm back here." From his new sense of harmony, Tony advises Paulie well: "You got to get beyond this petty bullshit, Paulie. You're part of something bigger."

The last montage contrasts Tony's new harmony with Paulie's alienation. In his garden, Tony sits by the pool that the ducks graced, then left (I, 1). His beneficent sky and blowing trees segue into Jason's boating scene, where Paulie cripples the "fuckin Mama's boy." Paulie turns his sentimental response to Helen Barone into violent jealousy of her son. Like the earlier cut from the picture of flying raptors to the birds circling over the Barone dump, the segue from Tony to Jason through the trees and heaven establishes a unity between the scenes and the characters, between the gangster and his prey, and between the reformed Tony and the self-damning Paulie. However, as Paulie hardens in his insularity, he storms off oblivious of the heavens, the wind-blown trees, and the church bells—that echo the earlier Browns's song—around him. Chase's editing establishes the unity that Paulie denies but Tony tries on for size.

If Tony's conversion seems implausible, there are at least two considerations in its support. One is the precedent set by Michael Corleone, in *The Godfather Part III*, who sought through religious association and charity to cleanse his family name—though he despairs for his soul. The other is antithesis. Tony's reform would be hardly more implausible than Paulie having a nun for a mother.

VI, 5:   Mr. and Mrs. John Sacrimoni Request

Written by Terence Winter. Directed by Steve Buscemi.

Johnny Sack requires a prison pass to attend his daughter Allegra's wedding. Tony urges Meadow to marry, but she seems to be cooling toward Finn. Tony returns to work. He initially refuses Johnny Sack's request to whack the troublesome Rusty Millio for him ("to point away from the family"). When Tony tells Melfi that his gang seems to sense his weakness, she urges him to act confident. So he picks a fight with his muscular young driver/bodyguard, Perry Annunziata, beats him up, and then retires to the toilet where he vomits from the strain. After he is spotted in a gay bar, Vito goes to the Maple Shade motel with a gun, calls Silvio at 3 A.M. to check in, and then disappears.

As the title suggests, the episode celebrates community and romance at two opposite parties, the Sacrimoni wedding and the gay club. Both celebrations conceal dark undercurrents.

The wedding involves various tensions, from family arguments over the seating arrangements to Johnny's own "I do" to the magistrate's stiff terms. He will be released for only six hours, accompanied by U.S. Marshals and with full metal-detection security at the church, all at his expense. With a capo's authority, he insists the groom call him Dad. But Johnny is humiliated when the police drag him away from the wedding early, in handcuffs, and block the newlyweds' car. The bride weeps and her mother faints. The strictures remind us of the illicit source of the $425,000 wedding reception at Leonardo's Dolce Vita hall.

In contrast, a private sensitivity underlies Vito's harsh exposure at the gay club. At the wedding, Vito is caught between opposite attractions when he admires both the "stunning" Meadow and "the young dentist all handsome in his Calvin Kleins. . . . Some beautiful grandkids these two will make." While his courtliness hides his homosexuality, his macho Joe DiMaggio reference recalls his attempt to force Finn into a baseball date.

Vito dances stiffly with his wife then brusquely orders her and their two children to leave the wedding early. When he later takes out his gun, he assures his wife, "Go back to sleep. I'm gonna take a shower." We expect he will try to come clean by killing himself. Had he stayed with his wife watching *Imitation of Life* (Douglas Sirk, 1958) on TV, the closet gay might have related to the family shattered when a black girl tries to pass as white in a prejudiced society.

But fired by the wedding romance, Vito, under the guise of making a collection, goes off to the gay club, where he dances in leather and chains until he's spotted by Sal, who is collecting money. Despite Vito's pleading "It's a joke," Sal vows to blow his secret. The Browns's religious ballad, "The Three Bells," which played against Paulie's coercion of Jason (VI, 4) here catches Vito's implicit fear for his unaccepted sexuality.

Other characters echo Vito's self-denial. As the Sacrimonis are unaware of their addictions, the bride seems too obese for the crooner's "Daddy's Little Girl" and her anorexic sister Catherine bristles at the family's obsession with food. Similarly, AJ's date smokes at the wedding but spurns the seafood buffet because of its toxins. Uncle Junior wavers in acknowledging his guilt: "I didn't shoot anybody. . . . The gun was on the fritz. . . . The fuckin gun malfunctioned."

Vito's vulnerability underscores Tony's, who collapses at the church entrance when the security requires he remove his shoes. Tony enjoys dancing with Carmela but is concerned about matching that wedding's scale when Meadow weds. His initial refusal there to kill Rusty Millio confirms his new softness. After Johnny Sack's humiliation, Tony defends him against Phil Leotardo's "my estimation . . . just fuckin plummeted." If the feds could make Johnny cry, Phil worries, "What else can they make him do?" Of course against outsiders, Leotardo defends Johnny: "An emotional man. He loves his daughter." Tony is sensitive to the weakened Captain: "I've seen tougher guys than John cry at weddings. Comes to daughters, all bets are off."

Tony is much softer with his women, too, as he snuggles with Carmela, confides to Meadow his desire for grandchildren, and returns to Melfi with a warm opener: "So let me ask you right off, is there any chance of a mercy fuck?" When Melfi asks about his feelings toward Junior, he, like Carmela, generalizes: "I got caught up in domestic violence." He prefers to discuss his disappointment in AJ. Melfi thinks Tony's shooting may have helped the boy. There are, Tony admits, worse ways to make money than by stocking Blockbuster shelves ("First stop on the Shitburg Express").

Back on the job, the softened Tony seems defensive with Perry: "I got to get back to the gym. . . . There was a time I could bench over three hundred." He restrains Perry's road rage. With the boys, Tony is embarrassed to scrape the onions off his bialy. He's irked that in the hospital he lost "goddam muscle mass not fat." Sensing the softness, Christopher presumes to match his chest scar against his boss's. He even questions his boss's judgment: "Farming [out Rusty's contract] is a pussy-ass manoeuvre." But for all his bravado Christopher is confused. He typically misquotes *The Godfather Part I* custom that no godfather can refuse a request at his daughter's wedding.

On his own, Chris cultivates his two Arabs. Muhammed and Ahmed pay him for 120 credit card numbers and security codes and bring fresh dates for Tony. The scene plays over Sexual Harassment's song "I Need a Freak." He also entertains their request for some semi-automatic guns: "Protection. It's a family problem. My former brother-in-law, actually." Christopher lacks the political awareness Tony let slip at the church door: "You'd think Ben Laden was getting married in there." But then Chris also thinks "allegra" is "a cold medicine," not Italian for happiness.

When Tony tells Melfi his friends sense his vulnerability—"People sense you're weak, they see an opportunity"—her advice is regressive. He should pretend confidence as if he weren't vulnerable: "People see only what you allow them to see." This echoes Gene Pontecorvo's failed strategy: "Tony and Silvio, all they understand is appearances" (VI, 1). Instead of advancing Tony's new sensitivity, Melfi recommends his old macho callousness. Her nonjudgmental counseling is as bad as Carmela's enabling of Tony. Even a sensitive sage can lapse into strategic pragmatism.

To demonstrate his old power, Tony picks the youngest and strongest gang member—and satisfies his initial jealousy of the muscular Perry. Despite his bravado outburst, Tony can't stomach his old violence. The high-angle shot on the seedy toilet deflates both the flash of the baroque reception hall and the furtive freedom of the gay club. Johnny's humiliation and Vito's fatal exposure parallel Tony's conflicted return to violence.

VI, 6:   Live Free or Die
Written by David Chase, Terence Winter, Mitchell Burgess, and Robin Green. Directed by Tim Van Patten.

Tony's new sensitivity is again tested when report of Vito's homosexuality provokes the crew's call for his killing. Vito flees with a coffee tin of cash and family photos. He finds refuge from the storm in a small New Hampshire town, Dartford. Carmela quarrels with her father over her spec house. Meadow quarrels with Finn about her family.

Continuing his sense of comfort, Tony enjoys his *Yachting* magazine by his pool, until deflected by the rattling tin lid on the garbage shed. In his office later, he's distracted from his *Robb Report* by Silvio's concern that Vito's safe return would encourage the crew to withhold more money from Tony. As Tony tells Melfi, "Regular life's got a way of picking away at" his sense of blessing. In particular, he has trouble keeping the lid on the gang, who would discard their homosexual friend like garbage.

Such betrayal is the episode's central theme. In her law internship, Meadow discovers that white-collar criminals are not persecuted like her family. Yet her office colleagues reduce the diligent intern to "Tony Soprano's kid." Meadow thinks Finn is "slamming my family" when he sneers at "John Macaroni," whose "pure harassment" by the Marshals at the wedding (VI, 5) still rankles her. Finn is pleased his own "Dad is so deracinated" (i.e., de-Italianized, a mayonnaise or white-bread wop), but Meadow has absorbed Tony's defence. Finn doubts Chris's assurance that if they find Vito, "It'll be okay. We'll get him to pay for some therapy." When Finn dismisses her "high horse about justice when they're going to mete [Vito's] out themselves," Meadow leaves: "This is untenable." For all its pacifying reputation, the lovers quarrel while smoking grass in bed. Like friends, grass cannot be depended upon.

Nor can family. Carmela feels betrayed by her father, who during Tony's hospitalization apparently stole her building materials yet waxes indignant: "You left it there to rot." When they blame each other for the failed construction standards he dismisses her: "Let her go. I've had a lifetime of her bullshit." Tony also abandons Carmela by failing to pressure the building inspector for her.

In contrast, Angie's independent career is booming. Her auto-body shop pulls her away from a lunch about the charity silent auction. With aggressive savvy, Angie suggests a live auction: "I say we get 'em liquored up, let 'em tear each other's throats out." Her donation of a $2,000 body job for the sale handsomely augments their $7,500 total. When Carmela finds Angie conferring with two hoods and putting money on the street, she and Rosalie feel betrayed: "She's one of us. Now she's like one of them." Where her Pussy flipped to the Feds, Angie has turned into a Family Husband. But in contrast to Carmela's delusion, Angie is self-sufficient.

In this episode, the major betrayal is either Vito's "playing with the pink team" or his family and friends' abandonment when he is discovered. After his suicide plan (VI, 4), here Vito appears in his beautiful, young black *goomah*'s beach apartment. He blames their yearlong abstinence on his blood sugar drop from his weight loss. He has clearly struggled to maintain his hetero front. When Silvio drops by to pump Vito's wife, she defends him as "a good father and a loving husband"—fully equipped with a *goomah*. But Silvio concludes: "My business, I'm around a lot of women. That one? Ain't getting laid." Silvio's tickets for a Blood, Sweat and Tears suggest his traditional values in rock as in sex.

The hoods' attack on Vito is selfish as well as hypocritical. After Carlo inherits Vito's construction business, he argues that Vito must be "put down . . . for the honor of the Family. . . . It's against our principles, Tony. A sin." If Vito returns, his crew would not take orders from him nor would the Captains talk to him. For Paulie and Carlo, the last straw is Finn's sight of Vito blowing a security guard: Vito was "catching not pitching." As in "Boca" (I, 9), oral sex is fine to receive but inadmissible to give.

Vito's in-law Phil Leotardo wants to "tear him limb from limb" because he made "a mockery of the whole sacrament." But with Vito's wife, Phil is strategically sensitive: "We can't be in denial no more, much as we love him." Has she any idea where Vito might be? "So we can get him back here, get him to do something about it." For the more candid Paulie, the news is "like a knife in my heart." Still suffering from the revelation about his mother, Paulie asks, "How much more betrayal can I take?"

In his new spirit, Tony initially defends Vito: "Enough of this fuckin rush to judgment." He dismisses Carlo's call to kill him with "fuckin Judge Roy Bean." "Let's be honest with ourselves here. We all know Vito's not the first." As he tells Melfi, "Who gives a shit? I got a second chance why shouldn't he?" He asks Paulie, "Are you going to care for his kids after he's gone?" To Silvio, Tony cites America's new liberal spirit: "It's 2006! There's pillow biters in the Special Forces." Tony tries to make his old language fit his new acceptance. As boss, Tony is torn between conflicting loyalties/betrayals. As he considers Vito's hard work and service, they "want me to burn that kind of dedication?" But to save his no-show jobs, Tony decides he can't turn the other cheek: "He's gotta go. Tell everybody I said so."

To save face, the men pretend not to have been fooled. Having rejected the first rumor, Chris now brags, "I fuckin called him, a long time ago." Chris also agrees now with Tony's import of Naples gunsels—"It's smart, Tony. The more I think of it"—and about considering Vito's children: "It's true. They didn't do nothing. Poor little guys." One is a girl. Yet Chris still acts tough, as he remarks at the AA meeting: "Human frailty—makes me sick sometimes."

Tony also claims, "Actually, I had him pegged all the time, but. . . ." It remains an issue, he tells Melfi: "He's a fa-a-a-ag." Tony admits to ambivalence. He finds homosexuality "disgusting," yet he appreciates the aesthetics of a lesbian show. "But don't forget I'm a strict Catholic. . . . If we let this stuff go too far pretty soon we'll be fuckin dogs." Of course, men in prison "got a pass" for "male to male contact," though he quickly adds: "Just for the record, my incarceration was very short term. So I never had any need for any anal—you know. . . . You think I'm lying, don't you?" In fact, Tony could have learned the direction of Vito's flight had he not sunk into homosexual insults with the black road worker who found Vito's cell phone.

As the homophobes grow nervous, they spring defensive gay jokes like those around oral sex in "Boca" (I, 9). Caparole "heard fat Vito is riding up the Hershey highway." Later, he's "an ass muncher." For Chris, "When he talked about greasing the union, who knew that's what he meant?" Some puns are inadvertent, like Silvio's "backstage passes" to Blood, Sweat and Tears and Tony's "Let's take this in the back." "The guys who are working for me are asking for head. I mean his head. What the fuck." Tony defends his "best earner" as "a come from behind kinda guy." The soundtrack adds ironic comment, from The Subways's "Rock and Roll Queen" to Patsy Cline's "Let the Teardrops Fall."

This vulgarity only heightens Vito's new sensitivity. A shot down his baby-sitter's cleavage implicates the viewer in a heterosexual eroticism far more problematic than Vito's. When his car breaks down in a storm (a pathetic fallacy if there ever was one), he dons an orange rain suit and waddles up the road, before collapsing on the fey four-poster of a bed-and-breakfast. At a diner one morning, over "addictive" johnnycakes and house sausages, he notices the comfy gay clientele and he eyes the cook. This scene of gay comfort separates two scenes of fractured family, Carmela's confrontation with her father and Silvio's pumping of Vito's wife, Marie, on the "romance department." Vito finds in the town a warmth and acceptance denied him by his lifelong friends. An elderly hiker says hello; the landlady offers to have her stepson tow Vito's car in the morning—and declines a tip.

Vito responds to that unaccustomed warmth. The rushing stream suggests bucolic beauty rather than a suicide venue. In the last scene, his admiration for an Arts and Crafts vase draws the (gay) owner's compliment: "You've got a good eye. The most expensive piece in the store. You're a natural." On a license plate, Vito reads the state slogan that gives the episode its title—and Vito a new self-respect: "Live free or die." The closing song celebrates his personal independence in the—however oft betrayed American tradition—"Hey Baby, take a walk outside. Hey Baby, it's the Fourth of July."

The Muslims in the episode figure on both sides of the betrayal theme. In the South Bronx Law Center, Meadow interviews an Afghanistan family who fled the Taliban only to suffer the U.S. government's "fucking over." The FBI arrested the son at school without cause and has held him incommunicado for four days, "like we're some third-world dictatorship." As for the girl, banned from skating with her headscarf on, "If she'd been wearing a yarmulke it would've been a different story, you can bet," her mother avows. Carmela's assurance—"There must have been some reason, Meadow"—rings false for a Family that itself claims government harassment. For Meadow, "9/11, 9/11, Bush is using it as an excuse to erode our constitutional protection, and you're buying into it."

Tony advises, "You oughta chill out about some of this." But he then asks Chris if his two Arab weapon-buyers might be Al Qaeda. The know-it-all begins, "You know, at one point it did cross my mind." His defence hardly allays our suspicions. Ahmad didn't like the infamous Danish cartoons but objected to the radicals' demonstrations that brought "bad attention to all Muslims." Muhammad's brother is "a government interrogator in Lebanon—or Syria." Besides, he and his girlfriend have a dog, a springer spaniel. Chris's logic is not persuasive. As the Afghanistan family exposes the U.S. government's betrayal of democratic values, the Arab gunsels may betray America—or expose our prejudice.

Amid all the betrayals real and feared, in bed Tony tells Carmela, his "busy little beaver," "You were right about my uncle, Car, all along. . . . And all this, you never once said 'I told you so.' "When Tony isn't yet ready for sex, Carmela applies vitamin E to his scar. In this intimacy, their mutual loyalty contrasts to the pervasive fear and betrayal. Though Carmela would really like Tony to call that building inspector already. . . .

VI, 7: Luxury Lounge
Written by Matthew Weiner. Directed by Danny Leiner.

Tony's Italian visitors kill Rusty Millio in his driveway. As Artie's restaurant faces competition from Da Giovanni's, his own declines in quality. He loses his American Express privilege after his new hostess, Martina, helps Benny Fazio sell credit card numbers. Meanwhile, Chris and Little Carmine meet Ben Kingsley in LA to court his participation in their film, *Cleaver.*

The episode is framed by the Neapolitans Tony imports to kill Rusty Millio. In the first scene, Corky gives them their instructions and guns. In the last, they fly home, exulting over the gifts—a watch, a Mont Blanc pen set—they have scored in America. For the Italians, keen to see where the

Twin Towers once stood, America is still a luxury lounge. The episode contrasts the luxury that the few enjoy to the misery of the many. Thus Chris compliments Lauren Bacall on her classic film *The Haves and Have Nots* [*sic*]. Among the episode's several contrasts between haves and have-nots, when the cloakroom girl informs on Martina, her sense of justice is tempered by our awareness that the plain, low-paid girl is getting back at a favored beauty.

Christopher is awe-struck at the luxury lounge where Ben Kingsley and other stars choose expensive gifts: "Is all this shit free?" He hides his greed under a cliché principle: "The coolest shit in the world to the people who need it least." Kingsley admits the practice is "obscene" but claims to give the gifts away to the homeless (!) and to charities. Besides, award shows give presenters $30,000 baskets. Chris nags Kingsley to get him into the freeloader line. Denied, Chris punches and robs the venerable Ms. Bacall. When Christopher gives Tony his "taste," the free golf trip to Australia ominously recalls Tony's arrest for giving Livia stolen flight tickets—and his rankling exclusion from the Cusamanos' club. Amid LA affluence Chris's reform crumbles. On the flight there, he "gave the stewardess an earful when she put down the champagne," but in his hotel room he reverts to cocaine and booze with a call girl. He loses his resolve.

Chris courts Ben Kingsley with embarrassing crudeness. Although "nobody plays a tough ruthless hard-hearted prick like" Kingsley does, Christopher *is* that violent brute who lusts for the trappings of class. He's delighted when he—albeit anonymously—makes *Variety*—with the Bacall assault. He is unlikely to impress Kingsley with his proposed screenwriter's credits: "*Nash Bridges, Hooperman,* and *Law and Order the SUV.*" Tony at least gets the show right when Carlo recommends hunting for Vito with a guy who "can track somebody from the corn in their shit": "I saw them do that on *CSI.*"

We are less surprised than Chris when Kingsley declines the film role, even though Chris enclosed "a muffin basket" with the script. Their cultural gap replays in the song over their tour of the luxury lounge, Zino and Tommy's "Gangstadog." His alcoholic anger back, Chris destroys the sunglasses he cadged from Kingsley. But Chris reports that "He was all over us but I don't think he's right." Kingsley may play violent characters but he shows class—especially in his so-British elongation of the polysyllabic "fuck" with which he notes Christopher's mean-eyed presence on the same flight home.

As Artie's restaurant fades, he blames the honesty his father taught him. His business down 40% from last year, now his debts have cost him his premium suppliers and the AMEX suspension will affect another 30%. "Life's not fair, but somehow I believed my dad about honest work. . . . He used to say, 'You'll see, it pays off in the end.' What a joke." In fact, at least his AMEX loss results from the gangster "buzz" he wanted and Charmaine opposed. Artie provides poor service at the dinner for the two new "made" men. The "new blood" includes his new rival, Giovanni, and Martina, the Albanian immigrant whom Artie has helped settle in and hired as hostess. When he sees her seduced by the married Benny Fazio, Artie withdraws his immigration help and starts to criticize her work. Like Artie, the vulnerable Martina decides she can no longer afford honesty. She confronts him with his sexual jealousy—"You stare at me like food"— and helps Benny steal the credit card numbers.

Again, Artie tries to turn into Tony. At the Badda Bing—over the Barbarellatones' "Fire of Love"—he wants Tony to screw a dancer on his behalf. Tony-like, he beats up Benny Fazio. Yet he also re-stokes his old resentments against Tony, as if their friendship has not paid off. Artie wisely refuses Tony's help but unwisely rejects his advice, for example, to can the "corny jokes and stupid stories" that only discomfit his remaining patrons. Artie initially rejects Tony's suggestion of offering "twofers" to rebuild its clientele: "I'll give it back to the bank before I turn it into a fuckin IHOP." But he gives in, greeting a line of new customers typified by the first question, "Do you have low-salt selections?"

Artie is friendly when he opens his staff meeting to solve the credit card mystery—"As family you will be treated with respect and, if need be, forgiveness"—but he stomps out in rage: "I don't know which one of you pieces of shit did this to me." Charmaine has to manage the mess before they open. As she advises, "The minute you use profanity you give them the high moral ground to do anything they please." Artie's tough gangster language only leaves him more vulnerable.

Under the strain, Artie snipes at Tony: "You want to help me so badly, try paying your tab." He resents Tony attending Phil's grandson's confirmation lunch at Da Giovanni's, where he also brings Carmela and her mother for dinner. To reconcile his friends, Tony compels Benny to hold his parents' anniversary dinner at Artie's. But in front of Benny's wife, Artie revives the feud: "Try the Martina. It's like a martini but it's from Albania. Well, apparently they go down real easy." In the kitchen, Benny shoves Artie's right hand into the boiling pasta sauce. As Tony poetically notes, Artie's scalded "skin came off his hand like a glove." Artie even rejects Tony's warm memory of Artie's generous welcome from the storm (I, 13). He sends him to Da Giovanni's: "See if he'll cook that bland shit for your shot-up pancreas."

However different their present situations and moods, Artie's last hope—like Tony, AJ, Christopher, and Carmela's—is to recover his self-respect. Having illegally shot a rabbit in his garden, he cooks it by his grandfather Angelo's handwritten recipe to serve a couple who arrived after the kitchen closed. That service recovers the generosity Tony recalled, as his return to his family tradition may suggest Artie's broader recovery.

When the same traditional music—Pepe Romero's "Recuerdos de la Alhambra"—plays over Artie's old recipe and the Italian hoods' flight home, the bridge recalls the immigrant's dream of American success and its troubled realization. So, too, the compromised Martina, whose family in Albania "was blown up waiting in line for an oil change." Her affair with Benny (and Artie's vengeance) has soured her American dream. As Artie threatens to blot her employment record, he unwittingly recalls his own American Express loss: "We lead the world in computerized data collection." Here his power is also his vulnerability.

Meanwhile, Tony shifts in and out of his new sensitivity. He deflects Phil's thanks for whacking Rusty, to distance himself. He turns on a measured force to reconcile Benny and Artie: "You don't shit where you eat. And you really don't shit where I eat." Urging Artie to see a psychiatrist, he summarizes Melfi's years of counsel: "In business, shit happens—playing field changes, whatever. You gotta do what it takes to somehow keep your dick up." Again, Tony adapts his old language to his new sensitivity.

With his new sense of responsibility, Tony advises Artie to stop going "around in pity for yourself": "You bitch and you moan and you blame everyone else for your problems." He stops Christopher: "How many times you gonna play the Adriana card?" Benny might not have sabotaged Artie had his boss, Chris, not been away on his Hollywood fantasy. Whether haves or have-nots, people here manage well until they discover they lack something or lose what they have. And in the gangster world the material matters more than the moral.

Indeed the little plastic credit card behind both Artie's troubles and Chris's new success is an emblem of the lust to have. In a pointed irony,

Chris's goon Murmur sells at a Jewish deli the credit card numbers that he buys from Hillel Teitleman at the Flyaway Motel. In I, 3, Hillel was the idealistic Orthodox Jew who warned his father not to deal with the Sopranos. Here he, like Artie and Martina, has been turned, whether by need or by greed. As Ahmed and Muhammed have been buying the numbers from Chris, the parallel contrasts two immigrant orthodoxies, the old and the new, the Jew and the Muslim. The with-it Arab buyers spurn the old-fashioned plastic: "We do Internet strictly." But this cycle makes the Jews and Arabs a miniature of Melting Pot America, their antagonistic cultures harmonized by corruption. When Murmur inflects the lyrics to Elton John's "Daniel"—"Hillel, my brother, you are older than me"—the episode draws a Biblical omen from the motif of American greed and crime. Perhaps the capitalism of Luxury Lounge America is like Artie's comparison of the restaurant business to keeping an elephant: "It costs a fortune and sooner or later it shits on your head."

In sum, this canvas of wants and frustrations indirectly endorses Vito's wisdom in fleeing to New Hampshire. This is contrary to the characters' rhetoric, like Christopher's "We were just discussing La Cage au Fat" and Phil's reference to his cousin's husband: "It's an honor to be among men, not faggot assed cornholing cocksuckers," like Vito; "He should fuckin die." True, without Vito, Marie can't control their children at Da Giovanni's. But the others' pursuits rather ennoble Vito's retreat to a town where his only luxury is openly to be himself.

VI, 8:   Johnny Cakes

Written by Diane Frolov and Andrew Schneider.
Directed by Tim Van Patten.

Having resumed his sex life with Carmela, Tony is perturbed when his pretence to fidelity holds true. AJ flubs his attempt to kill Uncle Junior. Vito is attracted to the diner cook Jim, especially after seeing the volunteer fireman rescue a child from a blazing house. By reflex he repels Jim, then takes him as a lover.

Tony's sex with Carmela is intercut with Vito, now "Vince," reading a muscle-man's magazine (*AB Attack*) in—as a license plate reminds us—the

Granite State, New Hampshire. The theme is hard-rock manliness. Vito claims to be writing a book on Rocky Marciano but includes Rocky Graziano—"You can't talk about one without the other"—because he's bluffing macho. In fact, he can't keep up with the diner boxing chat. Similarly, AJ sells his drums to a hard-rock group and plays the tough on the club scene, but he can't escape his father's reputation.

The episode's central tension is between the rock hard and the johnnycake soft, synthesized in short-order cook Jim. The muscular father, beer-drinking fireman, and hog-rider has a soft spot for "Vince" and makes marvelous johnnycakes. In softness, he first kisses Vito and in hardness he outfights his rejection. Although "Vince's" ostensible boxing book affirms his macho interest, he notes Jim's pat on his hand, remarking on the writer's loneliness, and Jim's ease with his young daughter.

Against Shawn Colvin's "Sunny Came Home," the community warmth prompts Vito to steal another tenant's cell phone to call his wife, Marie, to tell her where he has stashed $30,000 and to chat with his son. Wary in choosing his community, Vito avoids the other tenants' fey discussions of dishwashers but sends the firemen's table a pitcher of beer. Leaving with Jim, Vito instinctively rejects his kiss, calls him "some kind of fag," and punches him. Later, he carries a lonely pizza past the diner, then sheepishly returns for—of course—the tall stack of Jim's johnnycakes, that "you can't beat." Over Lisbeth Scott's "I Fall," "Vince" explains, "Sometimes you tell lies so long you don't know when to stop. You don't know when it's safe." The men bike out to the country to make love.

Tony's false fidelity also becomes—briefly—the truth. When he recovers his post-surgery libido, he brags to Silvio and Chris about the new "baguette in my pants 24-7." He assures Dr. Melfi that after Carmela's generous care any consideration of any "extracurricular outlet" is strictly theoretical. "The way she took care of me . . . you think I'd fuckin betray that?" But his resolve wavers when he muses about a flirtatious Bada Bing dancer and propositions the real-estate agent who wants to sell his warehouse.

The agent, Julianna, is a Melfi/Gloria type, a dark-haired, aggressive, independent beauty, with an alluring "low tolerance for boredom" that is antithetical to Carmela. Tony couches his first invitation—which Julianna declines because she is engaged—in his new hunger for life. As Tony's first medical crisis (I, 1) led to the medical insurance scam, this one justifies an affair. When Tony accepts her raised offer, she agrees to sign the papers at her apartment. Tony's new sensitivity gives way to his old self-indulgence.

After his 12-signature foreplay, they heave into ardour, but Tony abruptly stops and leaves. His fidelity to Carmela is here not a principle but a visceral impulse, a gut response, like his vomiting after beating up Perry (VI, 5). As Carmela buttoned his fresh shirt for his "real estate thing," Julianna's unbuttoning it snaps him back to his wife. Now Tony lives out Julianna's initial resolve: "For once in my life I will exercise a little self-control." As at the end of "Boca" (I, 9), when Tony staggers home, having done the right thing, the high-angle shot on him here assumes the superior feminine perspective, this time Carmela's. When he rails at her for not stocking smoked turkey, he seems to blame his wife for his rejecting Julianna. Here Tony relapses into his cold-cut phobia from seeing his father slice off Satriale's finger.

Tony's wavering sensitivity begins with the real-estate sale. Initially, he won't sell the warehouse, not just because of its future value but out of old-school respect for the chickens and eggs that his long-term tenant Caputo provides the community. "I don't want to sell out from under the guy." But to get at Julianna, Tony agrees to sell, without even warning the poulterer himself. At the loss of Caputo's kickback, even Patsy feels betrayed: "I got a kid in college." Tony sells out his principles for a possible affair.

Nor can AJ sustain his pose of hardness. The club staff and patrons play up to him because of Tony's power. The dwarf bouncer sends Tony regards, a kid wants Tony to lean on his uncooperative landlord, another an investment in sports drinks, and the blond masseuse pumps AJ for gossip about Tony and Uncle Junior. Though AJ plays tough with cocaine, his blackouts show he has also inherited Tony's weakness. He buys friends, as one $1,890 tab ("It's cool") suggests. At Blockbuster, he ignores a customer to practice martial arts with his colleague (new-age Rockys).

AJ happily shares beers and belches with his dad as they fish on the *Stugots II*, but he won't accept Tony's intention to leave Uncle Junior alone: "He's incarcerated for the rest of his unnatural life, so fuck him—a walking corpse." In the spirit of Michael Corleone, AJ visits Junior in the criminal ward but is arrested when his knife falls out—for all his Blockbuster practice. At first, Tony rages at his "stupid fuckin moron" but he softens: "I guess your heart was in the right place, AJ, but it's wrong. . . . It's not in your nature. . . . You're a nice guy and I'm grateful." Without

Tony's "connections," AJ would have been charged with attempted murder. Suppressing both his and his son's crying, Tony rejects *The Godfather*: "It's a movie. You gotta grow up. You're not a kid anymore."

The softness theme includes Melfi's scenes. Although Melfi warns Tony and Carmela to be consistent with AJ, Carmela slips him money for a suit and Tony insists Carmela not be told about his arrest. On AJ's immaturity, Melfi advises Tony that "true adulthood is delayed" by the new bombardment of information: "26 is the new 21." With her own therapist, she wants to discuss her father's premature aging but he sticks to his "tabloid level" interest in Tony: "Has he cried or reported crying at all?" Against Kupferberg ("This omerta concept comes from a pre-therapeutic culture)" Melfi affirms Tony's "more accepting" nature.

As Melfi defends him, Tony defends Vito against Phil Leotardo's hunger to avenge his family dishonor. "What am I supposed to do, put out an APB cause a guy takes it up the ass? . . . Fundamentally [*sic*] we're in agreement on this issue, but I'll handle it." Even the toughs pretend to sentimental principle. When a Seattle coffee-chain's new manager can't pay protection because "every last fuckin coffee bean is in the computer and has to be accounted for," Patsy concludes sentimentally, "It's over for the little guy." What the crook means is that the domineering chains don't allow for small-time hoods to enforce local protection charges, his "Protective Merchants Co-operative" offer of "all the supplemental safety net you need." At Tony's sale of the poulterer's building to a newfangled juice company, Patsy rails, "What the fuck is happening to this neighborhood?" The end-credits song, Ray Charles's "I'm Gonna Move to the Outskirts of Town," closes the episode on a note of sentimental liberation.

VI, 9:   The Ride
Written by Alan Taylor. Directed by Terence Winter.

Although Christopher's pregnant girlfriend, Kelli, offers to abort, he is so eager to have a family that he marries her instead. Paulie, operating the annual feast of St. Elzear, provokes the new priest Father Jose's concerns about the "criminal element." He refuses to lend the saint's traditional golden hat. When the festival teacup ride breaks down and injures several people, Paulie is blamed for skimping on safety. Also shaken by concern about his biopsy for prostate cancer, Paulie reconciles with his Aunt Nucci.

This episode's central metaphor may be the Ride of Life, with its loss of the holy in the secular and its provision of both danger and security. The religious patrons are so bored "they pay money so they can almost puke." So, too, Janice's baby cries when she's first taken on the ride, then again when it's broken so she can't go on. She's not mollified till Tony swings her through the air. The human craves danger.

For Janice, the ride embodies life's risks, to be exploited for drama or cash: "One second you're sitting there, enjoying a ride with your family. The next your entire world comes crashing down." While obsessing over her baby's danger, she dons a neck brace for maximal compensation. She goads Bobby into demanding $25,000 from the ride owner and then into attacking Paulie.

The festival reveals corruption beneath religious pretence. St. Elzear was a 14th-century Italian nobleman whose career combined political service, a wealthy estate, a happy marriage, and piety. The Sopranos want that ideal but are disqualified from it by how they choose to pursue it. The saint's day sinks to secular excess, such as the cannoli-eating contest (to Johnny Thunders's "Pipeline"). As Tony describes it, "Thousands of people, either praying—or eating." Nourishing Italian cuisine dwindles to the fair's signature *zepoles*, fried and sugared dough. The teacup ride adds a mad *Alice in Wonderland* note to the religious festivities.

The festival plumbs Paulie's fall from his altar boy origins. His very engagement is corrupt. For years, he has scammed the five-day festival through his "non-profit corporation," of which he is "recording secretary." Silvio, counting his own wad, declares him "Vice-President in charge of calzones." Now Paulie's authority is challenged by the new priest, who returns the gangster's coercion. Citing the festival's origin in "the spirit of giving," Father Jose wants the parish's "end" raised from $10,000 to $50,000, "a more equitable donation," or he will withhold the golden hat, made out of donated wedding rings. Paulie's "Fuck the hat" prefers his profits but its absence perturbs the faithful. Although Paulie taunts the deal-making priest—"Well it seems to me the church has plenty in its coffers for all those pedophilia lawsuits"—he still suffers his old religious conscience when the Virgin Mary appears to him at the Bada Bing.

Secular issues debase the festival. There, Carmela meets Liz LaCerva who is certain Chris killed her daughter, Adriana: "Carmela Soprano! How's your daughter?" Liz is broken: "Drunk? It's called depression. I haven't had a drink in years." With familiar hypocrisy, Tony deflects Carmela's suspicion of Chris with "Let's not sabotage his progress." At the religious festival, Tony offers Phil Leotardo a 50/50 split to sell a stolen truckload of multivitamins, proposing to "spare John the stress of having to hear about this." These St. Elzear celebrants add betrayal to their traffic in stolen pills. In context, the thefts of vitamins and wine are a fugitive play on communion.

The satire around the religious festival has topical currency. Tony wards off Carmela's suspicion of Chris with allusions to O .J. Simpson and "Scott fuckin Peterson." When Paulie tells Father Jose how expensive his festival is to run, Patsy adds the current concern, "not to mention fuel costs." Paulie greets someone's son just back from two tours in Iraq with "I'm proud of you, my friend"—though Paulie's every action affronts the soldier's mission. Confronting Paulie in the john, Tony parodies President Bush's post-Katrina slick comment of "You're doing a hell of a job there, Brownie." Tony orders Paulie to settle with Bobby for the ride, not for spiritual reasons, but because the religious feast is in "competition out there for the entertainment dollar" with DVDs and the Internet.

Even before the accident, the festival proves Paulie's tribulation. He strong-arms his advance rent payments, greets his Aunt Nucci with another profane assault upon her and his nun mother, and worries over his delayed biopsy results. Nucci blames the accident not on Paulie's greed but on his blaspheming his nun mother and omitting the saint's hat. The accident leaves Paulie ostracized at Chris's bachelor dinner.

Like the religious festival, Chris's wedding dilutes the sacred with the profane: "Drive to AC [Atlantic City]. Make a day of it." He cries with joy at Kelli's pregnancy because Adriana couldn't bear him children. As he assures Kelli, "I bet she's having some other asshole's kid, the fuckin tramp." When he immediately buys the house of his fancy, his "stately Wayne Manor," Chris sees himself a domesticated superhero, Batman—as if he would ever serve the law. So, too, he tells Corky he will "start a tradition," having his gunsels over for Christmas. When Chris announces his wedding, behind him a Bada Bing dancer snakes down the pole, an omen of his future infidelities. Chris piously declines Silvio's champagne: "Just water for me. My son will be my strength."

Chris's collapse begins with his caper with Tony, stealing the Viper gang's stolen wine. They steal to Free's "All Right Now" and they drive off to Buddy Miles's "Midnight Rider." As this ride is more visceral than the teacups, they revel in the cowboyitis against which Tony has warned Chris: "Yee-haaw." The escapade—"fucking Old School shit"—assuages the boredom that Tony describes to Melfi: "I told you my feelings. Every day is a gift. . . . It's just—does it have to be a pair of socks?" He goes on thoughtfully: "I'm joking. I'm joking. But what are you going to do? It's the human condition. . . . I dunno." Like Janice's baby, Tony and Chris crave danger. But as the boys relive their adventure, its excitement wanes. At the family dinner, Tony finds the wine has "lost its pop." Tony also revives his spirit at the religious fair—when he spots Julianna in a spinning ride high above the kiddies' teacups.

Tony shares his relapse when he coaxes on-the-wagon Chris to taste the stolen wine. Drunk, Tony and Chris express their love and Chris relives his traumatic report of Adriana's betrayal. That "love" ruins Chris's recovery. Although Chris sells his five cases of 1986 vintage wine for $300, his resolve dissolves. Just after he lectures the hood Corky—"You need to get your ass to rehab"—Chris snorts up himself. While Corky quavers for a fix, Chris lists the luxuries of his new house and car. As well as an impulse buyer, Chris is an impulse user. He spends the religious fair in a stupor, to the druggie mysticism of Fred Neil's "Dolphins," and vomits out of his car window (like Tony's religious thrill-seekers). The stray dog Chris befriends recalls Adriana's lapdog that he killed in an earlier stupor.

Like Tony, Chris's attempts at redemption seem doomed. Just before Kelly reveals her pregnancy, Chris is watching the horror movie *Saw II* on TV. The sepulchral voice intones: "How much blood will you shed to stay alive, Michael? Make your choice." The line anticipates the wine theft and Chris's focus on Corky's blood rising into his needle when he temptingly shoots up in Chris's car.

After these diverse rides, the episode closes on Paulie and his Aunt Nucci watching television in her smaller room at Green Grove. Despite Paulie's abandonment, she has not been evicted and she has a smaller TV than the plasma Paulie bought her then destroyed (VI, 1). They tacitly reconcile over a Norwegian folk dance ("Johnny Oslo Schottische") on the *Lawrence Welk Show*. Among the episode's rides, that is unexciting. As they silently recover their lost bond, the camera draws out their window into the wind and rain outside. From that stormy ride, Paulie has recovered his precious refuge.

VI, 10:   Moe n' Joe

Written by Matthew Weiner. Directed by Steve Shill.

An out-of-court settlement saves Johnny Sack from trial but leaves him in need of money. He asks Tony to negotiate the sale of a New Orleans business. After Janice complains of Tony's hatred of her, he makes Johnny sell her his mansion for half price. Vito moves in with Jim, who sees through his pretence to be a writer and gets him construction work. After they express their love, Vito, bored by his job, leaves for his former life. When he gets to Satriale's, he speeds away.

The implicit theme of this episode is loss of power. The clearest example is Johnny Sack's domination by the feds and by Tony. After the prosecutor offers him 20 years and a fine of 90% of his five million dollar assets, Johnny settles for 15 years in jail and a $4.1 million fine. Johnny's refusal to "flip" impresses even his lawyer: "Good, because frankly I don't represent turncoats." As Johnny tells his Jewish lawyer, "Being a rat—where I'm coming from, that's like asking a person where you're coming from to become a fuckin Nazi." But Johnny loses his gang's respect when he is forced to admit Mafia involvement. He should have stood trial "like a man." For Phil, the confession is "Fuckin nauseating. . . . You don't ever admit the existence of this thing."

With Tony, as with the feds, Johnny realizes that "beggars can't be choosers." For selling his silent share of a heavy-equipment leasing company in New Orleans, Tony raises his fee by 3%, then compels the bargain on Johnny's mansion. This, Johnny says, reduces Ginny to the pension she earned at the tie counter at Wanamaker's, where they met. Worse, Ginny sits stupefied while Janice brings through her decorator. Nor can Ginny draw consolation when the government, seizing Johnny assets, takes the Maserati for which Christopher paid her $25,000 cash. Clearly the Sacramonis' world has shrunk.

Bobby's silly model-train world, in which he fails to interest Bobby Jr., provides a comic version of reduced power. His engineer cap is a comic parallel to his son's compulsory bicycle helmet. The set assumes mock heroic proportions when Chase cuts from Vito's sex scene with Jim to Bobby's train entering a tunnel. The edit parodies the famous sleeping-berth scene in Hitchcock's *North by Northwest*. Bobby's adult life allows no such satisfaction. Janice's intervention with Tony advances her, not him. Distant from his children, dominated by his wife, still not a Captain at his age, Bobby finds refuge in his toy. When he is mugged and shot in the eye after a bookie pickup, Bobby futilely asks, "Do you know who I am?" Even when Bobby still gets Tony his payment, Tony rejects him: "Fuck that loyalty and honor shit. . . . It was his own fuckin fault." Bobby's only power is over his toy train.

The end-credits song, Chuck Berry's "Let It Rock," augments the train motif with rock energy. In this episode, the only successful rockers are the corrupt who exploit the Hurricane Katrina disaster. Hence, gangster Tony's zealous "Dick Cheney for President—of the fuckin universe." As in Season Five, the show equates the gangsters with the current presidency.

Like Bobby's train set, Vito's New Hampshire idyll fails to compensate for his loss of thrills and power. Vito and Jim work through some of their problems. Jim forgives Vito's lies; Vito, Jim's resentment when Vito, attending a fire call, cuts the power line to prevent the pastor's electrocution in a church basement flood. But Vito can't stand normal labor. For relief, the *nouveau schnook* secretly gambles. Despite their appreciation (and Toby Keith's "I Love This Bar"), Vito can't coax the firemen into a poker game. In an interior monologue, he assures himself the work time is passing quickly—but it isn't. To Dean Martin's "That's Amore," Vito makes Jim a romantic Italian dinner: "I fuckin miss this shit, I gotta say." The cuisine represents the whole Italian gangster community's lifestyle, with all its traditions and danger. To Sinatra's anthem "My Way," Vito drives away home, drinking. The shift from Martin to Sinatra signifies Vito's reversion from his new cool to his old criminal. When he collides with a parked station wagon, the victim insists on reporting the accident, so Vito kills him.

In contrast, Tony manages the games of his larger world relatively well. He confronts Janice's complaint that he is always insulting Bobby, as when he admires her baby's resemblance: "Baccalieris got no fuckin genes at all." Bobby "works so hard for you and what does he get? Merciless ridiculing about his weight, about his model railroading." She concludes, "There's nothing holding us together but DNA."

Yet Tony is as intensely bound to Janice as he was to Livia. With Melfi, he uncovers the source of his resentment. As a child, Janice once blackmailed him with a tape recording of his fight with younger sister, Barbara.

"Held that cassette over my head for a month! Fuckin extortion. . . . Got me to make her bed, get her shit." As a result, Tony admits, "I love it when I can take a shit on her and on her husband." As with Livia, Tony is outraged by Melfi's suggestion that Janice may have been the focus of his first sexual interest: "No guy wants his sister to be the town pump." Where Janice was always selfish—"Janice only does acts of Janice. Trust me."—Tony was dutiful: "I did what I was told." He still resents that Janice left home when he had to stay: "She gets nothing because I got the scars. So it's mine." As it happens, when Janice first reappeared in Tony's life (II, 1), she pretended to respect this very claim of Tony's.

The ostensibly new, improved Tony is still so uncomfortable with emotion that he can't handle Janice's crying in gratitude for the Sack mansion. When Meadow cries about Finn's detachment—"He doesn't fucking get it. I don't know what he's thinking lately."—Tony mentions her "living in sin" then sends her off: "Talk to your mother about this shit." At this point, he cancels Silvio's intervention on Carmela's real-estate problem, to restrict her to maternal duties.

As well, Tony still lies to Melfi and to Carmela. To Melfi, he complains that "even in bed she's [Carmela's] a million miles away." He claims Carmela has accepted a "don't ask, don't tell policy" on his "recreational life outside the home." He tells Carmela the building inspector resisted his pressure and urges her to sell her spec house.

Even the fringe victims lose their power. The long-exploited gardener Sal irks Tony by asking when he can stop doing Johnny Sack's yard for free. At first, Tony calls him a "selfish prick" (Carmela: "Such a mope"). Tony corrects Sal's belief in Johnny's confession: "He pled guilty. With this government no fuckin trial. . . . Don't besmirch the man, Sal." In this perverse order, believing a man besmirches him. Tony finally releases Sal only as a disservice to Janice, the new owner.

Like the hapless Sal, the New Orleans gamblers are shrunk by their debt to Johnny. His $50,000 loan for a gambling debt turns into a $500,000 share in the company that would now sap half the five-to-six-million-dollar sale price. "We're very different people," the " 'degenerate fuckin gambler" who is now reluctant to sell the company tries to temper Tony. Perhaps the unnamed Cajuns provide the episode title's replacement of the power fetish, Mojo, with two elided *schnooks*.

This episode presents the social order as a cycle of coercion, from which even Tony's new appreciation of life fails to remove him. As Johnny has an exploitative hold on his New Orleans partners, Tony and the feds sap him. As young Janice blackmailed Tony, he coerces Sal and now Johnny. This perpetual exploitation precludes any possible justice. Yet when Paulie's cancer appears to be under control by radiation, he assumes he has earned it: "Musta done good things in my life." Of that there is no evidence here.

VI, 11: Cold Stones

Written by Diane Frolov, Andrew Schneider, and David Chase.
Directed by Tim Van Patten.

After learning that AJ was fired from Blockbuster, Tony forces him into a construction job. Meadow moves to California to be with Finn. Carmela takes Rosalie on a holiday in Paris. Vito offers to pay Tony $200,000 for re-admission into the Family and requests assignment to the "much more tolerant atmosphere" of Atlantic City. In a challenge to Tony's authority, Phil has Vito tortured and killed. When his gunsel Fat Dom jokes about the torture, Silvio and Carlo kill him.

This episode's title completes the hard/soft tension introduced in "Johnny Cakes" (VI, 8). The cold stones over which we pass don't care about our hopes and our tragedies. They outlive us unmoved, untouched. That's what Carmela learns from historic Paris: "When you actually die, life goes on without you. Like it does in Paris, when we're not here." The ancient city prompts her to ask Tony's VI, 2 questions: "Who am I? Where am I going?" For all our petty conflicts and concerns, "In the end it all gets washed away. All of it just gets washed away." On the Paris cab radio, Rosalie and Carmela hear a French rap, "*Ouvre les yeux,*" that sets up their eye-opening experience.

In hardness, Rosalie finds strength. She brushes aside Carmela's invitation to talk about her son's murder: "He's dead. He's gone. What can I do about it? Light a candle. . . . Why would you bring New Jersey here? Why can't we just have a good time?" For her, the unexamined pain makes life bearable. So she dates Michel, a handsome 26-year-old French motorcyclist. In her own wilful naivety, Carmela photographs a neon pig sign, again finding Satriale's New Jersey in Paris.

322 • THE SOPRANOS ON THE COUCH

With her secularized religion, Carmela won the trip at the Feast's silent auction. Tony encourages it with a Louis Vuitton wallet stuffed with cash. But while he listens to her phone message, he eyes the Bada Bing pole dancer who will fellate him when he drives her home. The black-and-white moral code moves from her dancing to Giorgio Moroder's "Knights in White Satin" to the AC/DC song "Back in Black," where what seems to be Tony's heart attack is a blow job. This interlude demonstrates Carmela's compromises in her marriage and life, as it is intercut with her ritual observance in the Paris cathedral and reading the plaque for Resistance hero Jacques Martine. Against any temptation, the Sopranos show very little resistance. Thus, before leaving for Paris, Carmela encourages Tony to "do whatever it is boys do when they're on their own."

Vito is the tragic victim of the title's stone-cold humanity. As Tony watches Mickey Rooney energetically conduct an orchestra on TV, he seems to accept an alternative manliness. He feels for Vito and is inclined to let him sell meth and girls in Atlantic City. But Phil ends Tony's five no-show jobs on the Tidelands project. With Johnny Sack "folding laundry in fuckin Danbury," Phil is at full tide. When Phil complains that Vito is back despite Tony's promise to "take care of that fuckin finook," Tony walks off angry. The setting is the Lou Costello memorial where earlier Tony made peace with Paulie. Now, "If you want those no-show jobs Vito's got to go." To appease Leotardo, Tony agrees to have Carlo kill Vito.

But before he can, Phil flouts Tony's authority by killing Tony's homosexual Captain himself. In Vito's motel room, Phil literally comes out of the closet to confront the "fuckin disgrace." The rectal pool stick follows a tradition of homophobic torture in, for example, Marlowe's *Edward II* and the cited death of Roman Navarro. As the gangsters admire Phil's initiative, Patsy's only regret is that he hadn't borrowed money from Vito. Later, Silvio and Carlo explode at the insensitive Fat Dom's jokes: "The pool cue—I wonder if it was chalked. . . . You know the autopsy found a three ball in his side pocket. . . . Carlo's lipstick was on Vito's cock." Fat Dom's consequent murder threatens to launch the war with Phil that Tony gave up Vito to avoid.

To Vito's widow, Phil still plays sympathetic and innocent: "I loved him like a brother-in-law. But God moves in strange ways." Urging Marie not to dwell on Vito, Phil orders the TV shut off, discomfited by its male body builders. The gangsters' gay obsession recurs when Tony answers

Carmela's call with "Is Paris burning?" The phrase directly alludes to Rene Clement's 1966 film about the 1944 liberation of Paris (which Tony watched on the kitchen TV). But it also evokes *Paris Is Burning* (Jennie Livingston, 1990), a sympathetic documentary about New York drag balls.

The gangsters' callousness heightens Vito's tragedy. Even as he asks Tony's forgiveness, he denies his nature: "I'm not a fag. I never was," just affected by his blood pressure medicine. Tony rejects the idea of a doctor's confirmation: "A note from your doctor saying you didn't like to suck cock?" Pathetically, Vito has told his wife, Marie, "I don't have a problem. It's over with," and proposes they have another child. Vito tells his children he's with the CIA "working deep cover" in Afghanistan, but they ultimately read his exposure in the newspaper.

When the episode closes on the Thin Club photograph of Vito happily showing off the result of his diet (seen in the season's opening montage), his moment of joy and of self-respect underlines the horror of his end. The man of flesh was tortured appallingly by men of stone—in the name of higher values. Phil pleads a high moral code, despite his profound selfishness. As Tony knows, "All Phil cares about is fuckin money." His wife, Patty, endorses her priest's perhaps more ambiguous conclusion—"There's nothing gay about hell"—and feeds Phil's viciousness: "Vito has to be made to face his problems squarely." The last song gives Vito a sentimental valedictory. "As Time Goes By," from the *Casablanca* soundtrack, where Rick and Louie walk off together for "the start of a beautiful relationship," privileges the human exchange of a kiss over the cold calculations of stony time and politics. The fundamental things apply, whether Vito's "I love you guys" to his kids, his attempt to salve his abandoned Jim, Rosalie's hug of a weeping Carmela, or Carmela's resolve to tell Tony more often that she loves him. Against stone coldness the closing reaffirms the sentimental.

As Phil lies awake brooding over the murdered Vito, Carmela dreams she meets Adriana in Paris. The dream shows her discomfort over whacked friends and her denial of Tony's involvement. As she ignores the moral implications of her life, she is like AJ, "a complete stranger to the truth." What Tony calls his son's "deep down fuck you," Carmela declares "his dead, nihilistic streak. It chills me to the bone."

The AJ plotline here also engages the problem of hardness/softness. To rationalize his Blockbuster firing for selling promotional materials, he offers a cliché principle: "Maybe I care about the environment. Has that ever occurred to you? Wallace and Gromit, that weighed like fifty pounds. How many trees gave their lives for that. It just goes to the dump?" But like Phil, AJ is solely concerned with the money he could make from the movie ephemera. Similarly, when AJ dismisses Blockbuster as "fuckin religious fanatics," he abuses the criticism of the Christian Right that is implicit in the viewer's rejection of Vito's persecution. Like Carmela, AJ can posit a moral position but he remains committed to his luxuries, like his thousand-dollar champagne evenings. So Carmela, from eternal Paris, returns to her family's lavish laundry.

Tony tells Melfi he hates his own son because AJ doesn't conform to anyone's sense of a man. He regrets that Carmela protected AJ from his discipline. As Melfi reminds him, however, he resents Livia for not having protected him from his father. Melfi defends Carmela's motherhood: "He might have grown up with a desperate need to control."—like Janice, Livia, Tony, and Phil. But Tony blames AJ's frailty on "Carmela's side of the family. They're small people. Her father, you could knock him over with a fuckin feather." Tony respects only his own macho hulk.

Vito's bloody end prompts Tony to act against AJ's softness. He forces him into a rigorous 7 A.M. outdoor construction job: "I just want to see you do good. You're my son and I love you." Failure to comply would cost AJ his car first, then his clothes, then his room. As an earnest of his seriousness, Tony smashes the windshield on AJ's van, because AJ is too "fuckin little" to hit.

Paradoxically, Vito himself began in the outdoor construction work that Tony hopes will harden AJ. In contrast, Meadow escapes to California for a UCLA lab job that Finn's father gets her. Like Carmela with her spec house, Meadow remains dependent upon a father's help—but now it's not her own. Both young Sopranos take firmer steps outside their custom than Tony has managed to do.

VI, 12: Kaisha
Written by Terence Winter, David Chase, and Matthew Weiner. Directed by Alan Taylor.

After Carlo disperses Fat Dom's remains, Tony blows up Phil's wire room at Sheepshead Bay. Carmine Junior convenes a peace between

Phil and Tony, then explodes it by referring to Phil's brother Billy's murder by Tony's cousin. Phil's advisers urge him to whack Tony or someone close to him. Tony is warned by FBI agent Harris and saved by Phil's heart attack. Real-estate agent Julianna rejects Tony but starts an affair with Christopher, whom she met at AA. Together they sink back into drugs. AJ begins an affair with the construction company secretary, Blanca Selgado. A Salvation Army fund-raising letter to Adriana prompts Liz LaCerva's suicide attempt. When Carmela suggests hiring a private eye to find Adriana, Tony deflects her by clearing the building approval of her spec house.

The season's finale returns to the opening episode's theme of near-death and redemption, centering on the family's Thanksgiving and Christmas dinners *chez* Tony and on the sobering impact of Phil's near-fatal coronary. When he visits Phil in the hospital, Tony cites his own deathbed experience: "Believe me, nobody ever laid on their deathbed wishing they'd saved more no-show jobs." Warmly, he urges his enemy to recover and then to "focus on your grandkids. The good things." The last phrase echoes Tony's toast to his family at the end of I, 13 (recalled in VI, 7).

However, Tony reverts to a strictly materialistic resolution: "We can have it all, Phil. Plenty for everyone. Stop crying now." The line recalls the spiritual flourish when Tony accepted Johnny Sack's compromise (VI, 4): "Truth be told, there's enough garbage for everybody." As Tony continues to compromise his new sensitivity, the season comes rather to depict the *impossibility* of moral regeneration for such a self-indulgent society.

In the last shot, the camera draws back to a Christmas card image of a warm family gathered around the festive hearth. Earlier, Bobby Jr. flips the TV from the obligatory *A Christmas Carol* to the secular romance about integrity, *Casablanca*, specifically Rick's initial rejection of politics, the Jewish immigrant's (Cuddles Zackall) toast "to America," and the policeman's reminder that—as if unlike America—"in Casablanca life is cheap." As this progress suggests, the Sopranos' seasonal image of family harmony is false. Indeed Tony was with a shadowy woman— perhaps his ostensible "chiropodist"—when he got the cell phone report on the Sheepshead mission. So, too, he pursues Julianna with the promise of a property flip.

Carmela follows Tony's pattern. Her concern about Adriana and Liz easily fades into ordering roof tiles for her spec house. First, Tony argues that Ade fled her impossible mother, then that a private eye's investigation might be "an intrusion into Ade's personal life." "For all our sakes," Tony finally instructs Silvio, "my wife needs a career." After Silvio coerces the city planner's permission, Carmela hugs her enabling Tony: "This is the best Christmas present I could ever get." Carmela's house-pride defines her moral compromise and selfishness.

The episode opens on the isolated beach-house where Carlo retrieves Fat Dom's head and it closes on the Soprano's superior home. In the last exchange, Carmela accepts Blanca's "You have a gorgeous home" with "Thank you. [*pause*] We do." As Tony earlier consoled her, "You made us a beautiful home." Like Tony's embrace of the stricken Phil, her primary value remains luxury, however ill-gotten. Her caress of Tony's right knee parallels the stoned Julianna's caress of Chris's, suggesting the women's parallel addictions. At the end, Sinatra's "Silent Night" is drowned out by the Rolling Stones's wholly secular "Moonlight Mile," which played over Carlo's trip to the beach-house. That musical frame reminds us that Carmela's fine house and Christmas scene are based on the cold viciousness of the beach-house and Fat Dom's severed head. The idyllic *Leave It to Beaver* Cleavers' front is financed by the *Cleaver* ethos of Chris's film project. As Tony has failed genuinely to change after his near-death experience, Carmela pretends to a new integrity but remains corrupt.

The hypocrisy of failed redemption also characterizes Chris, who hugs and kisses his wife, Kelli, at the party but has betrayed her with Julianna and their drugs. He quickly loses the concern he expresses around Kelli's plans to decorate the nursery in "Morning Sunshine" and Disney characters. As he learned from *March of the Penguins*, "You sit on an egg for months. One little thing goes wrong and you're left with nothing." For once his proverb is directly apt: "Let's stop counting the chickens." Yet he tells Julianna, "I don't want a family with her. She's got no idea what I am."

In contrast to Chris's dishonesty, Julianna is self-critical even at the peak of their affair: "What are we doing here, huh? . . . How can you even like a person who sleeps with a married guy?" This self-knowledge aligns her with Melfi's mentor, Dr. Krakauer (III, 6), who, like Julianna, "comes from the Hannukah people" but is free from her destructive self-indulgence. In bed, she apologizes: "Sorry it's such a pigsty. I work a lot.

And I'm a pig." Julianna's honesty extends to her sensible response to Chris's film project: "Are you sure about the title, *Cleaver*? The Jerry Mathers connection?" Although Julianna appears solid when she rejects Tony ("Stick it in the lock box"), she proves as fragile as his Gloria. When she meets Chris at an AA meeting, Julianna reports that Tony's humiliating walkout drove her back to crystal meth. Even Tony's rare flash of virtue is destructive.

The lovers reject wiser counsel. As Murmur warns Chris, "Two of you together could be enabling. Bad habits shared." This "enabling"—as in Krakauer's advice to Carmela (III, 6)—means "debilitating." When Julianna's AA sponsor warns against those "sociopaths, murderers, actually," Julianna insists Chris is "sweet. He's good to me."

For once, Chris is properly wary of following Tony: "Weird, being where he's been." Though she insists, "Nothing happened," for Chris, "He's been there in his mind." That is to say, Tony sticks in Chris's mind. To Chris's "He thinks everything is his," Julianna replies, "But it's not" and kisses him. But even as the lovers try to evade Tony's hold, they slip into his destructive indulgence. Their relationship draws them back into drugs. At first, she is so wary that she refuses cough suppressants for their drug content. A ten-bag cup of valerian tea provides a Valium effect. But soon they are doing crack. As Chris rationalizes, it's "interesting" that they are "using again but integrating it into our lives." The "integrating" turns into dominance when they stop having sex.

One poetic montage intercuts their doing crack at home with their sitting stoned at a movie. The music evokes Hitchcock's *Vertigo*, in which a man's obsession destroys his fantasy woman. Chris initially tells Silvio and Tony that his new *goomah* is—"between us"—a black woman named Kaisha. He has not brought her around because of Paulie's "racial bullshit." By titling the episode "Kaisha," Chase emphasizes the characters' falseness, especially the phantom family bliss of the last shot.

Chris drifts from Julianna when he remembers how his "sacred oath" to the Family was supposed to give him the "higher power" or moral strength he couldn't get from his recovery groups. He denies her intuition he is leaving her, but he opts to follow her to an AA meeting instead of driving together. "I'm not a fucking parking spot," Julianna insisted, but when she took Chris and drugs, she abandoned control. As Chris returns to Kelli, the gangster creed that requires a *goomah* guides him back to his wife.

Chris tells Tony of his sexual relationship with Julianna—when they are no longer having sex. Tony is equally false in his reply: "I don't give a fuck. Do what you want with her." He tells Melfi he is angry that his "reward"—"I do not betray my wife"—is that "My fuckin turkey neck of a nephew ends up with his dick in" Julianna instead of his. Melfi applauds the new restraint on his appetites: "You don't have to eat every dish of rigatoni. You don't have to fuck every female you meet." But Tony's fidelity is now due to Julianna's rejection. When he notes his attraction to a certain type—"Dark complexion, smart, they smell a little bit, of money"—the latter detail signifies the class he craves. It also supplants the allure of danger or madness, admitting Melfi, as he continues to come "to hang out with you. Cause nothing ever changes for the therapy part."

For all Phil's family honor, he is taking his blond housekeeper to their tryst—"There's something I've got to get straight between us"—when the shop is blown up. His wife Patty's assurance—"God loves you"—is less comforting than Tony's blessing, criminal spoils. In their sentimental memory of last Christmas, Phil is still disgusted to recall Vito playing the piano for his daughter's "Oh Holy Night."

As Phil's heart condition initially masquerades as gas, Carmine Junior provides a verbal form of false pretences in his malapropisms at his "meeting of minds." That term avoids "the inclement negative implications" of "sit-down." "Certain incidents have expired lately. . . . Reasons I will discern in time. . . . A pint of blood costs more than a gallon of gold." It proves contagious, as in Tony's agreement, "Let the past be bygones," and Phil calling the East Indian doctor "Aryan prick." Here, language rings as palpably false as the characters' claims of redemption.

Perhaps the TV show about Lincoln summarizes the false peace throughout the episode. As a commentator remarks, "For some people, depression is a form of forced introversion." In varying degrees, most of the characters in this episode respond to depression. Phil's (perhaps guilt-induced) heart attack, Chris and Julianna reverting to drugs, Carmela's fleeting defence of Adriana, Tony's relapse, AJ adjusting to an adult job and relationship—all take different views into themselves to deal with depression.

The final shot's Christmas spirit is also undercut in its exclusions. The Jewish Julianna admits to habitual alienation. So, too, the two Arabs' season greetings to Tony, which he receives uncomfortably at the Bada Bing bar. There, Paulie recalls being distracted by a sexual partner's Santa hat.

Against this grain, Bobby Bacalla returns to Junior the cash he sent him but the ungrateful, Junior tweaks him about Tony: "He's still up on his cross, huh?" To command rather than to give gratitude, Junior slips the money to a ward orderly: "One hand washes the other." In context, the line suggests Pilate's and Lady Macbeth's guilt more than reciprocal service of Christmas spirit.

Nonetheless, there is hope of transformation. Although Meadow has not come home for the holidays, she has a warm phone exchange with Tony ("Love to Finn, huh?"). The episode's most genuinely warm scene may be Agent Harris's conversation with Tony over a Satriale sandwich. For once, Harris not Tony eats and Harris not Tony knows what is really happening—Phil's plan to attack him. Working in the anti-terrorist squad in Afghanistan, Harris also knows about illusions of peace: "Christmas is always potentially our busy season." To Tony's unprecedented "Thanks," Harris responds, "It's Christmas." On the one hand, Harris's intervention underlines Tony's vulnerability. On the other, these antagonists' new camaraderie once again confirms the possibility of character improvement.

More dramatic is AJ's evolution into a caring, responsible young man. Blanca initiates a date by giving him her phone number: "I left the last one off. If you want to find me, you got to work for it." On their first date, they watch *The 40-Year-Old Virgin* on TV, which reflects on both of them venturing into a new kind of relationship.

When the rowdy teens outside waken her baby, her previous lover—like Tony—"used to kick their asses." But AJ goes to his trunk for—instead of a gun or a baseball bat—his new expensive bicycle. When he buys them off with it, he both sets aside the vehicles of childhood and prefers a peaceful negotiation over Soprano violence. In his willingness to appear a "loser," AJ rejects Tony's habit of intimidation, which even Carmela has adopted. AJ's new maturity contrasts to how Chris first justified having a *goomah* when his wife is pregnant: "The playground's closed. A man has his needs." Chris's rationalization leaves him a child, while AJ matures.

The parents try to accommodate AJ. Tony tempers Carmela's concern that Blanca is ten years older than their son and a Puerto Rican: "Dominican. Maybe. At least she's a Catholic." More to the point, AJ bought her an expensive necklace with his own job money instead of drawing on his father's five-finger discount and Chris's compulsive "deal." After Blanca did AJ's "W-4—the Withholding" form when he joined the company, AJ has stopped withholding his emotions. In contrast, Chris refuses to share even at AA: "You learn as much from others."

At the Christmas dinner, AJ's evident comfort with both Blanca and her three-year-old, Hector, contrasts to the falseness in the other family relationships there, like Chris's with Kelli, Janice's with Bobby Jr., Carmela's father's absence or lateness, and Tony's chill toward Chris: "Are you going to hog all the ice?" Tony's son and his protégé Chris are natural contrasts, especially in how they reflect Tony. Where AJ establishes a new character of responsibility and commitment, as Tony was this season prompted to do, Chris, like Tony, backslides into his own destruction, returning to his marriage for the Christmas family show.

Conclusion I
(2002)

In the beginning are the credits.

The same montage opens every episode in all five seasons of *The Sopranos*. Its familiarity breeds comfort. The same song, the same images—the same intro provides the assurance of meeting an old friend. As we relax into the familiar title sequence, we're set up for the episode's surprises.

In addition, that ritual sequence has its own "content," its own meaning as it reflects the shows it prefaces. It collects meaning from the three seasons' experience. Basically, the visuals tell the same story as the title montage of our other great television-family series, *The Simpsons*: Good old Dad drives home from work. But where the cartoon series intercuts Homer's trip with his family's activities, here the focus is on Tony's drive. All we see is him and what he sees. Also, Tony drives from New York City to New Jersey, from the familiar crime-film setting into this show's unique territory. But the montage is not a literal route. It would take a "huge circle to get to all those places," director Henry Bronchtein remarks in his commentary on the Season II DVD (disc 3).

The first shot is up to the lights of the Lincoln Tunnel ceiling. Metaphorically, we emerge from a depth, a darkness that has been lit. From our experience of the series, that light represents the exposure of the Id or the suppressed impulses of our outlaw spirit. Literally and figuratively, the tunnel brings our hero from the underworld. The tunnel's artificial light sanitizes even its Freudian depth and makes it feel safe.

After we're directed to the New Jersey Turnpike we see Tony at the toll station, paying for his ticket to ride. In context, this shows him following the rules, paying his toll dutifully. He may take a bit of dangerous liberty—using both hands to light his cigar while driving—but so far our hero breaks no rules. According to director Allen Coulter's commentary on the Season II DVD (disc 4), Tony was intentionally veiled in a thick burst of cigar smoke and the cigar was intended to suggest "the prow on a ship" leading him home.

Most of the montage is what Tony sees. He looks down at his pinky-ringed hand on the steering wheel—and sees that it is good. He looks at the city reflected in a passing hubcap—and sees that it is good. What he sees outside his car-window must also strike him as good: a series of industrial sites, with long bridges across the abysses, smokestacks, familiar business logos, a statue of a giant worker, a Pizzaland store. Amid these emblems of business and industry there are quick glimpses of the Statue of Liberty and a church. From Tony's perspective this is an assuring survey of his kingdom, the world of blue-collar capitalism.

Especially as he passes his Satriale's Pork Store, where so much of his business is conducted—meetings, butchering, cold storage—and the site of his most shaping (that is, traumatic) boyhood experience. This shot disturbs the comfort of that montage; it connotes Tony's psychological vulnerability. That's where Tony saw his father chop off the debtor's finger and where his own panic attacks began.

This negative shot invites other questions about the montage contents. For example, where is the natural world? All we see is the man-made: factories, icons, bridges. The only animal we see is the fake pig atop Satriale's—a parody of animal life. Without vegetation and natural comfort Tony's industrial empire seems a wasteland. We only see other people in one quick shot, four young men walking abreast. Whether to work or from work or without work, they are a feeble balance against this non-human characterization of Tony's world. (Bronchtein remarks that shots of the principal characters were dropped from the montage.)

The human presence is implied when Tony passes through a series of residential neighborhoods. But we still don't see any people—just rows of uniform, modest houses, of diminishing class and comfort. They start with some traditional old-money homes and conclude with small, cramped bungalows. From them we cut to Tony's neighborhood, North Caldwell, with trees—and space—and the manorial scale of the new-money flash. It's a jolt to pass from the shabby bungalows to Tony's mansion. Aptly, Tony drives *up* to his home, as he leaves behind the drab, cramped, industrial world. Driving home from work, Tony takes us from the wasteland to the pocket of luxury that wasteland supports.

Although the meaning of those visuals may be subtle, the soundtrack has a clear and explicit impact. A3—a.k.a. Alabama 3—is a British pop group given new prominence by the show's signature adoption of their song, "Woke up This Morning." We get the first five verses at the start of each episode.

The lyrics fit Tony so well they could have come from his horoscope. He wakes up each morning effectively to live by the gun—even when others do his whacking. Tony was born under a bad sign (given Livia, Johnny-Boy, Uncle Junior) and he has a blue moon in his eyes—both that rascally gleam and the kind of good luck that a gangster maybe gets once in a blue moon. So he is looking good and feeling fine—and about to delve into his shame.

If his Papa did tell him about right and wrong he got the direction signs wrong. The Sopranos' value system seems a "world turned upside down." And as Tony's business does "turn shit green" (Massive's criterion for music in I, 10), when garbage provides his fortune, Tony has "that shotgun shine." As gangsters go, Tony is rather high caliber—though not a big bore.

As well as the lyrics, the voices set the tone. With A3 the Blues indeed walk us into their town. Their voices are low, rasping, "beat" in the 1950s sense of life-weary, like a trio of Tom Waitses. As they cling to the bass line, even their buoyant imagery hangs low.

The song ends as abruptly as the low-rent neighborhood. The last sound we hear is precisely ambiguous. It could be the phonograph needle ripped off in mid-note—where the pertinent *Public Enemy* ends with a record spinning after the song is over. Or it could be that other kind of forty-five—with a silencer. That's the gun in the show's brilliant logo, where the letter R—or the verb "are," to be—is replaced by a pistol. For the Sopranos, "Guns R Us." If Carmela *is* Tony's life, so are guns.

■   ■   ■

Though an extended TV series can deepen characterization and develop searching, shifting relationships, the industry has preferred to keep the formula secure, the plots simple, the characters shallow. In that respect, television has not changed much since Parnell Roberts quit the successful *Bonanza* series in protest against its static characterization (after which the show thrived and Roberts disappeared).

Occasionally, a series episode may rise to provoke a larger theme. Lucy, overwhelmed by the chocolate packing machine, articulates to the Chaplin-esque satire of modern man overwhelmed by modernity. The death of Chuckles the Clown raised *The Mary Tyler Moore Show* to a circumspect anatomy of the function of comedy and of our paradoxical emotions, when an absurd death provokes laughter and its poignancy frees tears. Sometimes a show may prove of prophetic form, like the self-referentiality of Ernie Kovacs, Sid Caesar, and *The Burns and Allen Show*.

But what is rare—perhaps unprecedented—is a series that springs from such a rounded and profound conception of its characters and experience that a single episode apprehends multiple views and themes. Here are characters so full that their behavior can be shocking, completely unpredictable, and yet completely consistent with the character as subtly established—like the Zen Janice's murder of Richie. The character ambivalence that *The Sopranos* brought television compares to the complexities that Shakespeare added to the simple dramatic structure of Lyly. *The Sopranos* may be a phenomenally successful television series. But—to twist Robert Burns—art is art for all that. For all its broad popularity, *The Sopranos* is a work of art for the ages.

Because of the show's strong central vision, there are innumerable links between the episodes. For example, in III, 3, when AJ is appointed defensive captain of his freshman football team, he faints. At the time it seems funny, especially since he only joined the team to wear the cool jersey and rode the bench for most of his first game, before he was blessed with a fumble recovery. But an implicit irony lurks behind the joke: His father has been fainting from panic attacks. But the incident stays a joke. The episode is recalled 10 weeks later. Only when AJ faints at the prospect of military school are the Sopranos informed about his football faint. Then they are properly angry that the school did not tell them. The school again put its (and their football team's) interests ahead of the student's and his family's. For the viewer, the III, 3, incident is not fully defined until III, 13.

In its every specific, *The Sopranos* turns conventional materials to expressive use. As we have often noted, the music comments on the action and themes. The series follows on the Scorsese gangster films' period pop soundtrack and Coppola's incorporation of Italian songs and opera. The key music—the opening and end-credit numbers—either encapsulates or ironically reflects on its themes. It builds on *GoodFellas*, which opens with Tony Bennett's "Rags to Riches," and concludes with Sid Vicious's deviant "My Way."

The show pays lip service to institutional religion, but deflates it. The Christian church in particular is characterized as weak, especially when its most respectable officer—the black priest in III, 12—is blatantly insensitive to Carmela's moral needs. Carmela's Father Phil and Paulie's "Protector" Father Felix are weak, secular, and of suspect dedication. The strongest religious spokesman is the Jewish psychiatrist, Dr. Krakower—with his Old Testament values and intellect—though he is balanced by Dr. Sam Reis, the ludicrous Jewish therapist who counsels Melfi's family.

That brings us to the question of the show's negative stereotyping of Italian-Americans. Does it? No more than it stereotypes black leaders as hustlers (for example, the Reverend James, Massive Genius) as often as solid citizens (Officer Wilmore, Jackie's chess-playing hosts). Or "the desert people," a.k.a. the Jews, as sneaky grubs, such as Jackie Jr.'s Ecstasy salesman, Dov Ginsberg, who leaves when his Reserve Unit is called up in Israel (III, 8). Even the Orthodox, Talmud–spouting Teittlemans squabble over the matching seediness of their marriage and motel. And all those—effective—Jewish lawyers. Even the warm and wise Hesh may have exploited his black singers.

As *The Sopranos* takes satiric aim at the moral ambivalence of our times, no ethnic group is sacrosanct. Certainly not the WASP-ish authorities in the high school, military school, or the professions (for example, Dr. Kennedy). In each community the series depicts, one can identify a moral ideal—Dr. Krakower, the senior Rev. James, Dr. Melfi—and the myriad pretenders whose rationalization and respectability make them dangerous. The series is a satiric representation of contemporary sin and folly—regardless of race, religion, color, and creed.

Penultimately, a word about the language. It is often delightfully rascally. If we are critical of Tony's treatment of Noah Tannenbaum, there's a guilty pleasure in his imaginative insults. Noah's mistreatment of Caitlin and Meadow proves that this series does not allow us easy moral judgments. Everything and everyone is ambivalent. So Noah's unfortunate behavior is paralleled by the exuberance of Tony's improper language for him: Oreo, the Hasidic Homie, Buckwheat.

Nor is the wall-to-wall profanity gratuitous. It provides an authenticity that any Bowdlerizing would destroy. The profanity provides an energy and insouciance that reflect the self-assertiveness of its characters' outlaw lives. They talk as they live, beyond the norm—and often the pale. From Jason's "motherfuckers" (after his mother's rape) to the somnambulant Aaron's sanctimonious "motherjumpin,' " the profanity plays sometimes poetic characterization and wit. Here Jason is honest and passionate, Aaron an opportunistic deadhead, and their language exposes them. The profanity tends to speak truth, unvarnished. Tony properly warns Junior that Carmela may cut him "another asshole" (II, 13), but Nils's euphemism—"I tore her a new one" (I, 1)—is a limp lie, because he didn't really excoriate the restaurant hostess, nor get her to seat him.

Finally: What about Tony? What are we to make of a show that warms us toward a fat, middle-aged man whose character falls off the scales of the heroic? He lies, he is unfaithful, he is insensitive and brutish toward his children, and he breaks most laws for what is a disgustingly excessive living. Oh, and he kills people.

First, this is not an amoral show. Portraying an immoral society should alert our moral vigilance. Its every sympathetic transgression is a moral test for the viewer. We have to struggle to upright our moral balance against the hero's sympathetic pull. In shading its moral spectrum so finely the show provides a rigorous exercise for our relativist age.

But *The Sopranos* goes even further. It humanizes the Other—what people don't acknowledge in themselves. We may prefer to think that the mobsters are—like Fitzgerald's rich—not like the rest of us. They readily do what we recoil from the idea of doing, what our every reflex of education and self-respect compel us to abjure. Or they do what we wish we had the *stugots* to do. In either case, they are still human. They are us.

The show's refusal to demonize its villains may perhaps be its moral benchmark. We can even empathize with the vile Richie Aprile for his touching sentimentality and the dignity of his Old School values. The scatterbrain Janice has a wolverine's compulsion to survive, in a world that is at once too sordid for her aspiration and too full of crackpot temptations to allow her rational growth. Even for the vicious Livia we can muster sympathy for her terror at being neglected, alone, hated, the very fate that her selfishness feeds.

And so to Tony. The man struggles to do his best, to meet his responsibilities to his family and to the Family, to keep his home and business wheels oiled and spinning and rewarding. He may not have our code but he has his. Tony is the best of men and the worst of men. He reminds us that whatever enemies we have, however threatening, if our antagonist is a human we have more in common than we have to fear. Indeed, what we may most fear is that disturbing part of ourselves that we project on an enemy. In restoring humanity to its villains lies perhaps the greatest spin of the show's dramatic irony and its greatest service to the viewer, both in self-knowledge and compassion.

With its rich style and the substance that constantly serves, *The Sopranos* is the rare television show that rewards multiple viewings. Other series have been enjoyable in rerun—*The Honeymooners, I Love Lucy, Dragnet, Alfred Hitchcock Presents, The Fugitive, The Prisoner, Star Trek, Seinfeld*—but that is usually to reexperience a familiar pleasure or to catch a missed episode. Re-viewing *The Sopranos* provides different rewards. It reveals new meanings, new connections, new ironies, new depths, or delights on each viewing. Happily, as it appeared when VHS was ensconced and DVD emerging, viewers can buy their own set, to backtrack or to replay to reconsider its riches. Perhaps this potential for re-viewing, for "reading" a television series over and over, like a Dickens novel, encouraged the producers' ambition to make this show so dense and to amplify the cross-references as the seasons proceeded.

What effect will *The Sopranos* have on North American television? The jury will be out on that for quite a while. The most obvious effects will probably be a loosening of the language, perhaps an increase in frontal female nudity, and an increase both in continuing series and in gangster programs. But that is small gnocchi. The big difference that this series will make—if we are lucky—is that the networks might realize there is a significant audience out there that craves adult drama, with sophisticated themes and treatment, with rounded, surprising characters and—above all—with moral complexity. They want to be provoked, not numbed. If that proves to be the effect of *The Sopranos*, then all those fictitious corpses and whacked television conventions will have died for a noble cause.

Conclusion II
(2003)

The fourth season opened, after a 16-month hiatus, to HBO's largest audience in its 30-year history, for the first time outdrawing the broadcast networks. The 13.4 million viewers topped the previous season's record premiere, 11.3 million. Though the finale audience dipped to 12.5 million, Season Four viewership averaged 11 million per week, up 22 percent over the third. More importantly, David Chase announced the show would return for a fifth season. In effect, then, we are in the midst of an unprecedented 65-episode drama. This five-season drama has the formal structure of a five-act play, which we can now make preliminary stabs at defining.

In his introduction to the *Sopranos* scripts, David Chase describes how the show is developed. He outlines story arcs for the season, which are then broken into thirteen episodes. Each episode interweaves three or sometimes four strands, centering on two. Whoever writes or directs the show, Chase governs the entire process, including the final editing. Obviously, each episode is subtly structured, with intro, climax, and denouement, balancing the interests of a continuing story with the stand-alone episode. Beyond that, each season is also significantly structured.

Season One introduces the characters and their various insecurities, with Tony the primary focus. After his opening squirm before the female statue, the season explores his relationships with Livia, Carmela, Meadow, Irina, his phantom Isabella, all guided by Dr. Melfi. Chase explores the proper nature of manliness, especially in relation to the feminine. The theme, implicit in the Sopranos' name (the feminine range of singing) and in Big Pussy's, makes Artie Bucco an extremely significant supporting character, as he struggles to define his integrity, torn between his wife Charmaine's moral values and Tony's. With Carmela so dependent upon Tony and Melfi professionally non-judgemental, Charmaine stands alone as consistently critical of the gang's values and conduct. If Artie is a key site for the battle between a brutish and a sensitive maleness, so is Uncle Junior in "Boca" (I, 9) and so are three "children" we watch grow through pains and temptations to their various maturity, AJ, Meadow, and Christopher.

The season moves from familial dysfunctions to the warm refuge from the storm at the end. The season's upbeat family union significantly occurs at Artie's, with Charmaine's reluctant allowance. The season's most dramatic episodes, "College," which interweaves Tony's family feeling and Family brutishness, and "Boca," which parallels Coach Hauser's license with Uncle Junior's self-reduction, are symmetrical, the fifth and ninth episodes, that lead up to the primary climax, Tony's assassination survival and his Isabella fantasy in I, 12. In the pivotal middle episode (I, 7), Tony remembers watching his father's arrest and Livia learns about Tony's therapy, key moments in the family's treachery.

In Season Two the central theme is how Tony internalizes his therapy and his failure to come clean through it. His multiple purge in II, 13, is an internalized parallel to the storm of I, 13. The major plot thrusts are metaphors for his self-examination. In confronting Richie he confronts his own most macho, violent nature and in Annelisa a female equivalent, in power, libido and will. As Christopher survives the acting and scriptwriting temptations and his near-death to recommit himself to Tony's world, Tony refuses to leave his old ways and places his mob duty ahead of his love for Pussy.

The central episode (II, 7) centers on Tony's vulnerability, with Pussy forced to wear a wire, Chris tempted to do a *GoodFellas* if not a Henry Hill on Tony, and AJ discovering Existentialism and other dangerous driving. In parallel scenes around this pivot, Carmela argues against Angie's plan to divorce Pussy but starts to entertain the idea (II, 4) and Carmela is tempted by the romantic paperhanger Vic Musto (II, 10). The common theme is emphasized by the episodes' place in the season, three before/after the midpoint.

A parallel placement between two seasons, the sixth episode in Seasons Two and Three, emphasizes Meadow's significance. In "The Happy Wanderer" (II, 6) her College Night success is directly due to Tony's plundering of her friend's father, David Scatino. This is also the point of "University" (III, 6), which intercuts Meadow's college success with the tragic life of Tracee, Ralphie's Bada Bing stripper. The parallel placement of the episodes emphasizes their shared theme. Whether she knows and likes it or not, Meadow's comfort (like Carmela's) derives from Tony's crime.

Season Three increases the number of violent climaxes, beginning with Tony's childhood flashbacks (III, 3). Chase explores how a boy grows into what kind of man, so the doomed Jackie Jr. joins AJ and Chris as Tony's "sons," all shadowed by Tony's scarred upbringing. In Episodes 4–6 we get Melfi's rape and Janice's assault, Bobby Baccala Sr.'s last hit and death, and Tracee's murder. The mid-season episode (III, 7) offers two responses to this violent ethos in the form of contrasting doctors. Corrado's Dr. Kennedy is modern, self-serving, unscrupulous, unreliable. In contrast, Melfi's mentor, the hard, incorruptible Dr. Krakower, stands solid against the three episodes of violence. As Tony's ensuing relationships with Gloria and Jackie Jr. follow Kennedy's easier path, their consequences validate Krakower.

In Season Four the middle episode (IV, 7) starts Tony's downfall. Here he beats Assemblyman Zellman, setting off the chain of events that lead to Carmela leaving him. He also starts his HUD scam, which causes his Family problems with Johnny Sack and Carmine. In addition to this pivot, every third episode seems heightened. "Columbus Day" (IV, 3) focuses on individual responsibility, from Ralphie abandoning Rosalie to the ethnic minority groups' historic sensitivities. In IV, 6, Tony is struck by Gloria's suicide and then, despite his campaign to be non-toxic, by Artie's suicide attempt. In IV, 9, Justin's accident affects Ralphie profoundly, but his burning of Pie-O-My drives Tony to kill him. In IV, 12, Paulie kills Minn, Tony's war with Carmine reaches new peaks, Furio departs, and Meadow's family dinner and Eloise tea redefine her relationship with Carmela. These dramatic episodes' rhythm drives the season, however topped by the Sopranos' split in IV, 13.

Overall, Dr. Krakower's significance increases when we note that III, 7, is also the exact midpoint of the five-season drama. From this point on, Carmela cannot say that she has not been told that she is enabling her monster criminal husband and compromising her moral integrity. Indeed, her climactic break from Tony (IV, 13) properly begins with Krakower's exposure of her rationalization of Tony's goodness and his exemplary rejection of her tainted money.

Though Tony is clearly the central figure of the drama, its major issue is how he is regarded. "So," the show continually tests us, "what do you think of our Tony?" Our response betrays our moral strength. Tony reads us by how we read him. Meadow and Carmela grow into Chase's perspective on Tony, when they define his vileness and grow to detach themselves, notwithstanding their affection. Where Charmaine remains Tony's fixed moral critic, Meadow grows into her awareness and responsibility. From cleaning up after her party at Livia's (II, 3), she grows to her volunteer legal aid work at college. In contrast, at the end of Season IV AJ still prefers Tony's discipline over Carmela's. Meadow's maturing echoes Mary's (Sofia Coppola) in *The Godfather Part III*, but Meadow is the more solid and independent of Mary's professional functions in her family foundation. Meadow clearly functions better outside her family than Mary is shown to do. (If Tony is slated to suffer Michael Corleone's tragedy, his loss will likelier be AJ.)

Ultimately Carmela's rejection of Tony (IV, 13) is prompted by a combination of his over-stepping with the one-legged Svetlana, Meadow's enviable maturity, and Carmela's heartbreaking loss of Furio. Leaving Tony for Furio might be a leap from one gangster to another. But Carmela leaves Tony in the absence of Furio, not to him. Moreover, Furio has been visibly changed by his experience of Carmela, especially since the death of his life-loving and love-loving father. Furio's jaundiced, then enraged, view of Tony (IV, 12) suggests that loving Carmela has converted him to fidelity and honor and even stilled his violence. Furio is the only male character to accept transformation by a woman, to have accepted the feminine instead of merely embracing women. In contrast, Artie disintegrates after leaving his marriage to Charmaine (though they still work the Vesuvio together, after their eruption). Jackie Jr.'s tragic error was to use Meadow to enter the Soprano world instead of as his way out. Except for the rehab, which Tony imposed, Christopher continues to resist Adriana's saving sentiments and instead draws her into his self-destruction. And overall, Tony rejects Melfi's wisdom and processes of self-examination even when he was taking her therapy. As the only male character who opens himself to the feminine, the new, improved and worthy Furio finds his salvation in Carmela and is the first to leave Tony.

In short, Tony is the central character of the drama, but Carmela and Meadow embody its primary theme: our problematic and self-revealing response to him. The series structure shifts our emphasis from Tony to the women in his family who learn to judge and to reject him (for the proper, not Livia's, reasons). In the five-season structure, as Dr. Krakower awakens Carmela's conscience at the mid-point (III, 7), Furio is introduced at the quarter-mark (II, 4) and Carmela first admits her love for him at the three-quarter mark (IV, 10). Similarly, there is the possibility of moral regeneration at the one-third point, where Chris comes out of his coma and Paulie is spooked to contemplate his Hell (II, 9), and at the two-thirds point, where Gloria's suicide prompts Tony's last attempt to overcome his toxic nature (IV, 6). But in both scenes the men refuse to reform after their experiences and so restore their amoral, unfeeling veneers.

Notwithstanding my definition of the series' five-act/season structure, David Chase and HBO have agreed to a sixth season of *The Sopranos* to run for 10 episodes. As Chase told the *Daily News,* "I'd planned out an arc for season five that would have ended the show. But as we're getting into it, we're finding there's a lot more material." And so the show's original five season/act arc is developing an epilogue.

Speaking at the Banff International Television Festival on June 9, 2003, Chase recalled that nobody starting the show had any inkling of its success. "We did it for ourselves," not for any imagined audience, and the principals on and behind the show are still fascinated with the material. Its audience has attended long enough to transcend the appeal of voyeurism. Now "a lot of people relate" to Tony's desire, which in Chase's view is not for redemption but to be liked, to ease his pain, to figure out his role in the complexity of modern life, and above all to serve his family—and his extended Family, despite the gangsters' juicily "warped point of view." Chase singled out Gandolfini's contribution to his character and to the show. The complicating factor of Tony's likableness saves *The Sopranos* from being simply a morality play.

The Sopranos continues to engage, provoke, and impress. David Chase has avoided the temptation to coast on any formula or just to replay successful strategies. Instead he delivers intense, nuanced episodes—and seasons. As in our richest literary and dramatic texts, the characterization is so complex and the interaction of elements so variable, casting new light as we view them from different points of view, that this work also gleams inexhaustible as life.

Conclusion III
(2005)

The fifth season opens on the decaying colors of autumn and closes on the freeze of winter. The first scene is a montage of the fall wind blowing through Tony's empty estate; the last leaves him in Carmela's refuge from the snow. Had David Chase not opted for an epilogue (yet to come), the ending of V, 13, would have been an appropriate conclusion to the five-act/season drama. Where in the series' first shot Tony cowers nervously before the Feminine in Dr. Melfi's office (I, 1), in the last he returns to Carmela's unseen solicitude.

But the feminine—whether in Tony or around him—has not won. Tony's macho callousness resists the understanding for which his therapy has struggled. Even Dr. Melfi, when her advice allows for Tony B.'s murder, shrinks to Tony's well-meaning enabler. He has completely subverted the feminine values of sensitivity and responsibility. Consequently, his victory in V, 13, is more shameful and bitter than a relief. Its high cost only extends his unfortunate career. Tony's frigid soul is imaged in that winter and his final discontent. Denied either the comic hero's victory or the tragic hero's redeeming death, he continues his death-in-life.

The fifth season chronicles the failure of Tony's nearest and dearest to escape his spirit. Carmela returns to be his most comfortable enabler. Their children ripen into his self-restricting rationalization. Christopher sacrifices his devoted lover and his own freedom to Tony's *omerta*. Most dramatically—and touching—of all, cousin Tony B., who tried the straight life, won a good woman's love, and reconnected with his twin sons, is defeated because he can't handle even *good* luck. When his windfall revives his taste for easy wealth, he loses his higher purpose. For both Tonys, misdirected success signifies failure. As the macho triumphs again, all its participants, men and women, are reduced. When Tony disappears into his house in the last shot, the *casa nostra* stands secured—from internecine warfare, against the fumbling officers of the law, but also against the alternative values of responsibility, self-respect, and humanity. Tony's survival is even for him a very mixed blessing.

With Carmela having left Tony, the fifth season was poised on the question of her freedom, both marital and moral. How would she live it? Could she sustain it? Would Furio return? He doesn't. The Old School killer who rediscovered his fertile heart disappears into hiding. Tony's memory of him is hotter than Carmela's.

Instead, Carmela's function is amplified by Tony B. Where earlier seasons gave Tony vile antagonists—e.g., Richie, Ralphie—Tony B. is someone he loves, the cousin with whom he grew up and for whose imprisonment Tony feels responsible. He is also a positive figure, a man of principle, conscience, and self-awareness. By casting Steve Buscemi, Chase ensured Tony B.'s substance and sympathy. He leaves jail intent upon an honest career as a massage therapist. That is, *contra* Tony, he wants to make his life by rubbing people the *right* way. But his ball-breaking humor, especially at Tony's and Chris's expense, suggests he may not make the leap. His sensitivity is only relative, within the Sopranos' constraints. Like the freed Carmela, the educated Meadow, and the ambitious Chris, Tony B. tries to transcend Tony. But paid the wages of sin, he fails.

Oddly, the season's first episode is titled "Two Tonys," but Blundetto is only mentioned. The title seems more pertinent to the season's general plot thrust than to its first episode. It derives from Tony's false claim to Melfi that he has a kinder, gentler Tony for her. As those two Tonys are really just one, perhaps the season's two Tonys signify just one, as well. Tony and Tony B. can be read as complementary halves. As the sensitive, ambitious ex-con, Tony B. becomes the suppressed, feminine side of Tony S. But when Tony B. made the heist and went to jail, Tony S. because of his feminine side missed the heist and jail, but was sentenced to the longer strictures of Boss. When the Boss kills his beloved cousin, he erases his living reminder of his own suppressed softness. Thus, too, Tony smuggled out Tony B.'s sperm to plant the twins. In their contrary ways of rubbing people and their mutual envy, each represents the road the other did not take. The only difference is Tony's power and attendant evil.

Indeed, the season's primary theme is the power of evil and the evil of power. The character with the most power, Tony chafes under the responsibility it imposes, especially when it requires he whack Tony B. But even this tragic murder turns absurd, when it shows Tony most selflessly dutiful and (in the gang's perverse logic) principled—in an action that is empty, inexcusable, and unnecessary.

Notwithstanding his Gleason imitations, Tony B. seems rather to live out Silvio's Michael Corleone *(Godfather III)*: "Just when I thought I was out, they pulled me back in." Tony B. may seem destroyed by the gang's arbitrary codes, beginning with his honor-bound avenging of Angelo Garepe and ending with his duty-bound murder by Tony. Or he may seem to collapse under external pressures: the losses of his daughter and his marriage, his twin sons' needs and his envy of Tony's grand life, and his despair at prejudice. But all that is Soprano-style rationalization. Tony B. crumbles because he is weak. Not even his generous career, his good woman's love, and his successful studies can counter the allure of easy money to which his windfall converts him. For all these external excuses, the real problem is his character. Tony B. lacks the strength of character to remain the family's white sheep.

That responsibility also applies to Adriana, Christopher, Carmela, and Tony, who explicitly asks: "Why the fuck does this shit always happen to me?" (V, 11). As Janice learned in Anger Management, "*It* doesn't make you mad. *You* make you mad" (V, 10). In fortune as in rage, these characters are their own victim, not any *its* or *theirs*. Good citizen Bob Wegler proves how easy it is to slip into the Sopranos' bullying—and how hard it is to make amends or to extricate oneself.

So the problems Carmela blames on her marriage are in her. She can't escape Tony's compromises because she has absorbed them. Wegler finds her as manipulative and unprincipled as she considers Tony to be. Then, when she can't counteract Tony's stratagems, rather than either continue her fight or surrender her luxury, she returns to her marriage. When Carmela takes Tony back out of resignation, not love or moral duty, her action resembles Tony B.'s relapse into crime and—more disturbingly—Finn's fatigued proposal to Meadow.

In their last chat (V, 13) Tony reminds Johnny Sack that the gang's whole objective is to feed and to provide for their children, for their future. For his part, Tony's legacy seems irredeemably poisoned. His children are growing into their father's ways. As Tony failed to save Jackie Aprile Jr. from his father's life, we catch AJ excited by violence and drawn to easy money in event/waste management. Meadow matures from her eyes-wide-open adolescence into her mother's willful denial. Meadow rationalizes the Family code as she draws Finn into Tony's world. Finn may avert Vito's seduction but not the double snare of Tony's generosity and Meadow's charm. As Carmela's cousin Brian was inveigled before, Finn is here. His proposal resigns him to Tony's luxury and moral lassitude.

So, too, the alienated Christopher is finally ready to "do a Henry Hill" (the spectre Tony raised in I, 1) by joining Adriana in the Witness Protection Program. Like the hero of *GoodFellas,* Chris has always wanted to be a gangster and he plans to write his memoirs. But when a glimpse of an ordinary small life warns him off, he betrays Adriana instead of Tony and saves/dooms himself.

In the characters' inability to leave the Tony ethos, Season Five dramatizes the grip of evil. By the old proverb, who touches pitch is forever defiled. Characters who try to escape lapse back into its thrall. New innocents are drawn in. Such is our own complicity with Tony that we relish the criminals' color, energy, and rakish delinquency, and we reject the more dutiful characters, like the Feds' snitches and the surrendering Carmine Jr., as traitors and a wimp, respectively. While bartender Georgie makes his break, we have yet to see whether he will stay free. When the other gunsels waver in their fidelity (V, 13), their detachment from Tony is only strategic, not a rejection of his values or a denial of his power. Even as Tony personifies the power of evil and the evil of power, he remains their most pathetic victim. For five seasons he has wrestled his demons. His every success deepens his failure. He can't escape his own corrupt power.

Only Charmaine Bucco remains uncontaminated. As the fifth season focuses on Tony's acolytes, she is largely marginalized until Tony briefly contemplates courting her. But she remains the drama's one clear ideal, the only character who resists Tony's temptation, rewards, and guilt. When Arty moves into Tony's house (V, 3), he is not just renewing their broken friendship but confirming his rejection of Charmaine's alternative. As Coach Molinari remembers Artie as the worst delinquent (V, 11), perhaps Charmaine saved him from a criminal life. He failed to let her secure him from it later. In his poolside sleep through Tony's seduction, Artie is in suspended moral animation. Among the minor characters, perhaps Artie best embodies the drama's major themes: his failure to accept responsibility for his moral choices; his confused criteria for honor, manliness, and humanity; the conflict between serving oneself and serving others, the dangerous models from popular culture; and the impediments to self-knowledge.

In this light, the season's core lies at its structural center, episodes 6, 7, and 8. In V, 6: "Sentimental Education," Carmela discovers with Wegler's rejection that she cannot flee her inner Tony, and Tony B. abandons his reform and reverts to Soprano. That establishes the season's thesis, the inescapability of Tony's evil/power. Episode 7: "In Camelot" proposes an antithesis, the mythologies in which we seek refuge from our embarrassing and disappointing realities. In particular, Fran and Tony cultivate the JFK myth for nostalgic refuge, and both deny their Johnny-Boy's betrayals. Episode 8: "Marco Polo" synthesizes the despair and the delusion. Carmela and Tony B. pragmatically use rationalizations or personal myths for a workable compromise by which to live. From Hugo's birthday party, Carmela finds reasons to take Tony back, Tony B. reasons to freelance against Tony's authority. In order to tolerate their situations both characters need a process of moral numbing and self-deception.

In addition—and like Flaubert's *Sentimental Education*—the fifth season also addresses the particular political tensions of its time. Of course, the idea of reading America through its films lies behind Carmela's-club study of America's greatest movies (V, 2). The season's references to the Iraq war anxieties, politics, torture, and strategies of post 9/11 survival gather in explicitness and force. They begin with Rusty Millio's fallacious prediction: "We go all out, we steamroll right over John, and I predict the guys on the street in Brooklyn and Queens, they'll welcome us as fuckin' heroes. It'll be easy" (V, 4). Christopher paraphrases (presumably) President Bush to assure Adriana: "We're gonna mop up the floor with the whole fuckin' world" (V, 5). Johnny Sack blames his Vespa thwart on Al Qaeda (V, 10). Tony stops barely short of President Bush's "Those who are not with us are against us" (V, 13). These allusions expand Tony's moral struggles to suggest America's bedeviled attempt to respond to "this fucked-up day and age" (V, 13).

In this light, the Sopranos' lawbreaking might be read as the nation's retreat from its international obligations and from its commitment to established law. Tony's Old School ethic may speak for America's determination to define its own way independent of other nations and past agreements, extending its frontier independence from European traditions. But Tony has a rare recognition of his wider community when he realizes America's threat from terrorism (V, 10). For the first time, he feels responsible to a larger community than his self-serving gang. His motives may still be more selfish than altruistic, but for the first time he realizes the national danger in his license. The terrorists provide the "outside threat," like the doomed waiter who reunited the squabbling Paulie and Christopher (V, 1).

In the last episode, when Tony pauses for breath en route home, from the school steps we hear America's future in the children singing. In the executive community, their angelic choir is antithetical to the inner-city school that Junior visits (V, 3). These singers represent the future Tony tells Johnny the gang is dedicated to serve. But there is no connection between his life and their value. They are another world, as yet untouched by the Soprano ways. Tony is their threat, not their security. Worse, he and his are frozen out of that world, with no means of entry.

When Tony admits that his nation is threatened by the very practices that he has exploited—lax customs, government contracts to friends, an authority based on intimidation and force—he realizes not just America's vulnerability but his implication in it. In this light, perhaps his Family's successes, moral failures all, can be read as America's having compromised the difficult balance she undertook between two powerful but conflicting ideals. One is vaunted individualism. The other is the responsibility to her own and the world community. This tension plays throughout America's most characteristic popular film genres: the Western, the gangster, the musical. The individual talent must assert itself even beyond convention, but only insofar as it serves the collective—the frontier community, the city streets, the production, respectively.

Without the overriding commitment to the community good, America's Rugged Individualist blurs into Outlaw, Gangster, the Rampant Ego. In the James Cagney persona, for instance, that is the moral continuum between his antithetical *Public Enemy* and his *Yankee Doodle Dandy* (Michael Curtiz, 1942). In the archetypal *Shane* (George Stevens, 1953), the difference between the two blood-handed gunfighters is that the hero (Alan Ladd) volunteers to defend the farming community, whereas Jack Wilson (Jack Palance) has been bought unscrupulously to advance the corporate Rykers. As this myth lies at the heart of American culture, it provides the rhetoric of American politics. But not usually the practice, as politicians typically talk populist but walk corporate.

The Sopranos' power argues the nation's need for a justice system that is blind in its fairness, not in corruption, and a capitalism that serves the social structure below the CEO class. As Tony drew from the headlines to complain, "We don't have those Enron-type connections" (IV, 1). Here every shot of the broken Sal Vitro recalls the victims of the Nortel and Enron fiascos, *inter alia*, and the preferential profiteering of Vice President Cheney's former company, Haliburton, in Iraq. As the Sopranos reflect the ostensibly respectable professions, religion, capitalism, and politics, they personify a troubled America, made newly vulnerable by its combination of brute power and unquestioning certainty.

Again, this political reading of *The Sopranos* derives from the debate current around the season's first airing. These allusions will no doubt be less striking when viewed in the future, outside the election year, and when the headlines and phone-ins have moved on to new fears and embarrassments. In that future climate, *The Sopranos* will perhaps speak less to concerns around the identity of the nation than to issues of individual conscience. The art will return from the topical to the exploration of human nature, our gender roles and tensions, our vulnerability to media influence, and our slippery sense of responsibility.

Finally, we have become increasingly aware of our leaders as actors, who convey an affected image rather than a genuine self. As leading players in Western business, religion, and politics have revealed the gap between their professed values and their action, *The Sopranos* explores the interplay between actor and role. This theme is especially clear in both the dream and the real worlds of "The Test Dream" (V, 11). It also appears in the casting of celebrities as "themselves" at the Executive Card Game (V, 4). The theme is played comic when Uncle Junior thinks an episode of *Curb Your Enthusiasm*—a series that itself flirts with the ambiguous overlap of actor and character—is a scene from his life (V, 3). In Tony's dream (V, 11), Carmela tells Tony his life *is* TV. That is, as the symptomatic product of the culture's mythology, he is as realistic as JFK was mythic.

For all their pretense to Camelot (V, 7), the characters compulsively live out Scorsese's *GoodFellas*, despite its exposure of the gangster myth. Scorsese is so important to this drama that in a cameo (I, 2), he is Chris's hero, gaining easy entrance where Chris can't. The myriad film and TV references, and the pointed overlay of popular music (also after Scorsese), warn against living out a script that pretends integrity but offers corruption, that in the name of freedom and individualism primarily serves the captains—whether of industry, church, government, or other forms of gang power. For all Tony's rationalization and charm, his code is corrupt, selfish, irresponsible—and as an icon more dangerous today than ever. He *is* "this fucked-up day and age."

In the interplay of actor and role, persona and self, reality and myth, what these characters do undermines what they profess to do—and even what they think they are. They have lost their integrity. Consequently, their every success advances their disintegration. For a culture and characters who deny their moral responsibility are bent upon self-destruction. And they can't blame any script for their choices.

Appendix

Godfather to The Sopranos

Of the various influences that have fed into *The Sopranos*, the most important is Francis Ford Coppola's monumental *The Godfather* trilogy (1972, 1974, 1990). Though David Chase exalts *GoodFellas* for its comedy, brutality, and realism (Season One DVD, disc four), the classical and operatic *The Godfather* was more popular among mobsters. *The Godfather* influence on *The Sopranos* is so pervasive that one writer, Stephen Holden, suggests that it is this series, "more than the wobbly, histrionic" *The Godfather Part III*, that is "the real sequel" (p. xvi) to the great first two films.

That the films were a remarkable achievement was immediately apparent. The first won three Oscars for Best Picture, Actor (Marlon Brando), and Adapted Screenplay (Coppola and source novelist Mario Puzo). *The Godfather Part II*—unprecedented for a sequel—won six Oscars, including Best Picture, Director, Screenplay, Supporting Actor (Robert De Niro), Musical Score (Nino Rota), and Art Direction (Dean Tavoularis, Angelo Graham, George Nelson). Coppola wanted to title the third film *The Death of Michael Corleone* but the studio insisted on the formula, *The Godfather Part III*. Though the third was considered a disappointment, it has grown into an emotional capstone to this epic trilogy. In 1981, the first two films were re-cut for a marathon television presentation, with their scenes rearranged into chronological order, as *Godfather: The Complete Epic, 1902–1958*, with 15 minutes of additional footage.

Coppola's *The Godfather* both revived and revised the gangster-film genre. Its dominant value was not the overweening individualism of the classic film but the corporate model that saw the Family as family and validated its criminal activities by principles such as family identity and fealty. It also played the criminal story as opera, with sweeping emotions, opulent settings, and a new emotional intensity. Coppola's trilogy proposed a nexus of crime, capitalism, and the family. That passed through Martin Scorsese's gangster classics—*Mean Streets* (1973), *GoodFellas* (1990), *Casino* (1995)—on to *The Sopranos*.

Coppola's influence on *The Sopranos* ranges from the passing to the profound. Holden notes the shared "crosscutting between scenes of extreme violence and domestic warmth, and interspersing the narrative with semi-hallucinatory flashbacks" (p. xvi). Clearly Coppola proved a major source for the vocabulary: *omertà, consiglière*, "sleeping with the fishes," "going to the mattresses," the men kissing each other in ritual greeting, the family/Family tension, the homage paid the Godfather, the politicians' and religious figures' collaboration with the criminals, the persecution by the Feds, the Families' rivalry under the power of New York, and so on.

In I, 4, Uncle Junior jokes about "the Chinese godfather" who makes an offer they could not understand, riffing off another famous phrase. The "offer you can't refuse" is quoted by—unfaithful—non-Italians: Hauser in I, 9, and Amy in II, 7. *The Sopranos* builds upon the detailed knowledge we have from Coppola. The Mob website Meadow shows AJ (I, 4) offers "The Sleeping with the Fishes Report." When Ralphie teaches Jackie how to cook spaghetti (III, 9), Chase upholds Coppola's inclusion of a good recipe in each film.

The Godfather influence operates in two general ways. One is the dramatic irony when the series parallels the earlier films. Sometimes it is incidental, like the family photographs formally taken in the first and third films and in II, 7. Richie's shame at his son's ballroom dancing career is an aptly cut-rate version of Michael Corleone's opposition to his son Tony's opera career. Tony's recovery from his assassination attempt parallels Vito's in the first and Michael's in the third. Carmela's irregular confession to Father Phil in I, 5 follows the reluctance and pain of Michael Corleone's irregular confession to the Pope in *The Godfather Part III*. Both begin with "It's been so long" and end in weeping.

More significantly, the I, 3, intercutting of Uncle Junior's assault on Christopher and Brendan with Meadow's choir performance of "All through the Night" parallels the climax of the first *Godfather* film, where the church organ unites the the baptism of Michael's godchild and the orchestrated assassination of the Corleones' rivals. The second and third *Godfather* films end by similarly intercutting a variety of fatal plots. In the Soprano version, Tony's paternal pride in Meadow's singing recalls the *Godfather* films, for the baby baptised in the first was Coppola's daughter Sofia. She plays Michael Corleone's daughter in the third, where they enjoy his son Tony's operatic success. The peacefulness of Meadow's "All through the Night" echoes the baptism music from *The Godfather* and contrasts to the violence of the third's *Cavalleria Rusticana* (ironically, meaning "rustic chivalry"). That's apt, given that Tony is uninvolved in Uncle Junior's vendetta. The opera ending of II, 7, similarly bridges Pussy's betrayal and Christopher's re-dedication to Tony.

The Sopranos' business trip to Sicily in II, 4, recalls Michael's trip to hide there in *The Godfather*, the family's flashback in the second and the aged Michael's return in the third, where he is hailed as *Commendatóre*. Indeed, the entire De Niro prequel in *The Godfather Part II* lies behind Tony's boyhood flashbacks in I, 7. The wedding in I, 8, recalls the opening scene of *The Godfather*, complete with a "Johnny Fontane" type singer. *Tony* (and hence son Anthony Jr.) Soprano may even be named in homage to Michael Corleone's son, Anthony. For that matter, the name of the increasingly troubled Catholic Carmela may derive from Father Carmelo, the priest briefly introduced at Anthony's communion dinner in *The Godfather Part II*, where the religious aspect is shaded by secular deal-making.

The *Godfather* context is especially pointed in II, 9, when the Hell-bent Paulie complains to his priest that 23 years of generous donations to the church did not buy him "immunity" from Hell. If Father Felix falls short of the Old School priest (for example, Bing Crosby, Barry Fitzgerald, Ward Bond), he is completely undercut when he responds—"You should've come to me first and none of this would've happened." This is almost verbatim what Vito Corleone (Brando) tells the undertaker Bonasera who comes for a favor to the Godfather-daughter's wedding in the first scene of *The Godfather*. Perhaps innocuous in itself, the echo recasts the priest as a godfather figure, precisely the protection-seller that Paulie is—and that Paulie requires the church to be. This allusion operates on the writer's level of irony, not the character's. Paulie's worldly, cynical, smoking priest seems to have stepped out of the corrupt, conniving Vatican of *The Godfather Part III*, which supports the *Sopranos*'s clerical satire and its sense that our respectable institutions mirror Mafia methods and values.

In the second form of *Godfatherly* influence, the characters cite the trilogy. In I, 4, the film is so dominant it does not have to be named. "In One" Pussy says, explaining the "Moe Green special" as a reference to the Bugsy Siegel figure in the first *Godfather*. Paulie corrects him with Talmudic fastidiousness: Moe Green was shot in the mouth because he squealed. "The eye is how Francis framed the shot. For the shock value." But Paulie is wrong—or his need for poetic justice overrides his perception. The shot is in the eye, as we see and as Hyman Roth (Lee Strasberg) confirms in *The Godfather Part II*.

In I, 10, both the white-bread Italian doctor and his friends ("How real was *The Godfather*?") and the black music hustler praise the films to ingratiate themselves with Tony and Chris respectively. In I, 1, Carmela tells Father Phil that Tony's favorite *Godfather* film is the second, where Vito returns to Sicily. Tony confirms this in II, 4, citing the sound of the crickets in Don Ciccio's courtyard. The scene is not as peaceful as he remembers it, however. But in his nostalgia for the Old School he sentimentalizes it.

Tony's choice is even more pointed. For that film has two scenes in Don Ciccio's courtyard. In the first, young Vito's mother is killed when she comes to beg Don Ciccio to spare her last son's life. Don Ciccio has ordered both sons killed so they won't avenge his murder of their father. In the second, the adult Vito (Robert De Niro) returns, receives the old Don's blessing, then kills him, now avenging his mother's, father's and older brother's murders. (Don Ciccio takes little pleasure in being proved right.) By choosing the second scene, Tony denies the one in which the hero's mother is killed. This coheres with his suppression first of his hatred of Livia, to the point of wishing her dead, then of her plot to kill him. Tony emphasizes the quiet crickets subconsciously to evade his mother's violence.

His choice also gives Tony the vicarious satisfaction of a hero satisfying his family's honor. This leads to Tony's second point of profound *Godfather II* influence. Despite Michael Corleone's assurance from his mother that "You can never lose your family," the thrust of the second film is indeed Michael's loss of his family and his familial comfort, trust, and honor. He loses his mother, wife, and children, is alienated from his sister and has his last remaining brother murdered. The joyful family flashback that concludes the film taunts Michael with what his advancement has cost him.

For whatever conscious reasons Tony dislikes the third film, one subconscious reason must be its depiction of Michael's pain at having lost his family. Not until his confession does he confront this behavior and its costs. He spends the third film trying to recover his children but dies bereft and alone. The trilogy supports Tony's grief at the loss of his ducks and his fear of losing his family.

Some characters' self-conception is based on those films. Hence, Silvio's recurrent impersonation of *Godfather III* Pacino: "Just when I thought I was out, they pull me back in." Ironically, this pretense at "getting out" demonstrates the character's deliberate immersion in the *Godfather* world. Silvio's party trick is part of his characterization. There is a powerful dramatic irony when he does "I know it was you, Fredo" for the traitor Pussy. If Tony needs any justification for lying to his wife about his love or business life, he finds ample precedent in Pacino's Michael.

In the same spirit of homage, Silvio's Bada Bing Club takes its name from the verbal riffs of Santino (James Caan) in *The Godfather*. Paulie's car horn plays the *Godfather* theme (I, 11). A variation is heard as background music at the restaurant to which Tony successively takes Irina and Carmela (I, 1). When Jackie Aprile Jr. sets up as a lower-level godfather, he has his own *consiglière* stand behind him, like Robert Duvall behind Brando. At Jackie Sr.'s funeral Uncle Junior pretends to the dignity of Brando's and Pacino's Godfather. In I, 7 Anthony Junior tells Tony that Jackie's funeral confirmed his suspicions of his father's criminal life because the guests and the photographing Feds reminded him of *The Godfather*.

When Livia dies (III, 2) the undertaker Cozzerelli dutifully—though unnecessarily—promises: "I will use all my powers, all my skills." This repeats Don Corleone's requirement of Bonasera, the undertaker in *The Godfather*, for the mutilated Santino: "I want you to use all your powers and all your skills. I don't want his mother to see him this way." In the event, the unmutilated Livia is left in a closed casket, adorned with her bridal photo, but Cozzerelli lives up to his (Coppola) role. The actor, Ralph Lucarelli, resembles Salvatore Corsitto, who played Bonasera (more or less the perfect name for an undertaker: loosely, "Good night" indeed.).

When Tony tries to soften Uncle Junior's leadership style by citing Octavius Caesar, he draws on Frank Pentangeli's comparison to the Roman Empire (*The Godfather Part II*), especially to encourage a traitor's suicide. The assassins model their attempt on Tony—gunning him down outside his newsagent's—after the grocery-stand attack on Vito Corleone.

Surprisingly, Christopher is inaccurate when dumping a body in the Meadowlands: "Louis Brasi sleeps with the fishes." Pussy corrects him: "Luca Brasi.

Luca, Christopher." Compounding the irony, Pussy will suffer the very fate he correctly cites here. The equally bulky Luca Brasi in *The Godfather* strategically pretends to switch to another Family but ends up "sleeping with the fishes." The difference is that Pussy's "flip" to the Feds is real. To Tony's conscience Pussy continues to sing as a fish.

As a result of these parallels and echoes we can often read *The Sopranos* against the context of the *Godfather* trilogy. The TV families flaunt the luxury of their homes, but none has the Old World character of the Corleones' estate. As the Sopranos' décor pales in comparison, they fall far short of their models. Where Brando's and Pacino's Don Corleone meet their colleagues and the people courting their help in a plush paneled den, even on their modern Nevada estate, Tony and his cronies meet in seedy little rooms, backstage at the Bada Bing or at ice-cream tables outside Satriole's pork store. The Corleones' life seems a Paradise Lost, to which the contemporary family/Family can aspire but not achieve.

Similarly, *The Sopranos* depicts an organization dedicated solely to its own benefit. In at least the first two *Godfather* films the Godfather provides valuable social services to the tight, helpless immigrant community. The current gangsters may value those films for they provide a value and dignity that they no longer have. After the generosity of the Brando and De Niro characters, however, Pacino's Michael turns from service to self-interest. Under Michael Corleone the Family turns from serving the underdog to promoting its own corporate interests. Even their munificent donations are self-serving.

The Sopranos extends Michael Corleone's corruption. The current gangsters don't help people unless there's something in it for them (for example AJ's Science grade boost if his teacher's car is recovered). Brando's Corleone would have settled the Teittlemans' problem (I, 3) amiably, for possible reciprocation in the future, but Tony immediately requires a continuing partnership in the motel. Tony's donations are as calculating as Michael's—and much cheaper. On the other hand, where in *The Godfather Part II* Michael hardens into a mask of unfeeling efficiency, *The Sopranos* depicts Tony's progressive humanizing, his softening and growth in self-awareness, along the lines of *The Godfather Part III* though without—so far—the father's emotional death on the murder of his daughter.

Some *Sopranos* characters may be read as variations on Coppola's. For example, Hesh recalls Robert Duvall's Outsider *consiglière* and counters the more treacherous Jewish figure, Hyman Roth of *The Godfather Part II*. He also evokes the parallel world of Jewish criminals in Sergeo Leone's *Once upon a Time in America* (1984). Christopher may fancy himself another Michael but his unpredictability and temper make him like the doomed Santino. Both are shot while in their car.

So, too, the women. Livia dramatically contrasts to Vito Corleone's wife (jazz singer Morgana King), who is peripheral to the business but a figure of compelling strength, dignity, and warmth in the family, and to Michael's sister,

Connie, who across the three films grows from spoiled princess into a tragic queen. Vito's wife actually prompts him to help his neighbors, establishing the base of his respect. Though Connie may ultimately grow beyond Carmela, the latter has more strength, character, and effect than the more marginal wives of the Corleone sons. No door closes on her as Michael's does on Kay (Diane Keaton). *The Sopranos* seems to redress Coppola's patriarchy by providing two such strong women, one positive, one dramatically negative.

When Carmela breaks down in I, 5, guilty for letting Tony's "evil" into her house and around her children, she presents an alternative to Kay Corleone, who aborted a baby because she felt her marriage and Michael were "evil." Where Kay leaves Michael, marginalizing herself in her children's lives, Carmela stays to help Tony become "a good man."

In I, 5, Meadow tells Tony that her friends prefer Scorsese's *Casino* over Coppola's *Godfather*, for the abiding grace of Sharon Stone and the 1970s fashions. That may reflect the New Woman's strength of character—or each generation's need to deny its parents' values. So Meadow's shallow preference proves *The Godfather* avatar of traditional values and ideals of conduct. So, too, when Chris violates Tony's grief at Boss Jackie Aprile's death by urging war against Uncle Junior (I, 4), he confirms his insensitivity and wrong-headedness by citing *Scarface* (Brian de Palma's 1983 remake). That's the wrong Pacino movie. As we have noted, Jackie's funeral restores the dignity—and FBI surveillance—of *The Godfather*.

Similarly, Ralphie's obsession with *Gladiator* is yet one more way he proves himself outside the tradition and disrespectful. In his most Gladiatorial episode (III, 6), he hurts Georgie and kills Tracee. Also in that episode, Noah Tannenbaum takes Meadow to see *Dementia 13* (1963), Coppola's first film, and uses that film as evidence that they should distance themselves from her hypersensitive roommate Caitlin. In III, 5 Gigi agrees to "control" Mustang Sally "with extreme fuckin' prejudice," paraphrasing Coppola's *Apocalypse Now* (1979; *Redux* 2001). In these cases, the characters lack the wisdom and character that the "right" Coppola film would have provided.

Throughout *The Sopranos* the aesthetic and moral benchmark is the *Godfather* trilogy. The last words of the traitor Sal Tessio (Abe Vigoda) in *The Godfather Part II* echo through the series: "It was never personal, just business." And for all the show's satire, cynicism, violence, profanity, corruption, and despair, through the exuberant liberty of *The Sopranos,* echo the first words of the first *Godfather*, the undertaker Bonasera's "I believe in America."

The Cast

Gloria	Annabella Sciorra
Lilliana Wasilius	Katalin Pota
Valentina La Paz	Leslie Bega
Miss Reykjavik	Tone Christensen
Branca Libinsk	Elena Solovey
Jackie Aprile	Michael Rispoli
Rosalie Aprile	Sharon Angela
Richie Aprile	David Proval
Jackie Aprile Jr.	Jason Carbone
Ralph Cifaretto	Joe Pantoliano
Father Phil	Paul Schulze
Neil Mink	David Margulies
Attorney Melvoin	Richard Portnow
Assemblyman Zellman	Peter Riegert
Newscaster/Anchor	Annika Pergament
Dr. Fried	Lewis Stadlen
Bobby "Baccala" Baccalieri	Stephen R. Schirripa
Bobby Baccalieri Jr.	Angelo Massagli
Sophia Baccalieri	Lexie Sperduto
Jimmy Altieri	Joe Badalucco Jr.
Albert Barese	Richard Maldone
Larry Boy Barese	Tony Darrow
Gigi Cestone	John Fiore
Beppy	Joe Pucillo
Raymond Curto	George Loros
Benny Fazio	Max Casella
Beansie Gaeta	Paul Herman
Little Paulie Germani	Carl Capotorto
Carlo Gervasi	Arthur Nascarella
Donny K	Raymond Franza
Murf	Val Bisoglio
Georgie	Frank Santorelli
Mikey Palmice	Al Sapienza
JoJo Palmice	Michele Santopietro
Patsy Parisi	Dan Grimaldi
Eugene Pontecorvo	Robert Funaro
Danny Scalercio	Bruce MacVittie
Marty Schwartz	Jerry Grayson
Chucky Signore	Sal Ruffino
Bryan Spatafore	Vinnie Orofino
Vito Spatafore	Joseph Gannascoli
Mike Waldrup	Will Arnett
Dino Zerilli	Andrew Davoli
Vin Makazian	John Heard
Dave Scatino	Robert Patrick
Dr. Bruce Cusamano	Robert Lupone
Jean Cusemano	Saundra Santiago

Skip Lipari — Louis Lombardi
Agent Harris — Matt Servitto
Agent Grasso — Frank Pando
Bureau Chief Frank Cubitoso — Frank Pellegrino
Deborah Ciccerone ("Danielle") — Lola Glaudini
Robyn Sanseverino — Karen Young

District Attorney — John Doman
Judge Whitney Runions — Randy Barbee
Prosecutor — Dan Castleman
Court clerk — Julie Ross

Hunter Scangarelo — Michele DeCesare
Caitlin Rucker — Ari Graynor
Noah Tannenbaum — Patrick Tully
Finn DeTrulio — Will Janowitz
Devin Pilsbury — Jessica Dunphy

Brendan Filone — Anthony DeSando
Matt Bevilaqua — Lillo Brancato Jr.
Sean Gismonte — Chris Tardio

SEASON ONE

Featured Performers

I, 1
MRI technician — Alton Clintoni
Nils Borglund — Phil Coccioletti
Sandrine — Elaine del Valle
Restaurant owner — Giuseppe Delipiano
Nursing home director — Justine Miceli
Beppy — Joe Pucillo
Father Phil — Michael Santoro
Emil Kolar — Bruce Smolanoff
Irina — Siberia Federico

I, 2
Bonnie Di Caprio — Johann Carlo
Perrilyn — Debrah Ellen Waller
Jerome — Mike Epis
Arnaz — Yancey Arias
US Attorney Braun — Tibor Feldman
Talk show host — Harvey Levin
Vincent Rizzo — Steven Randazzo
Counter person — Kate Anthony
Martin Scorsese — Anthony Caso
Joe — Victor Colicchio
Fanny — Marcia Maufrecht
Nude dancer — Desiree Kehoe
Bouncer — Michael Parr
Antjuan — Sharif Rashed

Truck drivers #1   Charles Santy, Manny Silverio
Mr. Miller   David Schulman
Special K   J.D. Williams

I, 3
Shlomo Teittleman   Chuck Low
Ariel   Ned Eisenberg
Hillel   Sig Libowitz
Russian man   Sasha Nesterov
"Nurse"   Bernadette Penotti
Russian man   Slava Schoot
Woman at party   Angelica Torn
Trucker   Joseph Tudisco
Miss Marris   Jennifer Wiltsie

I, 4
Kid #2   John Arocho
Lewis Pantowski   Michael Buscemi
Jeremy Piacosta   T.J. Coluca
Salesperson   Guillermo Dias
Kid #3   Daniel Hilt
Teacher   Ray Michael Karl
Stripper   Theresa Lynn
Yo Yo Mendez   Shawn McLean
George Piacosta   Sal Petraccione
Kid #1   James Spector
Woman   Corinne Stella
Lance   Anthony Tavaglione

I, 5
Fabian Petrullio (aka Fred Peters)   Tony Ray Ross
Peters' wife   Lisa Arning
Bartender   Ross Gibby
Admissions Dean   Mark Kamine
Gas station attendant   Michael Manetta
Bowdoin Student   Keith Nobbs
Lon LeDoyenne   Luke Reilly
Lucinda   Sarah Thompson
Peters' daughter   Olivia Brynn Zaro

I, 6
Batman   Freddy Bastone
Old man   William Conn
Waiter   Maurizio Conn
Old woman   Sylvia Kauders
Mr. Capri   Salem Ludwig
Mechanic   Prianga Pieris
Sammy Grigio   Salvatore Piro
Rusty Irish   Christopher Quinn
Card player   Dave Salerno
Guy on bridge   Donn Swaby
Eggie   Sonny Zito

I, 7

Johnny Boy Soprano	Joseph Siravo,
Young Junior Soprano	Rocco Sisto
Young Livia	Laila Robins
Contractor	Paul Albe
Pearl	Shirl Bernheim
Young Janice	Madeline Blue
Young Tony	Bobby Borriello
Rideland kid	Michael Jordan
Rideland kid #2	Scott Owen Cumberbatch
Father Hagy	Anthony Fusco
Byron Barber	Rob Grippa
Rideland cop	Jason Hauser
Jared	Greg Perrelli
Wiseguy	Nick Raio
Guy	Steve Santosusso
Mr. Meskimmin	Tim Williams

I, 8

Dr. Sam Reis	Sam Coppola
Bakery counter boy	Brian Geraghty
Comedian	Ed Crasnick
Bakery customer	Joseph Gannasoli
Aida Melfi	Barbara Haas
Jeffrey Wernick	Timothy Nolen
Bandleaders	Barbara Lavalle, Robert Anthony Lavalle
Bride	Brooke Marie Procida
Joseph Melfi	Bill Richardone
Emil Kolar	Bruce Smolan

I, 9

Bobbie Sanfillipo	Robyn Peterson
Coach Don Hauser	Kevin O'Rourke
Ally Vandermeer	Cara Jedell
Deena Hauser	Candace Bailey
Heather Dante	Jaclyn John
Bebe	Donna Marie Recco
Moldonado	Steve "Inky" Ferguson
Receptionist	Nell Balaban
FBI man	Moises Belizario
Taylor	Mary Ellen Cravens
Waitress	Elaine Del Valle
Delivery boy	Brian Guzman
Capman	Mark Hartman
Waiter	Patrick Husted
Becky	Marisa Jedell
Shelley Hauser	Joyce Lynn O'Connor
Contractor	John Nacco
Soccer referee	Bill Winkler

I, 10

Massive Genius	Bookeem Woodbine
Orange J	Bryan Hicks

Richie Santini	Nick Fowler
Vito	Gregg Wattenberg
Bass player	Chris Gibson
Drummer	Ned Stroh
Squid	Bray Poor
Jack Krim	Jim Demarse
Randy Wagner	James Weston
Eric	Phil Coccioletti
Rita	Terumi Matthews
Mullethead	Dan Morse
Wendy Krim	Alexandra Neil
Manager	Ken Prymus
Gallegos	Jessy Terrero
Barb Wagner	Elizabeth Ann Townsend
Police officer	Cedric Turner

I, 11

Debbie	Karen Sillas
Kevin Bonpensiero	Giancarlo "John" Giunta
Dr. Mop'n'Glo	Doug Barron
Girl	Veronica Bero
Traffic cop	Britt Burr
Bonnie DiCaprio	Johann Carlo
Feds	Ramsey Faragallah, Matthew Lawler, Chance Kelly
Male anchor	Bobby Rivers
Detectives	Tim Kirkpatrick, Peter Bretz

I, 12

Isabella	Maria Grazia Cucinotta
John Clayborn	John Eddins
Rasheen Ray	Touche
Nurse	Karleen Germain
Boy	Johnathan Mondel
Vendor	Jack O'Connell
Newscaster	Denise Richardson
Doctor	Bittu Walia
Donnie Paduana	David Wike

I, 13

US attorney	John Apreo
Janitor	George Bass
Police officer	Gene Canfield
EMT	Frank Dellarosa
Jeremy Herrera	Santiago Dorylas
Russian woman	Militza Ivanova
Ms. Giaculo	Candy Trabucco

SEASON TWO

II, 1

Barbara Giglione	Nicole Burdette
Manager	John Billeci

Proctor   Darrell Carey
Ernest Wu   Dan Chen
Dr. D'Alessio   Robert Cicchini
Caller #2   Mark Fish
Samantha Martin   Karen Giordano
Peter McClure   Bryan Greenberg
Philly Parisi   Dan Grimaldi
Caller #3   Philipp Kaner
Sylvia   Katrina Lantz
Caller #1   Wayne W. Pretlow
Kevin   Kevin Sussman
Lee   Robert Thomas
Tom Giglione   Ed Vassallo
Tom Amberson   Terence Patrick Winter

II, 2
Rev. James Sr.   Bill Cobbs
Rev. James Jr.   Gregalan Williams
Jack Massarone   Robert Desiderio
Protesters   Michael Broughton, Derrick Simmons,
                        Jay Lynch, David Lomax, Ron Van Clief,
                        Herb Kerr
Truck driver   James Collins
Arlene Riley   Catherine Dent
Therapist   Elizabeth Flax
Judge Greenspan   Sam Gray
Doctor   Timothy Huang
Duty nurse   Tertia Lynch
Ralph Georgio   John Mariano
Old guy   Tony Rigo
Surgical nurse   Laurine Towler
Nurse's aide   Kellie Turner
Funeral guest   Beatrice Winde

II, 3
Dr. Schreck   Matthew Sussman
Beansie Gaeta   Paul Herman
Beansie's mother   Antonette Schwartberg
Gia Gaeta   Donna Smythe
Miriam   Diana Agostini
Yoga instructor   Getchie Argetsinger
Nancy   Leslie Beatty
Comedian   Ed Crasnick
Nurse   Catrina Ganey
Partygoer   Marc Freeman Hamm
Joint copper   Linda Mann
Policeman   Joe Pacheo
Joey   Charles Sammarco
Big Frank   Mike "Scuch" Squicciarini
Hospital patient   Deirdre Sullivan
Pizza kid   Craig Wojcik

II, 4
Annalisa   Sofia Milos
Zi Vittorio   Vittorio Duse

Jimmie Bones	Mike Memphis
Partner	Jay Lynch
Nurse	Emme Shaw
Raffaelle	Ciro Maggio
Sontag family	Danton Stone, Melissa Weil, Jason Fuchs, Jessica Peters
Antonio	Gano Grills
Waiter	Anthony Allesandro
Host	Frank Caero
Manager	Ricardo Zeno
Mother	Pina Cutolo
Kid	Fausto Amato
Camillo	Raffaelle Giulivo
Nino	Antonio Lubrano
Pino	Guido Palliggiano
Prostitute	Alida Tarallo
Kid	Alex Toma
Tanno	Giuseppe Zeno
Hotel manager	Ricardo Zinna

II, 5

Dahlia	Linda Emond
Dominic	Stephen Payne
Rosie	Lydia Gaston
Russian man	Sasha Nesterov
Russian woman	Elena Antonenko
Cynthia	Oni Faida Lampley
Acting student	Scott Lucy
Omar	Ajau Naida
Mitch	Robert Prescott
Brenda	Phyllis Somerville

II, 6

Barbara Giglione	Nicole Burdette
Eric Scatino	John Hensley
Christine Scatino	Maureen Redanty
Fishman	Felix Solis
Sunshine	Paul Mazursky
Frank Sinatra Jr.	Himself
College rep	Adam Alexi-Malle
Gudren	Angela Covington
Mrs. Gaetano	Barbara Gulan
Hooker	LaTayna Hall
Hillel	Sig Libowitz
Cop	P.J. Brown
Priest	David McCann
Dealer	Carmine Sirico
Tim Giglione	Ed Vassallo

II, 7

Jon Favreau	Himself
Sandra Bernhard	Herself
Janeane Garofalo	Herself
Amy	Alicia Witt

Security guard	Arthur Barnes
Hotel clerk	Stephen Bienskie
Assistant director	John Devlin
Gregory Moltisanti	Dominic Fumusa
UTA receptionist	Andersen Gabrych
Hotel manager	Bryan Matzkow
Michele Foreman	Andrea Maulella
Bellman	Jason Minter
Matt Bonpensiero	Steve Porcelli
Stace	Elizabeth Reaser
Blaine Richardson	Asa Somers

II, 8

Joan Cusamano	Saundra Santiago
Therapist	Susan Blackwell
Secretary	Joseph Carino
Liz La Cerva	Patty McCormack
Stasiu	Marek Przystup
Gaetano Giarizzo	Stelio Savante
Gia Gaeta	Donna Smythe

II, 9

Jimmy	Brian Auguiar
Doctor	Seth Barrish
Detectives	Michael Cannis, James Sioutis
Daniel King	Tom Cappadona
Joanne Moltisanti	Nancy Cassaro
Quickie G	Scottie Epstein
Kevin Culler	John Christopher Jones
Father Felix	Peter McRobbie
Michelle	Judy Reyes
Felicia Anne	Lisa Valens
Nurses	Gameela Wright, Denise Burse

II, 10

Christine Scatino	Marisa Redanty
Frank Cippolina	Mike Squicciarini
Vic Musto	Joe Penny
Detective Giardina	Vince Viverito
Larry Arthur	Chuck Montgomery
Carole Arthur	Molly Regan
Detective Ramos	Antone Pagan
Ramone	Adrian Martinez
Fran	Olga Merediz
Karen	Janice Dardaris
Mother	Susan Campanero
Boy	Mitch Holleman

II, 11

Catherine	Mary Louise Wilson
Dr. Schreck	Matthew Sussman
Dick Barone	Joe Lisi
Helen Barone	Patricia Marand

Connie	Jennifer Albano
Bobby	Vito Antuofurmo Sr.
Tracy	Sabine Singh
Maitre d'	James Biberi
Woman smoker	Ilene Kristen
Man	George Xhilone
Agent Marquez	Gary Perez
Michael McLuhan	Ron Lee Jones
Sanitation worker	Louis Petraglia
Siraj	Remy K. Selma
Nurses	Janet Bushor, Lesli Deniston
Orderly	Robert McKay
ER Doctor	Amy Hart Redford
Dr Baumgartner	Roy Thinnes
Tom Amberson	Terry Winter
Guests	Frank Adonis, Alan Levine, Paul Borghese, Russ Brunelli
Chuckie	Gary Lamadore

II, 12

Victor Musto	Joe Penny
Dick Barone	Joe Lisi
Richie Aprile, Jr.	Andy Blankenbuehler
Ramone	Adrian Martinez

II, 13

Annalisa	Sofia Milos
Barbara Giglione	Nicole Burdette
Quintina	Barbara Andres
Flight attendant	David Anzuelo
Meadow's friend	Kathleen Fasolino
Airport guard	Ray Garvey
Vice Principal	David Healy
Hillel	Sig Libowitz
Sundeep	Ajay Mehta
Indian man	Jay Palit

SEASON THREE

III, 1

Agent Marquez	Gary Perez
Agent Tancredi	Neal Jones
Agent Jongsma	Jay Christanson
Agent Malatesta	Colleen Werthmann
Agent Theophilus	Dennis Gagomiros
Birgit	Erica Leerhsen
Jason	Etan Maiti
Rob	Matthew Breiner
Xavier	Tommy Savas
Colin	Ian Group
Egon Kosma	Mark Karafin
SET	Anthony Indelicato, Murphy Guyer

Judge Lapper	Jesse Doran
Coach Goodwin	David Mogentale
SET Lineman	Brian Smyj
FBI agent	David Raymond Wagner
Ed Restuccia	Robert Bogue
Stasiu	Albert Makhstier
Son	Anthony Dimaria

III, 2

Reverend James	Gregalan Williams
Barbara Giglione	Nicole Burdette
Cozzerelli	Ralph Lucarelli
Father Felix	Peter McRobbie
Mr. Zachary	Tim Gallin
Fanny	Marcia Haufrecht
Bobby Zanone	Vito Antuofurmo Sr.
Young man	Dimitri de Fresco
2–5/ 7–9	Marie Donato
Tom Giglione	Ed Vassallo
FBI techs	Gary Evans, Carlos Lopez
FBI agent	Michael Strano

III, 3

Johnny-Boy Soprano	Joseph Siravo
Junior Soprano	Rocco Sisto
Young Livia	Laila Robins
Security guard	Peter Byrne
Punked out co-ed	Megan Curry
Pizza customers	Steve Grillo, Jessica Ripton
Roy DelGuercio	Kevin Janicelli
Male student	Mario Lavanderia
Bill Owens	Steve Mellor
Coach Goodwin	David Mogentale
Football dad	Peter Napoliello
George Piocosta	Sal Petraccione
Operators	Frank Savino, Paul Reggio
Junkie	Johnny Spanish
Warren Dupree	Brian Anthony Wilson
Francis Satriale	Lou Bonacki
Young Tony	Marka Damiano II
Young Janice	Juliet Fox
Young Barbara	Elxis McLaren

III, 4

Arouk Abboubi	Shaun Toub
FBI techs	Gary Evans, Glenn Kessler
Edwina Fowley	Traci Godfrey
Clerk	Zabryna Guevara
ER doctor	Steven Kunken
Detective Piersol	Jill Marie Lawrence
Jesus Rossi	Mario Polit
News reporter	Bobby Rivers
Igor Parnasky	Igor Zhivotovsky

III, 5

Officer Wilmore	Charles S. Dutton
Bobby "Baccala" Sr.	Burt Young
Mustang Sally	Brian Tarantina
2 to 5/7 to 9	Marie Donato
FBI techs	Gary Evans, Glenn Kesler
Tina	Vanessa Ferlito
Receptionist	Sheila Gibbs
Carlos	Michael Martochio
Woman	Sheelagh Tellerday
Petey	Michael Variano
Manager	Erik Weiner

III, 6

Tracee	Ariel Kelly
Georgie	Frank Santorelli
Len Tannenbaum	Michael Garfield
Waiter	Daniel Booth
Homeless woman	Yvette Mercedes
Police officer	Richard Verdino
Mandee	Michette Ardente
Debbie	Kelly Kole
Strippers	Luiza Liccini, Marie Athanasiou
Jeff	Kenneth Franquiz

III, 7

Dr. John Kennedy	Sam McMurray
Dean Ross	Frank Wood
Dr. Krakower	Sully Boyar
Dr. Laurens	Ilene Landress
Dr. Mehta	Ismail Bashey
Paxton	Peter Davies
FBI man	John Fiske
Chooch	John Freudiger
Miles	Lorenzo Gregorio
RN Collins	Tony Hale
Dr. Enloe	Zachary Knower
Anesthesiologist	James Shanklin

III, 8

Aaron Arkaway	Turk Pipkin
Rev. James	Gregalan Williams
Caterina Cella	Annie Assante
Epsilon Zet	Kieran Campion
Joe	William DaRuffa
Dov Ginsberg	Michael Hogan
Lisa Cestone	Margo Singaliese
Tracee	Ariel Kiley
Frat boys	Kieran Campion, R.J. Reed

III, 9

Carlo Renzi	Louis Crugnali
Aaron Arkaway	Turk Pipkin

Little Joe	Joe Bacino
Guiseppe	Frank Bongiorno
Cops	Charles Trucillo, David Warshofsky
Matush	Emad Tarabay
Principal Cincotta	Daniel Oreskes
Egon Kosma	Mark Karafin
Father Nicolai	Bill Kocis
Rob	Matthew Breiner
Colin	Ian Group
Girl	Cyndi Ramirez
Xavier	Tommy Savas
Rocco DeTrolleo	Richard Petrocelli
Club kid	Gregory Russell Cook
Bouncer	Jay Boryea
Janitor	David Ross
Miami Relatives	Scout: Ashen Keilyn, Nigel Rawles, Rimas Remeza, David Weintraub

III, 10

Stava Malevsky	Frank Ciornei
Valery	Vitali Baganov
Dancer	Jana Januskova
Agron	Alik Sakharov
Igor Parnasky	Igor Zhivotovsky
Aaron Arkaway	Turk Pipkin
Kevin Bonpensiero	Dominic Charles Carboni
Young Jackie Jr.	Matt Cerbone
Mother	Domenica Galati
Little boy	Tyler Gubizio
Little girl	Loulou Katz
Debbie	Kelly Madison Kole
Second dancer	Rosie Chavolino
Cop	Larry Clark
Store employee	Capathia Jenkins
EMT	Diego Lopez
Man	Barry Shurchin
Waitress	Sian Heder
Donna	Randi Newton
Cook	Tony Rhune

III, 11

Valery	Vitali Baganov
Stava Malevsky	Frank Ciornei
Nurse	Crystal Fox
Rita	Dayna Gizzo
Ambujam	Deepa Purohit
Ilana	Anya Shetler

III, 12

Father Obosi	Isaac De Bankole
Sunshine	Paul Mazursky
Carlo Renzi	Louis Crugnali
Matush	Emad Tarabay

Dr. Rotelli	Victor Truro
P.A.	Joanie Ellen
Woman in car	Anna Mastrionni
Martin	Michael Lee Patterson
Service manager	Stephen Peabody
Roy Del Guerico	Kevin Janicelli
Cholos	Anthony Zayas, Freddy Martinez, Cesar Deleon
Card players	Paul Cicero, Jack Lotz

III, 13

Major Zwingli	Tobin Bell
Agent Deborah Cicerone	Fairuza Balk
FBI agent	Norman Maxwell
Detective Filemon Francis	Marc Damon Johnson
Mackenzie Trucillo	Danielle Cautela
Kelli Aprile	Melissa Marsala
Marie	Patricia Mauceri
Nucci	Francis Esemplaire
Cadet Delaunay	Ryan Homchick
Egon Kosma	Mark Karafin
Principal Cincotta	Daniel Oreskes
Mrs. Giaculo	Candy Trabucco
Father L'Oiseau	Dick Latessa
Ray Ray	Michael Kenneth Williams
Saleswoman	Monique Lola Berkley
Leena	Lekel Russell
Little Bruce	Geoff Wigdor
2 to 5/ 7 to 9	Marie Donato
Wiseguy	Phil Larocco
Cozzarelli	Ralph Lucarelli
Junior's friend	Dino Palermo

SEASON FOUR

IV, 1

Lt. Barry Haydu	Tom Mason
Joanne Moltisanti	Marianne Leone
Karen Baccalieri	Christine Pedi
Nurse	Gay Thomas-Wilson
Matt DeBlasi	Matthew Unger
Clerk	William C. Garvey
News anchor	Paul Messina
Flight attendant	Solje Bergman
Waitress	Andrea Ciannavei
Prison inmate	James Derrick Lawrence

IV, 2

Dr. Wendi Kobler	Linda Lavin
Jack Masserone	Robert Desiderio
Misty Giaculo	Danyelle Lahne Freeman
Student advisor	Chris Hogan

Laborer — David Lomax
The Swingin' Neckbreakers — Jeff Surawski, John Clark Jorgensen, Thomas Jorgensen

IV, 3
Dr. Sandy Shaw — Joyce Van Patten
Prof. Longo-Murphy — Roma Maffia
Montel Williams — himself
Phillip DiNotti — Joseph R. Sicari
Prof. Del Redclay — Larry Sellers
Maggie Donner — Alex Rice
Cousin Grace — Mary Aguilar
Reuben the Cuban — Yul Vazques
Joey the cop — Nick DiPaolo
Plains Tribesman — Robert Salas
Native American Women — Irma Estella La Guerre, Sami Sargent
Newscaster — Michael O'Looney
Radio reporter — John Mantone
Zi 'Pepin' — Carmine Mitore

IV, 4
Saskia Kupferberg — Julie Goldman
Joe Peeps — Joe Maruzzo
Frank Crisci — Richard Bright
Alfred — Stan Carp
Chris — Jeff Robins
Rose — Lisa Altomare
Lou "DiMaggio" Galina — Joe Castellana
Rahima — Soundis Bardu
Donna Parisi — Anna Mancini
Florida hit man — Stephen Sable
House boy — Ramon Fernandez
Bada Bing bartender — Elena Aaron
Restaurant bartender — Chris Mazzilli

IV, 5
Lois Pettit — Manon Haliburton
Alan Ginsberg — Stewart J. Zully
Don Rictora Jr. — Ben Lipitz
Teddy Genaretti — Santo Fazio
Nina — Sabrina Gennarino
Norman — David Pittu
Desk girl — Sharon Elizabeth Avendano
Inez Munoz — Rosa Nino
Jockey — Aaron Gryden
Veterinarian — Bruce Barney
Photographer — John E. Kelly
Joey (Giovanni) Cogo — David Copeland
Bartender — Joe Napoleone
Band — Christopher O'Hara, Danny Roselle, James Farrell, Walter J. Lockhart

IV, 6
Jean-Philippe Colbert — Jean-Hugues Anglade
Patrick Whalen — Paul Franklin Dano

Matt Tester	Cameron Boyd
Jason Malatesta	Ryan Hoffman
Elodi Colbert	Murielle Arden
Liz DiLiberto	Lauren Toub
Jessica	Vanessa Quijas
Eddie	Daniel London
Salesman	Tony Hoty
Cheokay	Omar Sharif Scroggins
Driver	Ronobir Lahiri
Security guard	Jason Furlani

IV, 7

Maurice Tiffen	Vondie Curtis Hall
Terri	Vanessa Liguori
Stan Gurman	Richard Ziman
Angelo Davis	Malcolm Barrett
Donna Parisi	Anna Mancini
Joanne Moltisanti	Marianne Leene
Liz La Cerva	Patty McCormack
Mecomia Williams	Messeret Stroman
Regina Hicks	Melissa Maxwell
Lenore	Sally Stewart
Loretta	Geany Masai
Felicia	Nichelle Hines
Saladin	Ephraim Benton
Keryl	Shawn Leggett
Jemilo	Philliph Oden
Darryl	Chad Tucker
Anklave	Matthew Weathers
Loan officer	Jay Alvarez
Attorney	Victor Matamoros
Salesperson	Bonnie Rose
Wino	Roy Milton Davis
Kid	Ali Wright

IV, 8

Charles Cirillo	Anthony Patellis
Lorraine Cirillo	Charlotte Colavin
Elodi Colbert	Murielle Arden
Cookie Cirillo	Anne Bergen
Minn Matrone	Fran Anthony
Miss Giacolo	Candy Trabucco
Robert Harris	Dennis Carrig
Uncle Maurizio	Nino Delduca
Etan	Modi Rosenfeld
Lois Pettit	Manon Haliburton
Stella	Roberta Wallach
Richard	Joe Narciso
Student	Rufus Reade
Dealer	Sam Guncler
Bernice	Marianna Paolo

IV, 9

Ronnie Capozza	Marissa Matrone
Dennis Capozza	Richard D'Alessandro

Lois Pettit — Manon Halliburton
Agent Smyj — Brian Smyj
Inez Munoz — Rosa Nino
Justin Cifaretto — Dane Curley
Shane Petrzelka — Samuel Allen
Elodi Colbert — Murielle Arden
Allison Pak — Susan Jhun
Print newsman — Rob Leo Roy
Newspaper reporter — Frankie Pad
Neighbor — Maria Ellen Ramirez
Policemen — Bruce Kirkpatrick, Gene Gabriel
Dr. Sharon Zalutsky — Ellen Orchid
Dr. Harrison Wong — Tim Kang
Dr. Donna Dechristafolo — Ava Maria Carnevale
Orderly — Debargo Sanyal

IV, 10

Dominic Palladino — Elias Koteas
Ronnie Capozza — Marissa Matrone
Albert Barese — Richard Maldone
Joanne Moltisanti — Marianne Leone
Eddie — Daniel London
Prabhat — Gurdeep Singh
Justin Cifaretto — Dane Curley
Doctor — Cristina Ablaza
Administrator — Heather MacRae
Brad Miller — Sidney Williams
Drug dealer — Carlos Pizarro
Street punk — Herman Chaves
Cabby — Burhan Uddin

IV, 11

Lisa — Crystal Allen
Joe Peeps — Joe Maruzzo
Vic Trifunovitch — George Spaventa
Dogsy — Kevin Interdonato
Anthony — Steve Santosusso

IV, 12

Alessandra — Aleksa Pallodeno
Minn Matrone — Fran Anthony
Cookie Cirillo — Anne Berger
Benny Fazio — Max Casella
Colin McDermott — Evan Neuman
Ellen McDermott — Elaine Bromka
Dave Fusco — Mark Lotto
Foreman — Chuck Lewkowicz
Dogsy — Kevin Interdonato
Alfie — Michael Geduti
Petey — Jeffrey Marchetti
Darlene — Marilyn Matarrese
Grey Erwitt — Brian McCormack
Uncle Zio — Marco Pane

Zi'Pepin	Carmine Mitore
Call girl	Natalie Jovan
Cocktail waitress	Jolan Boockvor
ER doctor	Buddy Fitzpatrick
Nurse	Gay Thomas-Wilson

IV, 13

Alan Sapinsly	Bruce Altman
Trish Reingold-Sapinsly	Liz Larsen
Virginia Lupo	Cynthis Dawlow
Credenzo Curtis	Curtiss Cook
Stanley Johnson	Universal
Marshal	Humberto Gettys
Petey	Jeffrey Marchetti
Betty Berman	Judith Anderson
Woman friend	Diana Brownstone
Delivery guy	Emanuel Loarca
Prosecuting attorney	Rosemarie Hue
Court clerk	Julie Ross

SEASON FIVE

Continuing Charaters

Lorraine Calluzzo	Patti D'Arbanville
Frankie Cortese	Tony Siragusa
Jason Evanina	Frank Fortunato
Angelo Garepe	Joe Santos
Dante Greco	Anthony J. Ribustello
Feech LaManna	Robert Loggia
Jimmy LaManna	Anthony Desio
Rusty Millio	Frankie Valli
Billy Leotardo	Chris Caldovino
Phil Leotardo	Frank Vincent
Jimmy Petrille	Vinny Vella Sr.

Jason Molinaro	William DeMeo
Joe Peeps	Joe Maruzzo
Uncle Pat Blundetto	Frank Albanese
Cousin Louise	Judy Delgiudice
Sophia Baccalieri	Miryam Coppersmith
Bobby Baccalieri Jr.	Angelo Massagli
Nicole Lupertazzi	Allison Dunbar
Violet Lupertazzi	Caroline Rossi

Aunt Quintina Blundetto	Rae Allen
Tony Blundetto	Steve Buscemi
Justin Blundetto	Dennis Aloia
Jason Blundetto	Kevin Aloia
Gwen MacIntyre	Alison Bartlett
Joanne Moltisanti	Marianne Leone

Barbara Giglione	Danielle DiVecchio
Tom Giglione	Ed Vassallo
Matt Testa	Cameron Boyd
Sal Vitro	Louis Mustillo
Robert Wegler	David Strathairn

Featured

V, 1

Officer Zmuida	Robert John Burke
Raoul	Omar Rodriguez
Officer Yorn	John Elsen
Reporter	Sukanya Krishnan
Manny Safier	Matthew Weiner
Pete	Jeffrey M. Marchetti
Fran	Maria Baan
Kim	Lisa Regina
Patti	Barbara Christabella
Bernice	Anna Maniscalco
Waiter	Bill Quigley
Woman	Laurie Rosenwald
Pierced girl	Ginger Kearns
Delivery guy	Jason Ongoco

V, 2

Jack Massarone	Robert Desiderio
Tina Francesco	Vanessa Ferlito
Donna Parisi	Anna Mancini
Agent Reyen	Triney Sandoval
Agent Jeffries	John Viscardi
Agent Jim Ashe	Kelly AuCoin
Ken Wu	Nick Bosco
Cop	Scott Johnsen
Waitress	Renee Franca
Uncle Zio	Drummond Erskine
Old lady	Rosemarie Dana
Joe Cogo	David Copeland
Paulie's friend	Joe Scarpinito
Mourner #1	Frank A. Vallelonga

V, 3

Aunt Mary	Anna Maria Gottfried
Tommy	Ed Setrakian
Dr. Harry Winer	Allen Enlow
Wanda	Hilda Evans
Nelson	George Odom
Charles	Dean Edwards
Curtis	Bill Rowe
Shabazz	Michael Isaiah Johnson
E. Gary LaManna	Michael Cavalieri
Dan MacDonald	Rich Hebert
Cops	Myk Watford, Devone Lawson Jr.

Alyssa Giglione   Madison Connolly
Stephane Giglione   Anthony Piccolo

V, 4
Dr. Ira Fried   John Pleshette
David Lee Roth   Himself
Lawrence Taylor   Himself
Bernie Brillstein   Himself
Supervisor Jimmy Curran   Michael Pemberton
Alan Ginsberg   Stewart J. Cully
Asa Silverman   David Little
Stewart Silverman   Leon Wieseltier
Andrew   Cal Robertson
Todd   Adam Rose
Lem   Gabriel Millman
Jonah Dangler   Michael Goldstein
Carl "Fat Carl" Carlo   Vincenzo Ameruoso
Tom Amberson   Terence Patrick Winter
Mary Bisacci   Fran Gennuso
Sukhijit Khan   Manu Narayan
Uncle Jack   Lenny Singer
Gillian   Susan Pourfar
Rich Alberga   Joseph Larocca
Stripper   Gina Lynn
Dealer   John Marinacci
Gunman   Jimmy Della Valle
Mook   John Lanzillotto
Valets   Victor Cruz, Jorge Pupo
Guests   Gillien Goll, Neil Levine
Bandleader   Valerie Romanoff
Starlight Orchestra   Choma Chidebelin-Eze, Caren Cole, Andrea
                                  Eigner, Erin Henry, Allison Miller, Deborah
                                  Pilley, Sue Terry, Susan Terwilliger

V, 5
Dr. Stokeley Davenport   Hill Harper
Dr. Rene Katz   David Deblinger
Dr. Fred Mosconi   Joseph Costa
Nurse Janet Petit   Christian Corp
Dante Greco   Anthony J. Ribustello
Corky DiGioia   Duke Valenti
Sicilian   Paul Paglia
Bing girl   Mia Troche
Mimi   Jamie Sorrentini
Chesterfield Kings   Andy Babiuki, Mike Boise, Paul Morabito,
                                  Greg Prevost

V, 6
Sungyon Kim   Henry Yuk
Tom Fiske   Karl Bury
Amanda Kim   Liza Lapira
"Iowa" Burgess   Mitchell Burgess

Ms Mary Bisacci — Fran Gennuso
Attractive woman — Michelle Huber
Clerk — Angela Bullock
Dealers — Kimberley Norris-Guerrero, Anthony Spina
Waitress — Suzy McCoppin

V, 7

J.T. Dolan — Tim Daly
Fran Felstein — Polly Bergen
Johnny-Boy Soprano — Joseph Siravo
Young Livia Soprano — Laurie J. Williams
Young Tony Soprano — Danny Petrillo
Chick Philips — Kevin Hagan
Dr. Henry Winer — Allen Enlow
Cesar — Charles Santy
Dealer — John Marinacci
Relief dealer — Anthony Spina
Burt — Artie Pasquale
Old woman — Carolyn Buccino
Uncle Zio — Fred Caiaccia
Cozzarelli — Ralph Lucarelli
Hysterical woman — Joanna Bonaro

V, 8

Dr. Russ Fegoli — Bruce Kirby
Edward "Duke" Bonpensiero — Philip Larocca
Freddy DiNovi — Frank Amirati
Lester DeAngelis — Vincent Stefani
Lena Fegoli — Barbara Caruso
Jerry Basile — Gerry Pastore
Dr. Onkar Singh — Samrat Chakrabarti
Heather — Erin Stutland
Muzzy Nardo — Vic Martino
Carmine III — Sam Semenza
Sommelier — Erik Schark
Delivery boy — Pablo Hernandez
Ecuadorian man — Rolando J. Vargas

V, 9

Alex — Aleksa Palladino
Felicia Galan — Paula Garces
Todd Herman — Bruce Kronenberg
Lee Nieman — Sid Davidoff
Petey — Jeffrey M. Marchetti
Dale — Jackson Loo
Louie Ramos — Angel Caban
Josette — Hilary Flynn
Security guard — Joe Moretti
Priest — Andrew Eisenman
Golfer — Joel Blum
Waiter — Demo DiMartile
Guy — T. Colby Trane

V, 10

Cheryl Kolpeki	Dawn Evans
Dr. Phillip Seepman	Remy Auberjonois
Evelyn Greenwood	Chandra Wilson
Terry Doria	Ron Castellano
Janet Petit	Christian Corp
Bradley Stafford	Jim Wisnieswki
Tom McMillan	James Flaherty
Security guard	Angelo Dimascio Jr.
Soccer mom	Finnerty Steeves
Soccer dad	Chris Juell
Referee	Richard Byrne
Bela Kakuk	Adam Grupper
Lissie Kolpeki	Gabby Pineo
UPS guy	Carl Palmer
News anchor	Andrew Siff
Gillian Glessner	Jennifer Rainville
Vinny Pitts	Gina Cafarelli

V, 11

Annette Bening	Herself
Mr. DeTrulio	John Heard
Johnny-Boy Soprano	Joseph Siravo
Coach Molinaro	Charlie Scalies
Jade escort	Didi Wong
Mirsa	Teresa Yenque
Store clerk	Chandler Parker
Plaza receptionist	Roslyn Ruff
Man in the crowd	Germel Younger
Face in the crowd	Mark McGann
Crowd leader	Eric Seltzer
Doorman	Patrick J. O'Connor
Woman	Sarah Ireland
Bellman	Angel Feliciano
Dot	Elaine Hyman
Harpist	Sylvia Kowalczuk

V, 12

Matush	Emal Tarabay
Kamal	Homie Doroodian
Gilbert Nieves	Santos
Liz LaCerva	Patty McCormack
Dr. Sarah Klum	Felicity LaFortune
Walter	Adam Sietz
Ship leader	Marc Damon Johnson
Sea Scouts	Jelani Jeffries, Eisley Tate
Secretaries	Adrienne D. Williams, Yvonne Jung
Teenage Tony Soprano	Danny Petrillo
Teenage Tony B.	Kyle Head
Bodyguard	Lou Savarese

V, 13

Jason Masucci	Paul Diomede
David Pasquale	Adam Scarimbolo

Patrick Whaley	Paul Franklin Dano
Estela	Bethany Pagliolo
Ignatz Pravalkis	Bob Shaw
Rocco	Richard Petrocelli
Technician	Charles Anthony Burks
FBI agents	Flint Beverage, Joe Rowley
Partygoer	Mike Zegen
Football player	Barrett Wall

SEASON SIX

Continuing Charaters

Jim Witowski	John Costelloe
Julianna Skiff	Julianna Margulies
Kelli Moltisanti	Cara Buono
Bobby Baccalieri Jr.	Angelo Masagli
Sophia Baccalieri	Miryam Coppersmith
Domenica Baccalieri	Kimberly and Brianna Laughlin
Liz LaCerva	Patty McCormack
Patty Leotardo	Geraldine Librandi
Deanne Pontecorvo	Suzanne Di Donn
Robbie Pontecorvo	Thomas Russo
Ally Pontecorvo	Grace Van Patten
Allegra Marie Sacrimoni	Caitlin Van Zandt
Catherine Sacrimoni	Cristen Milioti
Eric DiBenedetto	Adam Mucci
Anthony Infante	Lou Martin Jr.
Marie Spatafore	Elizabeth Bracco
Vito Spatafore Jr.	Frank Borrelli
Francesca Spatafore	Pauline Gerzon
Tom Giglione	Ed Vassallo
Barbara Giglione	Danielle di Vecchio
Aunt Dottie	Judith Malina
Nucci	Frances Esemplare
Mrs Conte	Sylvia Kauders
Rhiannon	Emily Wickersham
Beth Kaplan	Tracey Silver
Betty Wolf	Susan Blommaert
Monks	Henry O, Ho "Oyster" Chow, Simon Sinn
Emmerich	Antony Hagopian
Elliot	Daniel Ahearn
Ron	Jason Betts
Agent Ron Goddard	Michael Kelly
Agent Ron Gosling	Matt Pepper
Ron Perse	Brad Zimmerman
Dr. Lior Plepler	Ron Leibman
Dr. Budraja	Anjali Bhimani
Dr. Ba	C. S. Lee
Nurse Leontine Overall	Traci Lynne Kindell
Nurse Aquino	Luz Lor
Perry Annunziata	Louis Gross

Larry Boy Barese	Tony Darrow
Corky Caporale	Edoardo Ballerini
Albie Cianfione	John "Cha Cha" Ciarcia
Cary Di Bartolo	James Vincent Romano
Terry Doria	Ron Castellano
Fat Dom Gamiello	Tony Cucci
Carlo Gervasi	Arthur Nascarella
Burt Gervasi	Artie Pasquale
Albie Gianfione	John "Cha Cha" Ciarcia
Dante Greco	Anthony Ribustello
Peter "Bissell" LaRosa	Jeffrey M. Marchetti
Rusty Millio	Frankie Valli
Jason Molinaro	William DeMeo
Eddie Pietro	Nick Annunziata
Gerry Torciano	John Bianco
James "Murmur" Zancone	Lenny Venito
Ahmed	Taleb Adlah
Muhammed	Donnie Keshawarz

Featured

VI, 1

Jimmy Lauria	Greg D'Agostino
Eugene Pontecorvo	Robert Funaro
Ron Senkowski	Daniel Stewart Sherman
Teddy Spirodakis	Joe Canjano
Sushi waitress	Ai Kiyono
Bada Bing waitress	Lisa Sue Miller
Hostess	Amber Gross
Neighbor	Maria-Elena Ramirez

VI,2

Lee	Sheila Kelley
Perry Benedek	Allan Wasserman
Detective DeLeon	Danny Johnson
Detective Klinger	Ted Kocj
ER doctor	Christopher Evan Welch
Salesman	Lee Sellars
Psychologist	Jay Edwards
Bartender	Edward Watts
Bald guy	Scott Davidson
Nurse's aide	Barbara Pindle
Nurse Tuthill	Gary Cowling
Omni clerk	Austin Jones
African-American guy	Quentin Heggs
Tall man	Jon Shaver
Jock guy	Peter O'Hara
Clerk	Jay Russell
TV reporter	Amy Kean
Conference center host	Emily Vaughan

VI, 3

Man	Steve Buscemi
JT Dolan	Tim Daly

Bill Kurtis	Himself
Superintendent	Luis Ruiz
Nick "Spags" Spagnelli	David Francis Calderazzo
Nurse Alfeo	Carmen Lopez
Bartender	Edward Watts
Dr. Vahabsideh	Mueen Jahan Ahmad
Intern	Joe Delafield
EMT	Matthew Stocke
Colombians	Angel Fajardo, Chris Colombo

VI,4

John Schwinn	Hal Holbrook
Jason Barone	Chris Diamantopolous
Marvin	Treach
Da Lux	Lord Jamar
Bob Brewster	Rob Devaney
Mop	Mums
Charles Cinelli	Michael De Nigris
Helen Barone	Angela Pietropinti
Mother Superior	Lois Markle
Nurse Fiona Macken	Sandra Daley
Kenny Giacolone	Ivan Martin
Aaron Arkaway	Turk Pipkin
Catherine Lipman	Gina Tognoni
Julian	Alberto Vazquez
Rudy Diaz	Ash Roeca
Ramon	Marco Muniz
Dispatcher	Paul De Pasquale
Nurse	Fiana Toibin
Devonna	Felicia Graham
Marvin's girlfriend	Lila Blake-Palmer
Nurse Bruce	Gary Cowling
Nurse Gilbert Campos	Jojo Gonzalez
Armando	Gustavo Cunha
Blinged-out girlfriend	Sally Toussaint
Goon	Chazz Menendez
Driver	Michael Serratore
Grandma	Joyce Roach
Keshawn	Keith Brown

VI,5

Prosecutor Castleman	Dan Castleman
Zev Charney	Josh Pais
Judge Whitney Runions	Randy Barber
Deputy Feetham	Mike Pniewski
Deputy Mayweather	Jeffrey Joseph
Gianna Millio	Merel Julia
U.S. Marshals	Joey Vega, Tereze Meza
Judge Holzer	Robert Hirschfeld
Linda Vaughn	Alysia Reiner
Priest	Carmine Parisi
Gillian	Katie Lowes

Rick	Anthony Stropoli
Wise guys	Jimmy Smagula, Jared Dicroce
Kimmie	Faina Vitebski
Emcee	Phil Anastasia
Bridesmaid	Taryn O'Brae
Johnny's dad	Joe Iacona
Nurse Halsey	Erik Martin
Aunt Grace	Irma St. Paule
Aunt Louise	Jean Marie Evans
Bartender	David Coburn
Wedding guest	Jerry Russo
Jamaican nurse	Nikki Walker
Wedding singers	John Kozan, Shana Steele
Jabberers	Nico Hartos, Clayton Dean Smith, Stuart Rudin
Wedding band	Tommy Riccardo & T. R. Touch

VI,6

Michael Kardish	Adam Trese
Rae "Rafaeelo" Martino	Donna Villella
Mr. Fahim Ulleh Kahn	Laith Nakli
Mrs. Fahim Ulleh Kahn	Jacqueline Antaramian
Fifat Kahn	Afeefa Ayube
Kevin Mucci	Danny Mastrogiorgio
Carty	James Hindman
Local woman	Georgianne Walken
Flagman	Ray Anthony Thomas
Babysitter	Amanda Magnavita
Jill Dibiaso	Selenis Leyva
Don	Leo Daignault
Waspy housewife	Julia Montgomery Brown
Antique store owner	Michael Malone
Local man	Cal Crenshaw

VI, 7

Sir Ben Kingsley	Himself
Lauren Bacall	Herself
Wilmer Valderrama	Himself
Salvatore	Peter Alla
Italo	Carlo Giuliano
Martina	Manuela Feris
Sarah	Abigail Marlowe
Hollings	Brian O'Neill
Kloski	John Rue
Hianna Millio	Marel Julia
Jen Fazio	Kristen Cerelli
Benny Fazio Sr.	Mario D'Elia
Connie Fazio	Judy Prianti
Sandy	Dierdre Friel
Eden	Alicia Loren
Shelly	Ariana Delawari
Yael	Meital Dohan
Roxanne	Laura Niemi

Carla	Channing Pourchot
Erica	Dee Nelson
Janine	Enya Flack
Liaison woman	Angelle Brooks
Doorman	Dylan Bruce
Hillel Teittleman	Sig Libowitz
Alonso	Alberto Bonilla
Hector	Jose Sanchez
Men	Joe Abbate, Todd Wall
Giovanni Cappito	Filippo Bozotti
Elderly Man	Peter Salzer
Photographer	Bjorn Johnson
Boys	John Robert Tramutola, Joseph Emmi

VI,8

Hernan O'Brien	Vincent Piazza
Matt Testa	Cameron Boyd
Drew	Christopher Carley
Brandon	Evan Ferrante
Baz	James O'Toole
Bibi	Nikki Dinki
Nadia	Lindsey Kraft
Martha	Casey O'Brien
Vic Caputo	Joseph Leone
Coffeehouse manager	Jayson Ward Williams
Mom	Elizabeth Meadows Rouse
Otto	Noah Keen
Farhad	Richard Zekaria
Daryl	Piter Marek
Little Person	Nic Novicki
Evelyn McCone	Julie Boyd
Thad McCone	Malachy Cleary
Mrs Kimball	Susan Barnes Walker
Mr Bauer	Andrew Schneider
Warren	Stink Fisher
Orderlies	Samuel Smith, Aurelia Williams
Desk Sergeant	Steve Stanulis
Waitress	Chris McGinn
Locals	Robert O'Gorman, Nick Choksi, Jeff Keilhotz, Sgtephen Morrow, Alexandra Daddario
Hispanic kid	Rene Rosado
Store owner	Douglas Ryan
Patient	Stephen Brian Jones

VI, 9

Kelli Lombardo	Cara Buono
Father Jose	Jonathan Del Arco
Charles Russamano	Gene Ruffini
Dale Hutchins	T. R. Shields III
Eddie Lind	Dennis Predovic
John Campisi	Biagio Tripodi
Joan Gillespie	Susan Varon

Bikers	Jeremy Schwartz, Vic Noto
Judge	Lou DiGennero
Man in crowd	Sonny Passero
Old man	Salvatore Darigo
The Virgin Mary	Tanya P.
Teenager	Frank Carlo
Latino woman	Maria Hernandez
Old woman at parade	Diane Mortella
Old woman in church	Francis W. Erigo
Hispanic guy	Pietro Gonzalez
Latino kids	Gabriel Cano, Francisco Burgos
Cop	Michael DeLuca

VI,10

Paul Calviac	William Russ
Earl Bretanoux	Patrick Holder
Sal Vitro	Louis Mustillo
Pat	Chris McGarry
Omar	Rick Gifford
Judy	Kafren Lynn Gorney
Rene Cabot Moskowitz	Rebecca Wisocky
Nora Minter	Kate Buddeke
Jeep owner	Guy Paul
Kids	Qadir Forbes, Daveed Ramsey, Alex Mitchell, Matthew "Matlock" Rullan, Brian Gilbert
Federal Marshal	Joe Forbrich
Bookie	Sal Dipiazza
Butcher	Christopher Maggi

VI, 11

Hernan O'Brien	Vincent Piazza
Brian Spatafore	Vinnie Orofino
Caterina Cella	Annie Assante
Lori	Nathalie Walker
Photographer	Clyde Baldo
Photographer's assistant	Melissa Schneider
Michel	Alexandre Varga
Headwaiter	Michel Winogradoff
Gendarme	Doug Rand
Waiter	Luc Sonzogni
Shopper	Marni Penning
Priest	Gerald Hubert
Arab cabbie	Chaouki El Ofir
Senegalese	Stephane Soomongo, Christian Julien, Mamadou Sall

VI, 12

Blanca Selgado	Dania Ramirez
Butch Deconcni	Gregory Antonacci
Mr Caravalho	Rob Falcone
Stacey	Adira Amram
Jimmy Lauria	Greg D'Agostino

Dr Abu Bilal	Aasie Mandvi
Yaryna	Matilda Downey
Amy	Arabella Field
Aaron Schaffer	Neal Benari
Teddy	Ciaran Crawford
Scott	Eric Zuckerman
Warren	Stink Fisher
Orderly	Samuel Smith
Val	Suzanne Hevner
Another member	Jeff Williams
Teenagers	Anthony Garcia, Kelvin Santos, Jonathan Marino Cuellar
Hector Selgado	Kobi and Kadin George